Firstfruits

FIRST

a harvest of

The Jewish Publication Society of America

Philadelphia   5733 • 1973

edited and with an introduction by

James A. Michener

FRUITS

25 years of Israeli writing

with a foreword by Chaim Potok

Contents

Foreword vii CHAIM POTOK

Introduction ix JAMES A. MICHENER

An Enigma 1 BENJAMIN TAMMUZ

Hai's Well 10 ASHER BARASH

Tehilah 22 S. Y. AGNON

On Galilean Shores 56 YITZHAK SHENHAR

The White City 80 AHARON MEGGED

The Sermon 139 HAIM HAZAZ

The Wanderer and the Blind Man 157 YEHUDA YAARI

In a Son's Footsteps 182 HANOCH BARTOV

A Long Hot Day 221 AVRAHAM B. YEHOSHUA

Coming Home 253 NATAN SHACHAM

The Third Hill 266 HEDDA BOSEM

The Wild Plant 272 YITZHAK ORPAZ

Nomad and Viper 289 AMOS OZ

The Parched Earth 308 YORAM KANIUK

Next of Kin 330 MOSHE SHAMIR

About the Authors 345

Foreword

In this year of the twenty-fifth anniversary of the State of Israel, some of us in the offices of The Jewish Publication Society of America wondered what gift we might give the reborn land. Since we are a book-publishing house, we thought in terms of a book. We wondered what kind of book might best sum up the life of the new land during its first twenty-five years. Someone suggested a collection of the very best short stories published by its authors during those years. This book was born of that suggestion.

Science communicates facts about the world of nature; historiography communicates facts about the deeds of men; stories, serious stories, focus upon aspects of reality indiscernible to science and history, upon the invisible tracery of lines that connect human beings to one another and to the different worlds in which men live. It is these lines that the serious storyteller explores, the lines that bind each of us to our own inner being, to other beings, to bodies of ideas, to old and new loyalties, to neighborhoods and nations. Some explore these lines with the tools of satire, others with rage, still others with compassion. All explore with a sense of total commitment to their own private visions of the truth and with a hunger to communicate that truth to the world. Some hope to shock us into change by offering us brutally honest images of ourselves. Others are more subtle teachers. And still others do not purport to teach at all but to amuse and titillate and create beauty for its own sake. But no serious writer will ever use his gift solely for the sake of public relations.

The writers of the stories in this book represent the finest literary sensibilities living and working in Israel during the past twenty-five years. The stories have about them a searing honesty; they are like deep probes into the psychic soil that supports the land and provides its people with their hopes and dreams and hungers and nightmares. They tell of a people whose life-style has been shaped almost as much by its enemies as by its founders. More than anything else, they tell us how these storytellers themselves see this new land. These are tales born of the candor of people who are among this young country's most treasured possessions—its writers.

The stories were chosen with great care out of the many dozens of Hebrew stories that have been translated and published in English-language periodicals over the years. Those many dozens yielded an initial selection of about thirty after they were read by some of us working in the offices of the Jewish Publication Society. Those thirty were then sent to James Michener, who made the final selection that is this book.

With the focus on modern Israel, the final selection of fifteen stories reflects a wide range of talents. Some of the writers represented have written with stunning effect about other times and places. Notably, there is Amos Oz's remarkable "Crusade." For complex reasons it could not be included in this anthology, but we urge the interested reader to seek it out for its display of craft and imagination.

So our gift to the new land on its twenty-fifth birthday is this book of the very best stories it has produced in the quarter century of its existence—stories that are a kind of image of the land offered us by the best of the land's storytelling sensibilities. And because we are all of us the better for the private visions offered us by truly creative literary sensibilities, this book is our gift to ourselves as well in celebration of this joyous moment in the history of our people.

Chaim Potok

Introduction

Over a period of years in the sixties I frequently crossed and recrossed the Negev, the forbidding desert that stretches southwest from the lower end of the Dead Sea to the Gulf of Eilat. It is an authentic, perpetually valid part of Israel. It always impressed me with its somber beauty, its bleak outlines, its harsh horizons.

I could imagine myself in ancient days on a camel caravan in the Negev. The land speaks of Israel's heritage, of biblical times when shepherds came to this arid sandscape and made it their home.

I knew the Negev well. It played a vital role in my thinking. The bleakness conformed to certain ideas that were germinating in my mind, and influenced me in many of my historical interpretations.

I am a prisoner of whatever land I inhabit, taking from it concepts and constructs, and I always returned to this southern desert with affection. After Galilee, where I worked much, the Negev was for me the most significant part of Israel and I explored all its dimensions.

And then one March day in 1964 a most unexpected rain fell on this arid land, not much in inches, but enough to stir the Negev into an activity it had not known for a dozen years. There was excitement in the villages to the north. Two days after the rain fell I had the good luck to cross the desert again, from Beersheba down to Dimona and Sodom, and it was as if I had been transported to a wonderland.

Every inch of Negev was covered with flowers! There were blue and gold buttons, pink spikes, and yellow rosettes. They blended together into a solid carpet of color, stretching to the horizon and far beyond. It was an explosion of color and vitality, a miracle of rejuvenation. Seeds long dormant had been waiting a generation for this rain, and when it came they were ready. Seeds that should have been dead were mysteriously alive; the desert bloomed. I felt as if I were walking upon a rug of many colors, saved for this one happy day. The bare earth had shown once more what it was capable of.

Then and now I think of Israel in those terms. It was a land long dormant which sprang to abundant life. It was a desert of sorts which waited, sleeping, for the awakening rain. It was arid, but it held the secret of vitality. Mysteriously, it was summoned back to life.

For centuries the unborn State of Israel was only a religious vision. Hebrew prayer books reminded faithful Jews of a basic tenet of belief —"Next year in Jerusalem." Through the centuries this could be no more than a pious hope.

However, in the latter years of the nineteenth century a series of anti-Semitic events surfaced across Europe, generating wide reaction. The climax came when Polish and Russian officials launched carefully planned pogroms and when the French military sought to cover its own traitorous acts by assigning them to one Captain Alfred Dreyfus.

The vicious effects of the pogroms and the sordid Dreyfus case generated in the mind of Theodor Herzl, a Hungarian newspaperman who covered the Dreyfus trial in Paris, a specific plan for the reestablishment of a Jewish homeland. Thus political Zionism was born to implement a religious ideal. Any state which might result from such impetus would perforce be both a religious symbol and a political reality.

The Balfour Declaration of 1917, combined with the activist efforts of men like David Ben-Gurion, Moshe Sharrett, and Chaim Weizmann, turned the focus of Jewish effort on the ancient soil of Palestine. Henceforth there could be no other logical site for a homeland, even though Great Britain had proposed Uganda in Africa and Soviet Russia did later offer Birobidjan in Far Eastern Siberia. Israel was to be the new home.

It required four decades of toil, turmoil, and bloodshed to achieve the dream. It demanded the conviction of men and women, half farmers, half soldiers, who occupied the first kibbutzim along the frontier. It required the faith of those who came to build the cities.

It required the blood of the Haganah, the Palmach, and even
Gang before the outlines of the new state were fixed.

On a Friday afternoon in May 1948—the fifth day of Iyar in the
Hebrew calendar and the eve of Sabbath—in a small Tel Aviv museum these manifold efforts came to fruition. Thirty men pledged their
sacred honor to dedicate the new State of Israel. Hours later, American recognition assured, the new state entered the community of
nations. Israel, as a sovereign independent nation, was a reality. It had
two responsibilities to discharge: to be a homeland for the Jews who
occupied it and to be an ideal to which eleven million other Jews of
the world could subscribe and from which they could borrow spiritual
support.

A quarter of a century is so brief a time in the history of nations,
and these last twenty-five years have been so perilous for nations,
young or old, that the very survival of Israel is a kind of miracle. The
new nation has been beset by war, by deep ethnic problems, by the
economic transformation from an agricultural to an industrial state,
and by dramatic shifts in the world balance of power. Nevertheless,
Israel has not only survived but has grown strong, sometimes finding
its strength in the very problems that endangered it.

Its continued existence and the improvement of its patterns of life
have become a source of strength to Jews throughout the world. The
tailor in Leningrad, the merchant in Brazil, the newspaperman in
London, the taxi driver in Manhattan, the physicist at Harvard, and
the banker in Paris adds a cubit to his stature when in the council of
nations Israel raises her voice.

Together with her political image Israel has succeeded, during these
momentous twenty-five years, in carving out a cultural image of equal
stature. In the fields of art, music, literature, and theater the world
has acclaimed Israeli accomplishment; one might say that her artists
have provided Israel with one of the best weapons a nation can have,
a viable culture which demands international respect.

That I was able to witness part of this miracle has been one of the
major joys of my life. That I was able to write about some of the
accomplishments in those years of awakening has been a satisfaction

that will never diminish. I was not an actual part of the rejuvenation, but I listened and tried always to weigh the fulfillment on my own scales. I have had many experiences in my life which I do not understand and about which I have been unable to reach conclusions, but my experiences in Israel seem crystal clear to me, and about them I do know what I think.

I do not, for example, believe that prior to 1948 all was barrenness, with the Arabs and the British having achieved nothing. From what I could see of Haifa when I lived there I suspect that both the Arabs and the British accomplished a good deal and that if they had retained control of the Jewish homeland they might have accomplished a good deal more in a quiet, desultory sort of way, with swamps still swamps and water still wasting itself on its way to the sea.

I have no inborn feeling that Judaism is much superior to either Christianity or Islam as a national religion. I am sure that satisfactory societies can be worked out under any one of the three. Nor am I overwhelmed by mere technical achievement. I remember my first visit to Israel when proud Israelis showed me a new bridge, speaking as if its construction was something miraculous. I recall saying, "It may surprise you to know that Burma is building bridges, too. In fact, I haven't been in any nation during the last dozen years that wasn't building bridges."

But I was, from the start, impressed by the spiritual regeneration that accompanied the rebirth of Israel, and I was delighted with the thoughtful manner in which the soil was preserved and given a new chance for life.

I can think of twenty areas of human experience in which the State of Israel has broken new ground. Such is the obligation of any society. Life is better in Haifa and Beersheba now than it was fifty years ago, and anyone who denies this misses the essential contribution of Israel during the past quarter of a century.

I can think of twenty parts of Israel which were fifty years ago swamps or arid wastes on unfulfilled land and which are today havens of conservation and production. I watched many of these locations during their period of transition and thrilled to the imagination and work which achieved the transformation. It seems to me that a major responsibility of any organized society is to preserve and use its natural resources. Few societies have done this better than Israel.

On these two points alone Israel justifies itself at the end of its first quarter century. For these reasons alone this state had to be called into being. For these reasons alone its continuation is not only justified but demanded. We need the lessons that Israel can teach us, and in these two fields the instruction has been magnificent.

I realize that another observer might come up with other justifications, but I think it best to stick to what I know most surely—life enrichment and land reclamation.

I have always thought that the State of Israel was born spiritually on that spring day in 1948 when David Ben-Gurion faced up to the most severe moral problem yet to have arisen. A ship, the *Altalena,* filled with much-needed armor, was approaching Tel Aviv under the command of men not willing to subject themselves to the authorized rule of the new state. Prime Minister Ben-Gurion commanded the ship to obey his instructions. The command was ignored. With anguish of heart but without hesitation Ben-Gurion ordered his small air force to destroy the recalcitrant ship, and it did so. The unity of the central government was assured and its authority established.

With two conspicuous exceptions, the leaders of Israel have always been ready to face up to difficult decisions. When a seaport was needed where it was quite impossible to have one, they built Ashdod. When new towns were required for new citizens, they were willing to go onto ploughed land and build new cities like Kiryat Shimona. And where new concepts of living were needed, they were willing to sponsor kibbutzim.

If I lived in Israel I would certainly want to live in a kibbutz. I would be quite willing to turn my income over to joint management, for from what I have seen of the good kibbutzim they would handle it at least as intelligently as I do, and probably much better. I would thrive under group social arrangements and wonder why the rest of the world doesn't experiment in this area right now.

I was much impressed during the time I lived in Israel to find that whereas the kibbutzim contained only 5 percent of the total population, they provided something better than 50 percent of the political and military leadership. I am not surprised at this disproportion, nor am I surprised at the number of fine pieces of writing in this anthology which come from men and women trained in the kibbutz.

I am at heart a kibbutznik. It has been my bad luck that I have lived where kibbutzim did not flourish.

Nothing that I saw in Israel impressed me more than the way the state used an unfortunate necessity (the army) as a means of improving the total social life of the country (army education in civic matters).

I believe a superior nation is one that adjusts its desires to the inescapable facts that confront it. And in Israel's utilization of its army not only to defend itself but to educate the total youth population we have one of the finest examples of this truism.

Israel was perfectly free to have a standard-type, makeshift army from which young people emerged more disoriented than when they went in. (I must add here that my own country, the United States, has grappled with this problem, too, but much less successfully than Israel.) Instead, Israel used the necessity of its army as a heaven-sent excuse to educate its young people to a higher standard than they might otherwise have attained. This is one of the brightest successes of Israel's first twenty-five years, and one least appreciated by the outside world.

I am not in favor of army-supplied education. I judge it to be one of the worst ways to educate young people, but if total conscription is a necessity, especially when women too are included, then army education ought to be of the highest possible standard and directed to the highest possible goals.

I am struck by the number of writers in this anthology who had some of their education in uniform. I doubt if they liked it at the time, but the system of which they were a part seems to me the finest in the world, a prime example of converting necessity into virtue.

I am a writer, and writers live best when they live in the world of ideas. My principal concern with Israel has always been what is happening to its brains. Great institutions like Hebrew University at Jerusalem, Haifa's Technion, and the Weizmann Institute of Science in Rehovot have excited me since I first heard of them. They are a tribute to the spiritual determination of the nation. For a youthful state to have sponsored them is without parallel. Only a people dedicated to the Book could have done so, and I could if I were in an uncharitable mood cite a dozen other new states with greater financial means which have failed to construct even a first-rate high school.

I remember how amazed I was when I first moved to Haifa to find that that city alone distributed newspapers in some *ten* different languages, with the three best papers being quite respectable in coverage and editorial responsibility. By this I mean that Haifa, with a population of 200,000, had three papers which seemed to me better than those of many American cities with equal population but which usually had only one newspaper.

As for literacy in varied languages, I was, like most Americans, impressed by the ease with which individual Israelis handled three and four languages. In my day the Israel Supreme Court could hear, en banc, cases in six different languages—that is, each judge was proficient in each of the six languages—and by using smaller groups of judges could hear cases in some dozen languages. Surely no other nation could make a similar claim.

Of course, much of this language facility stemmed from the fact that Israel was then populated by people who had been educated abroad and had learned two or three other languages in other countries, but this did not account for the fact that the court could also hear cases in Hebrew and Arabic, two languages which had to be learned on the spot, often when the learner was of an advanced age.

I was disturbed later to find that among the sabras this language facility is not repeated, and I found quite a few sabras who believed that in the future Hebrew alone would be sufficient. A miserable miscalculation. I once said in a speech in Haifa that I feared Israel's destiny was to become a Nebraska of the Middle East. By this I meant a semiagricultural state in which everyone spoke Hebrew and let it go at that. Upon being questioned I said that I considered the people of Nebraska to be among the happiest in America and the most contented. But I wondered if that ought to be the destiny of a land which had a somewhat stronger tradition in diverse cultures and language facility.

There can be no other state on earth whose citizens have finer private libraries than the educated people of Israel had in 1964–1966 when I was in a position to judge. I doubt if any other citizenry has more or better phonograph records, certainly not the European or American ones I know. Partly, of course, this was because Israel at that time had few good public libraries and no television, but mostly it was because the educated Jew knew that he required good books and good music to stay alive mentally. I suppose some of the splendid family libraries have begun to deteriorate, but even so they must stand much higher than the average private library in other countries.

The level of Israeli conversation was unusually high, with topics of the greatest diversity being discussed with considerable expertise. This was partly due to the fact that Israelis came from so many distinct backgrounds, bringing with them broad interests. This might not have been generated within a small, insulated area, but it came in large part, I believe, because of an inherent Israeli interest in all aspects of the world picture.

The Israeli was educated in the widest sense of that word, and he used his education to good advantage. Some of the best conversation I've had in my life I had in Israel, and not always with university graduates. I found a recognition of local and national concerns which was most gratifying, and I believe that I myself was lured onto a somewhat higher lever of conceptual thought in Israel than I have been elsewhere, not because of any change which occurred in me but because of the germinative quality of the talk I participated in. I had to think to keep up.

Concerning the arts, three impressions of Israel remain most vivid. There never was a nation which has so loved music and which has been willing to support it in various forms. One of my happiest memories is attending the concerts given by the Haifa Symphony under Serge Comissiona's direction. Here was a town of less than medium size, by world standards, which had its own symphony and a fine hall in which to hear it. There may be other cities of similar size with an orchestra as good, but I do not know of them. Haifa supported its symphony because the citizens needed it, and if the brasses were not quite as good as those in the Berlin Philharmonic, they were as good as some I heard in Rome.

Israel's composers bring to her music a wide range of talents and specialties and many world honors. Of particular note are Menachem Avidom, Paul Ben-Haim, and Joachim Stutschewsky.

The Israel Philharmonic, of course, was then and is now one of the world's top aggregations, playing in a home hall of superb quality. So many great violinists were being produced in Israel that I supposed Tel Aviv would take the place of legendary Odessa, from where first violinists used to emigrate to all the great orchestras of the world, and in recent years this seems to have been coming true. First violinists may turn out to be Israel's principal cultural export.

There was music everywhere and of all types, many modern forms finding sources in the ancient biblical cantillations. Music was a part of daily experience and was familiar rather than esoteric. The only other nation which comes close to placing music in such a position of preeminence in daily life is Korea. In only one category was Israel inferior to other nations: it stood well below either Italy or Germany in its performance of opera, and there economic limitations may have been the cause, because Israelis who loved orchestral music also loved opera and would have supported it had they had a chance.

In the plastic arts Israel's production was remarkable, for it provided far more artists of first rank than its population would have warranted. Coming quickly to mind are such names as Reuvan Rubin, Anna Ticho, Nachum Gutman, Samuel Bak, Igael Tumarkin, Benni Efrat, and Shalom of Safed. The sales galleries in Jerusalem, when I knew them, contained the works of a score of artists of world rank, and in recent years men like Yacov Agam have attained the international recognition they deserve. The effects of their work were beginning to be felt in many aspects of Israeli life: in the architecture of new and daring buildings, in commercial design, in book illustration, and in public decoration. Not much had been accomplished in these important fields when I was living in Israel; from international exhibitions seen since then I judge a great deal must have been done.

And finally, the subject of this anthology: the manner in which the writers of Israel have caught the spirit of their nation. First I must pay tribute to the amazing accomplishment of the Israeli writer: the resuscitation of a language once nearly dead. Ireland tried to revive Irish and largely failed. Scottish nationalists tried to revive Gaelic and failed completely. Norway has struggled with its two versions of Norwegian and has found no satisfactory solution. And several nations in Africa have wanted to make their national language Swahili, without success. Only Israel has succeeded in this most difficult of ventures. Last year two-thirds of the books printed in Israel were composed originally in Hebrew, an astonishing accomplishment, and four-fifths of all books printed were in that language.

It is noteworthy that each of the selections included in this anthology was composed originally in Hebrew and first printed in that language. The reestablishment of Hebrew as the native tongue of the land of Israel is not an esoteric thing; it functions in both the marketplace and the library. A living language has been revived, a tribute to Eliezer Ben-Yehudah, the visionary who practically singlehanded brought the tongue of prophets to modern times.

I know few lands in which the role of the writer is so exalted as in Israel. When I lived there men quoted Bialik as evidence in an argument, they kept informed as to what Agnon was up to, they told me of Megged's latest work with a pride that indicated their participation in it.

How exciting it must be to be a young writer in Israel today! To know that you are part of a movement that is giving a new nation its base-literature, its foundation.

During the first quarter century of Israel's existence the writing has been very good, directed for the most part at precisely those subjects which most demanded attention. It has been less literary, perhaps, than similar writing done in France, less politically subservient than the writing of Soviet Russia, less polished than the writing of England and Germany, less encompassing than the best writing of America; but perhaps more vital than any of those.

It has spoken directly to the Israeli condition, which is the best thing national writing can do.

Israel's writing is about where one would expect it to be at this stage of development. In poetry it is excelled by the songs of no contemporary nation, either in abundance or quality; the Israeli poets, Yehuda Amichai, Leah Goldberg, Dalia Rabikowitz, and others must be among the best in the world today as far as impact and vibrancy are concerned, and as far as making Israel a singing nation. I cannot commend them highly enough, for they have done what the poets of England, France, and the United States have been unable to do—take poetry right to the heart of their society and make it listen.

In the short story, as exemplified by this anthology, Israeli writers stand with the world's best.

In the novel, perhaps because of the financial difficulty in publishing first in Hebrew and later in one of the world's major literary languages, Israeli writers have lagged behind men like the Russian Alexander Solzhenitsyn, the German Gunther Grass, or the Italian Alberto Moravia. Intellectually, there is no reason why this should be so; Israelis are natural storytellers and substantial forms come easily to them. Within the next quarter century I would expect some very great novels to come out of Israel.

Writers, publishers, governmental agencies, and particularly literary agents should direct their attention to the problem of winning a worldwide audience for Israeli writers, for if a writer's first obligation is to speak to his own people, he cannot fulfill that obligation until he also speaks to the whole world.

I am reminded constantly of what Ernest Hemingway once said within my hearing: "I could never be content with being the 'well-known Philadelphia novelist.' I wanted to go up against the world's best, Pio Baroja, Turgenev, Flaubert." I believe this is the legitimate desire of any serious writer; he is entitled to the widest possible translation and steps should be taken to ensure it.

In this respect the Israeli painter stands in a somewhat more favorable position than the writer, because the former can circulate his product to Paris, London, Berlin, and New York without facing the problem of translation, while the writer cannot evade this hurdle. It is regrettable that a man like me, who tries his best to follow what is happening in a land he loves, knows more about Israeli painting than he does about Israeli writing, and only because the former is available to him in many of the galleries he visits throughout the world, while the fine stories and novels find their way to him only accidentally.

Years ago the intellectual leaders of Holland decreed that henceforth no Netherlands university could grant a doctor's degree (the Ph.D. principally) unless the thesis was written in either German, French, or English; they did not want Dutch scholars to be talking merely to themselves. The fruits of Dutch scholarship would turn barren if only people who spoke Dutch could enjoy them. I am told that Dutch intellectual life jumped forward following this decision, and I myself have often gone to Dutch sources in recent years, whereas prior to this wise decision I would have been cut off from such learning.

There is a vast difference between a Ph.D. thesis and a short story which sings of local situations, and a rule which works well with the former might be disastrous if applied to the latter; but the problem of communication within the world community remains constant, and if someone has something relevant to say, the rest of the world needs to hear it. It must not be kept immured within the confines of any one language. Israeli writers are so good that their thoughts must be shared.

Earlier I referred to two areas in which the leaders of Israel were delinquent in facing reality. It has been the writers who have identified and grappled with these vital problems, and it is to their credit that they have done so.

The two problems are these: Israel's overriding intellectual concern, its everlasting confrontation, will be its relationship to the Arab world; the best brains of the nation should be directed at finding solutions and a modus vivendi. When I was in Israel it seemed to me that only the writers were bothering with this problem.

The comparable internal problem is less compelling but perhaps more gnawing: How can the Sephardic Asiatic minority be absorbed into full national life with justice and common sense? When I first knew Israel not even the writers were addressing themselves to this problem, whose ramifications were so obvious to the outsider; but during my stay they began to wrestle with it, long before their political compatriots were prepared to do so.

In recent years the writers have done superb work in exploring these two permanent problems and have outlined some of the psychological perimeters. Selections in this anthology reflect some of that thinking. Indeed, if a committee were to identify the top hundred stories written during the first twenty-five years of Israeli's existence, a fair proportion would deal with these two problems, and that is most encouraging.

I have not spoken of war. In other places I have twice written about Israel at war and I have nothing fresh to say. I do, however, read a good many stories written by Israeli writers and focusing on the three wars, and I have never read more compelling material. At its best it stands comparison with Stendahl and Tolstoy; its insights are profound; its humanity is at times overwhelming; and its impact is powerful. I do not see how it could be much better. Its only deficiency is scope, and among the forthcoming novels of the next quarter century I feel confident that some gifted writer will attempt the job of encompassing the outstanding work so far done in a comprehensive work which will shake the world.

There is a chance, I suppose, that the noble work I speak of may be written by some Arab currently brooding in Damascus. Great novels are not always written by the winners.

How does an outsider feel on Israel's twenty-fifth birthday, an outsider who has given some of the strong years of his life to a land he came to love passionately?

The land itself seems to be prospering. It is producing more food-stuffs, more minerals, more living space than ever before. Scars which obliterated some of its beauty have been erased and the monstrous building construction which has defaced much of America has been avoided. Water resources have been husbanded and vast concrete roads have not been encouraged to eat up the countryside. There is an abundance of trees and it is important, I think, to recognize that the rationalizing of certain political boundaries has given the entire land a better sense of balance.

I have never been a Nile-to-Euphrates man, for mere territorial aggrandizement is repugnant, but I used to feel strongly that the former arrangement on the road from Tel Aviv to Jerusalem was an abortion that simply had to be corrected. I am gratified that it has been. I felt the same way about the narrow waist northeast of Tel Aviv, and I am equally glad to see it repaired. I speak not as a nationalist but as a geographer. Geographical monstrosities ought to be corrected, and history usually takes care of the matter, for it does not like to see them indefinitely prolonged. The land is therefore in better *shape* than it used to be.

The people who occupy the land appear to be in good condition too. The new breed seems to have inherited the courage and quality of the old. I have often told my friends, "The most beautiful thing I ever saw in Israel were the original Russian immigrants. Men like Ben-Gurion, Shazar, and the irrepressible David Hacohen of Haifa. They were men of granite and laughter, perhaps the best single group of men I've ever known anywhere."

I remember a distinguished French Jew who lived in Tel Aviv telling me of her reactions to the 1956 war: "We French and the English among us were terrified at the prospect of war with Egypt, but those damned Russians . . . they marched off singing as if they expected to go right to Cairo and be back within a week. It was something to see, as if they were coming right out of the pages of the Old Testament."

I used to worry about what might happen when the old Russians died out. I was not too much impressed with their German replacements, but gradually I saw that the land of Israel itself modified people, and in the end the Israelis I trusted most to keep the spirit alive were the generation of Germans. They seem to have turned out even better than I expected.

Those friends of Israel who live abroad brood constantly about the ultimate place of Israel within the world's hierarchy, just as we brood about our own. It is the mark of an intelligent man that he be willing to speculate upon the future and of a concerned man that he contemplate not only his own future but that of others.

It seems to me that the status of Israel is quite secure, perhaps more so now in 1973 than it was four years ago in 1969. By slow and painful steps China, Russia, Japan, and the United States are approaching an understanding in the Far East, while the European community, Russia, and the United States are stumbling toward a comparable understanding in Europe.

Certainly any casual willingness to see things explode in the Near East has been diminished, and if Israel has lost something because of America's disillusionment over Vietnam, it has gained something because of Russia's desire to accommodate and sponsor a generation of detente. I am much more hopeful about the Near East than I was four years ago.

But the great problem remains: How to reach an understanding with the Arabs. I have long thought that one more war may be necessary before reason comes to this area, and the hopefulness I expressed in the last paragraph relates to my belief that in such a crisis Russia and the United States would keep hands off. I am not too hopeful that the insanity which has long gripped the Near East can be dissipated without one final confrontation.

But if I lived in Israel I would direct all my energies to the avoidance of such a conflict, and I would be willing to take steps which a generation ago might have seemed impossible, if taking them meant that reconciliation was moved one day nearer.

When I lived in Jerusalem it was apparent, even to a blind man, that this noble city was intended from the moment of its inception to be a central source of light for a very wide community reaching from

Cairo to Babylon. Here should be the great universities, Western and Eastern alike, educating experts in all fields who would return to their natal communities to improve them. Here would be the schools of medicine and optometry and dentistry and the research hospitals serving a vast area, staffed by men and women from Jaffa and the remotest village of Syria, the only requisite being intelligence and application.

Great libraries should center here, and schools of business, and industrial exchanges, and experimental stations for the betterment of all aspects of life. Religious experience would also center here, as it does now, and from Jerusalem would go forth Arabs and Jews and Druses and Circassians and all the citizenry of the various nations, to the profit of each.

My vision of such a city has not diminished. In previous days in different parts of the world, Paris performed such a service, and Bologna, and Berlin, and in its way the cluster of cities around Madrid, and before them Bagdad and Damascus and Cordoba. I expect to see Jerusalem performing such a service for the lands of the Near East, perhaps in the opening years of the next century when nationalisms have been arranged.

I speak of these things from deep-rooted personal conviction and commitment. In 1963, when I went to Israel on a trivial vacation, I had no intention of writing a long novel about the Jews. My studies over the preceding ten years had fitted me exclusively for writing about the Muslim world. I had lived for varying lengths of time in every Muslim nation from Indonesia to Spain, save Arabia alone, and I was about to start a novel on Constantinople. It might have turned out well, for I loved that city and had in my heart an appreciation of Islam, about which I knew infinitely more than I did about Judaism.

But on this vacation friends took me to the deserted ruins of Athlit Castle, north of Caesarea, and by accident I was left alone in the dungeon. As I looked at the ancient vaulting and saw the shadows of crusaders passing, an entirely different kind of novel sprang almost fully embodied in my mind, and I wrote not about the Arabs, whom I understood, but of the Jews, whom I did not.

The creative impulse is like that. It is a thing to be cherished, for it does not appear on demand.

This anthology reflects a young nation's vigor in the art of storytelling. Here you will find a depiction of life on many fronts: in the homes of Israel, in the fields, in the kibbutzim, in the cities and on the battlefronts. People of the most diverse character are portrayed and issues which cut right to the heart of Israeli life. This is the literature of a young nation; these stories show so much youthful vitality that the future seems assured.

The stories that follow have been written by men and women attached to a noble land and perplexed by permanent problems. They have much to say to all of us.

James A. Michener

Benjamin Tammuz

An Enigma

Mother and father went to the concert. The neighbours went along too, and the little boy was taken over to their house to be looked after by their big children. The house stood alone where the road slopes down, not far from the fields and the distant vineyards. When there was no one in it there was a deep silence all around.

Abraham, the neighbour's son, took two baskets of hay and set out into the courtyard to feed the animals in the cowshed and the stable. The little boy toddled along silently behind him. Deep in the court-yard old Whitey woke up and wagged his tail at them, his hoarse yappings proclaiming his delight. His iron chain clinked gently as it beat against the wooden wall of the stable. The little boy wanted to go over and pat him, but Abraham walked off towards the cowshed. After a moment's hesitation the little boy turned about and followed him. The two cows looked at them apathetically through the gloom. Abraham emptied his basket into the box in front of them and turned to go without saying a word to either. A hard boy he was, dark-skinned and surly, like his father with his heavy fleshy nose and the low forehead which wrinkled up without any reason. He wore, all the year round, a yellow shirt and grey trousers. When he bathed in the pool in summer, he would walk around naked, and return naked the whole length of the farmyard to the house. And he was nasty to everybody from the first moment. He was nasty towards the animals of the farmyard too. When he emptied the other basket into the horse's crib, he paid no attention to the quiver that passed like a wave over the animal's skin, and did not respond to its dumb entreaties for a pat on the back or a little scratching on its powerful bulging chest.

The little boy was afraid to do so, so he looked at the horse helplessly and in his heart promised him that he would treat him nicely when he grew up and had the courage to.

Abraham went back to the house with the little boy behind him. From the side of the path where the grasses grew, right under their very noses, a bird flew off like an arrow from a bow, straight towards the roof of the house. Before they reached the house they saw a big lizard, whose colour could not be made out because of the poor light. It was crossing the path in a hurry; and once again poor Whitey whined at them and clinked his chain.

"Want to eat!" Abraham ejaculated as he climbed up onto the verandah.

From the kitchen came a sound of stirring and the shifting of pots and pans, but there was no answer.

The little boy went over and entered the kitchen apprehensively, trying to make himself as unseen and unheard as possible so as not to attract the attention of Sarah, for fear she might send him out. She was frying potatoes, the thirteen-year-old girl, and the expression on her dark and roundish face was grave and concentrated. But there was none of her brother Abraham's bad temper. Apart from her dark skin there was no resemblance between the brother and sister. She was willowy and slender, and her eyes were soft and brown, hidden behind long lashes. Her nose was short and straight and her face was clean with a pattern of the kind you only find in flowers. Sometimes her face lit up with a smile which passed swiftly leaving the observer with a sense of wonder and melancholy like that which comes on a winter's day when the sun withdraws behind the clouds after it has warmed the earth a little.

She died suddenly that year, of an illness nobody knew; and her memory remained in the little boy's heart as a secret symbol of the gloomy autumn days that come down on the world every year, with a hot sun now and then peering out of them; and then he would remember Sarah.

But that evening he was not concerned with memories. That evening, as in all those distant days, his heart was charged with something hidden and mysterious towards Sarah; something which he knew, many years later, was what people call first love.

She was frying potatoes and the expression on her dark-skinned, roundish face was very grave indeed as with her fingers she placed the pieces one by one into the bubbling oil. From time to time she started back as the jumping oildrops leapt up almost into her face. Then she could not refrain from a mischievous childish smile. But, as she bent over the oil stove which shed a little ruddy glow, she reigned over the kitchen as she did over the grave game of Mummy and Daddy when they sometimes played together in the courtyard. Her small face and large eyelashes were lit up by the ruddy light, and were achingly pretty in the stillness of the empty house.

"Want to eat!" Abraham repeated from the verandah with an obstinate grumble. This time he rose, appeared in the kitchen and shuffled his feet. He looked surlily into the frying pan and burst out with forceful annoyance: "How long do we have to wait for a meal in this house?"

"As long as is necessary," said Sarah not looking at him.

"D'you think that if mother and father have gone out, then you're a whole queen right away?" Abraham boiled over and stared at the little boy as though it were all his fault. And when he received no reply, he added irrelevantly: "And this baby here too, wandering about."

Having said which he left the kitchen. If the little boy had had more courage, he would have taken hold of the skirts of Sarah's dress and hidden his face in the folds. But a few moments later he was at ease again. Sarah too recovered her spirits and said:

"Just sit down here beside me and don't pay any attention to that crazy fellow. In a little while we'll eat together."

"In a little while we'll eat together"—that was what Sarah said many, many years ago, and ever since the words have remained firm in his memory. They have been transformed into an inscription engraved on the gates of that universe which the children call the world of the grown-ups, the world of freedom, the world where you can do whatever you feel like doing, unchecked by the eyes of mother and father; the world where you can go to sleep long after nine, the world where a man grips the helm of life in his own hands.

"In a little while we'll eat together"—were those not the words which it seemed he heard twenty years later from the girl whom he intended to marry?

So they ate together that evening. Sarah set a plate and a little bowl. And into the little bowl she sensibly and concentratedly poured, biting her underlip the while, the sour milk out of the reddish jug.

"A good appetite to you," said Sarah and, raising her skirt till the bottoms of her white drawers could be seen, sat down in her place and took a long sideways look all round, like a conductor at his orchestra when he raises his baton before the crash of the music. They all took their forks, opened their mouths and began chewing silently. Abraham thrust the plate of potatoes away and began to drink the bowl of sour milk.

"First you have to finish these," said Sarah to him and pushed the plate back under his nose. Did Abraham actually sense the sanctity of the moment, of the solemn occasion? For he did not turn obstinate but acquiesced and went back to the potatoes without any refusals, his eyes alone barely darting hither and thither over the table in embarrassment. Sarah was the first to stand up when they finished. She gathered the dishes together and, when she saw that they remained where they were, awaiting her instructions, she deigned to say that they could do what they liked for a while until she finished washing up.

Abraham rose heavily from his seat like his father and took hold of his belt to ease his tummy, breathing deep in his father's fashion while puffing up his cheeks and wrinkling his forehead. But he did not belch like his father because he couldn't. He quickly fetched queer tools and rubber strips, and began to prepare a sling which needed straps to be tied to it, and a leather pouch.

A faint chill spread over the verandah. Whitey came close and scratched at the wooden steps with his claws, but did not dare to come up. When he received no response, he turned and went back as he came, his chain dragging through the grass of the farmyard, clanking against the stones and the buckets and the pots scattered around.

The little boy almost fell asleep with the heavy meal and for want of something to do, but he woke himself up at once. He slid off the chair and went back to the kitchen to observe Sarah's movements. She had finished and was wiping her hands on a towel hanging over the tin wash-stand. Now she turned the wick down a trifle and left water in the kettle, as her mother had instructed her before leaving.

Abraham could be heard on the verandah, murmuring to himself meditatively: "I'll catch sparrows . . . I'll kill lizards . . . We'll have a bonfire." Then he became silent once more. Sarah entered the house. The creaking of a distant door announced that she had gone to the bedroom. Before long her voice sounded from there: "Children, to sleep!"

The little boy's heart tightened in keen protest at this injustice, which so swiftly destroyed the entire adventure of being grown-up for an evening. "Actually I can manage without sleeping," he argued with her.

"You just lie down and go to sleep at once. And Abraham after you, and after that I'll go last, because I have to make the beds," firmly declared Sarah from the house, as befitted a person conscious of all the responsibility resting upon her.

Abraham, who seemed to have grown tired of playing, raised his head and looking straight into the darkness within the rooms said with open mockery: "And if I don't go to bed, what will you do to me? And if I hit you, what will you do to me?"

Sarah came out and stood in the doorway. Her brown eyes flashed with fury and her full lips were tight and quivering. But she did not say a word. Turning to the little boy, she took him by the hand and led him into the house. Her unexpected touch gave him a sudden sensation of happiness and started waves of heat running through him until his ears burnt. He followed her and heard her settling the matter with a pretended indifference which could not conceal her injured pride:

"Just as you like, Abraham, I'll tell father everything . . . And I myself and this little fellow will go to bed . . . You can do whatever you like."

The boy did not miss her "this little fellow," but he did not feel like worrying over painful things. He promptly promised her in his heart that he would grow up and be even bigger than Abraham, and then they wouldn't call him "this little fellow" and more. Yet all the same he would love her just as he did now, and would take her by the hand and lead anywhere she liked.

She held his hand firmly in hers, and took him into her little room, one window of which faced the roadway. It was absolutely dark. Sarah let him be for a moment. Groping over a ledge in the lower part of an unseen cupboard she brought something out. The little boy heard the scraping of a match, and light gleamed from a little wax candle.

"Hold it while I prepare the bed," said Sarah. The boy hurriedly took hold of the candle as he stood in the middle of the room with his heart beating and thudding like the motor in the orange groves sounding in his ears.

"My brother is an awful fool," declared Sarah with a smile mounting her face. "He'll be sorry yet."

She made the bed and gave a final decisive fold to the blanket. Then she decreed:

"And now turn to the wall and don't look until I tell you."

All the noises which had vanished from his hearing during those many moments now suddenly penetrated through the window and the door and surrounded him. He heard the scraping shoes of the horse on the floor of the stable. Whitey's whining seemed as though it had not stopped even for a moment. Through the door he could see a faint moon shedding light. It drifted through the wooden palings of the verandah and through the ornamentations to the guttering which descended from the roof in triangles and crosses and semi-circles. The oilcloth was gleaming on the table at which Abraham was sitting immersed in his sling-making. And whenever the howling of a jackal sounded from the distant fields, it seemed to him as though the sheen on the oilcloth trembled and the light flowing through the wooden ornaments quivered. He felt heavy all over. It seemed to him as though his feet were stuck to the floor and he would never be able to move them again. For a second time that evening he gave way to a kind of momentary slumber. When he woke from it, the floor had rolled under him and seemed as though it had vanished forever. He asked himself whether Sarah had already given him permission to turn round; but he said nothing, seeing in his imagination nothing but the gaze of her eyes resting on him like the eyes of some wild beast, a jackal or hyena; one of those he had seen caught by the watchman with something in their expression, a riddle you could never solve, which always seems to contain some sort of mockery mixed with a longing for you, the human being.

"You can look now," said Sarah.

When he turned back, Sarah was lying in her bed with her hands by her sides on top of her cover and her brown gaze peeping between her lashes. "You can sit by my bed until the candle goes out and I fall asleep," she said, and closed her eyes with a long, sleepy breath.

The little boy went and sat on the corner of her bed. He was holding his breath and the tender night air flowed from the window in dark and spacious gusts, while distant sounds came floating in. The candlelight dwindled steadily. It could no longer illumine her features properly. The melting wax was flowed over the child's fingers and hardened on his nails. He peered into the darkness. Only the little pillow shone white in front of him. On it could be seen her shadowy head, dark and quiet. He did not know whether she were asleep or awake, her round and heavy chin, and her purplish mouth, which seemed so like rose-petals that have dropped from the bushes and dried up, their colour scorched and almost black, stood out sharply.

The shifting of a chair on the verandah shook the silence, and Abraham, who was tired of being alone, entered the room. He looked at them silently for a long moment. Then he grinned under his nose.

"A lovely mummy and daddy," said he. "I'll tell everything . . . Do you think I don't understand anything?"

The little boy signalled to him that she was asleep and that he should not raise his voice, but at that moment Sarah answered quietly:

"If you had listened to me and gone to bed, I would have let you sit beside me as well for a little while till I fell asleep."

"Don't need your favours," responded her brother contemptuously. "And in any case, I'll tell everything."

"Tell then . . . Who cares . . . And get away from here now," answered Sarah and turned her face to the wall.

Abraham went out. From the other room came the creak of the bed as he flung himself upon it without undressing, falling asleep at once. Sarah turned her face round and lay as before; and as she did so, the little bed moved under her and the boy felt the movement as though it came from within him and were the touch of something alive.

The candle went out of his hand. With the absolute darkness, a gentle heavy sleep began to come down on him. Every touch of it gave his slumbrous imagination some picture for his disturbed spirit. Her face laughed at him. Her slender figure moved towards him and ran to meet him with the wind in the field. Her mouth said something to him which he could not hear, and he yearned to understand the meaning; but she slipped away and fled from him. Her arms caressed his neck and his eyes welled with tears. Sarah promptly looked at him with sombre gravity, and said: "Why are you crying; we are mummy and daddy."

And he fell fast asleep.

The laughter of the parents woke him up. They had lit a small light in the room, and the two fathers were looking and laughing together. He looked around and found himself lying on the cover beside Sarah, with her hand embracing his neck in her sleep. His head was so close to her widespread tresses on the pillow that they mingled with his breath, like the sand that penetrates into the nostrils of wayfarers in the desert.

His father bent and picked him up in his arms. The little boy clasped his neck and pressed his face against his cheek. The scent of fresh soap and the feeling of short and ticklish bristles quietened him. His father took him out of the room and carried him through the farmyard and the wicker gate and the vineyard which lay between the house of the neighbours and their home. His parents spoke together in whispers because they thought he was fast asleep.

But when he was alone in his bed he felt an anguish worse than anything he had ever known. He wanted to storm out of the house and go back to the little room where Sarah was lying in her bed, so as to make sure whether he really had been resting beside her all those hours with her hair so close to his face that he could have stroked and kissed it if he had wanted to. He grew very angry for having fallen fast asleep. He whispered her name into the darkness and assured her that he had not fallen asleep with any ill intent, and that it was not because he was little that he had not kissed her hand as it lay on his neck. He assured her and explained that it had been some devilish trick, something mysterious and cruel. He felt his neck and seemed to sense her hand resting on it. But he could not hear her voice answering him.

He could not know then that throughout all the coming changes and chances of his life this would return: that he would slumber and dream or sing of himself like this child, to whom the winds of slumber and dream had come by some mischievous trick of innocence at the time when happiness was swelling up all around.

The little girl became ill that year. Nobody knew what her illness was, and she died in a hospital far away in town.

No man ever sipped the warm smile of her mouth, and nobody ever breathed her hair again in his sleep.

Translated by I. M. Lask

Asher Barash

Hai's Well

In a poor little colony which lies high up in Lower Galilee there was a little man who had a little wooden hut, a dunam of land, and a wife and three children. The man went by the name of Nathan Hai. He was a farm-worker who had gone through all kinds of transformations in Judah and Shomron and Upper and Lower Galilee. He had fevered a lot and affectionately cursed the ways of the old and new Yishuv alike, besides using a sharp bachelor's tongue to tease the girl workers and mock at marriage. But, when he was thirty-five years old and looked like a dwarfed and wrinkled olive trunk, he took to wife the "Rosh Pinah seamstress," who was younger than he, and settled down in the little colony. Within five years they brought three healthy sons with good appetites into the world, and the burden of life rested thenceforward on the two of them.

How did he come to the name Hai? After all, he was not one of the Sephardim among whom that name is common, but a fellow from the neighborhood of Dubno. The truth was that the name "Hai" was short for "Hai vekayam" (hale and hearty). For that was his regular reply whenever anybody asked him how he was. "How are you, Nathan?" "Hai vekayam!" And to be even more precise it should be added that even this expanded name of "Hai vekayam" was only a translation made by one of his friends, who was hot for the Hebrew language and translated into it the Yiddish reply that he had been giving for several years, namely "Hai-gelebt!" (Hai-alive). Nathan cheerfully accepted the translation, but as time went on and he said less because his troubles were growing greater, he would simply answer, "Hai!" And so the short name remained and everybody from Dan to Beersheba knew him as Nathan Hai.

Like a dozen other fellows of his own type in the Second Aliya, he was a kind of monomaniac. And what was his particular mania? Water! The redemption of the land and hence, obviously, the redemption of the nation and the Ingathering of the Exiles depended only on water. If Eretz Israel could only get enough water it would be a paradise. And he had bundles of proof, both by word of mouth and in writing, from hundreds of sources. He would begin with a verse at the very beginning of Genesis, "And a river went forth from Eden to water the garden" (which goes to prove that if there had been no irrigation, there would not have been any Garden of Eden), and go right up to the famous phrase of Kaiser Wilhelm to Herzl as he sat on horseback in the heat of the day near Mikveh Israel: "It needs water, plenty of water!" And then he would add his own experience.

For Nathan Hai did not rest content with talking about water but was, so to say, the servant of water everywhere. He investigated the water situation in the country from the salt water in the sea and the exceedingly salt water of the Dead Sea to the waters of the rivers and the brooks and the wadis; spring water and flood water, underground water and rain water, upper water and lower water, water for irrigation and water for power. For months and years he took a hand with the well-borers in various parts of the country. For months and years he toiled in the motor cabins of the orange groves, working at draining and drying swamps and laying irrigation pipes. In brief, wherever there was water, there he was to be found. And they say that the old worker and writer who was the teacher of all the workers slapped him on the shoulder once and, speaking of him, quoted a verse from the Book of Job: "He gives blossom from the scent of water."

And now came something queer. This Nathan Hai, the water man, chose as his dwelling place a desolate colony in Lower Galilee, which was white with dust the greater part of the year, in order to raise his hut there and settle down. One might have supposed that in this way he wished to symbolize his great longing for water. For, if he had dwelt in one of the Sharon colonies where there is an ample water supply, the source of his longing would have dried up. But in the Galilean colony, swooning with thirst, the staff of his longings put forth blossoms like Aaron's rod in the Bible; and he never wearied of talking about water.

In the center of this colony there was a well with a wheel over it, whose water came from the rains in their season. If the winter was rainy, the well was full and it had enough water (only for man and beast and the few yards of green round the houses) until the beginning of August, after which nothing was to be brought up from the well bottom save mud and mire. If there was little rain in any year the water lasted until mid-June or, at most, to the beginning of July. After that there was work for the water carriers (and naturally Nathan spent no small amount of time on that job as well). Morning and evening they had to take the mule and the big barrel on two wheels and fetch water from the distant fountain on the Arab land, water that had to be bought for good money. If the water carrier came home late in the evening there would be a cloud on the faces of the colony people, as they asked themselves what they and their beasts would have to drink.

But Nathan was not the fellow to see folk suffering and do nothing. From the time he became an established citizen among all the others in the place (by right of his cabin and his dunam of course) he would get into touch with every "factor of consequence in the Yishuv" in order to raise the question of water for the Galilee settlements in general and, in particular, his own colony which suffered from the shortage more than them all. It cannot be said that Nathan Hai's efforts did not bear fruit. He set all the wheels in the Yishuv moving about this business of water, from the staff of the Baron de Rothschild in Palestine and abroad to the Jewish National Fund and all the departments of the Jewish Agency. He kept them all busy with letters and memorandums and interviews about the water without which the colony could not live. No excuses helped. They came, they investigated, they sent experts, they hewed and they bored, and they bored and they hewed, inside the colony, down on the hill-slope on the one side and then down on the other hillslope; a mile away from the house that lay farthest north and a mile away from the house that lay farthest south. They bored and they stopped, and they went back and they bored again. Drills were broken, workers were injured, and one who fell from the stand broke his spine and was crippled for life. But they did not find any water. In one spot they bored for six weeks and they found moist earth, and the pump even brought up a few pails full of fluid mud. Some of the local inhabitants began dancing an Arab "Debke" all round; but after they bored a little more it all stopped and once again the drill brought up only dry cold unfriendly gravel, to the disgust of the inhabitants.

But Nathan never ceased prophesying: "There is plenty of water in our good earth. It has an artery throbbing like the heart's artery in the human body. It is only necessary to find the pulse, to put up the drill at the right spot."

And one day (nobody quite knew how he managed it) Nathan fetched out of the Negev an Englishman with a little yellow beard, wearing a Bedouin *Kefiya* and *agal* round his head. This fellow had spent many years in the Sudan, spoke Arabic with an English accent and a lot of hard guggings, and he carried a little wand with which he walked about like a lizard, touching the surface of the ground, holding the wand and watching it trembling, and deciding accordingly whether there was water at that spot or not.

The Englishman decided on a new spot for boring a well. But after all the bitter experience and waste of money there was no longer anybody prepared to invest the first hundred pounds that were needed to begin the work. The local inhabitants fed the Englishman on the best to be found in the house of the *Mukhtar,* and also presented him with five pounds that they collected in the colony before giving him an honorable send-off. But no boring followed.

Meanwhile Nathan Hai lost his strength. He was already forty-three and four and five. His hair, which had been curly in the old days when the Rosh Pinah seamstress had stroked it with trembling fingers and whispered, "Nathan, you have nice hair"—most of that hair had fallen out, leaving a sunburnt scalp that was as smooth and gleaming as silk. The three children, all of them boys, did not make the little hut any quieter, particularly as she, Eva Leah, always had to be sewing with a machine in order to make most of the living. She used to sew for the Arab women of the surrounding villages too; and he, fully aware though he was of the husband's duties to his wife and those of a father to his children, earned very little. Sometimes he would have to go far away for weeks on end in order to look for work; and during his absence his dunam would suffer from jaundice and baldness.

Not that he ever became melancholy. That is, he looked miserable enough, particularly his eyes which had sunk deep and burned with repressed unhappiness. But his mouth still knew its job. He would make brief jokes, and when he came to talk about water it seemed as though his own trunk had been watered and the living water had entered his veins. His eyes would gleam and his tongue would serve his flights of imagination in lively fashion. "Before long any amount of water will come up to irrigate the land of the colony and make it yield. It is pouring along under our feet. Can't you hear it? Just listen carefully and you will!"

The listener would slap him on his shoulder, look him in the eye and ask:

"And what's the news with you, Nathan, about making a living?"

"We live, so-so—Hai vekayam. Hai!"

II

When their youngest child was six years old, after an interval of six years that is, it came about that Eva Leah found herself in the family way again, for the fourth time. The whole household became apprehensive. Nathan Hai himself also grew afraid. That was all that was missing! As it was the three they already had were wandering about like starving jackals, in rags and tatters. Eva Leah sewed for everybody, yet for her own children she could not sew shirts or a pair of linen trousers. She simply did not have the time. And if she were to take the time off to sew for them, what would she have to put in their mouths? And now this was coming! After they thought they were finished with any more children!

The local nurse and midwife scolded Eva Leah, abused her

thoroughly and demanded and insisted that she should go to town and do what had to be done. "Human beings aren't swine!" she permitted herself to say coarsely. She was an old maid with principles. (Once upon a time she had been one of those who had "gone to the people in Russia.") For a moment Eva Leah hesitated saying to herself: "Maybe she is right and it would be worth doing what she suggests." But when she said as much to Nathan he opened a pair of startled eyes at her, then spat for all he was worth and cried in a voice which was not his own:

"Listen to a block of dry wood like that? No, as long as I am Nathan Hai, you won't do anything so abominable!"

And the item was struck off the agenda.

It must be confessed that from that day forward there was a different mood in Nathan. He seemed to be transformed into a kind of tense machine on springs. He was on the move all the time, travelling to Tiberias or Haifa, to Afulah and Nazareth, even to Tel-Aviv and Jerusalem. He would spend a few days or weeks there, then came home fetching in his rucksack a few things that they required. Maybe some tinned food or some cloth or knitting materials and so on. And his tired-looking purse would also have a little ready cash.

So there was a little light in the hut. Nathan's face looked worse, to be sure. He grew thinner and seemed to shrink. The silken bald patch turned to a burnished copper, and his eyes flamed as though he had the fever. But he was in a good mood. Often he would answer those who asked how he was with his old phrase of, "Hai-gelebt!" but would at once correct himself: "Hai vekayam!" The children were dressed in more orderly fashion, for if he spent a few days or weeks at home he compelled Eva Leah to turn down a few customers in order to sew some clothes for them.

The day of the birth was on the way. They reckoned that the child ought to be born in the middle of August.

The ninth of Ab passed at the beginning of August and Eva Leah completed her full term. Everything was ready for the birth. They had already spoken to the midwife. Her fury had not quite died down at the "barbarism," but she had no choice save to accept the fact, and she came into the hut from time to time to see that everything was in order.

On the eighteenth of Ab the birth-pangs came. Nathan quickly filled two tubs of water. Although Eva Leah had not cried out, the nurse heard and came running, only to see almost at once that the birth was not in order. After an hour of sweat and toil she realized that the doctor had to be brought from the neighboring colony because the danger was increasing. She told Nathan so. He asked no questions, grabbed his stick and dashed off to the colony.

It was the forenoon, in the heat of the day. High up in the heavens sailed distant white wisps of cloud, enjoying a sun bath. The little colony was silent with its poor little houses. The few gardens were grey with the remains of scorched vegetables, looking like stains of rust on zinc. Only the pruned eucalyptuses at the wayside rose green with their young branches. The way down the slope to the wadi was thick with beaten dust. In the skies three vultures were circling in a triangle: One in the north, one in the west and one in the east. Nathan noticed them. It immediately occurred to him that they were coming from the water, one from the Kinnereth, one from the sea and one from the Jordan. This thought gave wings to his feet, so that he did not notice the sweat running down like a fountain of water from his head to his collar. It took an hour through the wadi to reach the big colony, but he ought to get there in half an hour, for he was running. Why had he not taken a horse or donkey? It simply had not occurred to him. Now it was not worth his while going back. He had already passed a quarter of the way.

Nathan passed the cemetery on the little hill. He glanced at the handful of scattered tombstones, two of which stuck out so importantly while the rest lay like stones in the field. He suddenly felt afraid at the sight of the cemetery, and the thought of Eva Leah twisting and turning in her birth-pangs, all in ever-greater danger. He went even faster down the slope, running with his stick ahead of him. The sweat poured from his head over his face, into his mouth, and down his neck and over the hair of his open chest. When he got to the bottom it was no longer so hot and he felt a little easier. He removed his hat, held it in his other hand and allowed his gleaming bald patch to absorb the sun.

All of a sudden at the entrance to the wadi, he felt a kind of slight stab in the head. His legs began to quiver. They seemed to grow light, lifted themselves a little from the earth and fluttered in the air. His heart beat as though it was running away with itself. The light turned suddenly dark. He fell on his stick, quivered a little, turned over at the wayside and slipped down into a shallow ditch.

III

Two hours and more passed but Nathan did not return. Neither did the doctor arrive. The midwife came out of the hut with her hair in disarray, and shouted in a way that the little colony had never heard since it was founded. Nathan's three children immediately stopped their play, startled; they sprang up and stood staring as though they were senseless. One by one came grownups from the houses. The woman shouted at them:

"What are you standing like blocks of wood for? Go and fetch the doctor quick! Eva Leah is dying!"

Within half an hour one of the local lads had fetched the doctor on his cart. But the doctor found Eva Leah lifeless. And the child remained within its mother.

A village Arab found the body of Nathan Hai in the ditch five days later. He saw kites busy and gathered round there. He approached and recognized the dead man. So he went and told the *Mukhtar.* When they brought him away from there his flesh was already going. His face and eyes had been pecked by the beaks of the birds of heaven.

They buried him as he was, without cleansing him, beside Eva Leah's grave. The three orphans were shared out to three houses, one to each. The little one was adopted by the midwife, who had fought like a lioness against death but could not prevail.

The colony mourned grievously. In one day three souls had been cut off and a family had been uprooted in the little community. Who can understand the cutter-off of life?

IV

Once Nathan Hai had been brought to burial after the fashion of Israel he was eased of the burden of his life, which had been beyond his strength. Eva Leah lay not far from him, her child within her, and rested forever. "There rest the exhausted of strength" and who was so exhausted of strength as to compare with Eva Leah? Even before her marriage, as long as she had been in Eretz Israel, she had been harnessed to the yoke of hard work; first as a worker, then as a domestic help, finally as a seamstress. Even after she had married Nathan and given birth to three sons one after the other, each coming before the other was big enough to look after himself, she had continued to sit bent over the sewing-machine which had sucked up the rest of her blood. But she was a good person of spirit and character, and no matter how she suffered she was never heard to make a complaint. Now she had gained the rest she deserved. The children had been orphaned of their father and mother, but were better off than they had been. Each of them was in a good home, his bread provided at the proper time and his clothes not lacking. Best of all was the little one. For the captious and bitter old maid gave him all her pity and love. He was small and tender in her eyes.

And he, Nathan Hai, had attained full rest. His bones, worn and broken with hard work, now took it easy. His brain, which had grown weary with concern and alarm for the souls depending on him, could also rest and devote itself entirely to the one thought which had filled him from head to foot while he was alive; the thought of water.

For days and days, for months and months, he lay listening, sending forth his will, one might say, like delicate antenna deep into the earth. He forgot everything. He forgot himself and the whole world. Somewhere, in some hidden place a pulse of water was babbling and throbbing, longing to be revealed. Summer passed, winter vanished, a new summer came, and his will grew tense as a violin string, while his water sense grew keener than ever.

The following summer, in the heat of the month of August, a year after he had fallen at the wayside, a faint sense of moisture reached

him. First he did not know from which side it came. He grew very
excited. He had to gather all the strength of his will in order to sense
precisely where it came from. At length he realized it exactly. It came
to him, a cold and pleasant stream, from one specfic point. There it
was! The vein of water gathered in his awareness. It was not far away.
He had had to labor with his awareness for a whole year until he found
the spot. Ha ha, it was certainly not the spot to which the English
water diviner had pointed! No, the fountain was here, below the
cemetery. Exactly ninety yards in a straight line west of his grave!
Ninety yards, according to the numerological value of *mayim,* the
Hebrew word for water!

All his bones rejoiced. Now he knew what he had to do. He knew.
A dream. The dream he had dreamed on earth had come about. Now
he knew what he had to do. The locked and sealed water must rise
up.

V

The following summer, during the hottest days of August, Nathan
Hai appeared in a dream to the *Mukhtar* of the colony for three nights
running. He appeared with radiant face, and this was what he said:
"Wake up and get up! Go out and bore! Exactly ninety yards in a
straight line west of my grave! Thirty-three yards down the water is
waiting for you. Don't delay! For a whole year I have been bringing
the water up to that point. Don't miss the chance. I shan't be able to
keep it there very long. Uncover it!"

On the first night the *Mukhtar* woke up and in the darkness told
his wife about the strange dream. They both decided it was nonsense.
But next day the man went about all day long not knowing what to
do. The dream would not leave him alone even for a moment. After
the second night, when the dream was repeated again, he told it to
several of the local people, and one of them went so far as to remark:
"It isn't just nonsense." After the third night the *Mukhtar* summoned
a meeting of the committee and they decided to try. Thirty-three
yards—the cost was next to nothing.

Now it so happened that not far away the water company was boring a well. They had already gone down more than two hundred meters. They had already been boring for three months. They had already made their way through two strata of rock, and now they had reached a third which was even harder. But there was no sign of water. Work had stopped three days before. The borers had simply grown tired and given up. Their tools lay where they were, like dead corpses.

Two committee members went to the company in Haifa and deposited thirty-three pounds, according to the number of yards that they wished to have bored. Next day the well-borers came to the spot, which was already marked with an iron spike. They dug a little, put up the stand for the drill and began to drill.

Lots of jokes were heard, as they worked, and the deeper the drill bit, the lower grew the spirits of the people and the smaller their faith in the *Mukhtar's* dream. After the drill had passed the thirty-yard mark they all but gave up, and felt that they wished to ask the workmen to stop; but were ashamed to do so.

And then, all of a sudden—

It was noon, the heat of the day, just the time at which Nathan Hai had run off to summon the doctor and had fallen while running and dropped into the ditch. White clouds were sunning themselves in the sky. Three vultures were circling in a triangle. The final thuds of the drill sounded in the silence of the colony—and the iron rod in the hands of the drillers suddenly beat, while a lapping sounded from the deeps. Before they could see what had happened a sound suddenly rolled and echoed all round. Water! Water! The little pump standing there suddenly emitted a jet of water, pure water from the hole. It gleamed like crystal in the sun, fell to earth and melodiously flooded all the neighborhood. And the pump went on pumping the precious fluid on the ground.

There was not a living soul in the colony who did not come to see the sight. All of them stood over the little pool, gazed through tears and trembled with excitement and joy.

The experts measured the force of current. There were two hundred cubic meters an hour. A fountain of salvation had been opened to plants and living creatures. Now the colony would begin to grow and flourish. The words of Nathan had come about.

VI

Before long a big reservoir was put up. It was big and tall and stood on five tremendous pillars, four at the corners and one in the middle. A proper pumphouse was also built. And the village water festival was held.

Many people came from settlements close at hand and far away to rejoice with the people of the colony, whose thirst had been quenched with much water. Each one brought his gifts of all wherewith the Lord had blessed him. Round the well they planted saplings and fresh flowers that were amply watered. The whole of the square intended for the rejoicing crowd had been besprinkled with water. Every white shirt, every white blouse, whether of man, woman or child, was adorned with a green twig. Neighbouring Arab horsemen took their places amid the horse-riders of the colonies. Tables on trestles stood ready, loaded with good things to eat and drink.

Three choirs of children from three schools in three colonies stood on the platform, the music teacher keeping them quiet with his conductor's baton. They were waiting to sing the song "And you shall draw water with gladness from the fountains of salvation."

In the front row, like pioneers before the choirs, stood the three children of Nathan Hai, each smaller than the next, all dressed in suits that were as white as snow.

In front of the pumphouse, over the iron door, was an inscription in large letters:

HAI'S WELL
This is the well of Nathan Hai, and such is its name and fame forever.

But one man, the man who writes this, looked sorrowfully at what he had added, while nobody had noticed, in chalk on the iron door in small printed characters: "Let Eva Leah also be well remembered."

Translated by I.M. Lask

Tehilah

Now there used to be in Jerusalem a certain old woman as comely an old woman as you have seen in all your days. Righteous she was, and wise she was, and gracious and humble too: for kindness and pity were the light of her eyes, and every wrinkle in her face told of blessing and peace. I know that women should not be likened to angels, yet her would I liken to an angel of God. She had in her, moreover, the vigour of youth; so that she wore old age like a mantle, while in herself there was seen no trace of her years.

Until I had left Jerusalem she was quite unknown to me: only upon my return did I come to know her. If you ask why I never heard of her before, I shall answer: why have you not heard of her until now? —It is appointed for every man to meet whom he shall meet, and the time for this, and the fitting occasion. It happened that I had gone to visit one of Jerusalem's celebrated men of learning who lived near the Western Wall. Having failed to locate his house, I came upon a woman who was going by with a pail of water, and I asked her the way.

She said: Come with me, I will show you.

I replied: Do not trouble yourself: tell me the way, and I shall go on alone.

She answered, smiling: What is it to you if an old woman should earn herself a *mitzvah?*

If it be a *mitzvah,* said I, then gain it; but give me this pail that you carry.

She smiled again and said: If I do as you ask, it will make the *mitzvah* but a small one.

It is only the trouble I wish to be small, and not the merit of your deed.

She answered: This is no trouble at all, but a privilege; since the Holy One has furnished his creatures with hands that they may supply all their needs.

We made our way amongst the stones and descended the alleys, avoiding the camels and the asses, the drawers of water and the idlers and the gossip-mongers, until she halted and said, Here is the house of him you seek.

I found the man of learning at home at his desk. Whether he recognized me at all is doubtful, for he had just made an important discovery, which he immediately began to relate. As I took my leave I thought to ask him who that woman might be, whose face shone with such peace and whose voice was so gentle and calm. But there is no interrupting a scholar when he speaks of his latest discovery.

Some days later I went again to the City, this time to visit the aged widow of a rabbi; for I had promised her grandson before my return that I would attend to her welfare.

That day marked the beginning of the rainy season. Already the rain was falling, and the sun was obscured by clouds. In other lands this would have seemed like a normal day of spring; but here in Jerusalem, which is pampered with constant sunshine through seven or eight months of the year, we think it is winter should the sun once fail to shine with all its might, and we hide ourselves in houses and courtyards, or in any place that affords a sheltering roof.

I walked alone and free, smelling the good smell of the rains as they fell exultantly, wrapping themselves in mist, and heightening the tints of the stones, and beating at the walls of houses, and dancing on roofs, and making great pools beneath, that were sometimes turbid and sometimes gleamed in the sunbeams that intermittently broke through the clouds to view the work of the waters—for in Jerusalem even on a rainy day the sun yet seeks to perform its task.

Turning in between the shops with their arched doorways at the street of the smiths, I went on past the shoemakers, and the blanket-weavers, and the little stalls that sell hot broths, till I came to the

Street of the Jews. Huddled in their tattered rags sat the beggars, not caring even to reach a hand from their cloaks, and glowering sullenly at each man who passed without giving them money. I had by me a purse of small coins, and went from beggar to beggar distributing them. Finally I asked for the house of the *rabbanit,* and they told me the way.

I entered a courtyard, one of those which to a casual passerby seems entirely deserted, and upon mounting six or seven broken flights of stairs, came to a warped door. Outside I stumbled against a cat, and within, a heap of rubbish stood in my way. Because of the mist I could not see anyone, but I heard a faint, apprehensive voice calling: Who is there?—Looking up, I now made out a kind of iron bed submerged in a wave of pillows of bolsters, and in the depths of the wave an alarmed and agitated old woman.

I introduced myself, saying that I was recently come from abroad with greetings from her grandson. She put out a hand from under the bedding to draw the coverlet up to her chin, saying: Tell me now, does he own many houses, and does he keep a maidservant, and has he fine carpets in every room?—Then she sighed: This cold will be the death of me.

Seeing that she was so irked with the cold, it occurred to me that a paraffin stove might give her some ease, so I thought of a little stratagem.

—Your grandson, I said, has entrusted me with a small sum of money to buy you a stove: a portable stove that one fills with paraffin, with a wick that burns and gives off much heat.—I took out my wallet and said, See, here is the money.

In a vexed tone she answered: And shall I go now to buy a stove, with these feet that are on me? Did I say feet? Blocks of ice I should say. This cold will drive me out of my wits if it won't drive me first to my grave, to the Mount of Olives. And look you, abroad they say that the Land of Israel is a hot land. Hot it is, yes, for the souls in Gehenna.

Tomorrow, I said, the sun will shine out and make the cold pass away.

"Ere comfort comes, the soul succumbs."

In an hour or two, I said, I shall have sent you the stove.

She crouched down among her coverlets and bolsters, as if to show that she did not trust me in the part of benefactor.

I left her and walked out to the Jaffa Road. There I went to a shop that sold household goods, bought a portable stove of the best make in stock, and sent it on to the old *rabbanit*. An hour later I returned to her, thinking that, if she was unfamiliar with stoves of this kind, it would be as well to show her the method of lighting it. On the way, I said to myself: Not a word of thanks, to be sure, will I get for my pains. How different is one old woman from another! For she who showed me the way to the scholar's house is evidently kind to all comers; and this other woman will not even show kindness to those who are prompt to secure her comfort.

But at this point I must insert a brief apology. My aim is not to praise one woman to the detriment of others; nor, indeed, do I aspire to tell the story of Jerusalem and all its inhabitants. The range of man's vision is narrow: shall it comprehend the City of the Holy One, blessed be He? If I speak of the *rabbanit*, it is for this reason only, that at the entrance to her house it was again appointed to me to encounter the other old woman.

I bowed and made way for her; but she stood still and greeted me as warmly as one may greet one's closest relation. Momentarily I was puzzled as to who she might be. Could this be one of the old women I had known in Jerusalem before leaving the country? Yet most of these, if not all, had perished of hunger in the time of the war. Even if one or two survived, I myself was much changed; for I was only a lad when I left Jerusalem, and the years spent abroad had left their mark.

She saw that I was surprised, and smiled, saying: It seems you do not recognize me. Are you not the man who wished to carry my pail on the way to such and such a house?

And you are the woman, said I, who showed me the way. Yet now I stand here bewildered, and seem not to know you.

Again she smiled.—And are you obliged, then, to remember every old woman who lives in the City?

Yet, I said, you recognized me.

She answered: Because the eyes of Jerusalem look out upon all Israel, each man who comes to us is engraved on our heart; thus we never forget him.

It is a cold day, I said, a day of wind and rain; while here I stand, keeping you out of doors.

She answered, with love in her voice: I have seen worse cold than any we have in Jerusalem. As for wind and rain, are we not thankful? For daily we bless God, saying, "Who causes the wind to blow and the rain to fall."—You have done a great *mitzvah:* you have put new life into old bones. The stove which you sent to the *rabbanit* is warming her, body and soul.

I hung my head, as a man does who is abashed at hearing his own praise. Perceiving this, she said:

The doing of a *mitzvah* need not make a man bashful. Our fathers, it is true, performed so many that it was needless to publish their deeds. But we, who do less, perform a *mitzvah* even by letting the *mitzvah* be known: then others will hear, and learn from our deeds what is their duty too.—Now, my son, go to the *rabbanit,* and see how much warmth lies in your *mitzvah.*

I went inside and found the stove lit, and the *rabbanit* seated beside it. Light flickered from the perforated holes, and the room was full of warmth. A lean cat lay in her lap, and she was gazing at the stove and talking to the cat, saying to it: It seems that you like this heat more than I do.

I said: I see that the stove burns well and gives off excellent heat. Are you satisfied?

And if I am satisfied, said the *rabbanit,* will that make it smell the less or warm me the more? A stove there was in my old home, that would burn from the last day of *Succot* to the first night of *Pesach,* and give off heat like the sun in the dog-days of Tammuz, a lasting joy it was, not like these bits of stove which burn for a short while. But nowadays one cannot expect good workmanship. Enough it is if folk make a show of working. Yes, that is what I said to the people of our town when my dear husband, the rabbi, passed away, may he speak for me in the world to come! When they got themselves a new rabbi, I said to them, What can you expect? Do you expect that he will be like your *old* rabbi? Enough it is if he starts no troubles. And so I said to the neighbours just now, when they came to see the stove that my grandson sent me through you. I said to them: This stove is like the times, and these times are like the stove.—What did he write you, this grandson?—Didn't write at all?—Nor does he write to me, either. No doubt he thinks that by sending me this bit of a stove he has done his duty.

After leaving the *rabbanit*, I said to myself: I too think that by sending her this "bit of a stove" I have done my duty: surely there is no need to go again. Yet in the end I returned, and all because of that same gracious old woman; for this was not the last occasion that was appointed for me to see her.

Again I must say that I have no intention of recounting all that happened to me in those days. A man does many things, and if he were to describe them all he would never make an end to his story. Yet all that relates to that old woman deserves to be told.

At the eve of new moon I walked to the Western Wall, as we in Jerusalem are accustomed to do, praying at the Western Wall at the rising of each moon.

Already most of the winter had passed, and spring blossoms had begun to appear. Up above, the heavens were pure, and the earth had put off her grief. The sun smiled in the sky; the City shone in its light. And we too rejoiced, despite the troubles that beset us; for these troubles were many and evil, and before we had reckoned with one, yet another came in its wake.

From Jaffa Gate as far as the Western Wall, men and women from all the communities of Jerusalem moved in a steady stream, together with those newcomers whom The Place had restored to their place, albeit their place had not yet been found. But in the open space before the Wall, at the booth of the Mandatory Police, sat the police of the Mandate, whose function was to see that no one guarded the worshippers save only they. Our adversaries, wishing to provoke us, perceived this and set about their provocations. Those who had come to pray were herded together and driven to seek shelter close up against the stones of the Wall, some weeping and some as if dazed. And still we say, How long, O Lord? How long?—for we have trodden the lowest stair of degradation, yet You tarry to redeem us.

I found a place for myself at the Wall, standing at times amongst the worshippers, at times amongst the bewildered bystanders. I was amazed at the peoples of the world: as if it were not sufficient that they oppressed us in all lands, yet they must also oppress us in our home.

As I stood there I was driven from my place by one of the police who carried a baton. This man was in a great rage, on account of some ailing old woman who had brought a stool with her to the Wall. The policeman took a flying kick, throwing the woman to the ground, and confiscated the stool: for she had infringed the law enacted by the legislators of the Mandate, which forbade worshippers to bring seats to the wall. And those who had come to pray saw this, yet held their peace: for how can right dispute against might? Then came forward that same old woman whom I knew, and looked the policeman straight in the eyes. And the policeman averted his glance, and returned the stool to its owner.

I went up to her and said: Your eyes have more effect than all the pledges of England. For England, who gave us the Balfour Declaration, sends her officers to annul it; while you only looked upon that wicked one, and frustrated his evil intent.

She replied: Do not speak of him so; for he is a good *goy,* who saw that I was grieved and gave back her stool to that poor woman.—But have you said your afternoon prayer? I ask because, if you are free, I can put in your way the *mitzvah* of visiting the sick. The *rabbanit* is now really and truly ill. If you wish, come with me and I shall take you by a short route.—I joined her and we went together.

From alley to alley, from courtyard to courtyard, we made our way down, and at each step she took she would pause to give a sweet to a child, or a coin to a beggar, or to ask the health of a man's wife, or if it were a woman, the health of her husband. I said: Since you are concerned with everyone's welfare, let me ask about yours.

She answered: Blessed be The Name, for I lack nothing at his hand. The Holy One has given to each of his creatures according to its need;

and I too am one of these. But today I have a special cause for thanking him, for he has doubled my portion.

How is this?—I asked.

She replied: Each day I read the psalms appointed for the day: but today I read the psalms for two days together.

Even as she spoke, her face clouded over with grief.

Your joy has passed away, I said.

She was silent for a moment. Then she said: Yes, my son, I was joyful, and now it is not so.

Yet even as she spoke, the light shone out again from her face. She raised her eyes and said: Blessed be He, who has turned away my sorrow.

Why, I asked, were you joyful, yet afterwards sad, and now joyful again?

She said, very gently: Since your words are not chosen with care, I must tell you, this was not the right way to ask. Rather should you have said: "How have you deserved it, that God should turn away your sorrow?" For in His blessed eyes, all is one, whether sorrow or joy.

Perhaps in future, said I, my words will be chosen with care, since you teach me how one must speak. "Happy is the man who does not forget thee." It is a text of much meaning.

She said: You are a good man, and it is a good text you have told me; so I too shall not withhold good words. You asked why I was joyful, and why I was sad, and why I now rejoice.

Assuredly you know as I do, that all a man's deeds are appointed, from the hour of his birth to the hour of his death; and accordingly, the number of times he shall say his psalms. But the choice is free how many psalms he will say on any one day. This man may complete the whole book in a day, and that man may say one section a day, or the psalms for each day according to the day. I have made it my custom to say each day the psalms for that day; but this morning I went on and said the psalms for two days together. When I became aware of this I was sad, lest it mean that there was no more need for me in the world, and that I was disposed of and made to finish my portion in haste. For "it is a good thing to give thanks to the Lord"; and when I am dead I shall not be able to say one psalm, or even one word.— Then the Holy One saw my grief, and showed His marvellous kindness by allowing me to know that such is His very own will. If it pleases The Name to take my life, who am I that I should grieve? Thus He at once turned away my sorrow. Blessed be He and blessed be His name.

I glanced at her, wondering to myself by what path one might come to a like submission. I thought of the men of ancient times, and their virtuous ways; I spoke to her of past generations. Then I said: You have seen with your own eyes more than I can describe in words.

She answered: When a person's life is prolonged for many days and years, it is granted him to see many things; good things, and yet better things.

Tell me, I said to her, of these same good things.

She was silent for a little while; then she said: How shall I begin? Let me start with my childhood. When I was a little girl, I was a great chatterbox. Really, from the time I stood up in the morning till the time I lay down at night, chatter never ceased from my lips. There was an old man in our neighbourhood, who said to those delighting in my chatter: "A pity it is for this little girl; if she wastes all her words in childhood, what will be left for her old age?" I became terribly frightened, thinking this meant that I might die the very next day. But in time I came to fathom the old man's meaning, which was that a person must not use up in a short while what is allotted him for a whole lifetime. I made a habit of testing each word to see if there was real need for it to be said, and practised a strict economy of speech. As a result of this economy, I saved up a great store of words, and my life has been prolonged until they are all finished. Now that only a few words remain, you ask me to speak them. If I do so it will hasten my end.

Upon such terms, said I, I would certainly not ask you to speak. But how is it that we keep walking and walking, yet we have still not come to the house of the *rabbanit?*

She said: You shall have in mind those courtyards we used to take for a short cut. But now that most of the City has been settled by the Arabs, we must go by a roundabout way.

We approached one of these courtyards. She said: Do you see this courtyard? Forty families of Israel once lived here, and here were two synagogues, and here in the daytime and nighttime there was study and prayer. But they left this place, and Arabs came and occupied it.

We approached a tumble-down house. She said: Do you see this house? Here was a great academy where the scholars of the Torah lived and studied. But they left this house, and Arabs came and occupied it.

We came to the asses' stalls. She said: Do you see these stalls? Here stood a soup-kitchen, and the deserving poor would enter in hungry and go forth satisfied. But they abandoned this place, and Arabs came and occupied it. Houses from which prayer and charity and study of the Torah never ceased, now belong to the Arabs and their asses.— My son, we have reached the courtyard of the *rabbanit*'s house. Go in, and I shall follow you later. This unhappy woman, because of the seeming good she has known abroad, does not see the true good at home.

What is the true good? I asked.

She laughed, saying: Ah, my son, you should not need to ask. Have you not read the verse, "Happy art thou who art chosen to dwell in thy courtyards"? For these same courtyards are the royal courts of the Holy One, the courts of our God, in the midst of Jerusalem.— When men say "Jerusalem" their way is to add the words, "Holy City." But when *I* say "Jerusalem" I add nothing more, since the holiness is contained in the name; yes, in the very name itself.—Go up, my son, and do not trip on the stairs. Many a time have I said to the keeper of the community funds that these stairs are in need of repair; and what answer did he give me? That this building is old and due to be demolished, therefore it is not worth while spending a penny on its upkeep. So the houses of Israel fall into disuse until they are abandoned, and the sons of Ishmael enter and take possession. Houses that were built with the tears of their fathers—and now they abandon them. But again I have become a chatterer, and hasten my end.

I entered, and found the *rabbanit* lying in bed. Her head was bandaged and a poultice had been laid upon her throat. She coughed loudly, so that even the medicine bottles placed by her bedside would shake at each cough. I said to her: *Rabbanit*, are you ill?—She sighed and her eyes filled with tears. I sought for words of comfort, but the words would not come. All I could say, with my eyes downcast, was: So you are ill and deserted.

She sighed again and replied: Yes, I am ill as ill can be. In the whole world there is no one so ill as I am. All the same, I am not deserted. Even here in Jerusalem, where nobody knows me, and nobody knows the honours done to me in my own town, even here there is one woman who waits on me, who comes to my room and fetches a drop of soup for my royal feast. What do you hear from my grandson? He is angry with me, to be sure, because I have not written to thank him for the stove. Now I ask you, how shall I go out to buy ink and pen and paper for the writing of letters? It is hard enough even to bring a spoonful of soup to my lips.—I am surprised that Tilli has not come.

If you are speaking, said I, of that gracious old woman who brought me here, she told me that she would come very soon.

Said the *rabbanit*, I cannot tell whether she is gracious: at least she is efficacious. Look you, how many holy, holy women there are about Jerusalem, who go buzzing like bees with their incantations and supplications, yet not one of them has come to me and said, "*Rabbanit*, do you need any help?"—My head, oh my head.—If the pains in my heart won't take me off quickly, the pains in my head will take me off first.

I said to her: I can see that speech is difficult for you.

She answered: *You* say that speech is difficult for me; and *I* say that my whole existence is difficult for me. Even the cat knows this, and keeps away from his home. Yet people say that cats are home-loving creatures. He finds my neighbour's mice more tasty, to be sure, than all the dainties I feed him. What was I meaning to say? I forget all I mean to say. Now Tilli is so different. There she goes, with the bundles of years heaped up on her shoulders, bundle on bundle; yet all her wits serve her, although she must be twice my age. If my father

—God bless his pious memory—were alive at this day, he would be thought of as a child beside her.

I urged the *rabbanit* to tell me about this Tilli.

And did you not mention her yourself? Nowadays people don't know Tilli; but there was a time when everyone did, for then she was a great, rich woman with all kinds of business concerns. And when she gave up all these and came to Jerusalem, she brought along with her I can't say how many barrels of gold, or if not barrels, there is no doubt that she brought a chest full of gold. My neighbours remember their mothers telling them, how, when Tilli came to Jerusalem, all the best people here came a-courting, either for themselves or for their sons. But she sent them packing and stayed a widow. At first she was a very wealthy widow, and then quite a well-to-do widow, until at last she became just any old woman.

Judging from Tilli's appearance, said I, one would think that she had never seen hard times in her life.

The *rabbanit* replied with scorn: *You* say that she has never seen hard times in her life: and *I* say that she has never seen good times in her life. There is no enemy of mine whom I would—bless—with the afflictions that Tilli has borne. *You* suppose that, because she is not reduced to living off the public funds, she has enjoyed a happy life: and *I* believe that there is not a beggar knocking on the doors who would exchange his sorrows for hers.—Oh, my aches and my pains. I try to forget them, but they will not forget me.

I perceived that the *rabbanit* knew more than she cared to disclose. Since I felt that no good would come of further questioning, I showed myself ready to leave by rising from my chair.

Said the *rabbanit:* "The sweep hadn't stepped into the chimney, but his face was already black." You have scarcely sat down in your chair, and already you are up and away. Why all this haste?

I said: If you wish me to stay, I will stay.

She made no answer, so I began speaking of Tilli again, and asked if I might be told her story.

And if I tell you, said the *rabbanit,* will it benefit you, or benefit her? I have no liking for tale-bearers: they spin out their cobwebs, and call it fine tapestry. I will only say this, that the Lord did a mercy to that good man when He put the evil spirit into that apostate, may her name be blotted out.—Why are you gaping at me? Don't you understand the meaning of Yiddish?

I understand Yiddish quite well, said I, but I cannot understand what you are saying, *rabbanit*. Who is the good man, and who is the apostate you have cursed?

Perhaps I should bless her then, perhaps I should say, "Well done, Mistress Apostate, you who have changed the gold coin for the brass farthing."—See, again you are staring at me as if I talked Turkish. You have heard that my husband of blessed memory was a rabbi, wherefore they called me *rabbanit;* and you have not heard that my father too was a rabbi? Such a rabbi, that in comparison with him, all other rabbis might rank as pupils of an infant school: and I speak of *real* rabbis, look you, not of those who wear the mantle and give themselves airs.—What a world, what a world it is! A deceitful world, and all it contains is deceit and vanity.—But my father, of blessed and pious memory, was a rabbi from his childhood, and all the matchmakers in the province bustled about to find him a wife. Now there was a certain rich widow, and when I say rich, you know that I mean it. This widow had only one daughter—would she had never been born.—She took a barrel full of gold dinars, and said to the matchmakers: "If you match that man to my daughter, this barrel full of gold will be his; and if it is not sufficient, I shall add to it!" But her daughter was not a fit match for that holy man; for she was already tainted with the spirit of perverseness, as is shown by her latter end, and she fled away from her home, and entered the house of the nuns, and deserted her faith. Yes, at the very hour when she was to be led to her bridal, she ran away. That poor stricken mother wasted half her fortune in efforts to reclaim her. Her appeal went up to the Emperor himself; and even the Emperor was powerless to help. For they who have once entered the house of the nuns may never go forth alive. You know now who that apostate was; the daughter of . . . hush, for here she comes.

Tilli entered the room. She was carrying a bowl of soup, and seeing me she said:

Ah, you are still here! But stay, my friend, stay. It is a great *mitzvah* to visit the sick.—*Rabbanit,* how much better you look! Truly salvation comes in the wink of an eye; for The Name is healing you every minute. I have brought a little soup to moisten your lips: now, my dear, raise your head and I shall prop up your pillow. There, my dear, that is right.—My son, I am sorry that you do not live in the City, for then you would see for yourself how the *rabbanit's* health is improving day by day.

And do I not live in Jerusalem? I said.—Surely Nachlat Shivah is Jerusalem?

It is indeed, answered Tilli. God forbid that it should be otherwise. Rather may the day come when Jerusalem extends as far as Damascus, and in every direction. But the eye that has seen all Jerusalem enclosed within her walls cannot get accustomed to viewing what is built beyond the walls as the City itself. It is true that all the Land of Israel is holy, and I need hardly say, the surroundings of Jerusalem: yet the holiness that is within the walls of the City surpasses all else. My son, there is nothing I have said which you do not know better than I. Why then have I said it? Only that I might speak the praise of Jerusalem.

I could read in the eyes of the *rabbanit* a certain resentment, because Tilli was speaking to me rather than to her. So I took my leave and went away.

Various preoccupations kept me for a while from going to the City; and after that came the nuisance of the tourists. How well we know these tourists, who descend upon us and upon the land, all because the Place has made a little space for us here! They come, now, to see what has happened; and having come, they regard us as if we were created solely to serve them. Yet one good thing may be said for the tourists: in showing them "the sights," we see them ourselves. Once or twice, having brought them to the City to show them the Western Wall, I met Tilli there. It seemed to me that a change had come over her. Although she had always walked without support, I noticed that she now leaned on a stick. On account of the visitors, I was unable to linger. For they had come to spy out the whole land, not to spend time upon an old woman not even mentioned in their itineraries.

When the tourists had left Jerusalem, I felt restless in myself. After trying without success to resume work, I bestirred myself and walked to the City, where I visited of my own accord all the places I had shown to the visitors. How can I describe what I saw? He who in His goodness daily renews the works of creation, perpetually renews His own City. New houses may not have been built, nor new trees planted; yet Jerusalem herself is ever new. I cannot explain the secret of her infinite variety. We must wait, all of us, for those great sages who will one day enlighten us.

I came upon the man of learning whom you already know, and he drew me to his house, where he set before me all his recent findings. We sat together in deep contentment, while I asked my questions, and he replied; or spoke of problems, which he resolved; or mentioned cloudy matters, which he made clear. How good it is, how satisfying, to sit at the feet of one of the scholars of Jerusalem, and to learn the Law from his lips! His home is simple, his furnishings austere, yet his wisdom ranges far, like the great hill ranges of Jerusalem which are seen from the windows. Bare are the hills of Jerusalem; no temples or palaces crown them. Since the time of our exile, nation after nation has come and laid them waste. But the hills spread their glory like banners to the sky; they are resplendent in ever-changing hues; and not least in glory is the Mount of Olives, which bears no forest of trees, but a forest of tombs of the righteous, who in life and in death gave their thoughts to the Land.

As I stood up to go, the mistress of the house entered and said to her husband: You have forgotten your promise.—He was much perturbed at this, and said: Wonder of wonders; all the time I have known Tehilah she has never asked a favour. And now she wants me to say that she wishes to see you.

Are you speaking, said I, of Tilli, the old woman who showed me the way to your house? For it seems to me that you call her by another name.

Tehilah, he answered, is Tilli's true name, that was given to her in the synagogue. From this you may learn that even four or five generations ago, our forebears would give their daughters names that sound as though they had been recently coined. For this reason my wife's name is Techiyah, or Reborn, which one might suppose to have been devised in our own age of rebirth. Yet in fact it belongs to the time of the great Gaon, who required my wife's great-grandfather to call his daughter Techiyah; and my wife bears her name.

I said: You speak now of the custom four or five generations ago. Can it be that this Tehilah is so old?

He smiled, saying: Her years are not written upon her face, and she is not in the habit of telling her age. We only know it because of what she once let slip. It happened that Tehilah came to congratulate us at the wedding of our son; and the blessing she gave to our son and his bride was that it might be granted for them to live to her age. My son asked, "What is this blessing with which you have blessed us?" And she answered him, "It is ninety years since I was eleven years old." This happened three years ago; so that now her age is, as she might express it, ninety years and fourteen: that is to say, one hundred and four.

I asked him, since he was already speaking of her, to tell me what manner of woman she was. He answered:

What is there to say? She is a saint; yes, in the true meaning of the word. And if you have this opportunity of seeing her, you must take it. But I doubt if you will find her at home; for she is either visiting the sick, or bringing comforts to the poor, or doing some other unsolicited *mitzvah*. Yet you may perhaps find her, for between *mitzvah* and *mitzvah* she goes home to knit garments or stockings for poor orphans. In the days when she was rich, she spent her wealth upon deeds of charity, and now that nothing is left her but a meagre pittance to pay for her own slender needs, she does her charities in person.

The scholar accompanied me as far as Tehilah's door. As we walked together he discoursed on his theories; but realising that I was not attending to his words, he smiled and said: From the moment I spoke of Tehilah, no other thought has entered your mind.

I would beg to know more of her, I replied.

He said: I have already spoken of her as she is today. How she was before she came to our land I do not know, beyond what everyone knows; that is to say, that she was a very wealthy woman, the owner of vast concerns, who gave up all when her sons and her husband died, and came here to Jerusalem. My late mother used to say, "When I see Tehilah, I know that there is a worse retribution than widowhood and the loss of sons." What form of retribution this was, my mother never said; and neither I, nor anyone else alive, knows; for all that generation which knew Tehilah abroad is now dead, and Tehilah herself says but little. Even now, when she is beginning to change, and speaks more than she did, it is not of herself.—We have come to her house; but it is unlikely that you will find her at home; for towards sunset she makes the rounds of the schoolrooms, distributing sweets to the younger children.

A few moments later I stood in the home of Tehilah. She was seated at the table, expecting me, so it seemed, with all her being. Her room was small, with the thick stone walls and arched ceiling that were universal in the Jerusalem of bygone days. Had it not been for the little bed in a corner, and a clay jar upon the table, I would have likened her room to a place of worship. Even its few ornaments—the hand-lamp of burnished copper, and a copper pitcher, and a lamp of the same metal that hung from the ceiling—even these, together with the look of the table, on which were laid a prayer-book, a Bible, and some third book of study, gave to the room the grace and still calm of a house of prayer.

I bowed my head saying: Blessed be my hostess.

She answered: And blessed be my guest.

You live here, said I, like a princess.

Every daughter of Israel, she said, is a princess; and, praised be the living God, I too am a daughter of Israel. It is good that you have come. I asked to see you; and not only to see you, but to speak with you also. Would you consent to do me a favor?

"Even to the half of my kingdom," I replied.

She said: It is right that you should speak of your kingdom for every man of Israel is the son of kings, and his deeds are royal deeds. When a man of Israel does good to his neighbour this is a royal deed. Sit down, my son: it makes conversation more easy. Am I not intruding upon your time? You are a busy man, I am sure, and need the whole day for gaining your livelihood. Those times have gone when we had leisure enough and were glad to spend an hour in talk. Now everyone is in constant bustle and haste. People think that if they run fast enough it will speed the coming of Messiah. You see, my son how I have become a chatterer. I have forgotten the advice of that old man who warned me not to waste words.

I was still waiting to learn the reason for her summons. But now, as if she had indeed taken to heart the old man's warning, she said nothing. After a while she glanced at me, and then looked away; then glanced at me again, as one might who is scrutinising a messenger to decide whether he is worthy of trust. At last she began to tell me of the death of the *rabbanit,* who had passed away during the night, while her stove was burning, and her cat lay warming itself at the flame—till the hearse-bearers came, and carried her away, and some-one unknown had taken the stove.

You see, my son, said Tehilah, a man performs a *mitzvah,* and one *mitzvah* begets another. Your deed was done for the sake of that poor woman, and now a second person is the gainer, who seeks to warm his bones against the cold.—Again she looked me up and down; then she said: I am sure you are surprised that I have troubled you to come.

On the contrary, I said, I am pleased.

If you are pleased, so am I. But my pleasure is at finding a man who will do me a kindness; as for you, I do not know why you should be pleased.

For a moment she was silent. Then she said: I have heard that you are skilful at handling a pen—that you are, as they nowadays call it, a writer. So perhaps you will place your pen at my service for a short letter.

I took out my fountain-pen. She looked at it with interest, and said: You carry your pen about with you, like those who carry a spoon wherever they go, so that if they chance upon a meal—well, the spoon is ready to hand.

I replied: For my part, I carry the meal inside the spoon. And I explained to her the working of my fountain-pen.

She picked it up in her hand and objected: You say there is ink inside, but I cannot see one drop.

I explained the principle more fully, and she said: If it is so, they slander your generation in saying that its inventions are only for evil. See, they have invented a portable stove, and invented this new kind of pen: it may happen that they will yet invent more things for the good of mankind. True it is that the longer one lives, the more one sees. All the same, take this quill that I have myself made ready, and dip it in this ink. It is not that I question the usefulness of your pen; but I would have my letter written in my own way. And here is a sheet of paper; it is crown-paper, which I have kept from days gone by, when they knew how good paper was made. Upwards of seventy years I have kept it by me, and still it is as good as new.—One thing more I would ask of you: I want you to write, not in the ordinary cursive hand, but in the capital letters of the prayer-book and the Torah. I assume that a writer must at some time have transcribed, if not the Torah itself, at least the scroll of Esther that we read on *Purim.*

As a boy, I answered, I copied such a scroll exactly in the manner prescribed; and, believe this or not, everyone who saw that scroll praised it.

Said Tehilah: Although I have not seen it, I am sure you know how to write the characters as is required, without a single flaw. Now I shall make ready for you a glass of herb tea, while you proceed with your writing.

Please do not trouble, I said, for I have already taken something to drink.

If so, how shall I show hospitality? I know: I shall cut you a piece of sugar-loaf; then you can say a blessing, and I can add, Amen.

She gave me some of the sugar. Then, after a short silence she said:

Take up the quill and write. I shall speak in Yiddish, but you will write in the holy tongue. I have heard that now they teach the girls both to write and to speak the holy language: you see, my son, how the good Lord is constantly improving His world from age to age. When I was a child, this was not their way. But at least I understand my Hebrew prayer-book, and can read from the Torah, and the

Psalms, and the Ethics of the Fathers.—Oh dear, oh dear, today I have not finished my day.

I knew that she meant the day's portion of the psalms, and said to her: Instead of grieving you should rather be glad.

Glad?

Yes, I said, for the delay is from heaven, that one day more might be added to your sum of days.

She sighed, and said: If I knew that tomorrow our Redeemer would come, gladly would I drag out another day in this world. But as day follows day, and still our true Redeemer tarries and comes not, what is my life? and what is my joy? God forbid that I should complain of my years: if it pleases Him to keep me in life, it pleases me also. Yet I cannot help but ask how much longer these bones must carry their own burden. So many younger women have been privileged to set up their rest on the Mount of Olives, while I remain to walk on my feet, till I think I shall wear them away. And is it not better to present oneself in the Higher World while one's limbs are all whole, and return the loan of the body intact? I do not speak of putting on flesh, which is only an extra burden for the hearse-bearers. But at least it is good to die with whole limbs.—Again I am speaking too much: but now what matters it, a word less, or a word more. I am now fully prepared to return the deposit of my body, earth back to earth.—Take up your quill, my son, and write.

I dipped the quill pen in the ink, made ready the paper, and waited for Tehilah to speak. But she was lost in her thoughts, and seemed unaware of my presence. I sat there and gazed at her, my eyes taking in every wrinkle and furrow of her face. How many experiences she had undergone! She was in the habit of saying that she had seen good things, and yet better things. From what I had been told, these things could not have been so good. The adage was true of her, that the righteous wear mourning in their hearts, and joy upon their faces.

Tehilah became aware of me and, turning her head, said: Have you begun?

You have not told me what I am to write.

She said: The beginning does not need to be told. We commence by giving praise to God. Write: *With the help of the Holy Name, blessed be He.*

I smoothed the paper, shook the quill, and wrote, *With the help of the Holy Name, blessed be He.*

She sat up, looked at what I had written, and said: Good; very good. And now what next? Write as follows: *From the Holy City, Jerusalem, may she be built and established, speedily and in our days, Amen.*— In conversation I only say "Jerusalem," without additions. But in writing, it is proper that we should bring to mind the holiness of Jerusalem, and add a plea for her to be rebuilt; that the reader may take Jerusalem to his heart, and know that she is in need of mercy, and say a prayer for her.—Now, my son, write the day of the week, and the portion of the Torah for the week, and the number of years since the creation.

When I had set down the full date, she continued:

Now write, in a bold hand, and as carefully as you can, the letter *Lamed.*—Have you done this? Show me how it looks.—There is no denying that it is a good *Lamed,* though perhaps it could have been a trifle larger.—Now, my son, continue with *Khaf,* and after the *Khaf* write *Bet,* and after it *Vav.*—*Vav,* I was saying, and now comes *Dalet.* Show me now the whole word, *Likhvod,* "in honour of."—Very fine indeed. It is only right that the respectful prefix should be attractively written. Now add to that, "the esteemed rabbi"—ah, you have already done so! You write faster than I think: while I am collecting my thoughts, you have already set them down. Truly your father—may the light of God shine on him—did not waste the cost of your education . . . My son, forgive me, for I am so tired. Let us leave the writing of the letter till another day. When is it convenient for you to come?

Shall I come tomorrow? I said.

Tomorrow? Do you wish it? What day is tomorrow?

It is the day before new moon.

That is a good day for this thing. Then let it be tomorrow.

I saw that she was inwardly grieved, and thought to myself: The day before new moon is a time for prayer and supplication, a time for visits to the tomb of Rachel our Mother; surely she will not be able to attend to her letter. Aloud I said to her: If you are not free tomorrow I shall come on some other day.

And why not tomorrow?

Just because it is the day before the new moon.

She said: My son, you bring my sorrow before me, that on such a day I should be unable to go to Rachel our Mother.

I asked why she could not go.

Because my feet cannot carry me there.

There are carriages, I said, and buses as well.

Said Tehilah: When I first came to Jerusalem there were none of these buses, as they call them now, and a foolish word it is, too. There were not even carriages; so we used to walk. And since I have gone on foot for so long, it is now hardly worth changing my ways. Did you not say you are able to come tomorrow? If it pleases The Name to grant my wish, my life will be prolonged for yet a day more.

I left her and went on my way; and the following day I returned.

I do not know if there was any real need to return so soon. Possibly if I had waited longer, it would have extended her life.

As soon as I entered, I perceived a change. Tehilah's face, that always had about it a certain radiance, was doubly radiant. Her room shone out too. The stone floor was newly polished, and so were all the ornaments in the room. A white coverlet was spread over the little bed in the corner, and the skirtings of the walls were freshly colour-washed blue. On the table stood the jar, with its parchment cover, and a lamp and sealing wax were placed at its side. When had she found time to colour-wash the walls, and to clean the floor, and to polish all her utensils? Unless angels did her work, she must have toiled the night long.

She rose to welcome me, and said in a whisper:

I am glad that you have come. I was afraid you might forget, and I have a little business matter to attend to.

If you have somewhere to go, I said, I shall come back later.

I have to go and confirm my lease. But since you are here, sit down, and let us proceed with the letter. Then afterwards I shall go about my lease.

She set the paper before me and fetched the ink and the quill pen. I took up the quill pen and dipped it in the ink and waited for her to dictate her message.

Are you ready?—she said. Then I am ready, too!

As she spoke the word "ready" her face seemed to light up and a faint smile came to her lips. Again I prepared to write, and waited for her next words.

Where did we leave off? she said.—Was it not with the phrase, *In honour of the eminent rabbi?* Now you shall write his name.

Still I sat waiting.

She said in a whisper: His name is Shraga.—Have you written it? I have written.

She half-closed her eyes as if dozing. After some time she raised herself from her chair to look at the letter, and whispered again:—His name is Shraga. His name is Shraga.—And again she sat silent. Then she seemed to bestir herself, saying: I shall tell you in a general way what you are to write.—But again she lapsed back into silence, letting her eyelids droop.

I see, she said at last, that I shall have to tell you all that happened, so that you will understand these things and know how to write. It is an old story, of something which happened many years ago; yes, three and ninety years ago.

She reached for her walking-stick and let her head sink down upon it. Then again she looked up, with an expression of surprise, as a man might who thinks he is sitting alone and discovers a stranger in his room. Her face was no longer calm, but showed grief and disquiet as she felt for her stick, then put it by, and again took it up to lean upon, passing her hand over her brow to smooth out her wrinkles.

Finally she said: If I tell you the whole story, it will make it easier for you to write.—His name is Shraga.—Now I shall start from the very beginning.

She raised her eyes and peered about her; then, reassured that no one else could be listening, she began.

I was eleven years old at the time. I know this, because Father, of blessed memory, used to write in his Bible the names of his children and the dates of their births, his daughters as well as his sons. You will find the names in that Bible you see before you; for when I came to Jerusalem, my late brothers renounced their right to my father's holy books and gave them to me. As I said before, it is an old story, three and ninety years old; yet I remember it well. I shall relate it to you, and little by little you will understand. Now, are you listening?

I inclined my head and said: Speak on.

So you see, I was eleven years old. One night, Father came home from the synagogue, bringing with him some relative of ours, and with them Petachya Mordechai, the father of Shraga. When she saw them enter, my dear mother, peace be upon her soul, called me and told me to wash my face well and put on my Sabbath dress. She too put on her Sabbath clothes and bound her silk kerchief round her head, and, taking my hand, led me into the big room to meet father and his guests. Shraga's father looked at me and said, "Heaven protect you, you are a pretty child." Father stroked my cheek and said, "Tehilah, do you know who spoke to you? The father of your bridegroom-to-be spoke to you. May the influences be happy, my child: tonight you are betrothed." At once all the visitors blessed me with happy influences, and called me "the bride." Mother quickly bundled me back to her room to shield me from any evil eye, and kissed me, and said, "Now and henceforth, you are Shraga's betrothed; and God willing next year, when your bridegroom comes of age at thirteen for wearing the *tefillin,* we shall make your wedding."

I knew Shraga already, for we used to play with nuts and at hide-and-seek, until he grew too old and began to study the *Gemara.* After our betrothal I saw him every Sabbath when he would come to Father's house and repeat to him all he had learned through the week. Mother would give me a dish of sweets which I would take and offer to Shraga, and Father would stroke my cheek and beam upon my bridegroom.

And now they began to prepare for the wedding. Shraga's father wrote out the *tefillin,* and my father bought him a *tallit,* while I sewed a bag for the *tefillin* and another bag for the *tallit* that is worn on a Sabbath. Who made the large outer bag for both *tallit* and *tefillin* I cannot remember.

One Sabbath, four full weeks before the day fixed for the wedding, Shraga failed to come to our house. During the afternoon service, Father enquired at the house of study, and was told that he had gone on a journey. Now this journey was made to one of the leaders of the *Hassidim,* and Shraga had been taken by his father in order that he might receive a direct blessing on the occasion of his first wearing of *tallit* and *tefillin.* When my father learned this, his soul nearly parted from his body; for he had not known until then that Shraga's father was of the Sect. He had kept his beliefs a secret, for in those days the *Hassidim* were despised and persecuted, and Father was at the head of the persecutors; so that he looked upon members of the Sect as if (God forbid) they had ceased to belong to our people. After the *havdalah* ceremony, at the close of the Sabbath, Father tore up my marriage contract and sent the pieces to the house of my intended father-in-law. On the Monday, Shraga returned with his father, and they came to our house. My father drove them out with abuse; whereupon Shraga himself swore an oath that he would never forgive us the insult. Now Father knew well that he who cancels a betrothal must seek pardon from the injured party; yet he took no steps to obtain this. And when my mother implored him to appease Shraga, he made light of her entreaties, saying, "You have nothing to fear: he is only of the Sect." So contemptible were the *Hassidim* in my father's eyes that he took no heed in this thing wherein all men take heed.

Preparations for the wedding had been made. The poultry was on order, and the house was cluttered with sacks of flour and casks of honey for the making of loaves and cakes. In short, all was ready, and there lacked nothing but a bridegroom.—My father summoned a matchmaker; another bridegroom was found me; and with him I went to my bridal.

What became of Shraga, I do not know, for Father forbade any of our household to mention his name. Later I heard that he and all his people had removed to another town. Indeed they were in fear for their very lives, since, from the day when Father ended my betrothal, they were not called to the Law in synagogue; not even at the Rejoicing of the Law, when every man is called. They could not even come together for worship, for my father as head of the community would not let them assemble outside the fixed houses of prayer; and had they not removed to another town where they might be called to the Torah, they would not have survived the year.

Three years after the wedding, I was granted the birth of a son. And two years later, another son was born to me. And two years after that, I gave birth to a daughter.

Time passed uneventfully, and we lived at our ease. The children grew and prospered, while I and my husband watched them grow and were glad. I forgot about Shraga, and forgot that I had never received a note of pardon at his hand.

Mother and Father departed this life. Before his death, my father of blessed memory committed his affairs to his son and his sons-in-law, enjoining them all to work together as one. Our business flourished, and we lived in high repute. We engaged good tutors for our sons, and a foreign governess for our daughter; for in those days pious folk would have nothing to do with the local teachers, who were suspected of being free-thinkers.

My husband would bring these tutors from other towns; and whereas the local teachers were obliged to admit any student who came, even if he was not suitably qualified, tutors who had been brought from elsewhere were dependent upon those who engaged them and under no such obligation. Coming, as they did, alone, they would dine at our table on Sabbath days. Now my husband, who because of the pressure of his affairs could not make set times for study of the Torah, was especially glad of one such guest and his learned discourses. And I and the children delighted in the tuneful table hymns he would sing us. We did not know that this tutor was a *Hassid,* and his discourses the doctrines of *Hassidism,* and the airs that he sang us, *Hassidic* airs; for in all other respects he conducted himself like any other true believer of Israel. One Sabbath eve, having discoursed of the Torah, he closed his eyes and sang a hymn of such heavenly bliss that our very souls went forth at its sweetness. At the end, my husband asked him: "How may a man come to this experience of the divine?" The tutor whispered to him: "Let your honour make a journey to my *rebbe,* and you will know this and much more."

Some days later, my husband found himself in the city of the tutor's *rebbe.* On his return, he brought with him new customs, the like of which I had not seen in my father's house; and I perceived that these were the customs of the *Hassidim.* And I thought to myself, Who can now wipe the dust from your eyes, Father, that you may see what you have done, you who banished Shraga for being a *Hassid,* and now the husband you gave me in his stead does exactly as he did. If this thing does not come about as atonement for sin, I know not why it has come about.

My brother and brother-in-law saw what was happening, but they said not a word. For already the times had changed, and people were no longer ashamed to have *Hassidim* in the family. Men of wealth and position had come from other towns and married amongst us, who followed the customs of *Hassidism,* and even set up a house of prayer for their sect, and would travel openly to visit their *rebbes.* My husband did not attend their services, but in other respects he observed *Hassidic* customs and educated his sons in these ways, and from time to time would make journeys to his *rebbe.*

A year before our first-born son came of age, there was plague in the world, and many fell sick. There was not a house without its victims, and when the plague reached us, it struck our son. In the end the Lord spared him—but not for long. When he rose from his sickbed, he began to study the practice of the *tefillin* from the great code of the *shulhan aroukh.* And I saw this and was glad, that for all his *Hassidic* training his devotion to the Law was not lessened.

One morning our son rose up very early to go to the house of study. As he was about to enter, he saw there a man dressed in grave-clothes, resembling a corpse. It was not a dead man he had seen, but some demented creature who did many strange things. The child was overcome with terror and his senses left him. With difficulty was he restored to life. Restored to life he was indeed, but not to a long life. From that day on his soul flickered and wavered like a candle flame, like the soul of a man at the closing prayer of the Day of Atonement when his fate is about to be sealed. He had not come of age for wearing *tefillin* when he gave up his ghost and died.

Through the seven days of mourning I sat and meditated. My son had died after the *havdalah,* at the ending of Sabbath thirty days before he came of age for *tefillin.* And at the end of the Sabbath, after the *havdalah,* thirty days before I was to go to my bridal with Shraga, Father had torn up the marriage contract. Counting the days I found to my horror that the two evils had come about on the same day, at the same hour. Even if this were no more than chance, yet it was a matter for serious reflection.

Two years later, the boy's brother came of age—came, and did not come. He happened to go with his playfellows to the woods outside our town to fetch branches for the Festival of Weeks. He left his comrades in the woods, intending to call on the scribe who was preparing his *tefillin;* and he never returned. We thought at first that he had been stolen by gypsies, for a troop of them had been seen passing the town. After some days his body was found in the great marsh beside the woods; then he knew he must have missed his way and fallen in.

When we stood up from our mourning, I said to my husband, "Nothing remains to us now but our one little girl. If we do not seek forgiveness from Shraga, her fate will be as the fate of her brothers."

Throughout all those years we had heard nothing of Shraga. When he and his people left our town, they were forgotten, and their where-abouts remained unknown. My husband said, "Shraga is the *Hassid* of such and such a *rebbe:* I shall make a journey to his man, and find out where he lives."

Now my husband was not the *Hassid* of this same *rebbe:* on the contrary, he was opposed to him, because of the great dispute that had broken out between the *rebbes,* on account of a cattle-slaughterer, whom one had appointed and the other had dismissed. In the course of that quarrel a man of Israel was killed, and several families were uprooted, and several owners of property lost their possessions, and several persons ended their days in prison.

Nevertheless, my husband made the journey to the town where this *rebbe* lived. Before he had arrived there, the *rebbe* died, after dividing his ministry amongst his sons, who went away each to a different town. My husband journeyed from town to town, from son to son, enquiring each son where Shraga might be. Finally he was told, "If you are asking after Shraga, Shraga has become a renegade and joined our opponents." But no one knew where Shraga now lived.

When a man is a *Hassid,* you may trace him without difficulty. If he is not the disciple of one *rebbe,* he is the disciple of another. But with any ordinary unattached Jew, unless you know where he lives, how may he be found? My husband, peace be upon his soul, was accustomed to making journeys, for his business took him to many places. He made journey after journey enquiring for Shraga. On account of these travels his strength in time began to fail and his blood grew thin. At last, having travelled to a certain place, he fell sick there and died.

After I had set up his tombstone, I went back to my town and entered into business. While my husband was still alive, I had helped him in his affairs: now that he was dead, I speeded them with all my might. And the Lord doubled my powers until it was said of me, She has the strength of a man. It would have been well, perhaps, had wisdom been granted me in place of strength, but the Lord knows what he intends and does not require his own creatures to tell him what is good. I thought in my heart: all this toil is for my daughter's sake. If I add to my wealth, I shall add to her welfare. As my responsibilities became ever greater, I found I had no leisure to spend at home, except on Sabbaths and holy days: and even these days were apportioned, half to the service in synagogue, and the other half to the reception of guests. My daughter, so it seemed, was in no need of my company: for I had engaged governesses, and she was devoted to her studies. I received much praise on account of my daughter, and even the gentiles, who make fun of our accent, would say that she spoke their language as well as the best of their own people. Furthermore, these governesses would ingratiate themselves with my daughter, and invite her to their homes. In due course, I called the matchmakers, who found her a husband distinguished for his learning, and already qualified for the rabbinate. But I was not to enjoy a parent's privilege of leading my daughter to her bridal, for the evil spirit took possession of her, so that her reason became unhinged.

And now, my son, this is what I ask of you.—Write to Shraga for me, and say that I have forgiven him for all the sorrows that befell me at his hand. And say that I think he should forgive me, too: for I have been stricken enough.

For a long, long time I sat in silence, unable to speak a word. At last, secretly wiping a tear from my eye, I said to Tehilah:

Allow me to ask a question. Since the day when your father tore up the marriage contract, ninety years and more have elapsed. Do you really believe that Shraga is still alive? And if so, has anyone informed you where he may be found?

Tehilah answered: Shraga is not alive. Shraga has now been dead for thirty years. I know the year of his death, for in that year, on the seventh day of Adar, I went to a synagogue for the afternoon service. Following the week's reading from the Prophets, they said the memorial prayer for the dead, and I heard them pray for the soul of Shraga. After the service, I spoke to the beadle of the synagogue, and asked him who this Shraga might be. He mentioned the name of a certain relative of the dead man, who had given instructions for his soul to be remembered. I went to this relative, and heard what I heard.

If Shraga is dead, then, do you propose to send him a letter?

Tehilah answered: I suppose you are thinking that this poor old woman's wits are beginning to fail her, after so many years; and that she is relying upon the post office to deliver a letter to a dead man.

I said: Then tell me, what will you do?

She rose, and picking up the clay jar that stood on the table, raised it high above her head, intoning in a kind of ritual chant:

I shall take this letter—and set it in this jar; I shall take this wax —and seal up this jar; and take them with me—this letter and this jar.

I thought to myself, And even if you take the jar and the letter with you, I still do not see how your message will come to Shraga. Aloud I said to her: Where will you take your jar with its letter?

Tehilah smiled and said softly: Where will I take it? I will take it to the grave, my dear. Yes, I shall take this jar, and the letter inside it, straight to my grave. For up in the High World they are well acquainted with Shraga, and will know where to find him. And the postmen of the Holy One are dependable, you may be sure; they will see that the letter is delivered.

Tehilah smiled again. It was a little smile of triumph, as of a precocious child who has got the better of an argument with her elders.

After a while she let her head sink upon her walking-stick and seemed again to be half asleep. But soon she glanced up and said: Now that you understand the whole matter, you can write of your own accord.—And again her head dropped over her stick.

I took up the quill pen and wrote the letter. When I had finished, Tehilah raised her head and enquired: Is it done now?—I began to read the letter aloud, while she sat with her eyes closed, as if she had lost interest in the whole matter and no longer desired very greatly to hear. When the reading was over, she opened her eyes and said:

Good, my son, good and to the point. Perhaps it might have been phrased rather differently, but even so, the meaning is clear enough. Now, my son, hand me the pen and I shall sign my name. Then I can put the letter in the jar; and after that I shall go about my lease.

I dipped the pen in the ink and handed it to her, and she took it and signed her name. She passed the pen over certain of the characters to make them more clear. Then she folded the letter and placed it inside the jar, and bound the piece of parchment over the top. Then she kindled the lamp, and took wax for sealing, and held it against the flame until the wax became soft; then she sealed the jar with the wax. Having done these things, she rose from her place and went towards her bed. She lifted up the coverlet and placed the jar under the pillow of the bed. Then she looked at me fairly, and said in a quiet voice:

I must make haste to confirm my lease. Bless you, my son, for the pains you have taken. Now and henceforth I shall not trouble you more.

So saying, she made smooth the coverlet of her bed, and took up her stick, and went to the door, and reached up that she might lay her lips to the *mezuzah,* and waited for me to follow. She locked the door behind us and walked ahead with brisk steps; and I overtook her and went at her side.

As she walked, she looked kindly upon every place that she passed and every person that she met. Suddenly she stopped and said:

My son, how can they abandon these holy places and these faithful Jews?

At that time, I still did not comprehend all she meant by these words.

When we reached the parting of the ways, she stopped again and said: Peace with you.—But when she saw that I was resolved not to leave her, she said no more. She went up by the wide steps that lead to the courtyard of the Communal Centre, and entered, and I followed.

We went into the Communal Centre, which administers the affairs of the living and the dead. Two of the clerks sat there at a desk, their ledgers before them and their pens in their hands, writing and taking sips at their Turkish coffee as they wrote. When they saw Tehilah, they set their pens down and stood up in respect. They spoke their welcome, and hastened to bring her a chair.

What brings you here?—asked the elder of the two clerks.

She answered: I have come to confirm my lease.

He said: You have come to confirm your lease: and we are of opinion that the time has come to annul it.

Tehilah was terrified.—What is all this? she cried.

He said: Surely you have already joined the immortals?

Laughing at his own joke, the clerk turned to me, saying: Tehilah, bless her, and may she live for many, many years, is in the habit of coming every year to confirm the bill of sale on the plot for her grave on the Mount of Olives. So it was last year, and the year before that, and three years ago, and ten and twenty and thirty years ago, and so will she go on till the coming of the Redeemer.

Said Tehilah: May he come, the Redeemer: may he come, the

Redeemer. Would to God he would hasten and come. But as for me, I shall trouble you no more.

The clerk asked, assuming a tone of surprise: Are you going to a *kibbutz,* then, like these young girls they call "pioneers"?

Tehilah said: I am not going to a *kibbutz,* I am going to my own place.

What, said the clerk, are you returning to your home country?

Tehilah said: I am not returning to my home country; I am returning to the place whence I came: as it is written, *And to the dust thou shalt return.*

Tut-tut, said the clerk, do you think that the Burial Society has nothing to do? Take my advice, and wait for twenty or thirty years more. Why all the haste?

She said quietly: I have already ordered the corpse-washers and the layers-out, and it would be ill-mannered to make sport of these good women.

The clerk's expression changed, and it was evident that he regretted his light words. He now said:

It is good for us to see you here: for so long as we see you, we have before us the example of a long life; and should you desert us—God forbid—it is as if you take away from us this precedent.

Said Tehilah: Had I any more years to live, I would give them gladly to you, and to all who delight in life. Here is the lease for you to sign.

When the clerk had endorsed the bill of sale, Tehilah took it and placed it in the fold of her dress. She said:

Now and henceforth I shall trouble you no more. May The Name be with you, dear countrymen; for I go to my place.

She rose from her chair, and walked to the door and reached up to lay her lips to the *mezuzah,* and kissed the *mezuzah,* and so went away.

When she saw that I still went with her, she said: Return to your own life, my son.

I thought, said I, that when you spoke of confirming the lease, you meant the lease of your house; but instead—

She took me up in the midst of my words. But instead, said she, I confirmed the lease of my long home. Yet may the Holy One grant that I have no need to dwell there for long, before I rise again, with all the dead of Israel. Peace be upon you, my son. I must make haste and return to my house, for I am sure that the corpse-washers and the layers-out already await me.

I stood there in silence and watched her go, until she passed out of sight among the courts and the alleys.

Next morning I went to the City to enquire how she fared. On my way, I was stopped by the man of learning to whose house Tehilah had led me. For some while he kept me in conversation, and when I wished to take my leave, he offered to accompany me.

I am not going home yet, I said. I am on my way to see Tehilah.

He said: Go; at the end of a long life.

Seeing my surprise, he added: *You* must live. But that saint has now left us.

I parted from him and went on alone. As I walked, I thought again and again: Tehilah has left us, she has gone on alone: she has left us, and gone on alone. I found that my feet had carried me to the house of Tehilah, and I opened her door and entered.

Still and calm was the room: like a house of prayer, when the prayer has been said. There, on the stone floor, flowed the last tiny rivulets of the waters in which Tehilah had been cleansed.

Translated by Walter Lever

Yitzhak Shenhar

On Galilean Shores

The path climbs up the hill, hedged by nettles and sharp-edged boulders. The boulders look as though blackened by some searing heat that is for ever scorching them from below. The path leads to the crooked and dilapidated spiked iron gate of the village.

From the road only four houses can be seen on the crest of the hill. They stand remote, anyhow, with the sun beating down on them. From there onwards the heavenly pastures appear to extend as far as the horizon, and anyone standing among the houses from afar looks as though he had stepped right out of the gate of heaven. The other houses are arranged in lanes on the yonder side of the hill, with the synagogue in the centre of the square. Every morning at sunrise the growling voice of prayer of Reb Jehiel Michel Schwartz, a founder and one of the village's first farmers, emerges. One by one his friends have left this world and have gone to their eternal rest in the small cemetery behind the village. Reb Jehiel Michel alone has remained behind, the grandfather of the place. He lives with the family of his eldest son in the "historical" red-roofed house that has remained unaltered ever since the early days. His second son has left and settled in one of the villages in the coastal plain. He writes to his father but twice a year, at Passover and the New Year. After the morning prayer in the synagogue grandfather returns home and begins slowly to rake and weed the vegetable garden. The synagogue remains empty. It is a high, narrow building, its whitewash peeling, and without any trees or shrubs surrounding it, as though proclaiming stoutly: I need nothing but the vault of heaven above! The small houses of the village stand at a distance, their faces averted. Most of them hide behind clumps of bougainvillaea all of which spell earthiness of reddish mauve: Only Dr. Hermann's house is unafraid and approaches the synagogue. This house is just a year old and still looks raw and unfinished. It is built half of brick and half of wood, half of it rests on the ground and the other half hovers in the air on poles. In the small garden in between the poles a brood of white chicks run about all day long, rolling about in the hot hollows of the dusty earth. On the Sabbath also Dr. Hermann's mare rests in the shade, half closing her eyes and watching the sun as it traverses the sky.

II

Dr. Max Hermann had been a solicitor in a small German town. He is a tall, energetic and forceful man, a man of the world. When catastrophe threatened the Jews of his native land, he did not wait until it was too late, but seized the opportunity and migrated to Palestine, taking with him his wife, his baby son Uri, and his modest savings. It took him just a fortnight after coming here to acquire a permanent suntan and to efface all signs of his profession; he shaved off his hair, took off his tie and sported heavy boots. On foot and on horse-back he toured the country's settlements and finally came to the conclusion that it would be good to settle in the neighbourhood of the Sea of Galilee, there being both sun and water to ripen the fruit which would have an assured market. So Dr. Hermann moved his family and settled in the small village. He built himself a house and bought a parcel of land on which he planted oranges and bananas. Now he spends the entire day in his orchard and with dusk returns home in his small cart, sitting upright on top of the green fodder which he is taking home for his cow. His coat is slung over his shoulders, the whip stuck into the side by the axle, his whole appearance a cross between the bailiff of a large estate and someone returning from a picnic. As he comes up to the village he lifts his straw hat and greets everybody.

His wife Susi is a capable woman, angular, with thin, bony shoulders. From the day she came to the village her mouth took on a permanently crooked expression and a single gold tooth glitters as a reminder of better days that are irrevocably gone. She works unremittingly all day long, her eyebrows drawn up to her forehead as though she herself is surprised at her present estate. Time and again she calls from the yard with a thin voice:

"Theo, please have a look what Urik is doing!"

Her brother Theo, a twenty-two-year-old young man who had spent two semesters at his native university in the faculty of humanities, shambles off in search of Urik. He is generally to be found standing with a nail in his hand, puncturing the wire netting of the balcony to admit the flies into the house. The child hugs his uncle's knees, grasping them like two pillars. He talks in a mixture made up of the language of the kindergarten and that of his mother who sees to it that he will not forget the European language. Theo cannot get over the queer contradiction of the child's flaxen hair and the broken Hebrew words spoken by his small mouth. It always makes him laugh to hear this talk and he swings Uri through the air in silent mirth.

Theo came to Palestine a year after his sister's family had settled in the village. He has already been with them for a number of weeks, but his brother-in-law has still not found any spare time to discuss his future in this country. The three spotlessly clean rooms of the house are filled with the heavy furniture brought in a "lift" from Germany. The elegant bookshelves overflow with law books and with works of Goethe, Schiller and Heine. Theo wanders aimlessly among the furniture. At times he reads a book with one leg thrown over the arm-rest of an easy-chair. At other times he immerses himself in the family archives, among pink letters, snaps of hikes to the Black Forest and albums of poetry dating back to his sister's girlhood. Dr. Hermann and his wife walk round him hurriedly, talking abruptly as though he, too, were an old and superfluous piece of furniture.

III

In the mornings Theo goes outside and walks up between the farm houses at the top of the hill. For a little while he stands among the ruts of the path and gazes at his surroundings. The landscape appears as a completely yellow pattern criss-crossed by bright blue and green stripes. The mountains send their greetings, their summits covered by strips of fields, their slopes weighed down by a string of isolated white houses like a heavily-loaded caravan of camels. Between the mountain clefts the blue hangs like a tapestry. The shadow of a feathery cloud climbs the slopes of the meadows. The palm trees nod their heads in the avenue which runs down to the lake like a column of nudists on their way to swim, carrying their clothes on their heads. The lake crouches between its shores like a basin of blue, little wavelets skip and hop on it; it appears as though it is not the sun that is reflected in them but a light that glows at the bottom of the water. Theo stands and looks, and the lenses of his glasses gleam in the sunlight. Every morning he gazes at the spectacle without it losing its novelty. A smile crosses his lips and comes to rest crookedly on his face.

At this time of day Geula passes by on her way to the cooperative store.

Geula smiles at him and asks: "Isn't it beautiful?" as though she had a personal share in the creation of the landscape.

"Beautiful," Theo answers with bated breath and squints as though blinking back a tear.

Geula continues on her way, lightly swinging the basket on her arm. She bends her neck a little on account of her heavy, wild mop of hair. Her tanned feet step out lightly in their sandals on the pointed stones of the path.

Geula is the granddaughter of Grandfather Reb Jehiel Michel, and this aristocratic descent imposes certain obligations on her. Geula is able to ride a horse bareback and excels at wielding a scythe. At the time of the disturbances she used to go up on the look-out on top of the water tower and spend days and nights with the men in the guard houses, and load their rifles. At village festivities she is called to the stage to recite poems, which she does in the correct oriental pronunciation without making any mistakes. Even so, she has no boy friend of her own in the village; she prefers her freedom to all the young men of the village. Her friends sometimes tease her that she will end up by having to call in a marriage broker. Geula wrinkles her somewhat broad nose, laughs, draws up her shoulders and in answer whistles the tune of:

"Hey, young man from the villages of Galilee!"

Theo follows her with his eyes and says to himself: There goes young Palestine. As uncomplicated as a wild sprig, perhaps excellent, maybe lacking in something, but in any event healthy and definite. It is a strange thing that there are people who search for the Land of Israel and do not know where to find it.

IV

Where the path bites into the road stands a leafy tree with an iron bench underneath. This is where Reb Jehiel Michel Granddad sits to rest himself from the heat of the day, and Theo comes and sits by his side. The sun has lost its fierceness and stray beams filter through the branches and come to rest on Grandfather's wrinkled face. His sparse, greenish-grey beard covers his open shirt. His neck threatens to creak with every turn of his head. Granddad's eyes have a habit of screwing up during the day-time, but towards evening they are wide open and their deep sockets reveal traces of light blue. Granddad straightens his black skull-cap and gazes into the distance towards Mount Hermon. The mountain looks at him from afar, its skull-cap a stationary cloud in the heart of heaven.

Reb Jehiel Michel chews at his remaining teeth and without any regard for chronology slowly tells about the group of nine people who had first come to settle in the place, about Isser Schechter who had been the consul of a foreign state in his native town, about brave Ze'ev Epstein who used to play the violin on the desolate hill and whose tunes rent the heart, and about Hirsch-Mendel Rabinov who, on coming to this country, used to examine every tree he happened to pass to see whether it flowed with honey. He came to mention the son of Meir-Leib Ashkenazi, the first watchman of the place, who was murdered and whose body was only found three days later, over there, between those hills. In the middle of these reminiscences the face of Herzl, whom he had the good fortune to see on the road between Jaffa and Jerusalem, surfaces in his memory, and he describes it as truly majestic. This led Granddad on to the troubles of the Turkish Holy War during the World War, of the *Badl* head tax, and with a bony finger he points to the place where the huts made of straw and dung stood, about the beams of which twisted large snakes. In one of those huts Sarah-Feige Goldenberg gave birth to twins, both of whom died one night. He quietly tells of disease, hunger and locust plagues; as he speaks his tongue slides over his palate as though tasting it. He pleasurably scratches the back of his neck; he does not care whether Theo understands all he says in Yiddish. The slat of sunlight moves across his face and settles on his forehead. Fifty years of activity confront him in all their minute details, from the day he departed for these shores on the boat "Iris" right to the present day.

Theo sits and listens, his hands quietly resting on his knees. Tough pioneers, he reflects. This grandfather and his comrades no doubt knew some secret that has been lost to the present generation. It must be that man has a certain sum total of spiritual and material life. When he makes no concession in matters of the soul, it is easier for him to renounce things of the body, to live in a hut with snakes, to suffer hunger and to give birth in the open field. But now men enjoy a measure of bodily comfort without which they cannot live, and they make their concessions in matters of the soul. Thus Theo reflects, for he tends to interpret to himself all the experiences he meets with.

Grandfather relates the incidents of a living past in which nothing is unimportant. The present is but ephemeral and unsettled and has no access to his heart. He only sees the men of his own generation, he does not notice that their children and grandchildren are leaving the village. Some of them have actually become shopkeepers in town, and have shaken off their earthy odour and their peasant origin. For the last twenty years Grandfather has served as honorary president of the village council and has not missed a single meeting; but he falls asleep as soon as the agenda is being read. Were it not for this, he would hear the constant complaint: A long time ago American Jews bought parcels of land, and since they themselves did nothing with them, they gave them to the farmers on loan; now that the price of land has risen they demand them back from the villagers. The farms might collapse, and the farmers declare with hoarse voices that they will rise up like one man with rifles in their hands to greet the tricksters. The confusion grows by leaps and bounds, causing jealousy and strife. But Granddad notices nothing of all this. Those purely transitory matters affect the upper sphere of village life while he has already descended to the lower sphere that is all confidence and unshakable reality. His mumbling at the dawn service is aimed at the people of the past who rest in peace in the little cemetery.

Meanwhile the day has waned and the mountains wrap themselves in silence. From the Lake springs a cool breeze that causes the palm trees to rustle in the avenue. The ramshackle bus that plies between the village and Tiberias has made its last journey and, blowing its horn, has clambered up among the stones and has fallen silent. Grandfather shakes his shoulders and coughs. He rises and goes to the synagogue for the evening prayer. With bent legs he climbs the hill; Geula his granddaughter walks down the hill, wearing a pink dress with a black belt round her waist. As he passes her, Grandfather places his hand on her shock of hair and ruffles it affectionately. Theo still sits on the bench and looks at them, his hands spread out motionlessly on his knees.

V

Theo and Geula walk leisurely along the road between green hedges and acacia trees. The day slowly gathers up its rich crop of colour and deposits it at the end of the horizon. The first stars are lit on the tops of the mountains and frogs tune up for the shore choir.

"You were born here, in this place?" Theo starts the conversation.

"Yes, I was born here and I have lived here all my life."

"Then you are wholly a product of the country," Theo answers happily and blinks through the lenses of his spectacles. "No doubt, you just take the life here, the landscape and everything else for granted."

Geula looks at him sideways and cocks her ears suspiciously. And what does this young man imagine, perhaps he means to allude to her being a *Sabra*. She immediately tries to think up a weighty answer so as to make things quite clear. "Perhaps you imagine that I have never heard of Freud?" she asks aggressively, blushes and turns her face away.

"No, no," Theo twists his face and waves his hands towards her. "No, not at all. I meant to say that you are a complete person, with your soul untorn, without the suffering due to changes of values. Something that has really sprung from the soil and not from some Zionist society."

He walks heavily, treading on his heels. Geula walks along at ease, fingering the thin gold chain round her neck which has come down to her from her grandmother. It does not occur to Theo that she only wears it in his honour, the necklace being worn only on festivals.

"And you, what are you going to do here?" Geula asks. "Are you going to settle in the village?"

"I think I shall go in for agriculture," Theo says and he himself is not aware of the hesitation in his answer. "We have not yet decided anything. I might start a mixed farm in partnership with my brother-in-law."

"And I want to go to town," his companion says, and unconsciously arranges the skirt of her dress that flares out in pleats.

"To town?" Theo stares at her perplexedly. "You are going to town? But why?"

"Why?" Geula answers with a question. "I too want to see life!" A car rushes past them; a woman's chiffon scarf flutters from its window. Geula follows it with her eyes until it disappears, and continues excitedly: "All your life you have lived in a town! But I? You have studied and have been in the great world; I have seen nothing and I know nothing. Here the days pass among cows and manure and petty worries; one just vegetates. It is a sleepy life, you are asleep, and when you wake up you are old without ever having lived."

Theo looks away from her. He bends down to pluck a blade of grass and chews it. The reflection of the sunset blinds the lenses of his spectacles and makes him grope his way.

"Take your grandfather, for example," he says after a pause. "I listened to him tell of past events. What a rich life he has behind him!"

"Oh, yes, Granddad," Geula says softly and leaves it at that. She thinks for a moment and continues: "And what does Granddad really know? All the young people make their quiet get-away, for it isn't worth their while to sit in this forsaken place. They leave for the towns and the *kibbutzim*. There are whole familes that have moved to a *kibbutz*. To a *kibbutz!* You understand? During the troubles there was an alert day and night until we dropped with fatigue because we had no one to relieve us. When a visiting lecturer comes out here once in six weeks he begins to stammer when he sees his audience and feels like running away."

They come to the little bridge that spans the *wadi* and sit down on the low stone parapet. A Yemenite rides past on the narrow path beside the road, quietly humming a tune, and his donkey steps out in a great hurry as though afraid of making a false step with one of his legs. The Yemenite greets the two, and Geula waves to him.

"New people have to be settled here," Theo resumes their conversation.

"By all means! But who would come here? Some farms do actually pass into new hands. That one and others like him," Geula says and points with her chain to the Yemenite in the distance. "They come here. Thank goodness we already have a number of Yemenites and Sephardim from Greece, new farmers in the village."

"They say they are important tribes of Israel. Hardworking, modest and frugal."

"Perhaps so, but what have I in common with them? Should I also put on red trousers that reach to my ankles like their women? New farmers," Geula says scornfully. She immediately regrets it and quietly adds: "Of course, if families like yours would only come here!"

"So you would simply leave the village where you were born and go off?" Theo says, half questioning and half stating a fact.

"And what is there for me here?" Geula shouts in a whisper and her nostrils quiver. "The mountains are beautiful and the Sea of Galilee is lovely, but very soon we shall be like the thistles by the road side and not know how to talk to people."

Theo wrinkles his forehead as if he is calculating carefully and the result does not come out right. "I don't understand," he stutters, and continues: "The suffering of adaptation might drive one mad. It is sometimes difficult, what with shortages, the pull of the past, the standard of living and all the rest of it. But the third generation of settled farmers, that is to say, a person rooted in the country, to all purposes free from all these troubles!"

Geula sits silently, crossing her legs, her elbows resting on her knees. This way of sitting elongates her neck and conceals her body.

The sound of singing is carried across from the shore of the Lake from the *kibbutz* camp that is barely visible in the distance. The *kibbutz* consists of veteran settlers and of members of the Working Youth; its economy is based mainly on fruit growing and fishing. A large area in front of the *kibbutz* buildings is planted with bananas. The fronds stand upright, well-tended and luxurious, with their greenish-yellow palm-like branches. Mats are stretched out in front of them as windbreaks, and walking among them you feel as if you have entered a room within another room until you come to the reception room. The camp itself consists of black huts and patched tents, only the animals occupying proper buildings. Red-painted boats bob up and down behind the camp by the bridge of the anchorage. By day the fishing boats glide on the Lake, their sails leaping about like birds with wounded wings that are sinking into the water.

Geula lifts up her head and listens. "They sing," she says. "They seem to be happy. You know, they never come to us in the village. It doesn't suit them to." She ruffles her mane of hair and adds with a smile: "They are not interested in me and in others like me."

"Why don't you join the *kibbutz?*" Theo asks.

"Why? So that I should wash laundry all day long, or push about huge pots and pans? Or so that dozens of pairs of eyes should peer into my heart and into my window until I do not know whether I am I, or not?"

Theo grieves in his heart. My teachers abroad taught me all that Zionism has to teach, he reflects, but they did not prepare me to answer a girl like this one here. Every theory can be learnt in no time provided you are interested, but if I should tell her that there can be no renaissance without soil, she is sure to laugh at me. Vision and reality don't go together. Vision goes straight and reality in round-about ways, they only have the same starting-point. Geula speaks of everyday things, and I have been here only a few weeks and know nothing.

Night falls and the two get up to go. They walk back along the shore. Their way is strewn with twigs and paved with small pebbles. A smell of decay rises from tree trunks that have fallen into the water.

"And in spite of everything you will stay with us in the village," Theo says.

"What do you need me for?" Geula chuckles silently, her face invisible.

Theo sighs, waves his two long hands about, not knowing what to do with them. The Sea of Gaililee has hidden its further shore and the water at a distance has turned dark. It ripples as it touches the shore, and the thick grass is in constant movement. Hidden creatures rustle, croak, hum and chirp excitedly from out of the darkness. Through the palm avenue the lights of the houses on top of the hill sparkle; small, lonely lights in the great emptiness of the night.

VI

The Hermanns have acquired a valuable black and white cow. She has been allotted half of the small shed that stands at the end of the yard. Little Urik can stand for hours upon hours at the entrance of the shed and gaze entranced at the huge beast stolidly chewing the cud. Mrs. Hermann has sterilized the milking apparatus; she intends to develop this new branch of the farm. The surprised look of her arched eyebrows has grown sevenfold.

"A nice cow," Dr. Hermann said when he came home in the evening. He had taken a shower, and as was his habit was sitting on the verandah in a plated bamboo chair, his shirt sleeves showing white on his hairy arms, all of him exuding the odour of field and soap. "Yes, indeed, a nice cow. It would be good to take her out to pasture before the great heat starts. But I am afraid to entrust her to the shepherd."

Mrs. Hermann hunches up her shoulders and breathes her protest that, after all, one single person cannot possibly do everything! She rises from the table, walks to the kitchen and begins clattering with her pots and pans.

Theo wriggles in his chair and says: "I'll go and take the cow out to graze." His brother-in-law glances at him keenly as though he had come across an interesting legal case.

"Meaning, that you are starting on your agricultural career," he smiles from the corner of his mouth.

Theo takes off his glasses and begins to polish them with a rag. He sits and squints with his weak eyes, and his brother-in-law's shaven skull gleams opposite him like a bare rock. He says: "What does it matter whether I begin one way or another. There is a certain job to be done, and no one else to do it except me."

In the morning Theo puts on a light grey linen suit which dates from a stay at a sea-side resort in Europe. He puts on sandals, and into the haversack on his shoulders he packs sandwiches wrapped in paper. He takes a stick in his hand and gets the cow from her stable. His sister accompanies him out of the yard and calls after him:

"If it gets too hot, bring her back home!"

Theo starts hopping round the cow to direct her, from the right side and from the left. He leaves the village street behind, passes the small cemetery and comes to the hills. He chooses a valley suitable for grazing, places the haversack on the grass and sits down. The cow immediately begins to munch the grass and the cord round her neck trails after her.

It is a fresh morning, the night dampness still covers the ground. The village with its houses has disappeared and the Sea of Galilee is hidden from view. There is only the sound of the well-pump, like a giant heart beating in the bowels of the earth. Theo considers himself far removed and hidden away, surrounded by sky, mountains, light and stillness—all of a piece. He stretches out on the grass and feels as though all his being is absorbed up by some great essence. He crosses his hands beneath his head and his eyeballs soak up the blue of the sky until they water. After a little while he notices that the grass has stained his light trousers. This pleases him and he says to himself: If you want to take it as such, it is some sort of omen, but in spite of that I would have done better to have brought along a book to pass the time. His eyes begin to explore his surroundings, searching for something on which to fix their gaze. He watches lizards gliding as though moving on wheels and, in contrast, the slow, heavy-moving tortoises carrying their world with them. He looks at them and ponders: If you want to become a man of the soil then you must learn not only how to do the job, but to inure yourself against boredom. Man's relation to time has to be cured, his fear of time must be mitigated. There is no room here for levity in life.

His attention is diverted from any kind of contemplation and thought as he feels the rays of the sun climb up his back. He sits and clasps his knees with his arms and softly calls to the cow in the manner of the Arab shepherd: "Hrdja!"

The cow turns her head towards him for a moment as though asking: What is it? and goes back to her appetizing chewing, the spittle dripping from her mouth.

Theo, smiling happily, once more calls out to her: "Hrdja!"

VII

As he returns with the cow the small children watch him in the street and begin to laugh. A grown-up person taking a single cow to graze! A whole gang of them run after him, barefoot and bare-headed. They throw dust at him and make fun of him. Their fathers and mothers, hearing the shouts of derision, scold the children. The noise and confusion in the streets mount to a crescendo, the cow becomes frightened, turns off the road and begins to gallop right to the end of the village, with Theo in hot pursuit. As he arrives by the four houses on the top of the hill she calms down again, and Theo, breathing heavily, strikes her in anger.

He looks up and sees Geula standing in front of her house, leaning one arm on the doorpost, her wild mane of hair coming down on her forehead. She must have witnessed the whole scene for her eyes were cold and without a smile of recognition. Theo blushed and began to adjust the hat that was pulled over his eyes and the empty haversack that swung over his shoulder. He pursed his dry lips in defiance to whistle to his cow, but all he produced was a wheeze. Geula walked across the threshold and said: "And why didn't you also take a flute to the pasture?" placing the fingers of one hand against her lips as though playing a flute.

Theo cleared his throat and said with a hoarse voice: "It's very nice up there among the hills." "Really?" Geula replied with a question and went back into the house.

Theo slowly led the cow home. His sister was already waiting for him in the yard; little Urik held the milking pail.

That same evening the village wits discussed the affair in front of their houses. They enjoyed it endlessly, embellishing the incident, and someone even bestowed the title "Shepherd of Israel" on Theo. This new title found immediate acceptance. Dr. Hermann found out about all this during a visit at one of his neighbours. It was from him that Theo learnt about his nickname; he did not outwardly react to the taunt implied in it, but he took it to heart.

That night Theo turned over in his bed for a very long time. In spite of being tired out from all the sun and the fragrance of the meadow, sleep eluded him. In reality the whole affair of the cow was of no importance and was not worth taking seriously, and yet it cut him to the quick. Something in his soul darkened and grew dim. It seemed that today his carefree time as a visitor to the country had come to an end, and from now there were going to be just working days, and the outlook was dismal.

Theo got out of bed, went to the window and quietly opened the shutters. A waning moon moved across the crests of the mountains, and a slight breeze blew over the tree-tops in the farm yards. The whole world appeared to be sleeping with open eyes. In a corner of the room a cricket chirped at the top of his voice, and from the adjoining room came the sound of Dr. Hermann's snores, the snoring of a man sure of himself and his way of life. Well, well, Theo smiled to himself, he has even managed to acquire a real farmer's snore! A slight grudge rose in his heart whose origin he did not know. He went back to bed and buried his head in the pillow to shut out the sound of the snoring, and contemplated: Not everyone enters the gate of work-a-day life by getting green grass spots on his white trousers! And before sleep overtook him, Geula's figure appeared before his eyes and her voice echoed in his ears: And why didn't you take a flute to the pasture?

VIII

Several days later Geula was going to leave for Jerusalem, where she intended staying with a family she knew until she found work. During supper the running of the farm was discussed, and it transpired that her younger brother and sister could fill her place. At first Geula was pleased that her absence would cause no inconvenience, but the discussion left her feeling surprised and hurt. For years and years she had been working and wearing herself out and in the end her presence proved not to be essential for the farm. Her mother did not object to her journey and said a little hesitantly:

"It might be good for a girl to see something of the world."

But her father grumbled and his face was angry.

"A single girl in town, how can that end? After all, a city these days is not what cities were twenty years ago. Times have changed and customs have changed and I do not like the idea of this journey one bit."

Her grandfather, Reb Jehiel Michel, listened to the conversation apathetically and it was only when he heard that Geula was going to live in Jerusalem with Rachel Yarkoni, a native of the village, that he bestirred himself and asked:

"Is that the granddaughter of Hirsch-Mendel Rabinov, peace be upon him?" He immediately started on his reminiscences, diverting the minds of his audience from the discussion and thus the subject of Geula's journey was decided in silence.

The journey became a central event in the village. When Geula went down to the bus, gripping a battered suitcase, many people came to see her off. Her girl friends stood round with linked arms, giggling with emotion. Some of the village boys had also assembled, dressed in their working clothes. They pushed their hands into their trouser pockets and stood about silently for they saw in this journey a hidden dart against them: That serves you right, boys, for not making sure that such a lovely shoot takes root among you!

At some distance from them Theo stood, shifting from one leg to the other, wanting to say good-bye to Geula and not finding the courage to speak. As the bus moved off down the slope, the boys turned and went their way; only Theo remained standing and waving his cap—and the lenses of his glasses shone in the sun.

IX

Geula was tense and excited on her journey to the city, but she could not visualize anything clearly. She pictured herself setting out for the bright lights, the grand parties, the abundance of colour and life.

Towards evening, with beating heart she knocked at her friend's door. The latter greeted her with a strangled cry, rose from the couch and came towards her with open arms. After a hug she put her hands on Geula's shoulders and examined her critically.

"A lovely girl," she said, "you don't even need lipstick." Geula laughed happily, a little embarrassed. "But we shall have to do something about your hair," she continued, her face assuming a serious expression. "You can't possibly walk around with your hair looking like the jungle of Abyssinia. Well, come and sit down and tell me just everything."

Rachel Yarkoni was Geula's senior by a few years. Her husband was a senior official in a commercial company, and Rachel counted herself among the elite of the city's society. She had furnished her flat according to the prevalent fashion, and had high standard lamps with painted parchment shades, light leather pouffes to sit on in the corners of the room, mahogany tea-wagons from which to dispense hospitality, and a small cocktail cabinet with sliding shelves. Rachel had two children of school age. The boy was given private lessons in English and the girl played the piano. Whenever there were visitors, the children were told to remain in their room and sit there quietly.

Mr. Yarkoni was a silent, good-hearted man who accepted Rachel's authority in all matters of social life. By dint of hard work and much effort she had succeeded in gathering round her a group of acquaintances, and with great pride she cultivated her handiwork. She would refer to this group as "our circle," and derived from it much joy and self-confidence in matters of taste, points of view and mode of life.

On the following day already Rachel fitted Geula into her daily routine. In the morning she went with her to a high-class hairdressing establishment, at eleven she rushed her to a café to be seen by all those women whom domestic help had freed from the kitchen. After lunch they both retired for a nap, and in the late afternoon they took tea in select company. Geula somewhat hesitantly asked Rachel whether she sometimes went to lectures or meetings, but Rachel laughed and said: "Our circle does not go to meetings. It has loads of interests of its own. Twice a year we arrange dinner-dances in a large hotel in aid of tuberculosis sufferers. These dinner-dances are the central events of the season and need a great deal of preparation. Sometimes we arrange bazaars in aid of playing-fields for poor children and also bridge parties in aid of an old-age home. You will see for yourself, there is plenty to do!"

In the evening when Mr. Yarkoni came home from his office, a group of them travelled to a country club outside the city. The building stood in a garden illuminated by coloured lanterns, and on a tiled platform couples were dancing. To Geula they appeared like creatures from another world whose life was one long wonderful holiday. As she walked along the dimly lit paths in the garden, she noticed that she was already trying to acquire a mincing walk and the fluttering movements of a butterfly, and she felt ashamed.

On Rachel's advice Geula bought herself two new dresses, one of a soft blue material with a white collar, and the other a white silk evening gown with silver dots. The only member of the group who was from Germany, an accountant at a bank, bald, and elegantly dressed, named the first dress "Ruth waiting for Boaz," and the second "Oh-la-la, we live." It was a jolly life, and Geula moved among this society as though intoxicated and with a permanent smile on her lips. The women of the circle treated her patronizingly and with indulgence.

A few days passed and Mrs. Yarkoni carefully inquired what Geula meant to do. Geula was not trained for office work, nor did she have the time at her disposal to acquire any of the professions followed by townswomen. After much discussion and deliberation in "our circle" it became clear that she could only be employed as domestic help. In her secret heart Geula wondered at this interpretation of her dream, and when she was offered the job of maid in the house of the advocate Harari she accepted it silently. But after a short while her shocked surprise dissolved and she tried to talk reason to herself. She said abruptly: "I'm not afraid of hard work. Not in the least. And I see no difference between one job and another. Oh well, I'll be a maid, so what? At least I shall earn my own living and be independent. Isn't that so, Rachel?"

While she way saying all this out of her confusion she glanced at her friend to see whether her expression had changed. Mrs. Yarkoni turned her head away and looked at her finger nails.

"You'll come to us in your free time, won't you," she said.

From now on Geula spent the mornings cleaning the house and cooking. In the afternoon, at Mrs. Harari's orders, she put on a nurse's cap and went for a walk with the two children in the avenue of the quarter. She was not given a room of her own, but slept in the spacious nursery. She took her meals together with the family, but she received her visitors in the kitchen. Quite naturally she ceased to be a novelty and very soon "our circle" stopped taking any notice of her. If she happened to spend an evening at the house of the Yarkonis, she would sit in a corner and watch the card games and no one would say anything to her.

These were dark days for Geula, days that began with suppressed annoyance, with the clatter of pots and pans, the beating of carpets on the balcony, and ended with sitting in a café among strangers who glanced at one another from table to table as though in search of something that eluded utterance. Sometimes, when she remained alone in the house, she would walk through the rooms and pretend to herself that the whole house belonged to her, the carpets on the floor, the silver on the sideboard and the china figurines on the shelves, and that she was one of the ladies of the city's high society, arranging dinners and going to parties. At such times she would recall sayings which she had come across in her reading such as to drain the cup of misery to the dregs, to swim in the sea of life with closed eyes, to watch the spectacle of the great world, and at the same time nodded her head and smiled to herself and her heart was agitated no longer. She would say to herself: never mind, such is life, such is life. And immediately she would turn on herself: and is that all there is to life? Sadness would take possession of her, the sadness of empty hours and of silence that produced no echo.

At first she saw the city as one wholly splendid and dazzling tapestry, but on closer acquaintance she saw that it was made up of successive strata of classes, divided by invisible partitions. It appeared to her that people were playing at some genteel game of make-believe, that they went as partners to a masquerade, but by secret agreement took care not to tear the mask from each other's faces. They did not wish to recognize each other; it was convenient for them to have this alienness add spice to their lives.

Upon one occasion she was invited to a select café that boasted an orchestra. As she sat there with a heavily made-up girl who had never been outside Jerusalem, and her flashy boy friend, a clerk in a government office, Mrs. Harari entered the café with a little group of her friends; she came past Geula's table, nose in the air, and with a rustle of silk said with astonishment: "What, Geula, you here too?" Not many minutes later Geula heard her complain loudly to her friends: "It seems that this café too is going down. It is becoming so common!"

Geula blushed. She, a granddaughter of Reb Jehiel Michel, third generation of pioneers and builders of the country's roads, spoil a café by her presence? But, as she considered her position for a moment, she felt to her surprise a sense of awkwardness, confusion at having come up against a barrier between herself and her mistress, and already in her heart there was a feeeling of inferiority that began by silently admitting the humiliating class distinction and developing into a sweet enjoyment of the very existence of such superior beings to whom one could look up in awe and reverence. Geula blinked her eyes and clasped her hands under the table. She was seized by a strong desire with one movement to wreck her stylish hair-do and to revert to her old mane; to get up and turn over the tables; to pull to their feet all the guests; to join hands with them in a circle and break into the heavy, stamping dance and to drown the false tinkle of the jazz by screaming "God will rebuild Galilee"; to tear off the elegant dresses and ties and all the empty externals round about. Something caught fire within her and her heart beat agitatedly to the rhythm of daring denunciation. Just then her companion bent close to her and whispered in her ear:

"Please, Geula, do just look at the dress over there, isn't it just too too daring!"

"Yes, yes," Geula stammered. "I don't think that my dress is daring enough!" The flame that had been kindled in her was extinguished immediately.

X

Geula spent three months in the city before she returned to the villlage with a little money and two new dresses. She reached home in the twlight, and found only her mother at home. Her mother was churning butter in the kitchen, her forehead covered with beads of perspiration from the effort. On seeing her daughter she interrupted her work and looked at her with tired eyes. Geula stood there gripping the suitcase.

"You never wrote that you were coming home!" the mother said with a snort.

"I made up my mind suddenly."

"What happened? Didn't you find there what you looked for? Tell me!"

"What is there to tell, mother? What do you think I looked for there and did not find?"

The mother bit her lip, wiped her hands on the wet apron and kissed her. "I think you have grown a bit, haven't you?"

"Maybe."

The mother was silent for a moment and stood bent and dejected. "You are very sad, Geula?"

"Sad? You can see that written on my face?"

"No, no, Geula," the mother smiled sadly. "Don't worry; it's not written on your face."

"If that's the case, why discuss it?"

"Oh dear, oh dear, and you are angry with me?"

"I am not angry, but I have only just entered the house this minute and I am already being carped at. Sad! What is it? I went away and spent a few pleasant weeks, and now I am back again, so what?"

"Do you really think you can make me believe that?"

Geula made no answer, she went to the other room and opened her suitcase. She sat on her bed, took out her dresses and spread them out to smooth the creases. She held up the dress "Ruth waiting for Boaz" and put it aside. She made a slight rustle with the evening gown "Oh-la-la, we live!" and considered: This is too long. If I shorten it I can even wear it here on the Sabbath. After that she dropped her hands into her lap and sat motionlessly. Dusk fell, and her heart seemed to her like the house, silent and empty, and the flies buzzed on the wire netting of the windows.

XI

When the grandfather, Reb Jehiel Michel, came home from the synagogue he showed no surprise at seeing Geula. He placed his palm on her head as he was wont to do and asked no questions. The younger sister embraced Geula and asked at once to see the new elegant dresses she had brought with her. The brother wanted to know how much money she had saved in the city and what she planned to do with it.

During supper Geula, without having intended to so so, related some episodes of her life in the city. Her mother listened with her hands folded on her apron, her head bent sideways and sorrow showing in her eyes. The father bent his face over his plate and moved his head up and down like someone who is burning to ask a certain question: Was the whole thing worth it?

After the meal Geula put on her old pink dress, gathered up her hair in the black ribbon and walked down the path. The stars were scattered over the wide sky, waiting for the moon. On the iron bench by the road sat Theo, his shirt gleaming white in the shade of the tree. He rose and eagerly moved towards her.

"Shalom, Geula, I heard from the driver that you'd returned."

"Yes, I have come back."

They stood silently and did not shake hands. It seemed as though Theo's body had grown even longer and leaner. Geula stood opposite him like someone who has jumped the distance from youth to maturity.

"Come, let us go," she said. "I want to see the Lake."

Together they walked down the avenue, and the palm trees nodded their heads after them. The dark-blue Sea of Galilee murmured as though counting the stars and constellations that it had gathered up in its bosom. Wavelets rippled from one shore to the other to bring the tidings of the night. The mountains stood up straight in the distance, ready to roll up the hem of the sky.

They walked along the shore in the shade of the trees. Theo wanted to tell Geula that a slight scent of powder still clung to her, but he did not. Geula wanted to say that she was no longer used to the darkness that surrounded them here, but she did not.

"Careful, there lies a cut-off tree trunk," said Theo.

"You are already more at home here than I," said Geula. She took his arm for support and touched his palm.

"Oho, you have callused hands," she said with a smile in her voice.

"Yes, I ploughed between the trees," he answered and felt his callused palm.

"Do they still call you 'Shepherd of Israel'?" she teased him.

"I don't know."

"And what about that mixed farm of yours?"

"My brother-in-law is still thinking it over. He is not certain of me and my ability."

"Really?"

For a while they walked in silence. They reached the little bridge and sat on it. A wide plain stretched round about on which not a living soul was visible. From the ends of the fields rose a bluish mist that enveloped the small houses of the village, and the lights in their windows were like eyes blinking hard to remain awake.

Geula said: "Don't be so silent, tell me your news!"

Theo hesitated for a moment and took a deep breath. He folded his hands between his knees and said: "Since the day you left I have not looked at a book."

"Because I went away?" Geula asked and laughed softly.

He did not reply to this, but continued: "I wanted to test myself to see whether I can stand up to all this."

"And are you satisfied?"

"I don't know. I sense the smell of the earth, I bring myself into close proximity with trees, plants and cattle, that's true, but I get no joy out of it."

Geula stopped her laughing and sat dejectedly. "That's so, we have no joy."

They sat quietly thinking.

"I have begun to be afraid of this country," said Theo.

"What do you mean, afraid?"

"I mean I am afraid that I may not make the grade and put it to shame."

"Ah yes, I understand."

"It is not a particularly pleasant feeling."

"No."

"If I fail, I shall have to start again from scratch since I have no place to go back to."

Geula thought for a moment and said: "You don't ask what made me return to this place?"

"No, I do not ask."

She looked at him gratefully.

Theo shook his head and repeated: "Yes, I am a little afraid of this country."

"Well, when one is afraid one has to sing." Geula bestirred herself and tried to get herself into a more cheerful mood. She slapped Theo on his shoulder and said: "Come on, let us sing together."

The two of them began to sing, she first voice, he second. But as they had started on too high a note, their voices broke and they stopped.

"You were right; we have no joy," Geula said and returned to her hunched-up position.

Both of them sat there dejectedly, deep in thought. At that moment the sound of singing carried across from the *kibbutz* camp. Geula neither lifted up her head nor moved from her place. "If you are not tired, let us walk on a bit," Theo whispered.

The two of them walked along the road, straight to the banana plantation. They turned right and walked among the stretched-out mats. They left them behind and walked round a piece of ground sown with clover and found themselves standing among the huts of the living quarters. No one was visible outside, only lines of washing waved on the ropes that were stretched out from one hut to the next. At the landing bridge on the Kinneret small waves dashed their heads against the heavy boats.

"Why did we come here?" Geula asked in a whisper.

"Let's listen how they sing," answered Theo, and pulled her to the large hut.

The *kibbutz* members had finished their meal, but were still sitting down together. Old-timers and youngsters, they sat leaning against the tables, their backs supported by the walls of the hut. They were all of them singing in unison, some with their heads thrown back, others with their heads bent down. The singing was spontaneous, solely for the sake of singing, without a conductor—as the cricket chirps and the birds twitter—about the sun that sets and the sun that rises, about the land that is held together by the bonds of toil, about life that goes on from today to tomorrow.

Theo and Geula stood in the darkness outside and gazed inside through the window and listened; and the touch of their bare arms felt warm in the coolness of the night.

Translated by Israel Schen

The White City

Everything was moving southwards. Like armored stallions thirsting for battle galloped trucks, jeeps, buses, bulldozers, cranes, tanks, stamped impatiently in their places, panting and neighing, and galloped again, biting one another's tails, separating and clashing, trolling backwards, breaking at crossroads like a river into tributaries. Sharp like an arrow glittering in the sun, facing forward towards its target. The noise of the vehicles cut through the once-quiet space now startled in the din. Far off in the fields white settlements lay peacefully, like flocks of white doves which landed to pick up seeds after the ploughing.

As the convoy stopped for a while, checked and deterred by the long pace, an army of heads rose above the vehicles' sides and then were thrown, from one group to the next: hands and caps waved in greeting, and hullos flew like swallows in swift volley from one end of the line to the other.

Then came the high and low hills and after them the broad flat plain, whose silence quivered like a string in the soft wind coming from the end of the world.

I ran to the sergeant's tent, and from there to the sergeant-major's tent, and from there to the quarter-master, falling into the ranks, swallowed up in them, like a coil in a snake, leaving them like an ant its colony, hurrying to the open square swarming with ants running and meeting one another and separating and returning to their rows and separating again in the quiet rustle which etched countless lines in all directions, and from there with my equipment and my belt and my arms to the pup tent.

I was one of a battalion, one of ten thousand, one of a nation. I shook people's hands, laughed, greeted people I didn't know. All of them were my friends.

Then I was alone on the hard, dry earth, and the muscles of my back, which were stuck to it, listened to the currents moving through its bowels, moving the muscles of its loins powerfully, reinforcing its bones like iron bars.

Then the earth was a large sea and I moved slowly over its broad waves, floating on my back from horizon to horizon.

I fell asleep. And when I awoke, I saw the first stars glistening in the sky and the sound of men singing far away. I got up and went outside. The camp was empty. Below, on the slope of the hill, a dense mass of men blackened the grey field. There the battalion was sitting on the ground, and the voice of its singing, which grew louder and louder in a single choir, sounded like the beating of iron wings in the clouds.

O Almighty God, what a miracle it was that war came along to save me from death!

I went down and seated myself at the edge of the large mass and pressed my body against its body. A soldier came up and put the palm of his hand against my shoulder so that he could sit down. At the touch of his hands a wave of warmth passed through my flesh. I wanted to shake his hand and thank him. Oh good people, I said to myself: an army of brothers who march together to conquer life!

"Officers, soldiers," the O.C. of the battalion said in his quiet voice, standing in the center of the mass, with his hands behind his back, "in another day and a night we shall face the great trial. We are already in the midst of the war, and at this very moment our army's advance troops are already deep in the enemy's territory, on the other side of his strongholds. Our task is to shatter his offensive positions, which threaten the integrity of our land and its very existence and to foil once and for all the enemy's aggressive plans. I will not dwell on the importance of this operation. All of you know this as well as I do. I will only say one thing: no country can put up with a state of permanent threat to its borders and unceasing attacks on its settlements. War is an unpleasant business, which involves suffering and sacrifice. But it is more unpleasant to live in constant fear, when at any moment the enemy is liable to flourish his naked sword and cut off your hand. Our orders are to attack the most strongly fortified sector of the enemy's front lines. On the border of this front is a dense chain of positions, separated by minefields and barbed wire fences. The enemy's forces include companies of infantry and tanks, and heavy artillery, mortar, anti-tank and armored car units. The General Staff has seen to it that for this attack sufficient manpower, tanks, light and heavy weapons have been concentrated at this point to overcome all the resistance the other side will show. I have no doubt about our victory, but it's up to you whether this victory will be gained with the lowest possible number of casualties. When I say that it's up to you, I mean that this depends on the bravery of each and every one of you, on the exhaustive use of all your battle skill, on the display of the right degree of daring, on the precise cooperation between the commander and his fellow soldiers in the unit, on the spirit of brotherhood which is the powerful force at our disposal, and with which the enemy can never compete . . ."

The enemy front was shrouded in darkness, and a dome of sky clustered with thousands of glittering diamonds hung over the whole earth. I knew no fear. I was proud of the trust the O.C. had placed in me. In me and in each of the hundreds of people who were sitting with me, whose faces I had never seen but whose voices I had heard when they sang together. I saw myself storming the enemy's lines with a drawn bayonet. Bursting into the lines, felling warriors all around me. I knew that no bullet would strike me and that I would enter, live and upright, into the conquered city, and my chest swelled with the joy of victory.

In the center of the camp, next to the headquarters tent, the radio brought good tidings from the distant desert, from the mountains of iron and copper, from the shores of an ancient sea. In the darkness, I could feel how the hundreds of bodies standing around me were bolt upright like drawn bayonets, and how the shudder of the electric current went from body to body until they became a single body yearning to thrust forward, to wherever their orders would take them. Then the racket made by the people, gay, laughing, greeting one another, patting one another on the back, slapping one another's palms, whistling, whispering, looking for their mates, hurrying to their tents, falling into line for food, eating from their mess tins, their arms making a clanking sound—which mingled with the noise of armored cars, gun-carriers, tanks, which ploughed the earth and the night with their roar, moving like a mighty steel beast southwards, somewhere. Everything was bound with a sound which injected fear-less strength. Left-right, left-right, like one man marched groups be-side the armored column in the darkness on the other side of the camp, left-right, and the dust of their steps turned to gold in the lights of moving vehicles. To march with them. To reach the battle-field. To run into the wall of fire, to fall and rise. To storm enemy positions. Face to face. To jump into them. To yell like an animal. Oh, another day and a night!

Suddenly the palm of someone's hand was placed on my shoulder again. This time it was the sergeant. "Come, let's go to the O.C.'s tent," he said.

Around the table, which was covered with a large sketched map, in the yellow light of three field lamps, sat the O.C. and five other officers. A strong heartbeat throbbed in my chest when my eyes fell on Debbele, who sat at the edge of the table. "You didn't think we would meet here," he said in his quiet, almost inaudible voice, and smiled a faint smile at me. The memory of my wife, the nightmares, the pistol, rose up in my heart like someone rising from the dead, but was immediately suppressed. Next to him sat Gabi and Yoram Nash. They hadn't aged at all. White khefiyas covered their necks, and their faces were dusty. Like then. Good God! As if it had been exactly at this place, exactly at this hour, around the table in a tent yellowed by field lamps. How everything repeated itself. And I as well. The hoarse, quiet voices, rasping from smoke and burning dust.

Yoram Nash shook my hands from his seat, and Gabi called out the name of my old company, as if uttering a slogan. We hadn't seen one another for eight years.

"We wanted to ask you if you are ready to go out on a patrol," the O.C. said.

"Yes, commander," I said, and a blush of pride came to my face.

"Tonight."

"Yes, commander."

"Do you know the terrain at all?"

"No."

"Go to the quartermaster with this slip, get your equipment, and come back here."

"Yes, sir."

About an hour later we went out into the silence, with submachine guns, pistols and hand grenades. There were four of us, apart from Debbele, who led the way. We were swallowed up by the darkness, and only the slither of our steps in the soft sand was heard. The terrain was flat, and we saw nothing in front of us, only Debbele, who set the pace with a rapid stride. No obstacles stood in our path, and it seemed that we could just go on walking like that until we reached the sea. An enormous land and we were its only rulers. If a bullet were fired, it would fly above us, to our right, to our left, but would not hit us. The war was a sport. The war was freedom. All man's power. I felt the power in my legs which would never grow weary, in my waist, braced by the weight of the belt, in my hands, strengthened by the iron of the arms, in my chest, which challenged the chill air, the darkness, the hidden anticipated fire. I was twice my height. A giant bestriding the earth. If a bullet hit Debbele, I would carry him on my shoulders as one carries a child. I would be the last to remain on my feet. I would be a whole people, whose love swelled within it until it choked in its throat. Oh, my many friends, thousands of them, who had gathered again into a single mass rooted to the earth. Oh, my name of which I was so proud. My father of whom I was so proud. My youth, of which I was so proud. Oh, the great night, on which I conquered my life anew.

Debbele got down on his haunches, and the rest of us did likewise. We crouched down like frogs, and listened to the night, so far and so close. Only silent nibblings could be heard among the thorns, the rustle of insects in the dry grass. The feeling of sawing legs in the stalks of straw. The quiet slither of a beetle over the soft earth. And from afar there was a surprised silence, like a calm before the storm. Before we left we had seen the two enemy positions on a sand table: like two giant tortoises sending out horny limbs in front and behind through their openings. Barbed wire fences, hidden cannon positions. A minefield sketched in crosses like the tracks of a beetle in the sand. A pock-marked, blocked road. Now everything was dark. We could easily fall on the fence before we came to it. Or fly up in the air from a mine exploding under our feet. Were we still far away?

Behind me Debbele hissed in a whisper, rose to his feet and marched. Again the plain was blind, without any obstacles. Oh, if only all of life was like that! Not in closed rooms. Groups of friends moving in the valleys or on the hills. Bearing a burden without growing tired. Each man for the other. And only a whisper going from man to man like a slogan, without any need to ask questions, because everybody understood. And no dark plots which called for duels. And everyone did what he was called upon to do, under the law of the single fate. If only all of life—

We stopped still. Two huge searchlights, far away in the West, sent long sickles to reap the broad darkness of the night. "Down!" Debbele ordered, when the light reached us, and we got down to the ground. The light was blinding, and the plain in front of us became hills and valleys for one sharp moment and then went dark again, even more so than before, and the sickle moved on and slipped away. We rose and marched, and from now on we froze in our places and knelt down every time the long sword of light was brandished. We felt our way in the darkness, unknowingly. Debbele slackened his pace, hesitating. He tried to examine what was in front of him in the ray of light, but this only revealed a mirage. Now he ordered us to sit and wait, and he himself went forward to the north, diagonally, until he disappeared from our view. We had strayed away, it seemed. No path crossed our way, and no sign indicating a paved road, as marked on the map and shown on the sand table. No sound of a dog barking, no clank of metal, no human voice. We put our ears close to the ground, straining ourselves to hear the sound of Debbele's footsteps. But there was no sound. Could he have lost his way and be unable to find his way back to us? The whistle of a distant bullet suddenly pierced the silence. Then came the rattle of a machine gun, with an explosive burst. A red star shone and grew in size, hanging in the air and opening out like a fan, splintering and dying out. The sound of an explosion on the ground, and a sheaf of light upwards. Far away in the south. Had the battle already begun without us? Or had the orders been confused? To go back? To wait? To run forward? To run towards the firing area? Where were we needed? Where was Debbele? Was this the battle already? But suddenly everything stopped, and became silent again.

Debbele returned and stood over us, without us noticing it. "Those are the sappers of the southern wing, blowing up the minefield," he said calmly. We looked to the south and waited for the resumption of the fire, but there was none. Again the broad, sharp stripe of the searchlight slid over us. "Follow me," Debbele said. "Have you found something?" "Yes. A long fold in the earth, a mound. A good place for an alignment of forces. Behind it are their positions, I think." Now we walked straight, and Debbele was our eyes. The sound of our steps grew louder in our ears, and we held the guns tightly. Why isn't he careful at all, when we are getting close to the enemy lines? Suddenly a black patrol will appear out of the ground, and we will fall before it like chaff before the reaper.

After ten minutes, we came to the mound. It was lower than we had supposed, but it was an event in the blank plain. We lay down on the ground and listened. Yes, now we could hear voices. A dull murmur from afar, the murmur of sea beating against the breast of the land and the sound of muffled bangs from close up. They were digging in. The enemy. Soon a volley of shots will burst out. We'll be a single corpse, on which the sun will rise in the morning, and a swarm of flies will hover round its mouth open to the heavens and the dry blood on its lips.

We lay down reclining and warm against one another, with Debbele next to me. I wanted to say something to him which perhaps I would never have a chance to say. To ask his forgiveness for the duel I had fought with him. To whisper to him that what had happened was no longer important to me, compared with the great war and the great, tremendous life, the power of which we now felt together. That really it was of no importance, that I had been a fool and had imagined things. That I loved him. That he was the country which I loved. That I was ready at that moment to get up and cross the track in order to throw a grenade at the enemy's sappers. And not to return. If he would just give the order.

Debbele ordered us to spread out along the length of the track, two to the south, two to the north, about five hundred paces to each side, and one of us to remain. To find the sand track leading between two positions. To mark the route of the attacking force to its objective. I walked along with Debbele and spoke to him in my heart. I told him that I could not go on living as I had until then. That after the war I would not return to my previous place of work under any conditions. That the smell of papers and the ink and the banknotes nauseated me. That I had to feel people around me, warm souls all bent on a single cause. Working together I told him that if we remained alive—and we would certainly remain alive!—we would organize, the five of us here and people from all different companies, and set up a new settlement in the south of the country. We would live in wooden huts. We would raise cattle. At night we would ride horses. We would be thirsty unto death in the burning sun. We would start everything again. We would form a pact. Like now . . . Suddenly he stopped, rubbed his shoe in the dust and said: "That's it." I felt it with my foot. Yes, it was a hard road, covered with sand. "That's it," he repeated, pressing my arm firmly. "This is the road we've been looking for. Let's go back."

The two men who had turned southwards also came back. We lay down on the ground again and crawled up on the low mound of earth. When we came to its peak, and the rays of light swung again in a broad bow over the open space, we saw the enemy's position. We saw it when it was shrouded again, in blind darkness. Fence poles. A hill of dust. Black openings. Gaping holes. Moving figures.

II

A night of splendor. A night of sparks and light. A night of a fiery river.

At 01.10 after midnight on the second night the force began to move eastwards, company after company, platoon after platoon, armed from head to foot, loaded on shoulders and back, marching in the darkness, stumbling through soft sand, carried on the crest of a rising wave, and we, the scouts, at the head of the column piloting its way to the objective.

We led the way, light footed, floating, knowing all the long way by heart, in the dark plain, halting every few moments until one platoon would take hold of the next one's tail, pulling again impatiently, westwards, westwards, thousands of feet behind us, as a dark forest of guns, a long beast whose inside was iron and whose scales clinked as it moved, pulling and hastening to get there in good time before dawn broke.

Far away in the south the fireworks in the air flew up and died, rushing on high as if on a festive night and falling into the tracks of the fire, sent up with shrill whistles, like thousands of slashing whips, with a quick, hunted rattle, snakes after snakes, the head of one in the next's tail, with the tinkle of stones falling and rolling down into the black abyss, splitting holes in the surface of the earth, with yells which cleft the heavens. There, far away in the south, the battle was already in full swing.

We stumbled on, getting heavier and heavier, and our steps pulling at one another's heels, and the hiss of short breathing like a bellows from row to row, and the sound of curt sentences coming from the telephones, strained like wire, torn and tied, and the wheels of light vehicles, somewhere behind us, moving and making a noise and churning up dust and moving again, and from the north we already heard the sound of tanks' chains.

I was a warlike knight. Happiness choked my throat like an anthem. It flowed through me like a river from the beginning of the column to its end. Sparks flashed between me and my comrades whenever my shoulders touched theirs. An incessant shudder rooted me to all the rows in front and behind me. All the chests shielded me, and my own chest was about to burst with pride. What a mighty mass of people, whose entire history marches with it when it goes out to fight back!

And when we reached the border, and the walkie-talkies sent forth staccato syllables and the row halted like a train of wagons, with a jangling of chains, creaking and sighing, and the force spread out to its breadth, platoons following brief commands, running bent-up under the weight of full kit and belt, the clink of parcels and metal, a flock of little foxes going out to hunt—I was like a bush squashed down, its roots stuck to its earth, and a soft wind passed hurriedly through my branches and passed on its rustles like a whispered slogan to all the long line of bushes extending to the end of the night from north to south. Spades were taken out and a brisk, diligent, panic-stricken clatter of dust passed along the entire length of the line, digging and throwing out, burrowing and deepening, like the patter of the rain, or the noise made by full sacks when one sack is thrown on top of another.

We waited for a signal, for the hail of fire from the heavens which would fall on the enemy's head and would set his fortresses and land on fire as in the destruction of Sodom and Gomorrah. On the southern horizon lightning flashed, and the din of battle flared up and died down there alternately. But in front of us was the ambush of silence in the plain, in which the rays of the searchlights roamed nervously, feeling along its length, stopping, hesitating, continuing to prowl around up and down, passing over our heads and going on to the dead areas, wandering purposelessly, feeling around without feeling. "Another twelve minutes," Debbele whispered beside me, looking at the hands of his watch. We looked up at the sky. Only a host of stars glistened there, thousands of light-years away.

Suddenly, the entire camp grabbed at its arms, at the sound of planes' buzzing and before the ear had caught it, three dull explosions split the womb of the earth, far apart from one another, north and south, and a third one in the midst of us, and the searchlights went out at once.

Oh, Great God! A buzz scratched the face of the sky, and immediately afterwards heavy thunder fell, flame catching up with flame, mighty thunder exploded and shattered in a din from one horizon to the next, scorching the whole earth. Twelve, twenty, twenty-eight, forty-two, sixty, one hundred! One hundred and fifty-eight!

Like a veteran war-horse, my body as one with the whole army, I plunged forward with the rows of infantry, and with the armored animal which rolled over on its stomach and came up to us, with the track cars which travelled beside us, stopping, retreating, moving again, kicking up a rocket, rumbling on an empty stomach gathering strength and advancing, and greetings and hasty orders cutting through the air as if there was no enemy . . .

And suddenly—from all sides, at one go, in front of us on both the right and the left, a sparking fire cut through the open space, fed by whistling bullets, vomited out of jaws in a hail of hoarse missiles, flaming and scorching, falling in shrapnel, and the whole enemy front suddenly took fire in an instant.

Oh, that was the battle already. And I felt no fear! As if my chest was made of armor and no fire could destroy it! The commands came out one after the other, companies collected together, putting machine guns, bazookas, mortars in position, and the whole earth was licked by fire, bullets hitting one another, passing with a screeching whirr to my right, to my left, above my head and bombs tore up the earth and a heavy banging, and the buzz of swarms of bullets, piercing and pointing in a thick net—and I knew no fear!

A burst from a light machine-gun passed on my left, a cry was heard, and a boy turned over on his stomach and doubled up. Cries of "Orderly! Orderly!" from all sides, and at once two people came running and put a stretcher down, and while I was still stunned, Debbele called out: "Forward!"

And I ran after him, bending down with a row of shadows intermingling in turn with the flashes of fire and firing in front of the row and falling in front of a high barbed wire fence. "Sappers!" came a call amid the constant rattling noise from both sides, and passing high above, and four or five or six men ran towards the fence and placed bangalores and called out warnings and retreated towards us, falling on their faces and a powerful explosion tore the wires with a screech and turned the poles upside down and forced a large breach, into which we ran, countless ones, pushing against one another and falling down and digging in again.

Oh, a night of a fiery river, a night of festive fireworks! Among the whirl of flashes and shadows I ran, attacking, falling and rising, as if in a dream. As if in a dream, Death had no dominion over me, and there was no time. My being was an electric flash in the night, unthinking, unknowing. The bullets shot out of my body, emerged in front of me, I knew not where. Had an hour gone by? Or three? Or a moment like a light-year?

As in a dream the noise suddenly died down. The enemy's jaws on the right were suddenly dead, and only one position still rattled away incessantly, with the music of mingled voices, making the earth shake around it, and it became an open target for our fire, which was directed towards it from all sides, continuous, insistent, vigorous, scorching the earth and puncturing walls.

And after hundreds of explosions, when the armored divisions turned to outflank the enemy in another direction, and the fire seemed to stop for a moment, came the order to spring forward, and again all the shadows rose up and began running forward, and at the sound of a loud explosion under my feet, I called out: "Debbele! Debbele!" running forward frantically. But I saw only a toppling fence and people running through it, and next to the bending pole a man's body was thrown up into the air and fell to the ground doubled up. "Debbele!" I called once more and froze in my place.

But amid the commotion of the rush towards the enemy position, in order to capture it by throwing grenades which exploded somewhere and the whistling of bursts of bullets, no one heard my cries. I knelt down beside the body and bent over it. I wanted to cry out again to the people running past me, to tell them that he was dead. Killed. Finished. No more. Everything stopped. But the cry froze on my lips. I shook his shoulders with all my strength and whispered: "Debbele, Debbele, listen, Debbele, Debbele, listen to me." But the body was stiff, lifeless. His chest was riddled with bullets, and the warm blood wet his whole shirt. His eyes were open, and in the darkness I could see them staring without any expression. His face was as hard as stone, and the palm of his one hand was clenched round the butt of his gun. Platoons of men ran past us towards the enemy positions.

I bent my head on to his forehead and closed my eyes. Around me the fire seemed to have slackened, or receded, and only stray bursts of fire passed with a sharp, desperate hiss, rushing and dying away when buried somewhere. Then my ears started buzzing. I heard nothing apart from the long, monotonous humming.

When I opened my eyes again, there was a pale dawn light. Everything was different and unbelievably strange. Unrecognizable. And impossible to grasp. And unlike anything that had been before. There were still stray bursts of fire, sounding like last sighs. Faint fire still hissed here and there, next to the opening of the enemy positions. People jumped into the communication trenches with dying cries. From afar I could see figures scurrying away as quickly as rabbits from the bullets whistling after them. Bodies lay on the grey, cloddy earth, which was just freeing itself of darkness. White smoke rose up here and there from the dust. Massive armored cars moved far off, slowly, as if in a nightmare. Opaque buildings, grey and brown, were scattered far off on the sand, and strips of road shone blackly between them. Lonely, sad trees with sagging fences. A tank sunk and lying on its side. A big land, burnt, naked, scarred. And more groups of people running. Where to?

A shiver ran through my flesh. The night had died, and the morning lay like a corpse. Like sadness, going from one end of the world to the other, without a sound.

III

When I had left Debbele alone, I ran after the last of the men towards the position whose fire had died down and, jumping into the communication trench, I sprained my ankle. The pain was so strong that it forced from my mind all the horrors of the night, and all the dangers of death were as nothing beside it. I stood pressed between walls of earth, and wanted to cry with humiliation and helplessness. Soldiers passed on the run in front of me, with their guns held in front of them and I didn't know what to do. I knew that it would be silly to call for a medical orderly at a time like this, when all the available orderlies were taking care of those wounded by bullets or mines. As I had lost my platoon, I also had no one to whom I could turn. I began stumbling after the running soldiers and pulling my one foot after me, and the pain grew stronger with every step. Eventually I became slightly used to it, feeling only that the ankle was fat and swollen, and like a heavy weight hanging on my foot. When I got inside the post, which was full of people, and in some miraculous way was already filled with the hustle and bustle of a command room, with communications facilities, maps and plans on the table, I threw myself on to one of the benches and lay down. The whole commotion around me, the running of the people going out and coming in in such a hurry, the sound of the commands being given to the messengers, the sound of jubilation, the whistling of bullets far above, outside, the chugging of the armored cars, the look of tinned cans lying about among the men's feet, the torn copies of illustrated weeklies, cartridge cases—all this now seemed a different, unreal world, like the hallucinations of a fever-ridden man. Everything was on the other side of an opaque wall, unattainable, inconceivable.

Fear seized me lest I be sent home, before I had seen the victory with my own eyes. I would reach home with a sprained ankle, limping, wretched and downcast. This thought brought me to my feet. I began walking up and down, placing the weight of my body on my aching foot in order to accustom it to carrying me. Slowly, the pain spread to the length of the leg, and seemed to become duller.

An hour before noon we entered the white city, in a column clanking in its armor, marching briskly, striking the stones of the long street rhythmically. On both sides of the column, standing with their backs pressed against the houses of earth and stone, the fenced walls, the bolted doors, stood the people of the town; slender youngsters, broad-waisted men, old men leaning on their canes, women with babies in their arms, bare-footed children with torn shirts clutching at their parents' clothes—long lines of angry eyes, torn with fear, stricken by shock. On all the roofs, on poles, broken branches, thin bars of iron, hung the white flags of surrender, rags, pieces of torn cloth, infants' diapers.

I kept in the lane, walking and limping as quickly as I could, dragging my sprained foot behind me in order to keep up with the marchers. But the pain grew and increased and pricked through unbearably. My strides slowed down more and more, and I began falling back row after row, trying to march together with every row and separating from it despite myself, until after a little while I found myself at the end of the column. I still tried to catch up with the last row, running and walking, walking and running, but I couldn't catch it up. My two feet were very tired by now, and straggled along with a heavy gait. The distance between me and the advancing line increased, until I formed a sort of line on my own, because from now on the eyes of the large crowd on both sides of the street were turned to me, and the glances of anger or amazement turned to looks of contempt. I saw the column advancing and drawing away from me, and the distance between it and me was like the distance between a drowning man and the ship receding and going on its way.

A low, white city. A great mass of people in tattered clothes, afraid, shaken. A line of soldiers drawing away from me. And I marching, walking and limping on my own.

Suddenly, I saw that all the people at the sides of the houses were drawing close to one another and pouring into the street, and in another minute the crowd closed around me and swallowed me up in it. The broad stream flowed after the column of soldiers, hurried after it to catch it up as if to watch some show or other, and I was drawn along with it, pushed here and there, shoved against, trying to hurry my steps, and to reach the head of the stream but the crowd pushed more and more until it became a single pressed mass, which moved a little bit forward and then stood quite still, and I was squeezed inside it from all sides, with all of it a wall between me and my battalion.

I drew myself up on the toes of my sound foot, and beyond the crowd's shoulder I saw a small square, a white house with a dome and arched windows. A lawn, with a fountain in the middle. Two palm trees, and a high pole between them. The column fell in line on three sides of the square. I made another effort to push myself forward and to reach my comrades, elbowing the people standing round me and asking them in a halting language to let me pass, but no one paid any attention and it was impossible to force my way though the dense crowd. I heard brief, brisk commands, the clicking of heels and guns, and then there was a hushed silence. An offier came up to the flagpole, stood with his hands behind his back, and made a quiet speech. At the side of the house with the dome stood a group of old men, broad-shouldered, with khefiyas on their heads and girdles around their waists, blinking because of the sun. The officer finished what he was saying, and a soldier came up to the group and whispered something into the ear of the oldest among them, a man with the bony face of a camel, a long chin and a narrow, prominent forehead lined with wrinkles. His eyes were sunken deep under the bone of his forehead and could hardly be seen. He nodded his head as if he understood, then went up to the flagpole twirled one end of his mustache and said a few words. His voice was hoarse and shattered. The first two or three sentences came out frantic from his mouth, as if he had learned them by heart. Then, he paused a while, blinked his eyes, and his lips and the ends of his mustache quivered. Again he uttered a few hasty sentences, and then whispered something to himself. At last he plucked up courage, said one long sentence, clear and plain, like a sort of blessing, and, when he had finished, looked around him, as if asking whether he should add anything. The sound of a command was heard, and a concerted click of heels. Two drums shook the air with quick beats like an alarm, and then a flag was raised up on a string; it climbed up to the top of the flag pole, opened and unfurled, and, when it came to rest, waved slightly in the midday breeze.

I looked up at the flag, as did the crowd around me, without pride, without joy. I felt only the pain in my ankle and humiliation at the thought that at a time like this fate had separated me from the victorious column.

Again curt commands were heard, which were answered by brisk clicks of heels, and then the crowd began to disperse.

I hurried to limp towards the square in order to find the men from my platoon, but none of them came my way. "Where's everyone going to? Where to?" I asked the soldiers, who had also dispersed in groups and went past me in various directions. They replied that they had been given leave for an hour, to stroll round the streets of the town, and the meeting place afterwards was the school at the end of the main street. They hurried on their way, but because of my limp I could not catch up with any of the group and remained walking by myself.

I entered a narrow street, and before taking many steps in it, some of the city's inhabitants gathered around me. At first some boys fell upon me and held out packets of cigarettes. I took two of the packets and put money in the boys' hands. Then several youngsters came along and began plying me with questions. As I stood and spoke to them in their own language, more people clustered around me, young and old, until there was a large crowd with me in the center. They asked me about the value of our money, the prices of various commodities, what was happening on other fronts of the battle, and I could only answer a few of their questions. Not far from me stood a shaven-pated man with a squashed nose and a split upper lip. He wore broad black pantaloons, and his large soles were encased in coarse, heavy shoes. He stood at the side all the time with legs astraddle, hands folded on his chest, and looking at me with a smile which, because of his deformity, seemed bitter, almost a sneer. When there was a moment of silence, he took two steps towards me and, standing in front of me with his hands folded, he asked me where I came from. I gave the name of my former kibbutz. He blinked a little, as if chasing a fly away, and grimaced, pursing up his thick lips. He asked me if I knew the village of A. "Yes," I smiled, seeing in front of me a group of huts the color of red earth, hugging the shoulder of a hill like a nest of wasps, surrounded by crude fences of prickly pear bushes. He asked me if I knew Bergmann's orange grove. For a moment I was speechless. Within me rose the strong, intoxicating perfume of the orange blossoms, the sight of the dense dark-green foliage, the cool pools of shade around the tree trunks, the dampness of the earth during the hoeing, the irrigation canals with their ends blocked with wet, rotting sacks, the flies above the dump of rotten fruit, the well house marked with spots of lichen and containing empty boxes, rugs, packing material with a smell of resin, a hill of sandstone on which blue beehives stood tilted on their sides in a field of wild yellow daisies with bees humming around them, the sound of the well being pumped in the great stillness of the afternoon. "Did you work there?" I asked. He didn't answer my question, but mentioned names—Rappaport, Zelkin, Schechtman, Abramski. This was a row of densely located orange groves lying next to one another along the side of the road. "How is Mr. Yakub?" he asked in my own language. Then he said: "Weeds, right? A lot of weeds there." The people around us stood open-mouthed, as if watching a conjuring show, and waited for me to say something. I was stunned and couldn't say anything in reply, and after my silence became prolonged, they began throwing cries at me from all sides, like stones: "Zeligman!" "Marmorek!" "Tannenbaum!" "Yavne!" "Moskowitz!" Now the close-shaven man smiled a smile of victory. He unfolded his hands and showed me one of the fingers of his left hand, whose upper joint was missing. "That's from a hoe," he said, looking at me as if waiting for my reaction.

I wanted to shake his right hand as a sign that we were friends, but at that moment the noise of a jeep was heard dashing in a great hurry from the end of the street. Inside it were men from the military police, and at once the crowd scattered in all directions, like a flock of chickens among which a stone has been thrown. The jeep stopped with a screech of brakes, and one of the soldiers asked me if I hadn't heard the order forbidding fraternization with local inhabitants. I said that I hadn't been at the parade because of my sprained ankle, and that I knew nothing about the order. The other policeman laughed at this in ridicule, and he warned me that I would be liable to arrest if I was seen talking to the people of the city again. I promised that it would not happen any more, and the jeep hurried on its way, sweeping the people standing in the street to both sides until they were forced against the walls of the houses and stood silent.

I limped to the end of the street, and turned into another one, a broad street of sand and low stone houses. The street was desolated and burning from the afternoon sun, and there was no one in it. My eyes hurt from the white light. There was a smell of salt in the air. I repeated to myself that I was the conqueror, the ruler of the city, but I felt no joy about it. There was a hot vapor over the sky, and this was like an ominous portent, like an eclipse of the sun. When I was halfway along the street, I saw a little girl, about eight or ten, carrying on her back a torn mattress twice as big as herself, which was slipping all over her body in all directions and covering her head. Her bare legs were sunk in the sand, and her back was bent like a bow, until it seemed that her head was touching the ground. I stood still for a moment. There was no one around. A burning silence possessed the street. I lowered the gun on my shoulder and limped towards her. I knew that she was returning from the sand dunes, like many of the city's inhabitants, who had run away there at night. Perhaps she was the only one left in her family, and was going alone to her empty home. She was so small compared to the mattress that I wanted to take her to wherever she wanted to go. Because of the bent-up way she was walking, she didn't notice me. I came up to her and said quietly: "Little girl." She lifted her head up slightly, and then her eyes opened in a deathly panic and the mattress slipped off her back, and she began running with all her strength to where she had come from. "Little girl!" I called again, and began stumbling after her, but she increased her speed, like a rabbit fleeing from a hunter, and disappeared in one of the courtyards. I retraced my steps, lifted the mattress on to my shoulders and began walking towards that courtyard. I went in through a wooden gate to a place strewn with donkey dung, where two red-feathered chickens were scratching in the dust with their feet. The chickens fled from me with a frightened cackling, overturning a tin in their flight. I couldn't see the girl. While wondering what I should do with the mattress, I heard from afar an approaching loudspeaker, announcing a curfew from ten until the following morning at ten; everyone found outside his house would be shot at. Four or five times the voice repeated this anouncement, each time in a different direction, until it vanished like an echo. The loud-speaker struck terror through the town.

I put my mattress on the ground and stood next to it, not knowing what to do. If I remained in the courtyard, the girl wouldn't find the mattress any more, and if I returned it to its place in the street, someone else would take it, or a car would run over it and ruin it. If I took it with me, I would only be laughed at. I knocked on the door of the house facing the courtyard. No one answered. A shutter of the window was lifted slightly, and immediately shut down loudly. I peered into the street. There was no one in its entire length. It occurred to me that the curfew might be meant for soldiers as well. I left the mattress standing against the wall facing the street. I placed a dry branch next to it, like a policeman guarding it against those who might want to steal it.

I turned back towards the square I had started from, moving along the sides of the houses. But I couldn't find my way. Everything was strange because there were no people around, and the city was shut and silent. The swollen carcasses of yellow dogs lay in the middle of the street, and when I went past them the swarms of flies which hovered over took fright and flew around my head. Here and there lay about, as if after a storm, filthy rags, crushed tins, abandoned pots and pans, limbs of chairs, shreds of wool, scraps of clothing. Pouches of bullets glittered in the golden sand. All the doors and shutters were bolted. I went past the shops locked with heavy bolts, past red and green signs, square courtyards surrounded by walls, low dens, houses. The later it got, the more panicky I become. A cold sweat covered my brow and my back, and trickled like ants between my armpits and my calves. My steps were the only sound heard in the street, scraping the stones because of my limp.

At three I reached the school, a whitewashed building two stories high, which stood in a large sandy courtyard, surrounded by a brick wall. Inside there was a great commotion, as if during an assembly parade in the camp. Everyone ran up and down in the corridors, with their knapsacks and equipment, and squeezed into the classrooms, grabbing places to rest and sleep. On the floor lay exercise books, textbooks, crushed pieces of chalk and scraps of food. In the room the pupils' chairs and desks were piled up in the corners, making way for green blankets, sleeping bags, boxes of ammunition, sacks of bread and tins of food. In the room at the end of the corridor, which was the headquarters, sat now, behind a table covered with green paper, on a high-backed chair, the O.C. of the platoon. On his right exercise books were piled high on top of one another: on his left were three thick books, and in the middle was an inkpot made of horn, a jotting pad, and a tray with paper clips and pins. On the wall behind him hung the picture of a man with a magnificent grey beard, with wavy hair surrounding his bald pate, a short nose and tightly clenched lips; underneath was the word DARWIN.

I explained to the O.C. the reason for my being so late and showed him my swollen ankle. After he had reprimanded me, as was his duty, he sent for a medical orderly. The orderly came, and led me behind him to a small room, in the corner of which stood a pile of books. I removed my shoe, and after he had examined my foot, which was swollen as if from a bee-sting, he brought a bucket, poured a kettle of hot water into it, and told me to bathe my foot in it. I did as he said. I took a book from the pile and glanced at it. Among the unintelligible lines were strewn chemical formulas and sketches of bottles, test tubes and joined instruments. A hand cut off at the root held a candle over the mouth of a test tube, and over it was written: CO_2. A glass bowl gave off vapors from its neck. A small bottle hung above a spirit lamp. Smoke issued from the end of a wooden stick. A pestle and mortar stood on a narrow shelf. A woman in a chemist's apron held a flame in front of her. Through the door, in the corridor, soldiers carrying guns hurried up and down.

The medical orderly returned, felt my ankle, buried his fingers in the soft, white flesh, rubbed the bone at the joint, took hold of the heel and moved the whole leg backwards and forwards, and then said: "There's nothing wrong with you. But to make you happy, I'll put a splint on you. Lie down for a few hours, and then you'll get up a new man." He bandaged my foot, and told me to go into the next room. This had been the teachers' common room, and contained two high black tables. I placed the tables next to one another, took my sleeping bag out of my knapsack, climbed up, squeezed myself inside and lay down.

The night of the battle now seemed something very remote, which had taken place a long time ago, half real, half a dream. A night of lightning and storm which had passed and calmed suddenly. A night without fear. Like a fireworks display in the sky. And the night was clean, and its showers purifying, leaving behind them a fresh smell in the air. A short but eventful holiday night, in the hot, hazy, endless desert of sameness.

But this was far away, a long, long time ago. And now the city was white, besieged, and I was trapped within it. And the burning, heavy skies, over which a sort of white fog had spread. And the awe of the hostile eyes along the houses. And the deep sand. And the filth of the corpses and the flies and the rags. And the sight of the people whose faces were like nightmares. And the feathers hanging on the barbs of the wire fences, as if after riots. And the scream of the little girl who had thrown the mattress away and run . . .

And the heavy skies, which boded ill, as if locusts were coming from the desert in enormous, countless swarms, covering the face of the sun and laying everything waste . . .

I wanted an earthquake to come suddenly and destroy all the houses and leave nothing alive—and one wouldn't be able to run away . . .

And now there was this school, with dust on its floors and exercise books lying strewn about the corridors and in the class-rooms. And the idle books in their piles. And the pieces of white chalk, crushed underneath the hobnailed boots. And the inkwell at rest.

The plaster of the ceiling was peeling in various wide-bayed islands. On the wall opposite hung a map of the country, with arrows pointing towards it from all sides. In Jerusalem was stuck a pole on which flew a green flag with a star and a crescent; it blew over the whole country. I felt no pain in my ankle. I sank into slumber.

I woke up to the sound of a cry. A man's cry, stunned, wild, broad, far away. And two shots cutting into it, one after the other, and the sound of voices receding outside. It was dark. "Who's there?" came a loud voice, angry and scolding, from nearby. I raised myself on my elbow. Beside me lay two other men, in their sleeping bags. "What happened?" I asked. The two of them also raised themselves. "An attack?" one of them asked. "They must have fired on the patrol," the other one said. The steps of four or five men hurried through the courtyard and receded. And then voices speaking, quickly and briefly, as if giving orders. "They can wipe us out as easy as anything," the one furthest away from me whispered. "One really big bomb in this building and we're finished." Then there was silence, and I heard only the hum of the sea.

The steps came close again, but were slower and quieter. Someone inside asked what had happened. And a voice answered him from outside: "Go back to sleep. Some nut thought they were aiming a gun at him from one of the houses. What an idiot!" A rustle of laughter went through the rooms. There was silence again, and the steps of two men walking in the courtyard calmly. "What's the time?" I asked. "About half past one. Go to sleep."

I tried to fall asleep, but couldn't. On the previous night, in the noise of the battle and the quake of the fire, I had not known fear. But now there was this silence. A great black silence which covered the whole city, blanketing it from all sides, tense as a bowstring, strangling cries, hiding eyes that looked out of their sockets. A hostile silence, which would soon tumble down like a high wall and bury us under it. If it wasn't for the silence, I said to myself, my courage would come back to me. But the fear of silence. Deep and black like an abyss.

And perhaps in the morning the whole mass would rise up against us in order to avenge its violated honor. Young and old, women and children would attack us, and we would retreat, one step after the other, until there would be nowhere to retreat to, and their pitchforks would be sunk in our flesh. A dog's death.

And the night of the fire would be like a shooting star flashing by in the darkness for an instant and melting and fading in eternity, and nothing would be left of it.

Again there were measured strides in the sand. A watchman's steps.

If the crowd did not attack us the next day, it would do it the day after, or the day after that. Or a week later. It had to happen. Some time, and not far off. A great mass of people. Thousands, tens of thousands, like locusts from the desert. Thirsting for blood, shouting for murder, drawing knives for the slaughter, the rod of their anger. No mercy.

And if the miracle should take place, and I returned alive? Where would I return to? From after, from beyond the mountain, I would always hear the sound of the crowd, like the flutter of locusts coming from the desert. Soon they would cover the face of the sun, and there would be darkness at noon . . .

I covered my head with the fold of the sack against these thoughts, but they crawled inside, like ants, like beetles, making my flesh creep.

When the first ray of dawn filtered in through the window, I got up. The soldiers were sleeping a tired sleep, and their faces were pale. The young men were children, and the old men were fathers. The young men did not know evil, and the older ones only knew worry. They lay in rows, rib to rib, wrapped in black and green blankets, up to the shoulders, up to the neck, up to the eyes, over their heads. Eyelashes pale as dawn. A hand covering an unshaven cheek. Hands crossed on a chest. Hands folded on a chest. A mustache quivering with breathing. An open, swollen mouth. A pinched mouth. A beard glistening like dewdrops. A worried, unrested brow. An innocent, peaceful brow. The breath of dreams. And there, somewhere, women were getting up in the house to kindle the first fire, to make food for the child. Babies waking up crying in their beds. Milkmen cycling from house to house. Women hugging their pillows. The steps of an early-rising worker, walking alone in the street.

The soldiers lay sleeping in long lines, and there was no war in their faces: children and fathers, and husbands and the vapors of their breath as if they were at home. The breathing of the morning like the spirit of a dream, hovering over the tired men.

I walked alone in the empty school, along the deserted corridor. In the second wing of the building were the empty classrooms. Rows of small tables and chairs, all facing the blackboard, on which was written in chalk:

28 : 4 = 7
32 : 4 = 8
36 : 4 = 9
40 : 4 = 10

I stopped at the threshold and could not take my eyes off the blackboard. All the sums were correct. The numbers were so innocent that they were the complete oposition of war. Abandoned and ignored, the blackboard gazed at the empty room and at the moment it seemed as if nothing in the world was sadder than an empty classroom.

In the next room two pictures of the human body, one flesh and blood, and one a skeleton, hung on the walls. One all muscle, muscles which were pink and tense, thick, tied to one another tightly by sinews, one above the other, and one below the other. A mighty man, proud of his strength. And the second one was the Angel of Death. A bald skull, with two gaping holes, a squat nose, clenched teeth laughing cruelly, a chin pointing forwards, and underneath this, the neck bones like a spring, the collarbone like an iron axle, hollow ribs like a camel's skeleton, things like the flat stones by the seashore, and very long hands, with heavy fingers, tied together with screws, held out towards someone unseen. On the one side was hung the diagrams of the heart, with its various chambers and its several arteries, as in a butcher's shop, the insides with their intestines writhing like earthworms, the kidneys and the spleen swollen, the lungs, the eyes, the ear drums, the brain, placed like a folded embryo, half plant, half swollen sponge.

In the pale morning light, in the desolation of the empty classroom, in which slivers of white dust covered the small tables and the black inkwells in them—the two people on the wall looked lonely and bewildered. The muscular man stood with his back to the room, with only half his face showing. His one foot was forward, touching the ground with the tips of his toes, and the other foot rested on its heel, like an athlete maintaining his balance. His face looked as if it was afraid to look inside, and the hands, which were held outstretched, at the sides of the body, seemed helpless. The skeleton man was filled with dread, not like a man carrying death but like a man who has a terrible fear of death. And the eye sockets, the cheekbones, the rows of teeth, which chattered against one another, as if from cold, wanted to cry out in a cry which was frozen in the bones, fossilized. The hollows of the ribs and the holes of the thighs were shocked by their emptiness. And the very long hands, like pitchforks, asked a question —like the burghers of Calais, when they handed over the keys of the city.

In a third room the chairs and tables were thrown about as if after a wild fight, and the teacher's chair was overthrown. But in an eternal peace, like the peace of grey morning skies, a map of the world looked down from the wall. This was the map in which two ellipses kiss one another, the eastern hemisphere and the western hemisphere. The map from Grade Four, when the world is still a mist-wrapped mystery and life the discovery of latent wonders. The great oceans, so clear and blue, endlessly broad, so that their horizons cannot be seen. The Pacific Ocean, so tranquil and foggy on both sides of the continents. The Atlantic Ocean, in the center of the world, was cut in half by the two spheres, and the lines of latitude and longitude in it seemed to indicate the paths of the many ships. Columbus, Magellan. Twenty thousand leagues under the sea. The warm Indian Ocean, whose waves washed the shores of the jungles. The South Pole. The huge continent of white ice. Captain Scott. Snow blizzards. Starvation. Pages of a diary lying about on the snow. The narrow North Pole, squeezed against the axis. Captain Byrd. Eskimos. Sharks. Whales. The equator and the sun travelling above it, around the earth, above dense primeval forests swarming with monkeys and snakes, above deserts of golden sand in which lions walked with quiet and terrifying tread. The Tropic of Cancer, along which the crabs ran on the land and in the sea, surrounding the whole earth. The Tropic of Capricorn, along which the goats leaped on the surface of the water. America, a large country of trains and herds of cattle and large cities. America of Charlie Chaplin and Shirley Temple. And of a girl called Suzie who spoke English and chewed gum during lessons and had a red bicycle at home and a Yo-Yo which jumped up and down at the end of a string, and the largest collection of stamps in the world. America, the country in which they rake in gold and lifts go up and down the buildings and the people wear checked trousers, puffed up below the knees, sing "Valencia, Valencia," and bang with their suede shoes on the smooth tiles. The great, much-desired America, stretching from ocean to ocean. And the many numbers at the edge of the semi-circles, outside the world, in the ether which surrounded it. Oh, for a morning like this, and a large map on the wall. And children dreaming of the strange, peaceful world, open as the heavens, enveloped in mystery.

The teacher's stool had fallen over, and the inkwell rolled among the upturned benches. On the floor, next to the blackboard, on which traces of a damp rag had made zigzag and blurred streets of chalk, lay two pieces of chalk, one white and one red. I picked up the white piece and wrote on the black board, in Latin characters:

MOON

and put the chalk down on the side of the board.

Then I went up to the roof. From there I could see the whole city. Flat roofs, narrow, mysterious streets. Courtyards. A chill ran through my body, and my shoulders shook. The white flags were still hanging loose at the heads of the poles and bars. The sky was cloudy, and a silent, quivering air from a cool breeze hung over the city and the sand dunes all around it. The town's shutters were pulled down and there was not a soul to be seen inside or outside. Among the red fences a dog padded slowly, walking along and sniffing. Inside the fences, in the courtyards, the sand had been swept by the night wind, and out of it projected pitted stones, dry, leafless stalks, ill-clad scare-crows, faded patches of cabbage, rusty tin hovels. On the far side were square land holdings, checkerboard fashion, surrounded by prickly pear hedges. In the streets, here and there, were tall, dark, palm trees. From afar, the salty sea air was wafted. There wasn't a person around. Only in the sealed houses did men, women and children, clad in rags, breathe the breath of a pale hour, the last before the morning rose.

As I went down to the corridor, I picked up an exercise book which had fallen creased and trampled, on the floor. I opened it and read. In a round, shaky child's hand was written:

$$11 \times 5 = 55$$
$$11 \times 6 = 66$$
$$11 \times 7 = 77$$

IV

In the middle of the day when the sun was already high in the sky, stoking up the white houses and the yellow sand, the officer commanding the platoon called me to the headquarters tent and asked me if I still felt pain in my foot. I said that the ankle had returned to position, and everything was all right. He asked if I was ready to go to the refugee camp and relieve one of the guards. "Yes, officer," I said. I took my gun and went off.

The curfew was in force, and the white city was empty, apart from the patrols of soldiers, which marched up and down the streets in twos or threes, looking like lonely trees in the desert in their green uniforms. I went past the same courtyard which I had entered the previous day. The mattress lay there in its place, as I had left it. When I came to the end of the unpaved street, and went up on to the sand hill, the camp appeared in front of me. It was an enormous block of dense tin dwellings, piled up on top of one another and touching, like tabernacles in the desert. In front of it, between the huts and a long barbed wire concertina fence, a great congregation of men, women and children squatted on the sand. Next to the fence stood five soldiers, with their guns aimed at the feet of the squatting people. Behind them was a small house, surrounded by a fence. A burning silence hung in the air, cut every two or three minutes by the short sharp whistles of bullets.

I wondered what they were shooting at, and only after standing there for some time did I understand. The crowd was hungry, and in the small building they were handing out rations of flour and oil.

Every now and then someone in the yard called out the name of a clan and the name of the village from which the clan had come. When they heard this, all the people of the village in question rose together, old and young alike, holding one another's clothes, with sacks and bags in their hands, hurrying impatiently to burst through to the other side of the barbed wire. The din of women's cries and babies' screams arose for a moment, and the collapse of people stumbling and being stamped on. Then the shots threw the crowd back to its place, until the silence was restored.

Again I heard the whistle of bullets, but only in order to frighten. Now the roll-call of clans and villages could clearly be heard in the midday silence. Family after family passed the narrow strip between the barbed wire barrier and the yard, flurried, bent and shirking, as if running on hot coals, holding one another, children hiding behind their fathers' backs as they passed under the butts of the guns, and the babies hiding their heads in their mothers' bosoms. When they reached the courtyard, they breathed in relief, as if grasping the horns of the altar at last.

When the names of the villages were heard, the villages of the coastal plain, one sight after another passed in front of me. The sight of thick, dark orange groves with the damp, hoed earth luxuriant with long-stalked creepers, twisting around age-old trunks spotted with lichen. The sight of fields of millet, shining in the sun, rustling in the afternoon wind. The sight of threshing floors and camels turning with panniers laden with stones. The sight of a market with its booths laden with slabs of juicy dates, loaves of sun-dried figs, jars of lemonade and honey water, sugary sweets, roasted chestnuts, dried apricot rolls. The sight of broad-waisted men wearing girdles, walking slowly, heavy with possessions. The sight of women in green dresses walking from the wells, upright like stalks and carrying jars on their heads.

Then I felt in my nostrils the smell of fine chaff, thrown with a wooden pitchfork, flying in the hot khamsin, and the smell of smoke and dung coming from afar, from the huts of sun-baked mud.

For a long time I stood like this, and the crowd of people squatting on the sand, so densely packed, now looked very tired, like sheep fainting in the midday heat. The babies' heads hung on their mothers' shoulders, and the congregation was dozing. Only a very faint humming in the air, like the rustle of leaves in an olive grove in the heat of the day. The soldiers were also too lazy to shoot.

From the top of the hill on which I stood the sight of the crowd squatting shoulder to shoulder, in its rags and white dresses, looked like a very ancient sight, from the time of the great desert. And dread hovered over it, as a falcon hovers in the sky, seeking its prey. For a moment, it seemed to me that the commanding officer had told me: "Come now therefore, curse me this people and extinguish it." And I stood at the head of the abyss, looking towards the desert, and saw the people lying there according to their tribes. I answered him: "Let my last end be like this." I was afraid to approach, and stood silent on the top of the hill, with the great noon around me.

But suddenly, I don't know how (perhaps something had been announced without my hearing it), the whole crowd rose up and moved forward with a great cry and burst towards the barbed wire barrier, and the soldiers ran hither and thither to stop them, hitting with the butts of their guns to left and right, shouting loudly, and amidst this shots were heard and the crowd retreated like a herd of cattle, falling back to its place, and when all the voices died down I saw a little girl fluttering in the sand like a slaughtered chicken weltering in its own blood.

Everything was silent now, and only a faint wailing could be heard from somewhere, like the chirp of a wounded bird, and in the air of the blazing noon the wailing circled round the heads of the squatting people, flying among the sand dunes, coming closer and then receding again, until it died away.

Then I saw a man climbing towards me through the sand. He walked barefoot, had long black hair, and wore a cloth robe, like a villager. He was young, about my age, only slightly taller and slimmer in build. When he reached me he stood calmly and gazed together with me at the large city of tabernacles, stretched out in the wilderness, and at the crowd squatting in it in dreadful silence.

In a whisper, so as not to disturb the silence, he asked me why I did not proceed to carry out what I had been ordered to do. I told him that I was afraid. Without looking at me he said that he had seen me on the night of the battle, and I had been as brave as a tiger. I said that then it had been dark, and in the sparks of fire it was impossible to see human faces. "Aren't you happy that you are the conqueror?" he asked me. "No" I answered, "there is no happiness in my heart." Then he asked me whether I loved my enemies. "They are hungry," I said, gesturing towards the crowd. He asked if I would like to be in their place. I thought a long moment about it, and then replied that I would not want to be among those guarding them with guns in their hands. "Are they so bad?" he asked, motioning with his head towards the line of soldiers. "No," I hastened to reply, "no, they are only doing their rightful duty." "Aren't you better than them?" he asked. "No," I replied, "certainly not. It's just that I haven't enough courage to see people suffer." Now, for the first time, he turned his head to me with a smile, put his hand on my shoulder and said: "Are you ashamed of that?" "Yes," I nodded my head, and a shudder ran through my body. "That's not good," he said. And after a short pause, he added quietly: "Go and do your duty."

Now I was more afraid to move my place. I repeated in a whisper and with quivering lips, as if pleading for my life, that I was afraid of the crying of a hungry or frightened child. That I couldn't stand it. "Aren't all the little children equal?" I asked. "Yes, they are," he said quietly, "but now go and do your duty."

The two of us stood and observed the silent crowd.

Suddenly he disappeared. There was only the burning sand around me, and the city of tabernacles hugged by the dunes.

V

The next day, at three in the afternoon, I was summoned to the Military Governor. When I entered the house with the dome in the central square, and went into the room, which was shrouded in semi-darkness, I was taken aback to see B. sitting in the arm-chair behind the table. Apparently he didn't recognize me, because without looking

at me he gestured to me to sit down on one of the chairs, next to four
other men who had apparently come for the same purpose. I tried to
catch his eye and to hint to him with a smile that we were old
acquaintances and that it was a happy occasion when old friends met
under these circumstances, so different from those we had known
previously, and so binding in comradeship. But he was busy giving
orders to the people coming in and going out, some of them soldiers
and others inhabitants of the city, and paid no attention to those who
were sitting and waiting for him. On his table stood a copper tray, on
which was a coffee pot and six blue china cups, a polished shell casing,
a large sea-shell ashtray and a pile of official forms. To the people of
the city he spoke in their own language, and these coming to him one
after the other, heard his orders with great submission, bowing
slightly, straining themselves not to miss a single word that left his
mouth and uttering only a few short sentences indicating agreement
or confirmation, or posing some practical question or other. On leaving the room they put their hands on their hearts and bowed a little,
with a smile on their lips, or touched their foreheads lightly with their
open palms. He spoke to them in a fluent and businesslike way,
without any formalities, as a man would speak to a colleague of his,
and without emphasizing his superior office. Like the manager of a
company, he gave instructions about operating the water pump, the
electric power station, the bakery, and other things which affect the
vital needs of a city. This simple, almost friendly, way of talking to
the men of the conquered city, which gave him a charm I had not
noticed in him before, aroused great affection in me and increased my
desire to attract his attention. If I can only find the right opportunity,
I said to myself, I will express to him feelings of appreciation for
behaving in such a humane manner towards the inhabitants of the
city, who are now his subjects. I thought in addition that I would draw
his attention to the question of the refugees who should be treated
with more sympathy so as to avoid unnecessary suffering. In his army
uniform, with two fig leaves glistening on his shoulders, one on each,
he looked sturdy and strong, and at the same time not like a regular
military man, perhaps because of his shirt, which was not tightly

clasped to his body, but hung rather carelessly, and perhaps because of his short grey hair and the look on his face, which displayed no tension, but a sort of alertness to everyday civilian affairs.

Eventually he sent all the supplicants away, ordered his aide to close the door and to remove everybody from the vicinity of the building, and, putting his arms on the table, he turned to us. "The inhabitants are cooperating in general, isn't that so?" he said with a smile, passing his gaze from one to another, as if seeking our confirmation of something we had just witnessed. He still didn't seem to realize who I was, because although I returned to him a smile full of agreement, and more than that, even filled with admiration, he didn't let his gaze linger on me. The others uttered a few words of agreement, both expressive of contempt for the local inhabitants and praise for military strength. "Will you have some coffee?" he asked, clasping the neck of the coffee pot. All of us smiled with pleasure, because hot Turkish coffee was a real luxury after the foul and lukewarm drinks we had been given the last few days. He poured coffee into the porcelain cups, and handed one cup to each of us with his own hands. "The stocks of food that we found in their army stores are enough for the whole country for a few months," he said, as we sipped the coffee. We laughed with him, and two of us added some descriptions drawn from their own experience. When we had finished drinking his face took on a serious expression, and he said: "This is about a rather unpleasant job. We have obtained a detailed list of the gangs in the city. I don't need to explain to you who they are and what their activities have been during the last few years: infiltrating, sabotaging, spying, killing, pillaging and so on. This list contains 32 people at present. Well . . ."

The rest of his words reached me like a distant hum. He said that we had to go from house to house, according to the list of addresses, to arrest the people and to take them in lorries to a place outside the city, where they would all be kept. When night fell we would have to finish them off. He added that the operation was secret and no one apart from us was supposed to know anything about it. We would receive more detailed orders during the course of the operation.

"Any questions?"

There was a long silence, which blended with the silence of the city, sunk in curfew, on the other side of the barbed window. Outside the stifling afternoon heat lay on the pavements like a tired dog in the doorway of a house. I felt that my face had gone very pale; my knees shook and my insides quivered. With all my heart I hoped for something, some miracle, which would avert the operation or release me from it. At first, when I entered the room, I had a feeling of pride that I had been chosen for the job, about which I hadn't known yet, and that I was one of a small group of five, which included a sergeant-major, two captains and lieutenant. When I saw B. I had been happy that in one operation we would be working together, bound by a link which could be everlasting, even in days to come as well. He was a man of duty, and when he spoke I knew that was only doing the right thing, which could not be avoided. But now I was caught in a trap. The choice was not in my hands. I had to do a thing more terrible than I had ever done; but this was my rightful duty.

"What will happen if someone displays resistance?" the sergeant-major asked.

"I hope this won't happen. I really hope not," B. said. "But that's what guns are for, isn't that so?"

The two captains sniggered.

"How will we find the addresses?" the sergeant-major asked.

"That's a good question," B. said. "You will be accompanied by one of the inhabitants. You can trust him."

"He's probably the person who gave you the list," one of the captains said.

"Allow me not to answer that question," he said. "Anything else?"

The four of them looked at one another and then at me. As if it was my turn to ask something. A shudder ran through my shoulders, I saw clearly that I could not escape the inevitable and couldn't stop at the edge of the abyss. That no miracle was going to happen. I was a soldier, and my duty was to carry out orders. Fear was not to be taken into account, and to reveal it meant surrendering one's honor. A badge of shame for all my life. Were there any moral considerations?

The gangs had to be wiped out, that was plain. Not only as a punishment, but in order to prevent disasters, clashes, murder.

My lips quivered.

"You said that we had to finish them off," I stammered in a faint voice. "Do you mean to kill them?"

B. sneered. It seemed to me that only then had he recognized me, and identified me with the man who had told him that he could not commit evil because he was afraid of the pangs of his conscience. As he didn't reply in my question, and the silence grew longer, I understood that I had uttered a hopeless slip of the tongue which had only aroused contempt or pity. I felt that the others, like him, thought me to be a fool for this reason, and were sure that it was a mistake to have chosen me as one of the five for this operation, which required men who knew what they were in for and understood much more than was said to them explicitly, and who were ready to carry out commands without hesitation and weakness. In addition to my previous fear, although it seemed opposed to it, I was not seized by fear that they would remove me from the operation.

"Any more questions?" B. threw a glance at all of us.

The others straightened up in their seats, as if indicating that they were ready to go off to action and everything was clear.

B. leaned backwards, and throwing a glance at the sergeant-major, he said:

"As I said before, this isn't the pleasantest of jobs. If any of you feels that it's not for him, because of a soft heart or moral inhibitions [he said these words with a contemptuous sneer, from which I realized that he was referring to me], or anything else, he has the choice of getting out of it, of simply saying, 'leave me out.' That's all. There will be no complaints. Of course, the order of secrecy will fall upon him afterwards as well."

Again there was silence, and although none of those present turned his head to me, I felt that they were wiating for me to reply. This was the fateful moment. The choice lay in my hands, and this was harder to bear than the state of no choice which preceded it. I had to decide. If I were to announce that I was withdrawing, I would forfeit my honor in B.'s eyes and the eyes of the four other men, whom I didn't even know. Perhaps this would never become known to more than this small number of people, although it could be lifted and my shame would become public knowledge. In any event, in B.'s eyes I would always remain a coward and a fool who would not succeed in any man's job. And B. was not only one man, but most of the society in which I lived. How would I be able to hold my head up afterwards? On the other hand if I did not withdraw, I would have to do something whose horror would haunt me all the rest of my life. I didn't know which of the two evils was worse . . .

"Well, then, everything is quite clear now," B. said, and leaning his fist on the table, he rose from his place.

All of us rose after him. Everything was plain, as the choice had been taken out of my hands.

When we stood in the square, the empty streets of the city glittered in front of us, white and still. After a few minutes the truck came and stopped next to us. Beside the driver sat one of the townspeople, his face covered by a filthy khefiya which hid his head to the forehead, throat and mouth. Only his nose could be seen and his black, hooded, frightened eyes.

At first the operation proceeded quietly. So quietly that the fear which had seized me when in B.'s presence was almost wiped from my heart. We would knock on the door of the house, go inside, call the name of the man we were looking for, inform him that he was wanted for questioning, tie his hands behind his back with a handkerchief or a piece of cloth, throw him into the truck, which was covered with a tarpaulin, and continue on our way. In the house there would be only shock, a silent shock, without any cry of protest or weeping, and the arrested people, all young men, accepted their fate without any opposition, silently, although with the silence of resistance, in which there was a sort of threat of revenge, which would come. Slowly I took heart, saying to myself that this was only a routine action, part of the reality of the first days of any conquest. I even avoided thinking about the last stage of the operation, which I would have to go through at the end. The knock on the door, the entry into the dark room, the firm but dry announcement by the sergeant-major about the arrest, the man's presenting himself, the silence of the relatives, who received it as the decree of fate, the click of our hob-nailed boots on the floor of the courtyard, then on the pavement, the lifting of the prisoner into the truck, throwing him on to the floor—all this was done with such polished efficiency and speed that it seemed more like a military exercise in the training camp than an act which had latent in it certain cruelty. The feeling of routine was augmented by the behavior of the sergeant-major, who sat next to me in the lorry: a short, fat fellow, with a bright face sprinkled with large freckles. For him it was a form of amusement, and during our journey he cracked jokes with the prisoners, spoke to them in Hebrew, made fun of them in Yiddish, asked stupid questions about their wives, promised them all the delights of life in the next world, and enjoyed the fact that they didn't understand a single word of what he was saying. In the semi-darkness inside the lorry we couldn't make out their faces.

Only when we came to the sixth house did the feeling of terror grip me again. The door was opened by an old man, short in stature, most of whose face was covered by the bristles of a white beard; his blue eyes were round and open like two lakes. Behind him, on the bed, lay a heap of rags, out of which peeped a little face, creased like sun-dried figs. An old woman lay there wrapped up in her tatters. A smell of chaff and of chicken droppings befouled the air. When the sergeant-major called the name of the person we wanted, the old man's face began shaking nervously as if saying no. The man was apparently deaf and perhaps also dumb, because no matter how loud the sergeant-major shouted he didn't answer, but only went on shaking his head. We were ordered to search the house, and overturned everything in it, including the bed, out of which the old woman rolled with a faint squeak. Only after searching the courtyard did we find the person we were looking for, hiding in the dog's kennel. The sergeant-major aimed his gun at him and threatened to shoot him if he wouldn't emerge, but he didn't budge. He was crouched on his belly, and when he looked at us, as we stood on the threshold of the kennel, he shrank still further, holding on with his fingers to the rear wall. The sergeant-major fired a burst of bullets into the ground in front of the kennel. The body inside shuddered slightly, but did not move. Then two of us crawled inside and dragged him away from the wall, by force. He was as heavy as a sack full of stones. When we stood him on his feet, we saw before us a boy of fourteen or fifteen. Black, smooth hair hung over his forehead, and his face was elongated and soft, like a plum. His eyes were red, and when they looked at us they glittered with stubborn resistance. I was taken aback by the look on his young face, and, holding his arm tightly, I said quietly to the sergeant-major, who stood on my left:

"Must be a mistake."

"No mistake. Take him away," he said impatiently, making a gesture as if chasing away a chicken.

"He's only a child," I repeated, nodding my head in his direction.

"Not a child. They're all the same," he continued, repeating the same gesture with his hand.

"Perhaps it's worth while checking," I whispered.

"I said take him away," he shouted. "All of a sudden he's taking pity on them!"

"Not taking pity," I said, still holding my ground, "but a mistake in name can take place . . ."   "Then why did he hide there?" he shouted.

"Perhaps he saw us coming and was afraid," I said.

"And why was he afraid? Why?"

"Seeing soldiers, he became frightened."

"Whom are you taking pity on? On whom?" He lost his patience with me. "And if there's been a mistake, so what? So another one will go? In war you don't examine identity cards. Do what you're told, that's all. Take him away."

The boy stuck to the ground like a stubborn root, and we had to hit him with the butts of our guns in order to drag him out of the courtyard. When we carried him away from there in our arms, we could still see the old man, standing in the door of the house shaking his head nervously all the time, as if saying no, no, no.

Apparently, despite the curfew, word of the arrests had gone from house to house, in some mysterious way, because from now on the people were not given up of their own accord, but hid in holes, in attics, in outhouses. From time to time the whistle of bullets flew overhead in the silent city. I felt a terrible weakness, so much so that my hands would not answer me, and I felt sick in my stomach, as I had felt once when a boy, after I had tried to kill a chicken in the courtyard, and the knife had been very blunt. The thought of the young boy who had been caught didn't leave me for a moment. It was clear that this was a mistake, on our part or on the part of the informer, but, whatever the reason, this mistake would cost the boy his life. When we sat in the lorry I didn't take my eyes off him, and I felt that I was personally responsible for him, in charge of him, as it were. But he didn't look at me. He sat hunched up, retired into himself, his head between his knees. Only his narrow back could be seen, the back of an adolescent boy, rounding over the curves of the shoulders, the spine protuding prominently with its joint continuing towards the narrow, smooth and swarthy neck. The thought that I wasn't doing anything to save him, that I didn't have the courage of doing this, to rebel against my commanding officer or at least to demand firmly an examination of the question in the first place, made me hate myself, and then filled me with a single desire to sleep. To forget. To throw myself down somewhere and to sink into a deep sleep. I carried out the commands without thinking, my limbs moving like those of a puppet.

When we came to the last house, the ninth, there stood in front of us a young, clear-faced woman, with two pigtails, thick as ropes, hanging down her back. At first she tried to smile at us and charm us with her beauty, but when she saw the sergeant-major aiming a gun at her father, she fell at his feet, embraced his ankles and swore to God that they didn't know where her brother was. He kicked her, and she rolled on to the floor, and when he saw a grimace of pain in my face, he cried: "She's breaking your heart, isn't she? See if she isn't lying, the bitch." and he was right, because after a few minutes we found the man, hiding in the hay in the attic. When we returned to the lorry, hot and breathing heavily from exhaustion and excitement, he burst out at me: "They're all like that, the bastards! Go and believe them when they swear by God. Do they have a God, those carrion?"

Now we went off to dump the load of prisoners at the concentration site. The road lay past the entire length of the silent city, left it and ran between the sand dunes, stopping before a long, yellow, oblong building with a rounded tin roof. On the other side of the building was the compound, surrounded by petrol drums and a barbed wire block. When we arrived there with our nine prisoners, fifteen or twenty others already sat on the ground together. All of them had their hands tied behind their backs, and their bodies were bent forward. Three soldiers stood next to the fence, holding guns.

We pushed the nine men inside the enclosure, and then the sergeant-major ordered me to stay with the guards. He and the three other men climbed into the lorry again and went off towards the city.

The sun was already sloping towards the horizon, and its rays gave a purple tinge to the silken waves of sand and the faces of the people squatting in the enclosure. Some of them were as black as Negroes, with ball-shaped heads and hair as curled as rings of iron wire, with slant eyes and mousy pupils. Some had smooth boylike faces, with tender mustaches soft with down and swarthy arms like rolls of copper, with round elbows. Others were stalwart, broad-shouldered, muscular, strong-faced, with feet as large as spades. Some were squat-nosed, harelipped, pockmarked, their faces gnawed by the climate and disease. Others had thin noses and sloping hairy cheeks, set in long faces, and their hair was like that of desert goats. Some of them dozed, with their heads on their chests; others whispered prayers to themselves, and others never took their eyes off us, with a harsh, rebellious look. There was the boy whom we had caught in the kennel, his hair falling over his forehead, as if he was returning from a wild game in the street; his eyes were small now, looking in front of them, like the eyes of a child who has been injured and is plotting to take revenge against his enemies.

The sun set, and a soft silence settled down over the curves of the dunes, with only a passing rustle of sand being heard from time to time. It was a calm twilight hour, and those people crouching down in the compound, who did not know of their impending doom, were like a community of worshippers. The pink light illuminated their faces, and when they looked towards the horizon whose light had died away, they were like dreamers. Sadness descended upon the stretches of sand, and I seemed to here a distant tune shivering in the still space. It was their last hour, and again the same man appeared before me, wearing the white robe of a villager and barefoot, approached them and whispered something. I heard words whispered like the rustling of the stand: "Our Father which art in heaven, hallowed be Thy name. Thy kingdom come, Thy will be done on earth, as it is in heaven."

After about an hour, when the last light died upon the hills, and the evening shadows lay in the hollows, the lorry returned, followed by a jeep. Three soldiers jumped out of it, and marching briskly towards us, observed the prisoners—who tensed in foreboding, as if wondering what was coming—strode to and fro, consulted one another in a whisper, asked something, went back to the sergeant-major, who took his five prisoners off the truck and ordered something curtly, and at this the sound of a loud shout was heard, and all the sitting men rose to their feet at once, and while they were pushed against one another, the soldiers urged them on in order to force them into the building.

Three of us were called into the building, and I remained outside. The door was slammed to, and a few minutes later, after what seemed like a very long time. I heard a rapid burst of fire and the sound of shattered groans.

But only for a minute, because at once everything became silent again.

VI

In the third watch of the following night I went out on patrol, together with an old private named Rivkin. It was completely dark in the city, and cold ruled the streets. We walked side by side, hugging the walls of the buildings, tightening the scarves round our necks and drawing our heads in between our shoulders. Our measured strides thudded on the pavement, and their dull echo followed us, spread to the alleyways and died away among the houses.

"There'll be rain tomorrow," I said.

"It's about time," said Rivkin. "The fields need it badly."

"Did you manage to sow?" I said.

"Yes, I did."

In my imagination I saw him trampling down water-soaked furrows with his rubber boots, striding with broad steps from one furrow to another. He was about fifty, short, broad-shouldered and energetic. He had a squarish face, in the center of which was a dense, colorless mustache, half grey, half white. His eyes were narrow and alert, always peering around inquisitively, hurrying to catch everything around them, in case they missed something, and when they smiled creases gathered at their corners, in the corners of his full lips, and then even his mustache shrank up and laughed. His hands and feet were always busy, walking, fetching, handling, doing something. During the three days we were together, there wasn't a single person we met who didn't call him by name, it only to show their affection for him or to win some humorous remark from his lips. They called him an old warhorse, since there wasn't a war for which he hadn't volunteered or that he hadn't forced his way into, like this war, for which he had left his farm and his wife and two daughters. But the image one had of Rivkin was more that of a work mule than of a warlike horse. The officers treated him with a certain amount of affectionate ridicule; but instead of minding this he used to ignore them, pointing out, half angrily and half jokingly, that they were novices and he was a veteran at the game. The privates never missed an opportunity of making friends with him, because he was always cheerful.

"There is good soil around here," he said. "But these people don't know how to make use of it."

"I've seen some well-cultivated plots," I said.

"Yes, next to the houses, but farther away they are fallow. They sow barley where they could have grown vegetables."

"There's probably a scarcity of water."

"There is water in the ground, but they don't pump it up. They should be taught some things."

"Meanwhile the vegetable gardens are dying," I said, "because of the curfew."

"It won't last much longer," he said. "Just a few days more. A week at the most. War is war."

We walked to the end of the street, and from there we turned into another street, whose two narrow pavements almost touched one another. Among the low houses, with their flat roofs, stood a broad house with a dome, on the side of which was a narrow, high tower. Behind it was an empty plot of ground, on which stood black shapes. We stopped and looked around us. The shapes did not move: apparently they were poles and barrels. Complete silence reigned as our steps died away.

"It's cold," said Rivkin, rubbing his nose. Then he stamped on the pavement to warm his legs.

We were silent. Then I said:

"I heard that they fired at people returning from the sand dunes."

"Who told you that?" he asked angrily, standing in front of me with legs astride.

"They said so this morning. Some of the inhabitants came from the seashore with raised hands and when they came close, some soldiers aimed their guns at them and finished them off."

Rivkin gave me a long, hostile look, and then said in a decisive voice:

"Don't you believe it. Just fairy tales."

And, turning away from me, he took several heavy steps in front of him. Then he turned round again and said:

"Don't you believe it. I tell you. They're just boasting. They like boasting. They think it's a sign of bravery. Let them pull someone else's leg. They killed people who came towards them with their hands raised? Just like that, eh? For the fun of it! I know our boys. Pure gold, that's what they are. No army in the world would have treated the inhabitants as we have at a time of occupation."

I walked a few steps behind him. We passed the plot, and then a row of shops close to one another, whose doors were shut with iron bolts and locks. He must still have been thinking about what he had just heard, for he stopped again and turned to me with an open stance, the butt of his gun peeping out behind his broad shoulder:

"Listen, you're a young man, aren't you? Thirty years old? Thirty-five? I've been through several wars already. Do you know how a victorious army behaves when it takes a strange city? Stealing, looting, raping, murdering. Never mind the Nazis. The English, the Russians, all of them. How can you compare it at all? Did you see anything of that here? Did they rape a single woman? Or rob a single shop? And here you have to deal with enemies who, if they only had a chance . . ."

He looked at me, blinked his eyes as if thinking with great speed, and then added, taking hold of the lapel of my jacket:

"Listen to what I'm telling you. If they had come into one of our cities, they would have slaughtered all of us. Do you hear me? All of us. Me and you and the women and the children. Keep this in mind!"

He was quiet for a while, and still holding my lapel and with his eyes fixed on me, his face beamed in a broad smile and he said:

"They fired on people returning to their homes, just like that, eh? You don't know them. They're boasting. That's all!"

And he pushed me away from him with force.

We continued to walk, until we heard the sound of steps from the other side of the street. We stopped and listened. The steps were measured, confident, one and one, one and one, iron on silent stone. "They're ours," Rivkin whispered. We gave the password and were answered. Two youngsters came up to us, strolling along shoulder to shoulder, with their hands in the pockets of their coats. When they reached us, they stopped.

"What's new?" Rivkin asked.

"Everything quiet," said the swarthier of the two.

"It's cold," said the other one.

"Tomorrow one platoon is going south, isn't it?" Rivkin said.

"We're staying here. Too bad," the swarthy one said.

"Don't you like it here?"

"Nothing to do. Curfew all the time."

"You want to fight, eh?"

"We came here to fight, didn't we? We want a bit of fun. Something to happen."

"Or else to go home, " the light-colored one said.

"So soon?"

"I got a wife and child. Got to be back at work," he smiled.

"You've just conquered a city," Rivkin said. "Now take it easy for a while."

"Call this taking it easy? It's getting on my nerves!"

"It's quiet in the city, isn't it?"

"The quiet makes me more nervous than the fighting. Like a cemetery. Especially with all these white houses."

"Last night there was some firing," the swarthy one said. "I heard that they finished off two of them."

"They fired on a patrol?" Rivkin asked.

"Before dawn. From a house not far from the square. Today our boys blew up the house."

"Really?"

"There are still a few terrorists in the city. Armed. Looks like they're trying to start something."

"No wonder. They're being treated with kid gloves," the light-complexioned one said. "We should have finished off a few dozen of them."

"Of women," Rivkin interrupted him.

"Just like that, a few dozen of them. To scare them a little. They don't seem afraid at all."

"You should really be going home already." Rivkin reprimanded him, and turned to go. "We'll be seeing you."

"Good night."

The sound of their footsteps receded, and again we heard only the click of our shoes. Rivkin walked a little ahead of me, and his broad shoulders, the shoulders of a man used to carrying loads, looked at me as if he could have put the gates of the city upon them and carried them up to the top of the hill. Now and then I squinted at the houses on both sides of the street and at the alleyways between them. When

we reached the square, we stopped and looked at it. It was the nerve
center of the city, which was so nervous under its calm skin. During
the day there was constant movement here of military men, vehicles,
representatives of the inhabitants who were allowed to move about
freely during the curfew. From here the orders went out. Here came
the reports from the other battle fronts and from the world beyond
the war. Jeeps which dashed through the city and stopped here with
a screech of brakes brought with them the dust of the desert or the
silence of the corpses. Here shining cars spewed out people wearing
civilian clothes, whose faces were silent, and whose stealthy movement presaged fateful decisions. Army lorries stopped here, loaded
with frightened people wrapped in filthy scarves, no one knowing
where they were brought from and where they were going to. High-
ranking officers came and went from the house with the white dome.
Under the surface of the open happenings, flickered the fear of a
conquered city, arrested in its silent houses. Fear of the unknown. A
blank waiting for what might happen suddenly, sudden thunder or an
earthquake.

The square now was lying under the night, small, shrunk in upon
itself, relaxed, sunk in a quiet sleep, after the troubles of the day. On
the other side the tops of the black palms moved a little, and next to
the entrance to the green lawn of the courtyard stood a guard who
did not trouble to ask who we were.

We circled the square and continued to stroll in a street of low
whitewashed houses. From the alleyways blew now a light breeze,
which sifted fine sand on to the pavement. Blind alleys led from the
street to dark quarters pregnant with evil. Rivkin slackened his stride.
Then we stopped near the ruins of a house. Two beheaded walls
leaned against one another, with a great heap of broken bricks between them. Between the sloping walls stood out a crooked iron bow.
The frame of a bed. The lintel of a door remained standing by a
miracle, upright, like the gateway of an ancient ruin.

"This must be the house they were talking about," said Rivkin.

I looked at the ruins, whose broken and shattered forms were like
a vision seen in a nightmare, and said:

"A lousy business, war. Even when you're the winner."

Rivkin thought for a while, his gazed fixed on the heap of bricks in front of us. Then he turned his head to me and said:

"Look, my boy. What are we anyway? A small plot of earth surrounded by a desert. All the time hot winds, sandstorms, armies of locusts, foxes and jackals come to destroy us. What should we do in order to continue working? Put up fences around us, build shelters, windbreaks. Sometimes this doesn't work. Then one goes outside and bangs on tins to chase the locusts away. Or one fires a gun to frighten the jackals. We want to live, don't we? We're entitled to live, aren't we? If so, then we shouldn't complain about the need for what has to be done. Necessity comes from God."

Necessity comes from God, I repeated to myself as we continued walking, necessity comes from God. I have to understand its laws and to surrender to them. If I don't understand them, then I am behaving like a fool. I have to understand its laws, in order to stay alive. Otherwise, I will again have need of the revolver hidden beneath the mattress of my bed. Is it still there? The choice does not lie between being good or bad, but between being strong or weak. The strong one becomes a necessity. He is able to fight all other necessities. The world is nothing but an incessant war between one necessity and the other. Oh, what darkness! How strange that I am thinking about the pistol hidden in my distant room, when I am holding a gun in my hands.

An early morning breeze passed by. The houses began shedding their darkness; they looked like phantoms wearing shrouds. In the sky could now be seen blocks of heavy clouds, travelling eastwards. In the courtyards were revealed barrels, poles, squashed bushes, dry, grey sand. Shutters and doors shone in their nakedness. Bubbles of dew covered the iron bolts. A frozen silence hung in the air.

Oh, if only everything was like this early morning, I thought to myself, silent and wrapped in grey mist, breathing a quiet breath, not plotting any evil, and in another hour the air would grow paler, and within the houses, so warm from the breath of children, women would get out of their beds, pattering across the floor in their bare feet, silently, so as not to wake anybody, to put a kettle on the stove, amidst the shadows of the kitchen, and the men would pull the heavy work boots out from under the beds, tying their laces slowly, feeling with a blind hand for the holes, trying to patch together the tatters of a vanished dream, and there would be no necessity to kill in order to live, or to tear a man away from his home suddenly in the afternoon or to stand on guard between the women and the flour, and it would be possible to go out to the courtyard and examine a cauliflower, to see whether the white head was hard already, and to say good morning to the neighbor on the other side of the fence, and the clouds would be clearer and perhaps there would be rain . . .

The shots froze my thoughts, and at the third a glint of fire flashed from the depths of the alleyway. "There!" Rivkin called out, running bent up along the side of the houses, holding his gun. For a moment I stood there, stunned. Where from? Where to? How? And then a sharp pain cut through my chest, and I fell down on my face. I felt a warm wetness spreading over my whole chest, and the pain also spread and grew blunter, like a stone. Hard. Hardening. Stone. That's it, that's it already, a voice mumbled inside me. It had to happen. Like a glass being shattered to pieces. The luck of a good man. Many people with goblets in their hands. What laughter. Moving and rolling all around. Round and round with the goblets. Where is my wife? The porch is falling. The pistol. That's it, the pistol. It's fallen into the jukebox, and is firing at a spinning wheel of elephants and monkeys, elephants and monkeys, moving at a great speed until nothing can be seen, only a crowd of white-clad people surrounding me with arms raised to hit and calling out. Necessity comes from God Necessity comes from God There is no God Rivkin There is no God Rivkin where . . .

Then everything went white and I sank into it as if in cottonwool, sank and sank in a wet pleasantness, sinking, only white and white, above me and around me, sinking into endless depths.

VII

A little bell, rather like a school bell, tinkled, and then the old man with the bushy mustache and the uniform took my arm and said that we had to go in. I got up from the bench and let him lead me to wherever we were going. Before entering I stopped and asked him what I was charged with. He shrugged his shoulders as if to say that he didn't know. Was I being tried because I had been killed? I asked again. "Perhaps," he said, taking my arm and pulling me inside.

It was a long and broad hall in an unfurnished building. The walls were unplastered and one could notice the cross-lines made by the bricks. On the floor there were many blobs of plaster. Above me I could see the tiles and the wooden beams which formed the underpinnings of the roof. The glass of the large windows, one on each side, was spotted with dabs of whitewash, and the light that came through them was grey as on a rainy winter day. At the far end of the hall was a long black table, with only one man sitting behind it. He wore a uniform, but as he was bent over his papers, I couldn't make out his face. On his right was the small copper bell. Two very long benches without back rests, facing one another, took up almost the whole length of the room, close to the walls behind them. The right-hand bench was empty, and there were some people on the left-hand bench. At once I made out Argaman, who was sitting hunched-up, supporting his chin with one hand. When I entered he looked at me intently through his large glasses, as if he was afraid he would lose a single flicker of expression on my face. On both sides of him sat the accountants, who exchanged whispers when they saw me, and a few other people, whom I did not know.

The old man led me to the center of the hall, a long distance from the judge's table, let go of my arm, and, walking slowly towards the empty bench, sat down on it, holding its edge with his fingertips. His feet did not reach the ground, and they waggled slightly. Standing in the center of the hall was torture, because I had nothing to lean against, neither behind me nor in front, and I didn't know how to stand or what to do with my hands. At first I let them hand down at my sides; then I folded them on my chest, but I was afraid this might be contempt of court and so I let them drop in front of me again, with my palms together and my fingers playing with one another. But then I was afraid of appearing nervous, and so I stopped playing with my fingers. Once the movement of the fingers stopped, it was worse than before, because I felt as if ants were crawling under my left foot, creeping to my leg and thigh and reaching as far as my groin. I shuffled my feet a little and the grains of sand on the floor made a creaking noise, which seemed to me to arouse the immediate attention of the spectators. Again I saw Argaman's high forehead with its two bays of receding hair on the sides of his head. He didn't take his eyes off me, piercing me right through and turning me inside out. The way he looked at me made me think that he had come here in order to confirm his beliefs, and that I was a sort of guinea-pig for him. I met Ben-Hen's eyes, but they didn't betray for a second that he knew me. When I managed to summon a faint smile, as if to say hullo, he immediately turned to his neighbor and whispered something to him.

The way all those people were sitting on the bench struck me as highly uncomfortable and increased my nervousness, because they also had nothing to lean against and their backs were either too straight or too bent, so that they looked quite unnatural. I looked around for Johnny, but he wasn't there. On the other hand, I noticed my neighbor from the first floor of our building: her broad face was flushed and she looked at me with wide-open eyes, eagerly awaiting whatever I would do or say. I became very embarrassed when I recalled that she knew a great deal about me, especially as I had borrowed the ladder from her. I wanted to ask her how my wife was, but of course that was quite impossible. Or perhaps I could get to her? I had an idea which seemed promising. Just whispering didn't constitute contempt of court and maybe I could whisper: "Is she at home?" Then she could answer with a movement of her head.

I had already motioned in her direction when the judge cleared his throat loudly, and when he raised his head from his paper I was stunned to see that it was B. His blue eyes were very cold, and then I knew what was in store for me.

"I hope you know why you were killed," his voice reached me form the other end of the hall.

I lowered my hands to my sides. Now it was obvious what they were accusing me of.

"It was an accident," I said in a weak voice.

"What's that?" he called out.

"It happened by accident," I repeated.

"No," B. said. Then, as if he was speaking from a long way off (I made out his words from the movement of his lips): "You didn't carry out the commandment: make haste to kill him who seeks to kill you."

When I understood this, I felt a sort of relief. The charge wasn't such a grave one. After all, my death was my own private affair.

As if he had heard what I was thinking he said: "Obviously, as a soldier your life is the property of the state."

Automatically I sprang to attention and saluted. I head a rustle on the bench and noticed that some of the spectators had straightened up and turned to one another to whisper something. B. made a movement with his hand to indicate that I could stand at ease.

"Well, what do you have to say to that?" he asked.

"To what?" I said. Now the rustle on the bench was louder than before. I could even hear the sound of faint laughter.

B. leaned his head forward and looked at me from under the cliff of his forehead. He waited for my answer. Perhaps I was wrong, I thought to myself. Perhaps it wasn't just chance that I was killed. I tried to remember the details of what had happened in the last few minutes before the sharp pain pierced my chest. The silence seemed to last very long, and I could see that all those present were losing patience with me.

"I couldn't shoot," I said. "My hands froze."

"Why?" B. fired the question at me as if he had been waiting for exactly this answer.

"Because it was morning already," I said.

"What difference did that make?"

"Well, it was light," I said, "and I can't kill a man when I see his face."

Ripples of laughter came from the bench. Only in Argaman's face could I detect any eagerness to listen: his face tautened with the effort. In the silence the rustle of papers from the table sounded like the rattle of sheets of irons. B. looked at some documents in front of him.

"You were sent to replace one of the guards in the refugee camp," he said, "and you kept at a distance."

"That's right," I said.

He removed a piece of paper from one heap and put it on another. The rustling sounded like the echo of thunder in a cloud.

"Your guarded the gangsmen," he said, "and then, when they were taken inside you remained outside."

My silence was tantamount to a confession.

"Why?" he asked.

"It wasn't fair," I said, "they couldn't defend themselves."

"Who, those murderers?" he fixed his blue eyes on me.

"They didn't look like murderers to me," I said, "perhaps because the rays of the setting sun shed a purplish light on their faces."

Again there came a laugh from the bench, and Argaman straightened his back and placed his palms on his knees. B. sniggered.

"In other words, you wanted to keep your hands clean," he said. As I didn't reply, he went on: "You felt relieved that the job was being done by others."

I could see heads nodding in agreement on the bench. Only my first floor neighbor continued to look at me with wide-open eyes, full of worry and concern. Her cheeks were flushed.

"Pure soul!" B. sneered. He bent his head down over the papers, turned a few of them over, then turned to me again, looked at me with his bright, glittering eyes, and said in a loud voice: "You saint! You were ready to sacrifice your brothers' lives in order to save murderers! If we had to rely on you, we'd be done for! What do you have to say in your defense? What?"

The echoes reverberated all over the hall.

I felt my legs trembling. I would never have thought that this moderate man could become so heated. The more I tried to move my lips, the less they responded. The glances thrown at me by the people sitting on the bench pierced me like arrows; they looked at me accusingly as if eager for revenge.

"Speak up!" B. shouted at me.

And as I still remained silent, as if paralyzed, he picked up the little copper bell and rang it angrily.

The old man got up from the bench and gripped my arm. I turned my head to the left and saw the spectators were getting to their feet and stretching themselves. It seemed strange that the court session had been so short, particularly as nothing had really been cleared up. Was the trial over, I wondered, with a sudden burst of fear? "Intermission," said the old man, leading me to the bench on which he was sitting.

I sat down. Next to the window which faced me sat the accountants, arguing among themselves. My neighbor continued sitting, her cheeks even redder than before and her eyes open wide. Argaman strolled up and down the hall, with his hands in his pockets.

I thought over what I had said and what I hadn't said. I was angry with myself. Why did I have to be tried? After all, my life and my death were my own private affair. Even if I was a soldier. A soldier who was killed in battle couldn't be tried. The state had lost nothing through my death, especially as in any case I had intended to commit suicide. Why didn't I have the courage to say what I had felt in the last few days, and what I really thought?

My eyes met those of my neighbor. "May I leave my seat for a moment?" I asked the old man who sat next to me. "Only for a minute," he said, wagging his finger in front of my face. I rose and walked over to the opposite bench. It seemed to be a very long distance, because everyone standing around noticed me, stopped talking, and looked at me with undisguised curiosity. I finally reached the place where my neighbor was sitting, and asked her in whisper: "Perhaps you know if my wife is at home?"

She shrugged her shoulders and smiled sadly.

"Hasn't she been there since I left?" I asked.

She placed a finger on her lips as a hint that I should be silent, and, turning round, I saw the old man coming up behind me. He took my arm, saying: "The minute is over!" and led me back to the bench.

Now I began worrying about what had happened to my wife. Perhaps she didn't know about my unfortunate accident. This supposition depressed me still more. As if I didn't exist at all. As if my life and death were worth nothing and nothing would remain of them, not even sorrow. And whatever I would say at the trial was also of no importance. Can one die twice?

A man in a shabby grey suit, with a black hat, was walking up and down near me, with his hands behind his back. From the way he squinted at me when he passed, I realized that he wanted to say something. He had a long, pale face, with a thin pointed nose and sad, watery eyes. Eventually he plucked up courage and sat down next to me, lifting the hem of his jacket.

"Excuse me," he said, "but how old are you?"

"Thirty-five," I said.

"Older than me," he said, "although I look older than you. Born in this country?"

"Yes."

"I thought so. You know very little."

He said this with a sad smile and sympathetically, but although I was so anxious for any of the spectators to come up to me and to offer me a word or two of encouragement, or even to ask me something, the few words he spoke had such a chilling effect that inwardly I wished he would go away and leave me alone.

"I can tell you a lot, but I will only tell you very little," he said. "I died three times." Here he held up three fingers. "But I shall only tell you about my first death."

I looked towards my neighbor and tried to catch some hint in her face. I was worried about my wife. Hadn't she been home for all those long days?

"Well, imagine yourself," I heard the monotonous voice, like the drone of a distant prayer. "Imagine me walking in the snow, in a long black procession. I was twelve then. A boy. On my right was my mother, with a large parcel under her arm. She walked and limped and walked, and I had to help her, otherwise she would have fallen in the snow. We came to a gate in a barbed wire fence, and they told us to stop. I was shivering with cold, and my mother wrapped me in a large scarf. Suddenly we heard screaming. People were being taken through the door. A soldier came up to us and took my mother away. She struggled with him and called to me. I ran towards her and tried to take hold of her. But they pulled me away. I shouted, without a voice coming out. I see her going away from me, into the large, open space surrounded by a barbed wire fence. I want to cry, but can't. And endless night. I have no one in the world . . . That was my first death."

"That's terrible," I whispered, "terrible."

"You understand?" He fixed his eyes on me.

"It's unbearable. Impossible. The human heart is too weak."

The little bell rang again. The audience hurried back to their places. The old man took my arm again and led me to the same place where I had stood previously. There was complete silence in the room. I crossed my hands behind my back.

B. sat hunched up over his papers, writing something. The creaking of his pen sounded like the scraping of a piece of pottery, and could be heard all over the hall. Two swallows flew swiftly after one another under the roof, and all the spectators looked upwards.

"Well, then, I understand that your intention was to avoid doing evil," B. said, turning his head in my direction. "Of course, something which you consider evil."

I moved my lips without uttering a sound. He looked at me closely, and then said:

"You probably remember your visit to my house. At the time you wanted to prove that you could also be wicked. Is that correct?"

"Yes," I whispered. "I was wrong."

"It's good that you admit it. Then you wanted to kill someone because you were under the impression that he thought you were a good man, so to speak."

"I was wrong in this too," I said.

"Wouldn't it be correct to say that at home, too, you behaved not like a good man but like a man who perhaps seeks the good but is not at all proud of it?"

The spectators on the bench straightened up and looked at me expectantly. For the first time Argaman turned to his neighbor and whispered something in his ear.

"Is that true?" B. raised his voice again.

At that moment I turned and was struck dumb to see my wife enter the hall. She walked in the direction of the right bench, bent over slightly and walking on the tips of her toes, as if afraid to be noticed or disturb the proceedings. She didn't look at anybody, but sat down next to the old man. She was holding a handkerchief to her nose, and her eyes were red.

"Naturally you caused your wife untold suffering by your foolish conduct," B. continued in a loud voice. "Conduct which was ostensibly good, but which led to evil, as you forced her to deny her real feelings. Were you wrong in this too?"

Tears choked me. I turned my head towards my wife, but she didn't see me. Her eyes were fixed on B. When I turned my gaze to the judge's table again, I saw that my neighbor from the first floor was whispering something in great excitement to those sitting beside her, who leaned forward to hear what she was saying.

Argaman nodded to his friends several times, as if in complete agreement with what B. had just said.

"Is that true?" B. asked again.

I swallowed the lump in my throat, and said: "Yes, commander!"

"And only here, in the midst of the war, you found the courage to refrain from hurting your enemies in order not to cause them suffering!"

"Yes, commander," I said.

"And to put an end to your life."

Here my wife broke into tears, and pressing the handkerchief against her mouth in order to check her outburst, she ran out of the hall.

The neighbor from the first floor also rose, bowed slightly towards the judge's bench, threw a reproachful look at me and went out, following my wife. Argaman gave me a contemptuous glance through his glasses, holding his chin in the palm of his hand. I felt very lonely.

B. took hold of the handle of the bell and lifted it a little from the table. I was seized by a terrible fear that that was the end of the trial.

"One moment . . ." I stepped forward.

He put the bell back in its place. The old man, who had already got up from the bench, sat down again.

"Well?" B. asked.

"I . . ." I began, but I couldn't continue. With great effort I managed to get the following words out: "I can't go on like this."

"Meaning what?" B. asked in surprise.

"Meaning . . ." I turned my head to the people sitting on the bench, hoping for some sign of help or encouragement. But they looked at me in indifference as if they no longer expected anything from me.

"Meaning that there's no end to it," I said. "Evil breeds evil and there's no end to it."

"What do you mean by that?" asked B.

"I mean," I said in a low voice, "that this has to be stopped once and for all. Someone has to stop it. At a certain moment. Because otherwise one murder will lead to another and one humiliation will lead to another and there'll never be an end to it. Who'll gain by this?"

"The strongest," said B.

"If that is the case, then there still won't be any end to it, because sometimes certain people are strong and then others."

"Well, so what should be done about it, in your opinion?" asked B., bending towards me impatiently.

"Perhaps simply to refrain from doing evil," I said.

"In other words, you would rather be killed than kill," he chuckled.

"After all, if I am dead or someone else is dead," I whispered, "the amount of suffering caused is the same. I'm not better than anyone else. At least I will know I haven't committed any evil. Perhaps in this way the amount of evil in the world will be reduced."

"Oh, that's going too far!" The voice came from the left bench. It was Argaman. He was saying it to himself, but his words could be heard clearly all over the hall. "It contradicts all logic!" he added, stretching his hands out to his fellow spectators.

"You want all of us to be saints," B. chuckled.

"As far as possible . . ." I said.

"To love our enemies and forgive them."

"We are not better than them," I said. "They want to live. Exactly as we do."

There was a commotion on the bench and a great deal of movement. I heard people saying that this business had to stop. B. gave them a look and waited until they had quietened down.

"That means you don't think that you are in the right," he said.

"To do what is right—that is my whole life," I whispered.

"Then defend your life! Defend it with all your might!" his voice echoed in the hall.

"When I kill others, my life loses its justice," my lips trembled.

"So you sought justice beyond life on this earth," B. scoffed. "I am sure you have found it. There, where all are equal, because they are all disembodied souls! Isn't that true?"

I was bewildered by his words and gaze, and could not answer.

"Justice is bought with force," he called out loudly. "Only a fool believes that justice and weakness go hand in hand! Do you understand this? Do you?"

He didn't wait for my reply any more. A sigh of relief came from the spectators' bench, and the hall seemed to sink in it. He lowered his head once more to the papers in front of him, took the pen and quickly wrote something on a piece of paper. While doing this he muttered, as if talking to himself:

"You wanted us to commit suicide and thus to bring salvation to the world. Fortunately our desire to live is greater than yours. You realize, by now, of course, that your death wasn't an accident."

My throat was choked. There was complete silence in the hall; the only sound that could be heard was the scratching of the pen. The spectators' gaze was now rooted to the slip of paper, as if waiting for the verdict to be given. I saw his sleeve move from line to line. Then he affixed his signature with a flourish, folded the sheet of paper twice, placed it in an envelope, pasted it down, wrote something on it, and summonned the old man to him with a motion of his finger. The old man came up to the table step by step, tiptoeing and took the envelope from B. Then he walked towards me, his back very straight. When he reached me, the bell rang.Everyone stood up. The old man handed me the envelope and said: "That's all."

"No verdict?" I asked fearfully.

"Here there are no verdicts," the old man said. "This is the routine procedure of registration of deaths."

I didn't know what to do. B. rose and walked past me on his way out of the hall, without giving me a glance. The accountants moved towards the door in a group, arguing heatedly among themselves. The moment I turned round to go, I was stunned to see Johnny come towards me, with a broad smile on his face. Was it possible that he had been there the whole time, without my seeing him? I wondered, blushing. He came up to me, shook my hand and said: "Thank you. You were wonderful. Fantastic. Exactly what I would have said if I were you."

"Were you here all the time?" I asked.

At that moment he disappeared.

I remained standing alone in the hall. The old man had also gone. Only then did I remember the envelope in my hand: I held it up and saw the words on it: "To deliver to Rivkin."

When I left the hall, it was bright light outside, and I blinded my eyes. From the look of the house on the other side of the sandy street I knew that I was in the village in which I was born. It was an old house, painted a faded brown, with a red-tiled roof and green shutters. A high avenue of cypresses led to its door, and inside the rusty, bent iron fence were dusty myrtle bushes. Clumps of weeds dotted the farmyard, and a low tap dripped, one drop at a time. A midday silence cast its spell around, and the sand burnt in the sun. From the door of the house a grey-haired man emerged, he stopped and scrutinized me closely. I wanted to call out: "Father!" But I was dumb. Apparently he didn't recognize me, because he turned on to the wooden pavement and went on his way.

Translated by Aubrey Hodes

The Sermon

Yudka was no speaker. He didn't make public addresses, never took part in the debate at general meetings or at conventions—not even to make a point of order. So he was considered a man whose strength was not in self-expression. And, even though he was not just as he was considered to be, his reputation had its effect; it became second nature to him, so that he quite forgot how to open his mouth in public and say something in proper form, whether it was important or no more than a jest. That was why the boys were astounded when they heard he proposed to deliver a formal statement before the committee; and the committee, whose proceedings were open only to its members and to individuals called in before it, was convened at that time for no other reason than to hear him speak.

The committee members sat in a single row at the green table, right and left of their chairman, all clean-cut and positive, like captains and heroes in council. They eyed Yudka curiously, waiting to hear him say something not yet heard or known, except the chairman, who gazed straight at the table, apparently dreaming or drowsing, with cool eyes.

The chairman dutifully spoke a few words of introduction, fell silent, and sat down, just as though he hadn't opened his mouth, and there were no one else in the room.

Yudka drew himself up stiffly, looking harried and confused, so much did he have to say and so little did he know how to begin.

It was shocking, how confused and how harried he was! This quarryman, who split rocks and rent mountains, and went out fearlessly on night patrols, no sooner had to speak publicly before his comrades than he lost himself completely from fright.

They waited, and he said nothing. Again the chairman spoke directly to the green-covered table: "Comrade Yudka has the floor."

Yudka stood there crumbling inwardly, drops of sweat glistening on his brow.

"You wanted to make a statement," the chairman prompted, glancing slantwise at him. "Well then, speak. We're listening."

Some of the committee members looked aside, some stared off into space; all were silent.

At last Yudka passed his hand over his forehead, and said in the soft, slurred accent of the South of Russia: "I didn't come here to make a speech, only to say something important. . . . Really, I shouldn't say anything at all. . . . Do you know what it is to speak when it's best for you to keep still?"

He looked down the line of seats, parting his lips in an injured smile, faint and sickly.

"But I must speak!" He fixed his eyes in a blank stare, his face clouding. "I don't understand anything at all . . . I no longer understand. It's been years since I've understood. . . ."

"What don't you understand?" the chairman asked him calmly, like a judge trained to be patient with the public.

"Everything!" Yudka called out with passion. "Everything! But that's nonsense. Let's leave that for now. All I want to know is: What are we doing here?"

"Doing where?" The chairman did not follow him.

"Here! In this place, or in Palestine. In general. . . ."

"*I* don't understand!" The chairman spread his hands wonderingly, and his lips twisted in a mocking smile. "Now *I* don't understand either. . . ."

"That's a different way of not understanding," Yudka rejoined. "That's probably your way of mocking me."

One of the committee members broke into a broad grin and tapped his fingers on the table top. Yudka felt his smile, but lowered his eyes, pretending not to see.

"Get back to the subject!" the chairman demanded. "Make the statement you want to make, without argument."

"I want to state," Yudka spoke with an effort, in low, tense tones, "that I am opposed to Jewish history. . . ."

"What?" The chairman looked about him to either side.

The committee members exchanged glances in astonishment. The one who had smiled at first could no longer control himself, and a short explosive laugh escaped him.

"I have no respect for Jewish history!" Yudka repeated the same refrain. " 'Respect' is really not the word, but what I said before: I'm opposed to it. . . ."

Once again the same comrade—a lively fellow by nature—burst into laughter and all the others joined in.

Yudka turned and looked at him.

"You're laughing," he said in a voice dulled and measured and serious beyond words, "because you took my wife from me. . . ."

At once they all fell silent and shrank back, as if from some imminent danger, and the comrade who had laughed was thrown into confusion. Shifting and slouching, he sat with bowed back and restless eyes.

The chairman struck four or five strokes with all his might on the bell, and then again three more from sheer shock and helplessness, with no idea of what to say.

"I think that's how it is," Yudka went on, after the ringing had ceased. "If I were in his place, I would laugh too every time I saw him . . . not straight in his face, but like that . . . it's a different kind of laugh! I couldn't help laughing, I wouldn't dare . . . I couldn't manage to do anything else or say anything . . . for I would feel terribly ashamed then . . . terribly ashamed! I couldn't talk to him freely, for example, let's say about literature. Or perhaps make my confession and weep . . . I can't explain it very well, but it's clear! I've thought it all out and made sure that that's how it is. But it's not important. . . ."

For a while there was quiet, a total, final quiet in the room.

Then the chairman stirred, beetling his heavy eyebrows, and spoke with gruff, ironical severity: "Comrade Yudka, I call you to order! If you have something to say, please, say it briefly, no wandering off the subject. And if it's history you want to talk about, then the university is the place for you!"

"It's on the subject, it's on the subject!" Yudka hastened to reply with a propitiating smile. "I can't proceed now without history. I've thought a great deal about it, many nights, every night when I'm on guard. . . ."

The chairman shrugged and spread his hands skeptically. "Speak!" he ordered, to cut it short.

Yudka became as before: confused and harried, as though at that very moment some ill fortune had befallen him and he had come to pain and torment.

"You've already heard that I'm opposed to Jewish history." He coughed in shame and unease, as he began the sermon. "I want to explain why. Just be patient a little while. . . . First, I will begin with the fact that we have no history at all. That's a fact. And that's the *zagvozdka*. I don't know how to say it in Hebrew. . . . In other words, that's where the shoe pinches. Because we didn't make our own history, the *goyim* made it for us. Just as they used to put out our candles on Sabbath, milk our cows and light our ovens on Sabbath, so they made our history for us to suit themselves, and we took it from them as it came. But it's not ours, it's not ours at all! Because we didn't make it, we would have made it differently, we didn't want it to be like that, it was only others who wanted it that way and they forced it on us, whether we liked it or not, which is a different thing altogether. . . . In that sense, and in every other sense, I tell you, in every other sense, we have no history of our own. Have we? It's clear as can be! And that's why I'm opposed to it. I don't recognize it, it doesn't exist for me! What's more, I don't respect it, although 'respect' is not the word, still I don't respect it . . . I don't respect it at all! But the main thing is, I'm opposed to it. What I mean is, I don't accept it. . . ."

The storm within him made him shake from side to side like an ox refusing the yoke. He swung his hands about as if he were moving stone or sorting lumber, and he was so swept along in his speech that he could no longer halt.

"I don't accept it!" he repeated, with the stubborn insistence of one who has come to a final, fixed opinion. "Not a single point, not a line, not a dot. Nothing, nothing . . . nothing at all! Will you believe me? Will you believe me? You can't even imagine how I'm opposed to it, how I reject it, and how . . . how . . . I don't respect it! Now, look! Just think . . . what is there in it? Just give me an answer. What is there in it? Oppression, defamation, persecution, martyrdom. And again oppression, defamation, persecution, and martyrdom. And again and again and again, without end. . . . That's what's in it, and nothing more! After all, it's . . . it's . . . it bores you to death, it's just plain dull! Just let me mention one fact, just one little fact. It's well known that children everywhere love to read historical fiction. That's where you get action, see, bold deeds, heroes, great fighters, and fearless conquerors. In a word, a world full of heroism. Now, here now, in Palestine, our children love to read, unless they're stupid. I know this for a fact. I've looked into it. Yes, they read, but historical novels about *goyim,* not about Jews. Why is that so? It's no accident. It's simply because Jewish history is dull, uninteresting. It has no glory or action, no heroes and conquerors, no rulers and masters of their fate, just a collection of wounded, hunted, groaning, and wailing wretches, always begging for mercy. You can see for yourselves that it can't be interesting. The least you can say is it's uninteresting. I would simply forbid teaching our children Jewish history. Why the devil teach them about their ancestors' shame? I would just say to them: 'Boys, from the day we were driven out from our land we've been a people without a history. Class dismissed. Go out and play football. . . .' But that's all in passing. So, let me proceed. I'm sure you won't take me wrong. I know that there is heroism in the way we stood up to all that oppression and suffering. I take it into account. . . . But . . . I don't care for that kind of heroism. Don't laugh . . . I don't care for it! I prefer an entirely different kind of heroism. First of all, please understand me, it's nothing but the heroism of despair. With no way out, anyone can be a hero. Whether he wants to or not, he must be, and there is no credit or honor in that. In the second place, this heroism after all amounts to great weakness, worse than weakness, a kind of special talent for corruption and decay. That's how it is! This type of hero sooner or later begins to pride himself on his 'heroism' and brags about it: 'See what great torments I withstand! See what untold shame and humiliation I suffer! Who can compare with me? See, we don't merely suffer torments. It's more than that, we love these torments too, we love torment for its own sake. . . . We want to be tortured, we are eager, we yearn for it. . . . Persecution preserves us, keeps us alive. Without it, we couldn't exist. . . . Did you ever see a community of Jews that was not suffering? I've never seen one. A Jew without suffering is an abnormal creature, hardly a Jew at all, half a *goy*. . . . That's what I mean; it's just such 'heroism' that shows our weakness . . . suffering, suffering, suffering! Everything is rotten around suffering. . . . Please notice, I said *around,* not *in* suffering. There's a tremendous difference. . . . Everything, everything around it rots: history, life itself, all actions, customs, the group, the individual, literature, culture, folk songs . . . everything! The world grows narrow, cramped, upside down. A world of darkness, perversion and contradiction. Sorrow is priced higher than joy, pain easier to understand than happiness, wrecking better than building, slavery preferred to redemption, dream before reality, hope more than the future, faith before common sense, and so on for all the other perversions . . . It's horrible! A new psychology is created, a kind of *moonlight* psychology. . . . The night has its own special psychology, quite different from the day's. I don't mean the psychology of a man at night, that's something separate, but the psychology of night itself. You may not have noticed it, perhaps, but it's there, it's there. I know it. I feel it every time I stand guard. The whole world behaves quite differently too in the day, nature moves in a different way, every blade of grass, every stone, every smell, all different, different. . . ."

"Yudka," the chairman cut in, half jesting, half beseeching, "your thoughts are very fine, but have pity on us. Why did you have the committee convened?"

"Wait, wait," said Yudka hastily, "I haven't come to the main thing. You don't know yet . . . I have something in mind, I have something in mind. . . . You'll soon see. Just be patient a little . . ."

"Let him talk," spoke up one of the committee, "let him talk."

"But . . ." the chairman began dubiously.

At that moment Yudka unintentionally shouted at him: "Quiet!" The chairman was cowed and submitted in silence.

"I'm not wandering from the subject. I'm speaking about principles, about basic things. . . ." Yudka fumbled wide-eyed, his earnestness written on his face, his mind obviously entangled and exalted, laboring and driving toward something.

In a short while, he began again:

"I've already told you, and I beg you to remember that a special, perverted, fantastic psychology has grown up among us, if I may say so, a *moonlight* psychology, altogether different in every way from other people's. . . . We love suffering, for through suffering we are able to be Jews; it preserves us and maintains us, it proves we are bold and heroic, braver than any people in the whole world. I admit, I am forced to admit that this is heroic indeed, in a way. People, you know, abuse many fine and noble words . . . in a certain sense suffering is heroic. And in a sense even decay is heroic and degradation is heroic . . . that is exactly the kind of people we are. We don't fight, or conquer, or rule. We have no desire, no will for it. Rather, we submit, we suffer without limit, willingly, lovingly. We actually say: You shall not conquer us, nor break us, nor destroy us! There is no power on earth strong enough for that . . . because power has its limits, but there is no limit, no end to our suffering. . . . In fact, the more we are oppressed, the greater we grow; the more we are degraded, the greater we think is our honor; the more we are made to suffer, the stronger we become. For this is our staple food, it is our elixir of life. . . . It's all so beautifully arranged! A character like that, imagine it, a nature so perfected . . . and that explains everything: Exile, martyrdom, Messiah . . . these are three which are one, all to the same purpose, the same intention. . . . Doesn't it say somewhere: 'The threefold cord'? . . ."

" 'And the threefold cord is not quickly broken,' " contributed one of the committee.

"That's it!" Yudka seized upon the verse excitedly. "Not quickly broken! Not quickly! Never, never. . . . These three support each other, aid and abet each other, so that never will the Jews be redeemed in all the world . . . so that they wander from nation to nation and country to country, age upon age to the end of all ages, the weight of the laws falling upon them, the fury of the lawless rising against them, everywhere trials and tribulations and foes and hatred on every hand. . . . Exile, exile . . . Oh oh, how they love it, how they hold it fast! This is the most sacred thing, the most beloved, intimate, closest to their hearts, nearer and dearer than Jerusalem, more *Jewish* than Jerusalem, deeper and purer. Far more, there's simply no comparison! Is this a paradox? But that's how it is. . . . Wait now, don't talk!" He hurriedly gestured to each side, though nobody made any attempt to interrupt. "Let me tell you how I look at it. . . ."

He rubbed his hand over his face and lips, as though coming up out of a tub; he muted his voice and whispered, as though it were a deep secret.

"The Exile, that is our pyramid, and it has martyrdom for a base and Messiah for its peak. And . . . and . . . the Talmud, that is our Book of the Dead. . . . In the very beginning, as far back as the Second Temple, we began to build it. Even that far back we planned it, we laid the foundations. . . . Exile, martyrdom, Messiah. . . . Do you grasp the deep cunning hidden in this wild fantasy, the cold *moonlight* with which it flames. . . ? Do you grasp it? Just think, just think! Millions of men, a whole people plunging itself into this madness and sunk in it for two thousand years! Giving up to it its life, its very existence, its character, submitting to affliction, suffering, tortures. Agreed that it is foolish, a lunatic dream. But a dream, that is, a vision, an ideal. . . . What an uncanny folk! What a wonderful, awful people! Awful, awful to the point of madness! For look, it scorns the whole world, the whole world and all its fighters and heroes and wise men and poets all together! Fearsome and blind! A bottomless abyss. . . . No, one could go mad!"

He formed the last words soundlessly on his lips and stood as though in trance, pale, with his mouth open and a fixed stare.

The chairman invited him to be seated. "Sit down," he said, pointing to an empty chair.

"What?" He came to himself, speaking as out of a maze. "But it's not just a fantasy, it's more than fantasy . . . fantastic, to be sure. But a necessary fantasy. . . . Why necessary? What is its purpose? A very necessary purpose, let me tell you, a vitally necessary purpose! This madness is practical, it is very deliberate, it has a clearly understood aim, and it is thought out to the finest detail. . . . Look here, here we have a single element, as slight as can be, a trifling anecdote, with consequences as grave, as far-reaching as can be . . . I'm speaking of the belief in the Messiah. That's a typical Jewish fantasy, the most typical of all! Isn't it? . . . A single myth, all that is left of the whole past, the closing speech of all that great drama, after the Judges, the Prophets, and the Kings, after the First Temple and the Second, after the wars and wonders—well, and all the rest of it. . . . And that's what we are left with—a single, simple legend, and no more. Not much, you say? You are mistaken. On the contrary, it is a great deal. It is far too much. You might think, it's no more than a trifle, a kindergarten legend. But it's not so. It's by no means so innocent. It has such a cunning, do you know, like that of well-tried, ancient men, a cunning of the greatest subtlety, so fated, so *podlaya*—that is, so corrupt a cunning. . . . Let me add, by the way, it's a wonderful legend, a tale of genius, although—apart from the philosophy and symbolism in it —not free of caricature, you know, not without a biting Jewish wit and humor; he comes on an ass! A great, a colossal, a cosmic image —not on a snorting steed, but precisely on a donkey, on the most miserable and insignificant of animals. . . . And this was enough to determine a people's fate and chart its course in the world for endless ages, for all eternity, this, and not the disputes of the schools of Shammai and Hillel. I'm not familiar with these things, I never learned Talmud, but it's quite clear. . . . It's an obvious thing, a certainty that if not for this myth it would all have been different. For then, they would finally have had to go right back to Palestine or somehow or other pass on out of the world. At any rate, they would have had to think of something or do something, somehow or other, to bring it all to an end. . . ."

Once more the chairman thought of making him bring his speech to an end, for it seemed to him that the whole discussion was out of place in the committee. He turned to both sides, consulting the committee members with a glance: "What do you think?" They signed to him to let him go on. He acquiesced and settled back.

Yudka did not notice the exchange of signals at all, but went on: "Now there is no need. Now they needn't think about anything or do anything, not a single thought or the slightest action. King Messiah will do it all for them, and they have nothing to do but sit and wait for his coming. In fact, it's forbidden to get involved in the whole matter, to force the end. Forbidden! What can this thing mean?" His voice shook. "What can it mean? . . . Under orders, under orders to stay in Exile until in *Heaven* they decide to redeem them. Not by their own will or their own acts, but from Heaven; not in the way of nature, but by wonders and miracles . . . you understand?"

His eyes passed down the seated line, and he stood there marveling, momentarily struck dumb.

"Do you understand?" he repeated, out of wonder and oppression of mind. "They do nothing, not an effort, nothing at all, just sit and wait. . . . They invented a Messiah in Heaven, but not as a legend out of the past, as a promise for their future. That's very important, terribly important—and they trust in him to come and bring their redemption, while they themselves are obliged to do nothing at all and there you have it. . . . How can they believe in such a thing! And so to believe! To believe for two thousand years! Two thousand years! . . . How, how can men who are by no means simple, who are no fools at all, on the contrary, very shrewd men, men with more than a touch of skepticism, men who are practical, and maybe even a bit too practical, how can they believe something like that, *a thing like that* —and not just believe, but trust in it, pin their whole life upon it, the whole substance of their life and survival, their national, historic fate? . . . And quite seriously, in full earnest! For truly they believe with perfect faith . . . the whole thing is that they really believe! And yet, and yet, in the secrecy of their hearts, you know, deep down, in some hidden fold, some geometric point down there in their hearts—*somewhat* they don't believe, just the faintest hint; at any rate, that he will come now, at this very moment, that he will come during their own

lives, in their day, and this, of course, is the core of the matter.
. . . It would not be possible for them not to *not* believe, even though,
generally speaking, they believe with perfect faith! See? . . . This is a
Jewish trait too, a very Jewish trait: to believe with perfect faith, with
the mad and burning faith of all the heart and all the soul, and yet
somewhat not to believe, the least little bit, and to let this tiny bit be
decisive . . . I can't explain it well. But that's how it is. I am not
mistaken! How complicated it all is! . . . Redemption is the chief of
all their desires, the whole substance of their hopes, and yet they have
bound themselves, locked their hands and feet in chains, and sealed
their own doom, guarding and observing their own sentence with
unimaginable pedantic strictness, not to be redeemed for ever and
ever! Well, now then . . . now then . . . the birth pangs of Messiah.
. . . That's an entire, separate chapter, a very interesting chapter.
. . . Why must there be, according to the folk belief, why must a time
of great troubles come before the end of days? What for? . . . Why
couldn't they do without the troubles? After all, he is Messiah and he
has unlimited power. . . . Why couldn't he come amid joy, with
goodness and blessings, in the midst of peace? . . . And look: It's not
troubles for Israel's enemies particularly, for the gentiles, but especially for Israel! Nor are these troubles such, let's say, that would
make them repent and so on, but just troubles for the sake of trouble,
with no rhyme or reason, a whole flood of troubles, plagues, and
oppressions and every kind of torment, until the eyes of Israel grow
weary with beholding the grief and agony, till they can no longer bear
it, and they despair of redemption. . . . What is this? A *Weltanschauung?* Historic wisdom? Or is it perhaps what one dare not hint: simply
their own fear of redemption? . . . I am just lost!"

He really looked lost, standing there. He seemed for a moment to
have forgotten himself completely, and not to know where he was.

"It seems to me," he said, with a vague, sickly smile, "I once heard
there was a sage or a pious man, I forget which, who said it already:
'Let him come, and may I not see it,' or something like that. . . . Maybe
it was a joke, a cynical remark, or just chatter. Or maybe it was a great
truth, revealing a secret deep, deep buried. . . . How was this myth

ever invented at all? Not invented, no . . . I don't mean to say that . . . because in the beginning surely there was nothing but hope and longing for the kingdom of the House of David. . . . But how did it become what it turned into afterwards, the classic creation of the people, one might say the creation of its highest genius, the eternal creation of the people of Israel? What made it, more than any other myth, sink so deep and spread so wide in the folk-mind that it became common to everyone, rabbis and thinkers and the mass of people, scholars and illiterates, man, woman and child? What was there in it to let it dye our very heart's blood, and rise to a kind of dogma of faith and religion, the foundation of the whole people's life for all ages, our national idea, our vision in history, our political program, and so on? Whatever the answer—it did! That's the fact. It means there must be a profound kinship, a fundamental bond between this myth and the spirit of our people, if it thrust so deep! It means there is a basic harmony, a full and perfect unity between it and our people's ideal, between it and the people's will, and the direction it desires to go! . . . There's not the least doubt: it's quite clear!"

He stopped for a moment, and his face turned dull and pale. It was quiet in the room, as quiet as in the season just before the rains come, a waiting, oppressive, gloomy quiet.

"Ye-es . . ." he said with a long, groaning breath, as if speaking from his very heart, "such is that wild, enthusiastic, *moonlit* fantasy of theirs . . . the fantasy they need for such practical purposes, for their well-understood ends. Just as I've already told you . . . because . . . because. . . ."

He halted and could not speak on. But even half-paralyzed, he looked from one to another in a sort of driven frenzy.

"Because they don't want to be saved!" he blurted out all in one breath.

Again he was still, looking from side to side like one who fears he has been trapped by his own foolishness.

"Because they don't want to be saved!" he repeated, seeking assurance in speech. "That is the deliberate intent of this myth, that is its practical effect, not to be saved, not ever to go back to the land of their fathers. . . . I don't say that it is conscious, necessarily. But if it's unconscious, it's even worse. . . . They *really* believe redemption will come, I repeat it, again, they believe in all truth and sincerity, they hope for it, aspire to it, and yet they *intend* that it should not come. This is not deceit, it's not duplicity at all. I'm sure of it, I'm sure of it. . . . Here something is at work beneath the surface, something rooted in the depths of their heart, something unconscious. . . . It's not for nothing that that myth became so beloved among the people, and holds such sway that they became like some kind of poets, not concerned at all with the world as it is, but altogether given up to dream and legend. Two thousand years it has consoled them, and for two thousand more they will live by its warmth, in dream, in mourning, in expectation, and in secret fear of it, and never will they tire. And that's the whole essence of Judaism, the whole character of Israel, and of its love of Zion, and the holiness of the land, and the holy tongue, and the end of days, and everything altogether. . . . But let's leave this now. For what if they really have something to fear? What if it's true that Judaism can manage to survive somehow in Exile, but here, in the land of Israel, it's doubtful? . . . What if this country is fated to take the place of religion, if it's a grave danger to the survival of the people, if it replaces an enduring center with a transient center, a solid foundation with a vain and empty foundation? And what if this land of Israel is a stumbling block and a catastrophe, if it's the end and finish of everything? . . ."

A queer, weary and ill-defined smile flickered on his lips.

"Well? . . ." He turned his eyes on them as though waiting for an answer. "What if they're right? What if their instinct doesn't deceive them? . . . Just see how here, here, in Israel, they are against us, all the old settlers, all those pious old Jews, simple Jews like all those that ever lived in any other place or time. Don't their very faces tell us plainly: 'We are no Zionists, we are God-fearing Jews! We don't want a Hebrew State or a national home. What we want is to go up peacefully to be buried on the Mount of Olives, or down to pray at the Wailing Wall undisturbed. . . .' Now, that means something! I won't talk about our Mizrachi people, those little naïve semi-sophisticates of our Zionist movement. I'm speaking about the people, the people of the root and foundation. Well, then? . . . I'll tell you! To my mind, if I am right, Zionism and Judaism are not at all the same, but two things quite different from each other, and maybe even two things directly opposite to each other! At any rate, far from the same. When a man can no longer be a Jew, he becomes a Zionist. I am not exaggerating. The Biluim were primarily very imperfect Jews. It wasn't the pogroms that moved them—that's all nonsense, the pogroms—they were falling apart inside, they were rootless and crumbling within. Zionism begins with the wreckage of Judaism, from the point where the strength of the people fails. That's a fact! Nobody has yet begun to understand Zionism. It is far deeper, far more pregnant with vast and fateful consequences than appears on the surface, or than people say. Herzl expressed no more than the rudiments of it. Ahad Ha'am said nothing at all, just another idea that came into the head of an inquiring Jew. At most, he went around advising Jews who had somehow determined to establish a new community that they'd do better to set up a Jewish study circle or build a school or cemetery first. . . . What?" He turned to one of the committee who had opened his mouth to speak.

"Oh nothing," the interrupter chuckled, "I just remembered something. I had an uncle, he was a clever fellow. The Bolsheviks killed him. For nothing, just killed him. He used to say: 'Ahad Ha'am is the Habad school of Zionism.' "

The committee enjoyed the remark, but the chairman felt it his duty to reprove him. "Don't interrupt!" he said.

Yudka may not have heard, or may not have understood; he stood bemused and smiling.

"I'll finish soon," he said with a deprecating smile.

For a while he waited, collected his thoughts and sought a new beginning.

"Yes. . . ." He coughed two or three times. "Right away. . . . What was it I wanted to say? That is . . . about Zionism. Yes! In a word,

no one has yet said the right . . . the . . . the hidden, the deepest
. . . no one has revealed, or explained, fully . . . just talk, elementary
things, banalities, you know, empty, meaningless phrases. . . ."

"Oh, they've explained," one of the committee broke in, jesting.
"The Brith Shalom, the wise men of the University and all the other
little professors. . . ."

"You can't prove anything by idiots," another spoke up in an
offhand manner.

"Ernest Fig . . ." went on the first, referring to a public figure who
was regarded as something of a fool and an exhibitionist.

"Ernst is' nicht fähig, und Fäig is' nicht ernst . . ." rejoined the first
with a witticism.

"I ask you not to interrupt and not to talk across the table!" The
chairman straightened up and took over control. "Please continue."

"All right." Yudka began again, struggling with the words. "Of
course I'm not the one to say what Zionism is. I'm not the man for
it. Even though I've wracked my brain and thought about it for a long
time. But that's not important. . . . One thing is clear. Zionism is not
a continuation, it is no medicine for an ailment. That's nonsense! It
is uprooting and destruction, it's the opposite of what has been, it's
the end. . . . It has almost nothing to do with the people, a thoroughly
non-popular movement, much more apart from the people than the
Bund, more than assimilationism, more even than communism. The
fact is, it turns away from the people, is opposed to it, goes against
its will and spirit, undermines it, subverts it and turns off in a different
direction, to a certain distant goal; Zionism, with a small group at its
head, is the nucleus of a different people. . . . Please note that: not new
or restored, but *different.* And if anyone doesn't agree, well, I'm very
sorry, but either he's mistaken or he's deluding himself. What? Perhaps it isn't so? I believe that this land of Israel already is no longer
Jewish. Even now, let alone in the future. Time will tell, as they say.
That's its hidden core, that's the power it will yet unfold. Yes! At any
rate, it's a different Judaism, if you choose to fool yourselves and keep

that name, but certainly not the same as survived for two thousand years, not at all the same. That is . . . well, nothing. You understand? And nothing will help, neither grandfathers and grandmothers nor antiquities, nor even Hebrew literature which has grown like a crust on the past, and clings to the old small towns of our Exile. All wasted! *Kaput!* I'll take the liberty of mentioning one detail, not directly related, but it has some bearing, a tangential bearing . . . a fine expression, you know," his lips twisted in a smiling grimace. "So round and smooth: tangential. . . . Well, then, it's well known that we're all ashamed to speak Yiddish, as though it were some sort of disgrace. I intentionally said 'ashamed.' Not that we dislike, or fear, or refuse, but we're ashamed. But Hebrew, and none other than Sephardic Hebrew, strange and foreign as it is, we speak boldly, with a kind of pride or vanity, even though it isn't as easy and natural as Yiddish, and even though it hasn't the vitality, the sharp edge and healthy vigor of our folk language. What's the meaning of this? What's the reason for it? For no reason at all, just to take on such an immense burden? But it's quite simple: This community is not continuing anything, it is different, something entirely specific, almost not Jewish, practically not Jewish at all. . . . In the same way, we are ashamed to be called by the ordinary, customary Jewish names, but we are proud to name ourselves, say, Artzieli or Avnieli. Haimovitch, you will agree, that's a Jewish name, entirely too Jewish, but Avnieli —that's something else again, the devil knows what, but it has a strange sound, not Jewish at all, and so proud! That's why we have so many Gideons, Ehuds, Yigals, Tirzahs . . . what? . . . And it doesn't matter that we had the same kind of thing before, that was with the assimilationists, that's easy to understand. There we were living among strangers, people who were different and hostile, and we had to hide, to dissimulate, to be lost to sight, to appear different from what we really were. But here? Aren't we among our own, all to ourselves, with no need for shame, or for hiding, or anyone to hide from? Well then, how do you expect to understand this? . . . That's it! That's the whole thing, point by point. It's obvious, no continuity but a break, the opposite of what was before, a new beginning. . . .

A little detail, quite unimportant, it didn't deserve going into so much, but it is a symptom of far more . . . I've gone into side issues. I won't keep you much longer. I'm finishing. In a word, this is the aim: one people, and above all, a people creating its history for itself, with its own strength and by its own will, not others making it for it, and history, not the chronicles of a congregation, anything but *chronicles,* that's how it stands. For a people that doesn't live in its own land and doesn't rule itself has no history. That's my whole idea. I've already told you and I repeat again, and I'll say it again and again, day and night . . . is it clear? Is it clear?" And all at once his words ran together and his voice broke and sputtered with feeling, his eyes flickered to and fro like one who doesn't know which way to go. "With this I've said a great deal, the whole thing . . . everything I had on my mind . . . and now I don't want to say anything more. I have nothing more to add. . . . Enough!"

He noisily pulled back a chair and cast himself heavily into it, wiping the sweat off his face with his palm, and sat there all in a turmoil, with his face flaming, his heart pounding, and his temples throbbing.

It grew quiet, like the stillness after a quarrel. The men were silent and sat uncertainly with changed faces, not sure in their hearts nor easy in their minds, as though in doubt whether something might not be lost or lacking, or as if they were in mid-passage between where they had been and where they were going.

Then the chairman lifted his eyes and spoke with a certain strain: "Have you finished?"

At that, Yudka sprang to his feet with a jerk.

"Right away, right away . . ." He spoke hastily and with some panic. "I said much too much. . . . That's not how I meant it, not the way I thought. It came out by itself. The devil knows how . . . such nonsense! Trifles, side issues like that, about Yiddish there, and the names. . . . It was ridiculous, quite unnecessary. I see it myself. . . . But just those side issues, those unimportant details, you know, they come to mind immediately. . . . Well, it's all the same. What I mean, I really just wanted to explain . . . I no longer know how to tell you . . . the main thing, what I'm after. It's not just . . . yes! Well, now. Now to the main thing. I beg just a few more minutes of patience. . . ."

The boys all straightened up in their chairs and felt more at ease, as though he had saved them from a great worry—especially the chairman, who bowed his head and sat staring at his finger nails.

"Say what you want," he said, "and let's see if we can't do without the philosophy. . . ."

Translated by Ben Halpern

Yehuda Yaari

The Wanderer and the Blind Man

At first I thought of telling you these things in the manner of a legend: "Once upon a time there lived a man in a distant land, etc., etc." But who has the strength nowadays to sit down and read legends? Therefore I shall describe the events as they happened.

It was a plain week-day; not one that the Bible called good twice, nor one not called good at all; not a day ordained for celebration, nor one fated for calamity, God forbid. An ordinary day between summer and winter. On such a day, if you are in high spirits, you may sense the aroma of a coming drizzle; but if you are in a bad mood, you sigh and complain, "Oh, when will this summer end?"

There are times when a man rises, looks out the window, and upon seeing a cloud lowering in the sky, says apprehensively, "I'd better not get up today. A day like this appears to be ill-fated." At other times everything he sees and hears seems to bring him glad tidings.

When I got out of bed that morning, I did not hope for any glad tidings, and my heart had no sense of foreboding, God forbid. I arose immediately after sunrise, as is my wont, and did not even look out the window. I dressed neither quickly nor slovenly, washed, and did all the things a working man normally does before going off to work. After breakfast I did not clean the house. I didn't even clear the table or shake the crumbs off the tablecloth. For such is my custom: on a day when my work load isn't heavy and I anticipate returning home during daylight, I usually do all these things when I return. I put on my jacket, following the custom of Jerusalemites who wear an outer garment summer and fall, took my hat, and went out—all was as usual, just as on all other days.

In order not to skip any of the details that have been fixed in my memory, I should mention one event of that morning—something rather extraordinary. When I opened the door, I did not find the morning paper on the threshold. This happens rarely, perhaps two or three times a year, when the newsboy is sick, for instance, or is late owing to some mishap. So I paid no particular attention to this. In any case, I don't usually read the newspaper attentively until I return from work—and after I have eaten my meal and cleaned the house. Moreover, I still might meet the newsboy on the street, take the paper from him, and during a break at work casually scan the headlines. But no matter, I thought as I left the house, the news won't grow stale during these few hours.

The clear bright sky bewildered and amazed me. I was sure I would see clouds, for while in the house I fancied that a certain dimness lay without. Yet my shutters were open, for I close them only during a hot summer day against the sun and on winter nights against the raging wind. Perhaps, indeed, the wind had raged during the middle of the night and I had risen to close the shutters but had forgotten this owing to my sleepy state. Who knows! I suppressed my amazement and set out to depart.

Once outside, I was overwhelmed by a host of morning noises. Here a man tried to start a stubborn car, there the milkman dragged his wagon full of clanking bottles. Further off stood a beggar rummaging through the garbage cans, trying to pick out any valuable objects before they were carted away. On the balconies of nearby houses women were busily airing their bedclothes, dusting furniture and the like. At that moment I somewhat envied my neighbors whose wives devotedly set their houses in order at the beginning of the day. Just because I don't have a wife, am I not worthy of finding my apartment orderly and clean when I come home from work? I made up my mind that henceforth I would meticulously arrange my house each morning before I left, regardless of the amount of work awaiting me that day. Having decided this, I proceeded on my way.

After taking several steps, I saw three men dressed in dark gray suits and black felt hats. They walked hesitantly, as though unsure of their way. The youngest held a sheet of paper; they were apparently looking for the house listed on it. Even though these men were unobtrusive and not known to me by name, they were easily recognizable by the people of Jerusalem. They were from the Burial Society, and it was well known that any house they enter, there was someone dead. I watched them for about a minute, but restrained myself from asking them whose house they sought.

From my youth I have had the following habit. When I see someone walking along the street and looking for a house, I approach and ask whom he wants, in case I might be of some assistance. From the day I settled in Jerusalem I continued this habit. In those days it was very difficult for a stranger to find a house in Jerusalem without the aid of one of the residents. Some of the streets had no names at all, and some were known by several names. Not to mention the houses which had neither numbers nor names—these houses were known by the names of all the tenants. Since I had become expert in the streets, alleys, and lanes of Jerusalem and, what is more, since I loved to spend my free time walking through the city, I made it a custom to help people who were lost to find the house they wanted. I'm not telling you this in order to boast. Whoever is afflicted with this habit knows that it is not one worth bragging about. Only rarely would I hear a word of thanks from the person I had helped. Generally speaking, each man prefers finding the house he is looking for unaided. Occasionally, if you approach a man suddenly and ask him what address he is looking for, he may even tend to be angry, as though you were asking him to reveal a big secret. At times, after I had pointed out the right house to a man, he obstinately entered the next house—only to leave it a few minutes later and go into the house that I had originally shown him. No, this habit wins for one neither medals nor acclamations of gratitude. On countless occasions I have vowed to rid myself of it but have not been successful. The habit had become second nature. I could tell you fascinating stories regarding this, but this is not the place, especially since I am not telling you the story but writing it, and I still do not know how this document will reach you.

And so, this time I overcame the force of habit and did not approach the men to ask which house they wanted. From this one can learn that feelings are more powerful than habit; for even *I* successfully conquered the habit which had become second nature just to avoid the Angel of Death's entourage and not help them in fulfilling their task. At this point I must actually beg pardon of these men for speaking of them in this fashion. They, who continually perform acts of unreciprocable kindness with the deceased, they surely do not see themselves as members of the Angel of Death's entourage, nor, frankly, do I usually see them in this light. But what shall I do? That is the way they appeared to me that morning. They will certainly find what they seek without my help, I said to myself. They will never come too late. And so I continued on my way.

When I reached the corner I saw the well-known black wagon with the white-lettered phrase, "Righteousness shall go before him." It immediately became perfectly clear to me that these men had indeed come here in order to tend to a dead man. From this it should not be assumed that I hadn't been sure of this previously. I just purposely sought to cast doubt on it. Is it a heavenly decree that these men must only deal with corpses? Isn't it also possible that they had come to gather donations for widows and orphans, or were on some similar mission? Thus I sought to delude myself, for I had known from the very beginning that at this hour of the morning men don't usually go from house to house soliciting donations. Now that I had seen that black wagon, my fancied doubts vanished and I had nothing more to say. Even members of the Burial Society would not dream of using this wagon for anything but funerals. I turned to see which house they were entering. My street is a small one and its houses are few. I know almost all of the tenants well and at least once a day exchange greetings with them. So it was only natural that I wanted to see in which house the death had occurred. I stood fixed in my place and followed the men with my eyes. I saw them stopping in front of the house where I live. The youngest of the three, the one who held the paper in his hand, called out, "This is it!" Immediately, all three entered and disappeared into the courtyard of my house.

I grew frightened. What's this? Had someone died during the night in my house? Is it possible? And I did not know of it? I live on the ground floor and immediately hear the slightest sound made by my upstairs neighbor, especially if it takes place during the silent hours of the night. Can it be that I had heard nothing? Yet perhaps, perhaps I had heard it, which is why I rose in the middle of the night to close the shutters. I had heard the sound of wailing and had risen to close the shutters because I thought the wind was wailing. Still, I don't at all remember getting up in the middle of the night to close the shutters. And who was it that died? Who could it be? Perhaps I ought to return and see.

I don't know why, but I did not return. On the contrary, I slipped away from the place like a thief. While walking I looked this way and that, hoping to find the newsboy, for if someone had died during the night in my house there would certainly be some item about it in the morning papers. Since I could not find him anywhere, I tried to forget about the entire matter. "May it be as though I had not seen these three men entering my house at all!" I whispered, then decided to go to the bus station with no further delays or regrets and proceed to work as was my daily custom.

At that moment a phrase by Yosef Chaim Brenner I had read some years ago floated up in my mind: "Soon we shall set out; soon we shall begin our journey." I latched on to it in order to exorcise another verse that had attached itself to me: "Righteousness shall go before him" —the white-lettered words painted on that black wagon. And so I continued on my way, humming to myself and saying rhythmically, "Soon we shall set out; soon we shall begin our journey," until I reached the bus station.

At that hour a long queue of passengers serpentined in the station, as it did every morning when working people go to their daily tasks. I stood at the end of the line as though nothing plagued my heart and I murmured softly to myself: "Soon we shall set out; soon we shall begin our journey." In front of me a man held a newspaper. I raised my head and tried to read the headlines, but just then our bus arrived.

The man quickly folded the newspaper and placed it in his briefcase. All the people on line began to press forward and enter the bus. I too pressed forward along with them.

I had hardly reached the door when a thought began to plague me. What would I do if a passenger who knew me and knew where I lived were to ask me about the death that had occurred in my house? Could I reply that I knew nothing? And even if I did say this, wouldn't courtesy oblige me to leave the bus at the next stop in order to run home to console the mourners and hold their hands during the funeral? No, I cannot ride on this bus, I decided, and left the queue.

I left the queue but I did not hasten to leave the station. I stood on the side contemplating what to do. Should I wait for the next bus, or should I indeed return home? Why *should* I return home? Am I really certain that someone had died in my house? More likely the entire matter was one round of errors. The members of the Burial Society chanced upon the place today by mistake, the house was not the one they were seeking, and the street was not the right street. There was some blunder here. And no wonder, I smiled to myself; in a city where they continually change the names of the streets, even the Angel of Death is likely to get confused and err with an address.

Meanwhile two or three buses had left the station, and since I missed all of them, I said: Today I shall walk to work. Yes, that's what I shall do. I shall walk. There's nothing like walking on a day like this, which is neither Indian summer nor pre-autumnal. It was neither cold nor warm; the air was clear—an absolute delight. During my youth, when I was still a day-laborer, I would leave my work on such a day and hike to the outskirts of Jerusalem or walk around the Old City walls from Jaffa Gate to Shechem Gate. But now it is no longer possible to walk around the walls, and moreover I am no longer young, nor a day-laborer. But why shouldn't I take off an hour on a day like this and walk to work? Who would say a word if I came late? Do I say anything to anyone when on my own I work late into the night several times a year? I don't keep score, but it seems I could allow myself to be late once, if only for my own pleasure. And, in any case, whether I walk or go by bus, it was clear that today I wouldn't accomplish very much. These thoughts ran through my mind and strengthened my resolve and I began walking from the station.

I left the bus station and chose not to follow the usual route, which at that hour was full of the fumes and noise of speeding cars. Having already decided to walk, why not make it a pleasure? Therefore, I left the main street and entered a quiet side street, intending to take a short cut. On my way I passed the municipal park. If I cut through it, I thought, it will not only make the walk more enjoyable but save time as well.

The park appeared desolate and forlorn, as though it had not been watered for years. Its dusty trees stood motionless and seemingly petrified. Their shade was no shade and their light no light. The park was empty except for the gardener who slowly walked on the grass, filling a can with bits of refuse and litter that visitors had discarded during a recent holiday. Seeing the gardener, I remembered that when I was a child I wanted very much to become a gardener when I grew up.

In the city of my birth there was a large, beautiful park that belonged to the baron. The townspeople would visit it summer and winter: during the summer they would walk along its path enjoying the aromas and breathing clean air; in the winter they would come and feast their eyes on the wonderful sights. When they were snow-covered, the carefully tended trees with their carefully trimmed tops looked like magnificent crystal sculptures, such as only the heavens are capable of executing.

During my childhood I too would frequent that park which stretched along the river bank not too far from our house. Sometimes I came there with my mother who loved to stroll in the shade of the trees; sometimes I came to play with friends my own age; and sometimes I would flee there to hide from both my parents and my friends. The old gardener who used to tend that park, pruning the trees and watering the flower beds, was my ideal when I was a child, and I wanted to model myself after him.

Every time I came there, whether with friends or alone, I would see him walking among the trees and the flower beds, hoeing, weeding, pruning, gathering. He appeared to me then to be a sort of walking plant. His clothes were of green linen, his wild grown hair was the color of dried hay, and his never-trimmed mustache hung down over his mouth. Whenever I saw him, it seemed that a lovely bird would come, nestle on his head and lift its voice in song. How envious I was of that gardener and how much I longed to be like him! Nevertheless, I knew—yes, even then I knew—that I would never achieve that ambition; but great is a child's desire which is its own satisfaction.

I had never told anyone of this ambition, even though it stirred within me more than once as I grew up. But when adults used to ask me what I would like to be, unlike other children I didn't have a ready answer. My reply would be: "I don't know"—which is why members of my family considered me a backward, unimaginative child. Had I told them the truth they would surely have thought me a little fool, but to you I can reveal my secret. *You* will not say to me that I am unimaginative or foolish, God forbid.

And so I followed the gardener and helped him gather up the rubbish from the lawns into the can he was holding. I did this not because I felt sorry for him or to make his task easier, but because there is nothing more disgusting and irritating than dirt in a park, and because I was constantly thinking of the old gardener in my home town. I forgot that I had entered the park only to take a short cut to work and to make my walk more pleasant. When I remembered this we already found ourselves standing at the gate.

But to my utter amazement and sorrow I saw that the gate was the very one that I had entered. Evidently the gardener had followed a round-about route and I, immersed in my thoughts, had gone after him without realizing this. I had planned to take a short cut, but found myself immeasurably lengthening my way. Hours had passed and I stood at the place from which I had started out. What should I do now? Was there any purpose in my going to work now? By this time my colleagues had probably reconciled themselves to my absence and my work had been done by another. If someone had indeed died in my house, they had already read about it in the morning paper and ascribed my absence to this event; and if not, they probably assumed I was ill and lying in bed. In either case, by appearing at work at this hour I would confuse my colleagues and myself as well. No, there was no sense going to the office now. However, I could not very well wander about outside either. My colleagues were assuming that I was either sick or visiting mourners, but what was I doing now? Gathering rubbish in the park and recalling longings from the days of my childhood! I ought to return home and that's that! As a matter of fact, I don't know what sort of ill wind had got into me and prevented me from doing this at the very beginning.

I immediately bade the gardener goodby and left in haste. The man had already returned to his work and did not respond.

II

Once again I walked along my street, which now seemed very strange to me. I was like a man who returns to a place he had already left; even though he finds no tangible change, it appears to him that everything has changed. Nevertheless, I was neither amazed nor confused. Every man who finds himself suddenly walking the streets at an unusual time has a similar feeling, I thought. I have lived on this street for years and never had the opportunity of seeing it during the week at this hour—which was neither a time of departure to or return from work, nor a time for a stroll or a visit. Thinking thus, I proceeded confidently, head high like one who has already managed to finish his work early in the day and was returning home to spend the rest of the day relaxing, reading, and reflecting. At that hour the street was quiet; only a few people were on it. The black wagon I had seen in the morning on this side of the street, now stood on the opposite side. Some people whom I could not easily identify were gathered around it as though waiting. I pretended that all this did not concern me at all and entered the courtyard of my house.

I entered my house and—ah, woe is me!—found my door open. What's this? Hadn't I locked the door upon leaving the house in the morning? And why had I not locked it? Had the miserable newspaper which was missing so confused me that I forgot to lock my door? What had happened here?

Frightened, I rushed inside. At first I saw nothing. Not only had my eyes dimmed but the entire apartment was immersed in the sort of darkness found only in a cave. I closed my eyes, unable to bear this two-fold darkness, and stood in the hall trembling and agitated. After a while, I opened my eyes and saw in the adjoining room several people wrapped in a light that was not light. Some sat, some stood. On the floor in the middle of the room lay a corpse at whose head burned two candles. He was covered with a prayer shawl. I recognized the prayer shawl as mine. It had come down to me from my forefathers, and out of deference to it I had stored it away in a closet. Even during holidays when I go to the synagogue it was not my custom to wrap myself with this prayer shawl but with a smaller and plainer one.

I entered the room silently and tried to expunge the signs of terror from my face and to assume the countenance of a mourner, as if I were a relative of the deceased who had come to pay him last respects. The people in the room paid no attention to me as I entered—it was as though they had not seen me at all. Only one of them, an aged man who sat in a corner weeping over the book in his hand, closed it when I came in and said, "Now we can go. The hour is late, friends." But I did not know if he said this because he saw me or because he had just then completed the chapter. The assembled company immediately rose and began preparing themselves to remove the dead man.

I froze in my place, terror-stricken, wanting to scream. No, no, I did not *want* to scream; I actually did scream, but my voice—like a man who screams in his dream—was not heard at all. "There must be some mistake, a terrible mistake! I live in this apartment. No one else lives here. And I'm alive, alive! Look and see, I'm alive!" I yelled with all my might, but no one heard me. If I remained here any longer, I thought, I'd give up the ghost and these people, who had come to tend one dead man, would in the end have to deal with two corpses. So I collected my thoughts and silently left the apartment. Just as they paid no attention to me when I entered, so they paid no attention when I left. And since at that moment the door to the kitchen was wide open, and a bright light filled the room, I glanced in and saw that my table was not cleaned and the cloth not shaken of its crumbs. Everything had remained just as I had left it in the morning. Even the two cans of olives which I had been pickling and preparing for the winter, even they gleamed on the shelf next to the table. At that moment I felt sorry for the olives.

For a number of years now, with the onset of winter, I prepare pickled olives for the entire year. At the end of every summer, when the olives are ripe, I go out to the fields near my house, and from the trees abandoned during the war, I pick a bagful of beautiful olives, and then I crack, salt and pickle them in cans. For myself I set aside one can, which provides me with olives for the entire year; the other is reserved for relatives and friends. I derive unimaginable pleasure from this annual task. With the passing of time these neglected olive trees had become like good friends, and even though I could not attend to them constantly, I was concerned for them and occasionally thought of them. A rainy year, when they produced fruit in abundance, made me happy; a year of drought, when their yield was small, saddened and distressed me. Even the process of pickling gave me satisfaction, for it reminded me of my forefathers' custom of making from fruits and berries all kinds of preserves and liquors that would delight men's souls during the hard winter days.

I fled from the house and had no time to think. But I left with the feeling that I would not return. For how could I return after what had happened? Nevertheless, at that moment I felt sorry not for myself or anything else but only for those two cans of olives standing abandoned on the kitchen shelf. I felt sorry only for them. What would happen now to these good olives which had given me so much joy when I picked and pickled them, and which I had tried so diligently to prepare well? What would happen to them? Believe it or not, this was the only thought that plagued me as my feet touched the threshold of my house.

III

I don't know how I reached the other side of town. Don't I really know? Is it possible? Of course I know. The truth is that I know my goings about on this day more than on any other day. But the trouble is this: all that happened to me that day, everything I did and everywhere I went, I know down to the finest detail. Not only that, but when I recall these things I even see a certain logic in them, as though they had rightly happened as they did. Nevertheless, I still cannot rid myself of the feeling that in fact I know nothing. I simply could not comprehend these events. I had become completely confused. Even time had become flexible: now it dried up and shrank until all the days seemed to be one day, and then it stretched and spread until I no longer knew when yesterday had fallen. But why should I burrow into something I know nothing about? It would be better to continue telling what I know.

When I went outside after seeing what had taken place in my apartment, I was terror-stricken. It was a disembodied terror, unrelated to any other sensation. No, not even fear. Fear? What was there to be afraid of? "Get out of here!" a voice ordered me from the depths of my soul—"Get out and run quickly! Where? What do you care, even across the border!" I wanted to run, but I strained every muscle to walk calmly so as not to attract the attention of people on the street. For what would they say—those who knew me and those who didn't—if they suddenly saw me running at breakneck speed? Would I be able to stop and tell them what had happened to me?

I walked with deliberate calm. One leg urged me on; the other held me back. Every step I took cost me enormous effort. Here, it seemed to me, one was intentionally staring at me though reading something from a tablet hung on my heart; there, another was standing and looking through me as through transparent glass. I lowered my eyes like a man deeply immersed in mourning who wants no one to trouble him. And thus I continued my efforts for a long while until I left my neighborhood and was quite a distance from my house.

Here my terrror gradually subsided. Now I no longer had the will to run—hence, I no longer had to strain to walk slowly. Walking alone, I made a path for myself in the shadow of the walls at the sidewalk's edge. I raised my eyes and began to consider what I should do and where I should turn. At first I thought of taking the first bus I saw to wherever it would lead me. I chanted that line of Brenner's —"Soon we shall set out; soon we shall begin our journey"—until I reached one of the bus stops along the way. I looked at the station sign not to learn the bus route but to fix my eyes on something specific— anything, as long as I would not have to see the passersby. As soon as I read the sign: To the Mount of Quietudes Cemetery, I immediately abandoned my plan. I slipped away from there like one who slips away from his ambushers and returned to my path at the edge of the sidewalk.

As I walked thus in the shade of the walls, tired and empty of all thought, I noticed an old acquaintance of mine walking toward me from afar. Behind him came another and right after him yet a third. Seeing them a great fright came over me.

I knew these men from the days when every worker in Jerusalem would befriend his colleague and share the same fate. Whenever they met me they wouldn't merely content themselves with a perfunctory hello, but would stop me in the middle of the street and ask me all sorts of questions. They would recall events from the old days and tell me stories of nowadays. What should I do if they stopped me now, I asked in a fright, and one of them began to ask his questions and tell his stories? What should I say to him? And who knows what he was likely to ask now! Even if he only asked what I was doing here at this hour and where I was going, what sort of answer would I give him?

But this time they did not act in their customary fashion. They did not stop me, not one, not the other, not the third. They did not ask any questions, they did not even say hello. They passed by me, all three of them, and did not see me at all.

In that case, you might say, I was instantaneously rid of a great fear. My problem had been solved of its own accord, at which quite natu-

rally I should have rejoiced, right? However, not only was I not happy
—but quite the opposite; my fear grew; it squared and cubed itself.
Had these friends of mine indeed not seen me? Not one of the three?
Perhaps they knew something I did not know and only pretended not
to see me. I wanted to run and shout after them: "What's wrong with
you, friends? Why don't you see me?" But I restrained myself. Why?
I shall not hide it from you. I restrained myself because I was afraid
to reveal the truth, and because I was about to do something that just
isn't done. Therefore, I held back.

Oh, how much I wished at that moment to assemble the passersby
and ask them, "Tell me good people, please tell me, do you see me?"
But who would dare do a thing like this? I was in a quandary. If the
people could not see me, my question would terrify them. And if they
could see me, why, then, they would consider me mad! And when all
is said and done, what do I know? If they could not see my face, very
possibly they could not hear my voice, either. What do I know?

I suppressed my cry, and my urge as well, and continued walking
silently. I no longer walked in the shadow of the walls at the sidewalk's edge, but by the light of the sun in the middle of the path. I
walked like a somnambulist—yes, like those sleepwalkers who during
moonlit nights walk on the roofs of high houses while fast asleep, and
if someone comes and calls them by name they immediately wake up
and fall. I too felt this way, as though I were walking on the verge
of an abyss, and if someone were to recognize me and call me by my
name I would immediately collapse and plummet downward. But,
nevertheless, I longed for someone to see me, for a friend to come and
greet me. My soul split into two, as it were, and I was like two people:
one exceedingly afraid lest people see him, and the other yearning for
someone to see him and call him by his name. And thus I wandered
about the outskirts of town, a man who had become two, a man whose
entire existence hung in doubt, until I reached the edge of the city.
This is what I had said previously: I know quite well how I reached
the other side of town, but nevertheless I know nothing.

IV

When I reached the edge of town, near the border, it seemed as though I had come to another world. Again, I did not know if I was still linked to the bounds of the day, or if I had already sailed into the domain of tomorrow, or returned to the past.

Here it was raining, a fine rain that fell softly and raised wonderful scents from the ground—scents that appear only once a year: on the day of the first rain. I did not say: it began raining, for I did not see it coming, and was not aware that it had begun. But I suddenly felt the rain around me, and when I looked up I saw the edges of the sky like a blazing fire—and the rocks in the field across the way, like a congregation of phantoms that had just emerged from the bath. I do not understand why people say of a lonely man that he is as lonely as a stone. I had never seen anything so bound and united as those stones in the field.

I sat on a stone fence at the edge of the path that separated the Hanna-David quarter from the no-man's land by the border, and refreshed myself with the bountiful rain and pleasant aromas waiting from the ground. A terrible silence encompassed me. Not a man was to be seen anywhere—possibly because of the rain, possibly for fear of the border. I sat alone, my eyes wandering back and forth, from the walls of the area on this side, to the sparkling stones in the field on the other. At that moment I felt I was clearly seeing a dream I had dreamt in bygone days. I tried to remember where I had dreamt this dream and when. In so doing, I recalled a terrible tale I had heard from a man who had sustained my soul with stories during my childhood.

In my home town there was a man named Kalman. He was a carpenter. I don't know if this Kalman excelled in his work and made attractive things—I was a small boy at the time and a complete ignoramus in such matters—but I know for certain that he was a master storyteller. During the winter, when the days were short and the nights very long, he would come every Saturday night to our house where a distinguished group of relatives and friends of the family gathered to mark the departure of the Sabbath with the telling of stories. There were several storytellers there, each an expert after his own fashion. But the outstanding one was Kalman the carpenter who with his stories would enchant his listeners, especially the children. His style was to tell one story in various versions. If once he would tell a story of the Hasidic *zaddik* A, another time he would repeat it with *zaddik* B as hero. When one of the boys would complain (children are rather uncomfortable when a long familiar story is changed): "But you told this very story about another *zaddik!*" Kalman would reply: "Yes, you're right. Which goes to show that it's not the man in the story who is most important but the story itself. Isn't it possible that what happened to this *zaddik* also happened to another *zaddik?* And even you, my son, when you grow up and become famous in the world, perhaps they will tell this very same story about you, too."

During my childhood I heard many of Kalman's stories; some made a lasting impression on me, others I forgot with the passing of time. But one of his stories remained with me for many days. And although it frightened me at night and even brought me to tears during the day, I asked to hear it again and again. With this story a change of version did not disturb me.

This was the story that I remembered now as I sat alone at the edge of the path between the border and the Hanna-David quarter, and beheld the image of the dream I had dreamt long ago.

Once upon a time there was a man who had died but did not know he was dead. He would continually walk about among the living as though he were one of them. Once he appeared at a wedding party and cast his fear upon the celebrants. Then he came to the synagogue and frightened the worshippers. Another time, he attached himself to a group of merchants who were traveling to the market and thoroughly confounded them. A pall of fear lay over the entire city. Children cried with fright at night, and old people wept all day for it reminded them of the day of death. Finally, a *zaddik* came whom the dead feared but who was not afraid of them. He commanded this man to quickly depart from among the living for he was dead, and to return to his resting place in the world of the spirits.

I told myself this awesome story that I had heard during my childhood from Kalman the carpenter. I told it to myself once in this version, and when I began to retell it in another version, it suddenly became clear to me that I was telling myself my own story. A great fear immediately overwhelmed me and the entire world seemingly darkened for me. I sat and trembled, and fancied that even the stones beneath me were trembling, too.

I don't know if I fell asleep there on the stone fence. In any event it is not out of the question, for I was literally dead tired. When I awoke from this doubtful sleep, I saw that the rain had stopped, and that the day that had previously appeared to be waning had apparently renewed its strength. The blazing heat had disappeared from the sky, and from the walls of the quarter came strange and varied sounds. These persistent, monotonous sounds of speech and strident melodies were evidently coming from radios. I turned this way and that, wondering how I happened to get here. I pricked up my ears on the chance that I would hear an answer to my questions from those sounds. And then I saw a bespectacled man with a white beard leaving the quarter and slowly stepping down the path. He held a white cane in one hand, while the other moved to and fro as though it were arguing with an invisible disputant.

This man was Reb Yankele. I recognized him at first glance, and immediately jumped up and ran toward him.

But before I tell of this meeting with him, I shall tell of the man and his ways and of the many times we had met previously.

I first met Reb Yankele a few days after my arrival in Jerusalem. A new quarter was being built in those days outside the Old City walls and my friends and I (the people called us "pioneers") laid the foundations and participated in its construction. We did all the menial labors —we were young in those days and had not yet been trained to do skilled work—while the specialized tasks were performed by local master craftsmen. To these men Reb Yankele was an apprentice.

Sometimes he worked alongside the builder, sometimes the stonecutter. At still other times he helped the glazier and, on occasion, he worked with the carpenter. He did many different types of labor but was never a fullfledged craftsman. From his youth he had been nearsighted, and a man with defective eyesight certainly cannot master a craft.

Reb Yankele was unique in our group of construction workers. His manner of dress was odd and his behavior strange. On several occasions we caught him singing and dancing during work. Once, we also found him sitting on the scaffolding of the building, crying and talking to himself. Reb Yankele was a Hasid, one of the Hasidim of Reb Nachman of Bratslav. He lived in the Old City, and the stamp of Jerusalem was engraved on his face as on one of the hewn stones one occasionally finds in the Old City walls. My friends and I were drawn to him because of his wonderful nature and his conversation that flowed as out of an ancient spring. It was he who had taught me to find my way in and out of the winding alleyways of the Old City. He was the one who had taught me to love the city—and it is well-known that one must be taught to love Jerusalem—and he it was who brought me to the humble prayerhouse of the Bratslav Hasidim to hear their prayers and to listen to their talks. And it was he who had told me the wonderful tales of Reb Nachman of Bratslav. Perhaps this is why I immediately recognized him as he merged from the quarter, for just then I had been thinking of Kalman the carpenter and the stories he told me during my childhood. But very likely I would have recognized Reb Yankele anyway. A man whose identity is stamped into him like a hewn stone is immediately recognizable even if you meet him in another reincarnation.

Our work in that quarter lasted about two years. Once we had finished building and paving the roads, our group separated and each went his own way. But even after we had separated I would on occasion meet Reb Yankele, at first quite often and then less frequently. Sometimes we met by chance, when I would stroll about on the outskirts of Jerusalem. Sometimes I would go to visit him at home or in his little prayerhouse on Hebron Street. I loved my meetings with him. His talk and stories were always a delight.

The last time I had seen him was during the riots that preceded the
War of Independence. One day I happened to be in the Old City with
a group of defenders. My special assignment was to organize the
evacuation of the sick and the women and children before the battle
intensified and the city came under siege. All day long I ran from lane
to lane and from courtyard to courtyard, and I didn't even think of
Reb Yankele. At a time when the ground is seething underfoot, a man
is likely to forget not only his friends but himself as well. Once, when
I chanced into a courtyard near his house, I suddenly remembered
him and immediately went to see him. I found him lying ill in bed.
His eyes fevered behind his glasses and his thinned-out beard once red
as copper had turned completely white. I felt that his sickness was due
to hunger, and accused myself for having let him come to this. There
was no time to indulge myself in guilt feelings and begin with questions and answers. I told him briefly why my friends and I had come
to the Old City that day. "If you agree," I said, "I can arrange that
you too leave this place and be admitted to a hospital in the new city.
Please understand that this is the last chance; very likely tomorrow
the city will be completely surrounded and inaccessible." Hearing
this, Reb Yankele trembled. He raised his head from the pillow and
shouted in a whisper, "The Lord preserve me! All my life I have lived
within the walls of the Old City and now that the hour of tribulation
has come for Israel, shall I get up and flee? God forbid! So long as
there is soul within me I shall not move from here. Our sages of
blessed memory said that the Divine Presence never departs from the
Western Wall. If it is good enough for the Divine Presence, it is good
enough for me." These were the last words I heard from him. I left
him some food I had brought with me, bade him goodby, and went
out to continue my work.

I had not seen Reb Yankele since that day. During the war that
broke out shortly thereafter, Jerusalem came under siege. The Old
City was doubly under siege until it fell and became widowed of its
Jews. Recalling the words that he had told me when I left him the last
time, I assumed he was no longer alive and forgot him.

Nevertheless, I was neither surprised nor amazed when I now saw him walking out of the quarter. On the contrary, it seemed to me as if I had been waiting for his arrival. I almost wanted to say that I had come here with the premeditated purpose of meeting him. But I prefer not to exaggerate, for as I said at the beginning of my story, I would describe events as they happened.

When I saw him leaving the quarter and recognized who he was, I immediately jumped up from my place with youthful speed and ran toward him. Here was the man I was waiting for, I said to myself. To him I could tell the entire story. He would certainly see me.

"Shalom, Reb Yankele!" I called out excitedly even before I managed to get close enough to shake his hand.

Reb Yankele smiled the way he used to during his younger days. He lifted his hand like one who greets his friend from afar, and said in the language of the Bible: "Come near, I pray you, that I may feel you, my son. Is it you? Shalom!" and he called me by my name. What shall I tell you? When I heard my name being uttered, a spark of joy, the likes of which I have never known, leaped within me.

"What? You do see me?" I asked, overawed.

"See—not exactly," he answered calmly, his smile not leaving his lips. "I recognized you by your voice. For a number of years now I have been blind, may you be spared the like. I am completely blind. Nevertheless, every day between the afternoon and evening prayers, it is my custom to go outside to meditate a while and to feel Jerusalem. I come to this place, for at this hour there are neither people nor machines here and I can talk to my Maker without hindrance."

"And how do you live, Reb Yankele?" I asked, because I could not bring myself to utter the question bubbling on my tongue: "Are you alive?"

"Ah, that's a difficult question, my brother, for is there any man who knows how he lives? But if you ask regarding my livelihood, I shall tell you. Come, let us sit down here under the tree and I shall tell you everything. It is difficult for me to stand in one place. My legs, too, are not what they used to be. Come!" he said and began to pull me to the field of stones on the other side of the path. Henceforth I had the feeling that I was the blind man and he the one with sight who was leading me.

"Do you see?" he added, as he felt his way with his staff in one hand and led me with the other. "There in the field are two olive trees which stand for the two great things that Reb Nachman taught us. You're laughing, eh? But you remember me from the old days and know that this has always been my practice—in everything under the sun I find a sign and hint of the teaching of our rabbi of blessed memory. And what are these two great things our rabbi taught us you know. I think I already told you. Of course I've already told you, but I shall tell you once more. The first thing is never to despair. Even if a man has come to the very end it is forbidden to despair. And the second thing is to begin each time anew. What did you ask before? How I sustained myself? Well then, I shall tell you. After the light of my eyes had been taken from me, my fellow Hasidim came to console me. When they saw how bad things had become, they did not rest until they found me a little niche in one of the abandoned houses on the Street of the Prophets and there they set up a little shop for me. I sit there constantly, selling newspapers, magazines and books. From this I draw my livelihood. Thank God, I have permanent customers who come to me from near and far. This one comes daily and buys a paper, that one comes once a week to take a magazine, another man comes from time to time to buy a book. There are some who come regularly not to buy anything, but merely to spend some time listening to me and telling me news of the big world. All my life I was anxious to hear news of the world; how much more so now that I can no longer use my eyes. I always used to urge you, too, to tell me the latest news. Do you remember? Today a man came to me and told me of a radio bulletin he had heard which actually made me tremble. Perhaps you have heard it, too. No? Come, I'll tell you about it, if you won't be shocked. But let us sit down first. Here are the trees. Let's sit beneath the other tree where there is a large rock comfortable for two."

We sat beneath that abandoned tree. I mounted a sloping branch and he sat opposite me on the large rock. He leaned against the trunk, closed his sightless eyes, and sat silently like a man who had fallen asleep by himself in the field. A wonderful tranquility came over his face. Fallen olives, the crop of several years, were scattered on the ground around us. Seeing them I became vexed, for I remembered the pickled olives I had left in my house. At that moment the desire to tell him the entire story was once again stirred up in me.

"Reb Yankele!" I called, as a sort of prelude to the things that would follow, but I had no chance to add a word for he said:

"Oh, you thought I had fallen asleep? No, my brother, I was not sleeping. I was thinking about that bit of news they told me today. Wonder of wonders! Listen! These scientists who sit in observatories and follow the movements of the stars report that their instruments have recorded signs of conversation from another world. Which means that the upper worlds have opened a dialogue with our own humble one. That is what they told me. Do you understand what's happening here? From now on the world will no longer be what it was. Everything will begin anew. Now that there is a link between our world and the perfect world, a great reformation will begin. Let us call upon all the worlds to come to our aid. That's what I meant when—"

I could no longer restrain myself. I broke my silence and asked: "What did you say, Reb Yankele? Are you by any chance telling me again that it is forbidden to despair? I want you to know that I am capable of despair even when I see the fallen olives rolling here beneath our feet. You come and tell me about the link between our world and the upper worlds. How does that help me? I no longer know if there is any link between me and other human beings, if I am alive or dead."

"In that case, you are certainly in need of compassion," Reb Yankele answered, sighing. "Woe, woe! I did not realize that things have reached this state." He sighed once more and then remained silent for a long while. Tears fell from his eyes. I got down off the branch, sat next to him on the rock, and placed my hand on his. Sensing my presence, he turned to me, stared at me in amazement, and I honestly felt as though he saw me, saw into me.

"It is good that you came to sit next to me," he said. "Warm me, my brother, I am very cold. A sign that the sun has already begun to set. Soon I shall have to leave here. Since I became blind I go out only during daylight so that other people can see I am blind and will not stumble because of me, God forbid. But before I go I would like to tell you a story:

"Several years ago I once got up from bed and did not know how to begin the day. I was empty of everything. My prayer was no prayer, and my deeds no deeds. Everything I took in my hand fell from it and broke.

"It is customary among our Hasidim that when one feels dejected and his deeds are not what they are supposed to be, he goes to a friend and pours out his heart until the other strengthens him with words and helps him emerge from his perplexed state. But how could I come to my friend and tell him that I no longer knew if I was alive? What shall I tell you? I wandered about in a world of chaos. I knew that I was in need of compassion but I could not even pity myself.

"But late one night I walked on the outskirts of the city in the darkness. When I reached Hebron Street, not far from our prayer-house, I heard voices coming out of the dark courtyards, simply the voices of people one hears every night, everywhere in the world: the sighing of an old man who could not fall asleep, the screams of a woman frightened by bad dreams, the crying of a hungry baby. And when I heard these sounds my heart was filled with great compassion for the world, for the people of the world, and for myself as well. Then I knew I was alive. I began to weep. I entered the prayerhouse where I sat alone all through the night and wept. With the coming of morning everything was no longer the way it was the day before. I no longer asked how to begin the day. I began it.

"Now that I have told you the story I shall go. Give me your hand and I will rise. Perhaps I shall still manage to get to the evening prayer in time. Shalom!" he said and departed.

Reb Yankele went on his way, but I did not accompany him. I remained alone there beneath the tree. I sat on the huge stone, spread out my hands and legs, and placed my head in the lap of the tree. I hardly had time to reflect on all the things that I had seen and heard when darkness fell. With the darkness a deep sleep came over me.

Who knows how long I was immersed in that heavy slumber! When I awoke, a thick darkness surrounded me; it seemed that I had slept thus days and nights. Since I had dreamt much during my sleep, and since all my dreams revolved about the events that had befallen me that day, I thought that perhaps the entire incident from beginning to end was but a horrible dream. But if all this was only a dream, what was I doing here and what was this awful darkness that surrounded me like a wall?

I rose from my place and took a few hesitant steps in order to convince myself that I was not in the bottom of a pit. In so doing I saw a cold pale light breaking forth from between the houses of the quarter opposite me, and I immediately began walking toward the light. I walked carefully, on tiptoe, for I knew that this place was near the border and was concerned lest the guards on either side see me and consider me an infiltrator.

I reached the quarter without incident. No one harmed me, not when I was outside the quarter, and not when I had already entered it. For a brief while I stood beneath a lamp post and looked this way and that. If there was a night watchman in the vicinity I wanted him to take a good look at me so that he'd immediately realize that I was lost and not an infiltrator. After that I began to walk along the streets of the quarter. I proceeded slowly at the edge of the road, thinking of Reb Yankele who one night long ago walked on the outskirts of the Old City and heard the voices of human beings emanating from the courtyards. I pricked up my ears. Perhaps I too would hear voices from the houses—but I heard nothing. Not the sighing of an old man, not the scream of a woman, not the crying of a baby. The quarter was silent. It slept its sleep without a sound.

Nevertheless, I too felt full of compassion at that moment. I felt compassion for Reb Yankele, the light of whose eyes had been taken from him, and who spent his days sitting in a little niche and listening to news from another world; I felt compassion for the people of the quarter who slept their sleep without a sound; and I also felt compassion for myself for wandering about outside at such an hour. To you I can reveal what I would not reveal to any human being: I stood there and wept. But I did not enter the prayerhouse. I did not even know where the prayerhouse was. I stood on the street, in a dark corner, and wept until I heard someone calling to me from afar. I do not know if it was one of the guards, or someone from the nearby houses who had been awakened by my weeping.

"Who's there?" a voice called from the darkness.

"I!" was my reply and I walked away silently.

And nevertheless, nevertheless, I still do not know anything. Perhaps you can provide the answer? I beg you! The coming day is approaching and I still do not know how to begin the day. Where shall I go from here, where shall I turn?

But perhaps, for all that, I should go and return home?

Translated by Curt Leviant

In a Son's Footsteps

Each day, when the hurrying, bustling women had left his store, Reuveni would clean and tidy it, working quickly, with flowing movements. He took the tin boxes of sweets and biscuits from the long counter and placed them carefully on stools which he had brought in from the front of the shop. He lifted the cylindrical lead weights and piled them onto the scales; then he took a rag from the sink, wet it and wiped the spotted marble slab, wrung it out, dried the slab and returned the boxes to their places. He went to the shelves, putting each jar and box back in its place and tied up the sacks containing flour, sugar and vegetables.

He was careful not to miss any grease spot on the counter, on the big refrigerator or on the two small tables at the entrance of the shop, on which he served snacks for workmen. But when he reached the tables and saw crumbs of crust and two thick drops of sour milk on the oilcloth his movements grew heavy. As he wiped the oilcloth he heard again the voices of the two boys who had sat here. Their young faces were unshaven, their clothes were sweat-stained and their nails long and black; they had leaned their rifles against the iron shutters.

"People here don't know what war is! They just sit in their village, in their shops, and make money!" said one, raising his voice so that it should reach the ears of the shopkeeper who was serving them. His companion added: "Oh, I would rub their noses in it, those pigs." He had not gotten angry, for they were only boys, and who knows where they had spent the night. But his thoughts were diverted from his daily routine.

Those long limbs, the grey eyes, that tanned face etched with fine lines were so like Yigal. He saw the resemblance in everything, in their build, in their speech and in their destiny.

He roused himself from his reverie and returned to his work. He took a pail of water and washed the floor of the shop. When there was nothing left to do and no more customers came, he took the morning paper and sat in front of his shop beneath the canvas shade, it was nearly noon. The road lay in front of him, dusty and trodden. At its edges pieces of paper and yesterday's rubbish lay in muddy water which he and his neighbors had thrown out. Two old men walked contentedly from the synagogue, their prayer shawls under their arms. A woman passed by, returning from the market, dragging her tired legs heavily. The road seemed to sprawl in the heat like a dog.

He turned to the newspaper and began to read slowly, so that no important detail would escape him. He had already read everything in the morning and knew where there had been fighting, which places had been shelled, where the enemy had been defeated and where our soldiers had been wounded. But there was no casualty list. Now and again one would hear in the village about one of the boys, and when there was no information rumors flourished. Soldiers arriving on leave would tell about someone who was missing, someone else who had been wounded. There were also rumors about unidentified dead. But no one came to him, no one brought him regards or information or asked him about his son. Even Dvorka was silent. He wondered why she was silent and why no one came to him to shake his shoulders and shout: "Reuveni, you have a son! Write to him and forgive him while you still have him!"

From sheer perverseness Reuveni still struggled with himself, although his whole being yearned for his son. He put the newspaper down and went into the neighboring shop. "Good morning, Berkovitz," he said.

Berkovitz, dressed in grey overalls and a cap whose peak had become black from the contact of greasy fingers, was bent over an open notebook, computing his accounts.

"Good morning," Berkovitz replied, raising his cap to reveal beneath it his long face with its pale, protruding eyes and tufts of black hair peeping from his nostrils. "Actually, I was just going to come to you; I want to talk to you."

"About what?" Reuveni asked tensely, fearing that this would be a continuation of the thoughts which pursued him.

"And what have we got to talk about?" Berkovitz asked. "The synagogue, of course."

"By all means," Reuveni answered, smiling. It seemed strange that this should concern Berkovitz now. Feeling that it would be a good idea to divert his mind a little he said: "We heard that you are preparing a revolution in the underground."

"You? Who is 'you'?" Berkovitz kindled. "Don't say 'you,' but all of us. Except for Stern, that is. Stern would treat even the Almighty as a union member—if He will not provide him with all that he requires, there'll be a strike! But we must do something constructive."

"What?"

"These are stirring times; the hand of God can be seen everywhere. Our synagogue should not be merely an insignificant assembly."

"The main thing is that every man should be able to communicate with his Creator."

"That is not so, Reuveni. The synagogue must be a magnet, so that young people will come inside. Look, twenty years ago, when I came to the village, no one would dare to smoke in public on the Sabbath; but today, even our own children, our own flesh and blood—"

The children; he could not avoid thinking and speaking about them. What did these people care about the children, and what did they want from them? Suddenly he loathed the dusty walls of the shop, the barrels of fish in front of him and the cupboard of empty boxes; he despised Berkovitz, who talked on while the tufts of hair in his nostrils glistened, and he hated himself. How could he ignore the terrible war that was being fought around them? During the last few days, when there had been nothing but bad news, he had felt the war in his body, like an illness which gnawed and consumed him. How could they talk about the children?

His wife, Dvorka, appeared at the window.

"Hello, Berkovitz," she said, hesitating in the doorway, looking small and fragile. "Nathan—"

He followed her. While walking she took off her head scarf; she hung her purse on a nail in the store and scurried about, tidying up and talking.

"That great philosopher, Berkovitz. While you listen to his stories he fills his shop. When we will be left without money or stock he will bring sugar, flour and oil from under the counter. Berkovitz! The synagogue!"

Reuveni did not answer. He listened silently and was glad when someone entered the shop to make a purchase and broke the flow of Dvorka's speech. But as soon as the customer left, Dvorka continued. He could not understand what she wanted or what it was that had roused her this time, but he did not ask for he already knew what her reply would be. She would talk about the others, about Gordon the Baker who had bought three plots of land and was building a second storey on his house.

"And what are we? I am sick of living a dog's life, Nathan, sick to death. I am entitled to a shower in my home after twenty-four years. For how long will I have to run out to a broken hut in the yard?"

Reuveni heard her, but he was no longer listening; he was long past caring about what she said.

"If it wasn't for me . . ." she was saying. That was how she ended every speech for the prosecution. If it wasn't for her they wouldn't have a shop and would starve to death. Really. If it wasn't for her he wouldn't have become a shopkeeper and he wouldn't have heard what the soldiers had said. Why didn't she talk about Yigal? He himself had forbidden the mention of his name, but today there had been bad news from the front. Dvorka, however, knew only one thing, to scream for more and to envy others. Then, with a fiendish smile, she said: "Mr. Gold promised to visit us, with Mrs. Gold."

"Why on earth did you call me?" he asked suddenly, in order to be rid of her.

"Taxes," she said, handing him a piece of paper. "More taxes. We are being skinned alive. Reuveni has his finger in every pie; whenever they need a donkey to work for them in Civil Defense or the Merchants Association they remember Reuveni, but if we should ask them to reduce our taxes, then it's nothing doing! Road, water, education, security—what good do your friends do us?"

"My friends?" he joked. "But you are the friend of all the important ladies—Mrs. Gold, for instance, and Mrs. Weiss."

"Are you laughing at them? You?" Dvorka was overcome with rage. "Of course they are important ladies; they live like human beings and they have what human beings should have. How can you laugh at them when you can't give me even half of what they have?"

That was it, she was always quick to throw his inability in his face. All right, he was not able, neither did he want, to give her anything. He did not want to provide her with all the things which she saw in the homes of the other women. Suddenly he felt his heart shrink or stretch, and start to beat violently. He had to silence her and stop her talking; he could not stand her voice any more. What did he have in common with her, or with the shop, or with the village?

"Be quiet!" he shouted. It was a high-pitched shout, sharp and shaky, the shout of a man who is past caring what others will say. "For once just shut your mouth!"

Dvorka stood dumbfounded by the counter, an open box in her hands; her lips were parted, revealing her teeth. Reuveni sat bent on a stool, his hands clasped round his knees. His small, fine-featured face was yellow and his eyes, ringed with deep lines, were dim like cloudy glass. He looked as if his stomach was torn with pain, as it had been in the days of his illness. Dvorka was frightened that something was not right. Had he really spoken like that? She did not deserve it in the least.

"Be quiet?" The insult had brought the tears to her eyes. "So this is what you have come to. As if you had taken me in from the street. Next thing you will be beating me, sending me out of the house." And suddenly, as if an external force had seized her, she added: "Like you sent Yigal."

"Be quiet!" he shouted hoarsely. "Be quiet and don't mention Yigal's name."

"I didn't send him out of the house," said Dvorka, refusing to give in.

"Oh, I hate you. Oh, how I hate you."

At that moment everything became clear; he had spoken and relieved himself at last. He really hated her, and the shop, and the village. He hated this life which had caused him to lose his beloved only son. He had hit Yigal and sent him out of the house because he was his. It was his right to do so because he loved him; he was his.

"I am going to Yigal," he said in a low voice. Dvorka shook; his words and appearance frightened her. His lips were tightly closed and bloodless and all his limbs trembled. That was how he had been on that day of madness when he had sent Yigal out of the house; he had remained sitting in his place, his whole body trembling. Since then it had been forbidden to mention his name. She knew that Yigal had not forgiven him; he would not want to see him even if he came to him now, in the midst of war. He had been a boy and had worked with his young hands to support the whole family because of his sick father. And he, that madman, had not for a moment considered that they would be left without food, he had never thoüght about that. "I will work at something, I will manage without him," he had said. Him, with his crushed, operated-on stomach. When at last she had managed to open the shop, through the charity of friends, it had seemed that he had calmed down and that he saw things more clearly now and a light shone in her heart; perhaps now Yigal would come back. She wanted it very much; without him the house was not a home. Reuveni was always running around occupied with public affairs, he was hardly ever at home. But neither father nor son had forgiven one another.

She had met her son secretly in town: he had matured and grown taller, his arms had become hard and muscular. He had been glad to see her but had said: "No, Mother, I will not come back home." But maybe this wasn't true, for in every letter, which one of his friends would bring her secretly, he would mention his father and ask about his health. With pain and envy Dvorka recalled that it had always been like that, his real, deep love had always been for his father, although the whole burden of rearing him and caring for him had fallen on her.

"Go to him!" she mocked him defiantly.

"I will go. I'm going today!"

"How can you say such a thing? How will you get there if the road to Tsurim is blocked? And even if you get there," she added, out of the same bitter envy which governed her, "even if you get there, I'm quite sure Yigal will send you away."

"I will get to him!" he said, and his chin quivered as if he had a nervous tic. Suddenly he burst into tears; he cried aloud, in bursts, like a child or a beaten dog. Two inquisitive passers-by poked their noses into the entrance of the shop, but were startled by the sight and retreated. Dvorka stayed where she was; she knew that she should go to him now and soothe and appease him, but she had never known what to do in a crisis. To tell the truth, she was repelled by the sight of the man crying, so she stood looking at him, but did not move. Gradually Reuveni's crying diminished and stayed at the back of his throat, then he got up and went out of the shop.

II

Berkovitz and a woman were standing at the entrance of his shop. The road was deserted, the wide courtyards were hidden beneath eucalyptus and cypress trees, houses with peeling plaster dried up in the sun; it was a hot and heavy summer. Reuveni walked in the middle of the road in the direction of the village. His back was hunched and he ambled at a sick and unceasing pace, as if he had been moonstruck. The two spectators sighed, shaking their heads.

"Only half an hour ago," Berkovitz said, "we were talking as we usually do, and suddenly he had an attack. It's terrible."

"Terrible, a man of forty-five suddenly bursting out shouting and crying. It's terrible."

"Well," sighed Berkovitz and entered his shop, the woman following.

Reuveni heard wild sounds crashing in his brain, his heart and all his limbs, and one sound soared upwards above them all: "Yigal, I must see Yigal." At that moment the track of his life changed. His blind, uncontrolled yearning for his son pushed him stormily towards his true self. Suddenly everything was all right, suddenly he became radiant with contentment in the midst of the storm. He was going to his son, whose body grew like a tree and on whose forehead lines of wisdom were marked. The road was cushioned with cattle dung, horses munched from sacks, the wooden pavement squeaked beneath his feet. How was it possible that he suddenly felt relaxed, as if it were the Sabbath, as if nothing had happened? His mind grew clear and he saw the courtyards which, trodden on for half the summer, had become as heavy and unfeeling as lead. Yigal, Yigal! One vision gave rise to another and smells aroused memories. How had it been that day when Yigal had run away from home? What had happened then? It had been a summer Sabbath, the morning of a summer Sabbath. . .

. . .The rotted, moldy wooden blinds, with their cracked boards, were closed. In the big, over-furnished room it was night, but the early, cruel sun already lanced fine, burning rays into his bed. He turned and changed his position but was unable to escape. Dvorka lay at his side on the adjoining bed, sleeping in a night-shirt, without moving a limb. His nerves were taut, he had had a sleepless night and now he could feel his temples throbbing. Sweat oozed from all his pores and something heavy lay on his chest. You are healthy, Dr. Hamburg had said, the operation assures you a long life on condition (and he had raised a warning finger) that you look after your nerves. Ha! He did not want to get angry, the anger came by itself, in that respect he could not say that there had been any improvement.

He raised himself and sat up in bed. Needles pierced deep in his chest: he scratched himself angrily. The chimes of the clock beat at him, striking and shocking his temples. Reuveni looked up and in the dimness distinguished the hands of the clock. It was half past five. How many hours had he lain awake while at his side Dvorka slept like a log? Nothing disturbed the routine of her life; she worked in working hours and slept in sleeping hours. Only he could not be put right. He was a potter's vessel which had been smashed and shattered and was not worth the bending to collect the scattered fragments. Around him life flowed as usual, the strong marched onwards and he was thrown up by their feet like a sod of earth. He was as important as someone who had died—even worse, for the dead could not feel. He went out to the kitchen to wet his dry throat. As he opened the door he saw Yigal sitting at the table, wearing his blue work clothes and drinking coffee. When he heard his father enter he turned around to him and smiled.

"Why did you get up so early, father? It's Saturday."

There was pity in his smile, Reuveni said to himself. Why did you get up so early? As if he distinguished between Sabbath and weekday; he did not work so could lie in bed all day. It is Saturday today, Yigal said to him, like a father speaking to his son; for he bore the burden of financial support and was the man of the house.

"And you," he said, "why don't you rest at least today?"

"We have military training today."

Suddenly a suspicion grew in Reuveni's heart. One wore khaki for training, why was he wearing his blue work clothes?

"These clothes are dirty in any case, it's a shame to wear khaki, we have field training."

He was not yet convinced. On the contrary, once the suspicion had been aroused it did not leave him and found new vantage points. It fastened onto Yigal's smile—a smile of pity but also of secrecy and repudiation. He was always smiling and secretive and there was no knowing what went on in his heart. "Hello, father," "How are you, father?" and nothing else. And when he was not at the factory he would sit over his books, his hands covering his ears; or he would go off to his friends or to matters about which it was impossible to know the truth.

"Why are you so concerned about the khaki? You have to wear khaki."

"What are you so worried about all of a sudden? I've already told you once, I'm going to training, that's all."

"Yigal!" What a way to speak to one's father, impatiently, insolently, as if a father had no right to know where his son went.

"I told you that I'm going to military training. How many times do I have to tell you?"

Yigal had lowered his voice but Reuveni felt that he did it only with great effort. He had no significance for him; since his son supported him he had relieved himself of all his burdens. How could he use that tone of voice: "What do you want of me!" "How many times do I have to tell you!"

"Yigal, how can you talk like that to your father!"

"How do I talk?"

"Insolently."

"Don't start with me now, father."

"Be quiet! Where did you learn to talk like that? Is that what Rafi has taught you?"

"What are you talking about—Rafi? Where does he come into this?"

"Fool, don't tell me what is relevant and what is not. Don't think that just because you have started to work I will let you do anything that comes into your head!" Yigal did not answer, he simply got up from the table, put his cup in the sink, took his knapsack and turned to go, as if his father had not spoken. "As long as I live I will not allow my son to associate with Bolsheviks. No, not as long as I live."

Yigal stood in the doorway facing his father, who was blocking his exit.

"Where are you going?"

"Let me pass."

"Where are you going?"

Suddenly the blood rushed to Yigal's face and darkened it. He threw the knapsack down and placed his hands on his hips, above the pelvis, as if he wanted to provoke a quarrel.

"If you are so keen to know," he said, enunciating the words coldly and cruelly, one by one, "I'll tell you: I am going to work, I work every Saturday, I am going to the factory. What are you going to do about it?"

For one moment there was a deep silence in the kitchen, it hung over the whole street and the whole village, the silence of a Saturday morning. Only the heavy breathing of the sixteen-year-old boy and his father could be heard. Strange, devouring eyes bored into Reuveni; Yigal was declaring war, feeling his strength in the seven pounds he brought home each week. His eyes clouded and his fingers grasped the edge of the door.

"Stubborn and rebellious son," he whispered. "Go. I don't need your detestable profane work. Get out of my house."

But Yigal did not move. He remained standing with his hands on his hips, his expression one of mockery.

"You don't need it, eh?" he jeered. "And on what will you live if I don't work? You and your Sabbath—your nonsense! Do I work for myself? I work to pay for your illness. Then you come to me with your Sabbath. You make me sick."

"You support me, you—" his sick voice choked.

"Yes, me. Who else?"

"Be quiet!"

"I will not be quiet."

And then, when he hit Yigal, everything ended.

"Reuveni!" The voice made him tremble and he left the electricity pole on which he was leaning. He saw Gold, all smiles, apart from his watery eyes, coming down the steps of his drug store.

"Hello, Mr. Gold," he said, and his hand reached for his hat.

"What's the matter—pains, pains?"

"No, nothing," and he started to go. "I was just standing for a moment."

"Where are you off to?" Gold asked, clutching a corner of his jacket.

"To town. You know, things to arrange—"

But Gold did not let him go. He held his jacket and his eyes examined Reuveni.

"Aha. Indeed, I understand that it is not pleasant for you to be seen suffering. But we are friends, there is nothing to hide, Reuveni. Something here," and his fingers lightly touched Reuveni's protruding stomach, "something here is not as it should be. And as for the whites of your eyes—one must not neglect such things, Reuveni."

"I am perfectly all right."

"Don't say that, you are not all right. There are few doctors who can diagnose as I can. Come with me and I will give you some good medicine, or perhaps you can come in the evening with Dvorka, eh?"

His fingers touching his coat, the eyes spying on his body, aroused nausea in Reuveni. What did they want of him, were they all the guardians of his fate? He muttered something and turned to go, but Gold's voice still followed him.

"Reuveni, just a minute. There is something . . . important . . . as an old friend, you could say, I feel it is my duty." He hesitated, as if seeking the words which would lighten the seriousness of what he had to say. "Reuveni, just the same, these are not ordinary times but days of emergency—war. And all of us feel this in our very bones . . . as you know, I give a First Aid course three times a week, two hours an evening. And each one of us gives according to his abilities. But the sons, the sons are at the front, and the war is hard. . . . and I thought, about your Yigal—"

Reuveni closed up within himself; not Yigal. They could at least leave him his son for himself. Gold felt this immediately and linked his arm in Reuveni's to appease him.

"No, no, Reuveni, please don't misunderstand me. I am not talking about forgiving and forgetting, but why don't you just write him a letter? These days, who knows . . . and he is in that kibbutz which they say is besieged. Just a letter, eh?"

Even in this they wanted to get ahead of him; even his moment of forgiveness and self-abnegation they wanted to take away from him like they had taken away his identity, his personality and the desires of his heart. First aid! A little letter! No wonder that Yigal had hated the village and all these people. No wonder that he had run away from here.

"I am not going to write any letter," he said, hearing the shout echo in his voice as if he wanted everyone to hear and be amazed. "I am going to him—now."

"What?" Gold put out his other hand and held Reuveni by his shoulders. "The road is blocked, there is no entry or exit. How will you get there?"

"I will get there."

"Reuveni!" Gold no longer spoke softly but chided him as one does a simpleton. "What a strange idea, there is a war on, with shooting and shelling. What is the point of your getting up and running, an old man like you. And anyway—there is no road through at all, even the mail doesn't get through. But as far as that's concerned," and he again adopted a soothing tone, "as far as that's concerned, I am able to help you."

"No, I'm going to him." A letter was nothing; he had to see him face to face; he had to hold him and know that he was his son and belonged to him. Meanwhile a question arose in his mind.

"What about the letter? How would it get through?"

"Well, well" the wide smile between the fat, swelling cheeks enjoyed its powers of persuasion. "I have always said that although Reuveni is a little hot-tempered he is a wise man, and in the end . . . give me the letter. The rest is my concern and on my head be it."

"Who will bring the letter?" His temper was getting short and he could no longer stand Gold's prattling.

"Why should you know? I will arrange everything." But when Reuveni pressed him he said: "A friend of my Rina is a high officer, one of those who go on the convoy. Although, between you and me," he bent to Reuveni's ear, "he's a youngster, a child."

"Where can I see him?" Reuveni could contain himself no longer.

"Still got that bee in your bonnet?"

'I have one son, Gold, one son. I have nothing apart from him." Against his will, tears flooded his eyes once more. "Help me, Gold, just this time."

"All right, I will," Gold stammered, confused at the sight of the tears. "But it's no easy matter."

III

"I've told you thirty times: go to headquarters, go to the government, we can't help you here," the boy at the gate of the police station said.

"For three days I've been running from one office to another, from one officer to another, they all told me that there is no road through."

"There really isn't any road through."

"But here, in this place, they can do something."

"Sorry, you're wasting your time."

Reuveni, confused and despondent, looked around him. The guard, a boy whose limbs had suddenly lengthened and on whose face no beard was evident, only a kind of thin, pale weed and a mustache of adolescent spots, sat astride a box, leaning his back against the wall of the police station. Several soldiers loitered nearby, listening; one sat on a stone, two stood in the gateway and a fourth casually practiced aiming stones against a pole on the other side of the road. Reuveni's appearance at the gate of the police station had relieved the monotony of the day. He stood in front of them, his face miserable and dusty with a sprinkling of tangled, bristly hair, unshaven for several days while his small arms hung limply by his sides. He had been standing there for a few hours arguing with the guards, a ridiculous and foolish old man. Those civilians, the boys said to one another, think that war is an insurance company. Whoever heard of a father coming to the front to look for his son? Even if they could they wouldn't help him, what if everyone started to get visitors—heaven forbid!

"Tell me," he said insolently, his right thumb playing with the safety catch of the Sten. "You understand that this is the front?"

"I know," Reuveni was encouraged. If the boy had renewed the conversation there was a ray of hope. That was what that boy had told him in Gold's house. "Go to the police station in Bet Anav. There, in the brigade headquarters, they could help you if they wanted to."

"But I was told," he added confidently, "that sometimes they go from here to there."

The guard burst out laughing, enjoying the old man's foolishness. From the force of his laughter he smacked his knees with his hand.

"Uzi," he said, turning his head to the left, to the one who was throwing stones at the pole. "He heard that they go to the other side."

Uzi, one-tenth of whose body seemed to consist of shorts and a torn shirt, and nine-tenths of curly black hair, glanced an all-knowing look in Reuveni's direction, scratched his head with a stone and pronounced:

"Get the Cadillac ready for him, Chaimke."

"Let him wait till we have taken the road," added the soldier sitting on the stone.

"Meanwhile, let's attach him to our unit," suggested one of those leaning on the gate, as his own contribution.

"That's good!" cried Uzi and immediately raised his voice and shouted into the courtyard of the police station: "Shimeleh! Shimeleh!"

While they joked and employed their inventive powers Reuveni stood silent. He did not participate in their joy; as if he did not know that the front was here! But he had definitely been told that it was possible to get through, and he had been really happy when he had actually reached this place. And even now, although they laughed at him, he was still happy to be here. How different it was from the village and from all his life until now. He suddenly did not care if they attached him to their unit, he would not even stand on ceremony, for they were heroes, Yigal's friends and companions.

Shimeleh appeared in the gateway. He was small and slight, older and sterner than the others. His nose was crushed flat and his narrow, grey eyes were fixed above high cheekbones.

"What's going on here?" he asked.

"We've got a new recruit for our unit," replied Uzi, pointing at Reuveni.

"One of the veteran settlers," said Chaimke.

"What is all this? What is this civilian doing here?" His voice was confident; it was clear that he was the superior of these boys.

"Excuse me," said Reuveni, "are you the officer here?"

"What's the matter?"

"It is not their fault, I wanted to go in."

"It's a hell of a story," Chaimke spoke up, "he doesn't want much. He has a son at Tsurim and he only wants to look in on him to say good night. I told him that the enemy is up there on the hill, so he said: if others get through so can I."

"I haven't seen my son for three years." Reuveni's voice was choked with pleading.

"Who told you they go through?" roared Shimeleh, and if Reuveni had not known his rank yet, he was sure now that he was the officer here. "Those pigs! Who told you they go through, I want to know!"

"It was by chance," he said, "an officer at home, in the village."

"Didn't I know it? They're walking around in the streets and talking. If they don't slaughter this whole army one day then I don't know what—"

"But it's my son." Reuveni wanted to bring him back to the matter in hand. "For three years—"

"Oh, you have a son. Really? And were all these boys made in a factory? So what if you have a son?"

"With us it's something special. My son and I—"

"You love him, eh? You have to! Doesn't Chaimke's father have to? And doesn't my father have to? Take my advice and go back home, wait patiently and pray that he will return."

There was nothing left for him to say. He sood facing the boys and looked up towards the low hills continuing eastward until they became mountains, the hills which these boys would climb to force a road through. What silence there was from here to the mountains! "There is shooting and shelling," that fool Gold had said. No, there was silence, the plains were dumb. From here the road continued on its empty, mysterious way. And could this strange, square, sealed police station be the front? These are children, almost like Yigal had been that Saturday. Should he tell them what had happened, why he had to hurry to reach him? They would laugh their heads off. Maybe Yigal would be like that too if he got through, even if he reached him he would be unattainably distant, mercilessly indifferent. What are you doing here, he would say, go back to the village, the shop is waiting for you, Berkovitz is waiting for you. Maybe it would be best to get up now and go back.

"Shimeleh," the one who was sitting on the stone said suddenly, "whatever happens, doesn't he have to eat something?"

"Listen, Turk, we don't need your advice. I know what to do."

He sat on a stone with mess tins in front of him, one filled with cold tea, the other with thick slices of black bread, a cube of margarine, a slice of yellow cheese, a spoonful of jam and a tomato. It was already three in the afternoon and he had not yet eaten all day. He ate ravenously, with appetite, forgetting the doctor's admonitions. The boys sat facing him, watching his mouth and between bites and gulps he answered their incessant questions. He did not mind answering; on the contrary, it was as if he waited eagerly for the questions and relieved himself by his full and detailed answers. He found himself quite openly and simply laying before them his whole life, the story of his relations with his son, his need to see him and to tell him what was in his heart. He had not sat like this for many years. Here he was in a remote field with a group of youngsters, eating from mess tins, without burdens, without inhibitions, without torment in his soul. And as the youngsters probed more and more deeply with their questions, and as he answered them, that complicated tangle of attitudes and relations with which he had been at odds for more than twenty years was released from his heart.

"So," said Turk, "so all this began because you didn't want him to join the youth movement?"

"He was quite right," said Chaimke, "they just confuse kids. My father also said: first of all learn and develop your own ideas, politics comes afterwards."

"Be grateful for your father," said Uzi, "my father didn't care in the least if I went to the youth movement or hung myself. All that mattered was that I shouldn't eat so much or make a noise in the house. If he could he would have sent all my brothers to some kibbutz."

Shimeleh appeared again in the gateway of the police station.

"Listen, uncle," he said, "in another hour a car will be leaving for Tel Aviv, you are going back in it."

Going back? That is, back to the village. He looked at the group of boys in front of him and suddenly the thought that he should get up and leave them and return to his shop was strange. Even if it was impossible to reach Yigal, where should he return to? They too waited in silence for Reuveni's reaction. Chaimke was sure that Reuveni was a little soft in the head; nevertheless he was attracted by him and

found the thought that there could be such contentiousness, such a
storm of emotions, between father and son, intriguing and fascinating.
At home everything was certain and planned, all decisions were taken
by his father. "First finish your studies in high school. After that study
medicine, I have not yet decided whether in the United States or in
Switzerland. And remember, a man who wants to achieve something
with his life must work hard not to be led astray by foolish things."
And when the war broke out he had said: "Chaim, you must enlist
at once; it is a patriotic obligation. I will see to it that you receive a
task befitting your education and abilities." But meanwhile he was
already in the brigade and everything was cut and dried. And as for
running after his son—that would never enter his father's head.

Uzi, whose father spent his days sitting on a stool at the door of
a cafe on the border of Jaffa, also considered Reuveni to be a strange,
amusing creature. What's his hurry, why does he have to see his son
just now? A father like that . . .

Turk knew his father only from the stories which his mother had
told him. His father had been a nobleman and had loved his wife and
son. Perhaps his father might also have run after him to the front.

"I've got an idea," said Turk. They all turned to him.

"Let him try to talk to the commander."

"What is this, a madhouse?" Shimeleh thundered at him. "You
think that everyone should just go and talk to the commander?"

"What's wrong with it? Let him try, then at least he will go home
with the feeling that he did all he could."

"What feeling?"

"What do you care," Chaimke chimed in, in support of Turk, "let
him try, the commander is not God."

The commander was due to leave on a tour of the outposts and it
was agreed that Reuveni would wait for him at the gate and try to
speak to him as he went out. Reuveni paced excitedly backwards and
forwards on the road; just a few minutes more and the commander
would come out. Reuveni was no longer filled only with the desire to
get through to his son's kibbutz. Everything was suddenly as clear and
plain as the deserted distance. There was no more madness, no longer

the dim yearning within him pulling towards worthless things, like jackals in summer at the back of their house. He was not old, only forty-five years of age, he was a man with good years still before him. And if he had wasted his time, if he had erred, then here was the moment of reckoning. He remembered a distant night at the edge of the village, there had been a track of loose earth between the acacia and cypress trees, pungent odors had emanated from the orchards and the vineyards were pleasant. Black shapes lay curled up beneath the stars, dogs of a new country. I will say to the commander: if they go, I will go too, I am not afraid. And if not, then I will wait, you will have an extra soldier, the road will soon be broken through. The officer would give in; with such a burning will as his, the heavens would help him.

"Pssst, the commander's coming," Chaimke whispered, "the commander and the information officer."

The two men strode energetically in step, as if they were going to the reviewing stand. One of them, a pace in front of his companion, was broad, with clipped hair and a belt that had slipped down over his stomach. His companion was thin, with a long neck and a disproportionately large mustache. While Reuveni was still hesitating, not daring to approach, the two had already climbed in and were sitting in the jeep which was waiting for them at the side of the road.

"Mister," cried Reuveni, and raised his hand to stop them.

The two turned towards him and waited.

"The commander," he said, "Which one is the commander?"

"I am," said the clipped one, "what's the matter?"

His face was hard and his lower lip was cracked. He gave Reuveni a serious, searching look, waiting for him to speak. Reuveni was struck by the fact that even though he was the commander he was still a young man, certainly not yet thirty. Hurriedly he laid his story before him, taking care not to omit any important detail and speaking quickly so as not to tax the commander's patience. The commander sat with his left hand on the wheel, his right on the gear lever and his face turned partly to Reuveni, partly to the road. There was no knowing if he was listening, if he understood. Suddenly the other one, the one with the mustache, said:

"Yigal's father? Reuveni?"

From where did he know this boy? And actually from where was less important than the fact that here was someone who knew him and his son and who would perhaps assist him.

"Don't you remember me?" smiled the information officer. "This mustache hides me, my name is Rafi."

Rafi? He suddenly saw him in his room at the kibbutz, outside the village. What a quarrel that had been, how he had defied him. Rafi would not help, he would remember only the ill will, he would only raise obstacles.

"Do you know Yigal?" Rafi asked the commander.

"What a question! He was in my division," he said, smiling at Reuveni, and creases spread down from the corners of his eyes along his cheeks; it was strange to see creases on the face of a young man. And then it was as before, a face that played a role. "Don't worry about Yigal, he is perfectly all right. But as regards your plan—no, not till the buses are running on the roads."

But Reuveni did not give in and, drawing strength from the fact that both of them knew Yigal, suggested the plan he had developed.

Rafi smiled and the commander looked at him and smiled too; it seemed as if Rafi was winking. Suddenly the commander said: "All right, stay here tonight . . . hey, you there," he called to Chaimke, "see that this man has blankets and a place to sleep."

When they were traveling between outposts Rafi told the commander what he knew about Reuveni. The commander said:

"In the morning I'll see that he gets to Rehovot. Neither I nor Yigal have the patience for tearful scenes."

"It's hard to know," said Rafi. "That man has aged a lot in the last few years, since his son ran away from home. I would like Reuveni to stay here with us."

"No," said the commander, "even without him the brigade is too full of strange characters."

"He won't be like them, he will free a young soldier for battle-duty. And besides—I would enjoy it very much."

"Have you an account to settle with him, Rafi?"

"No," laughed Rafi. But later he added: "Actually, yes, although he seems to be settling them on his own now." After a long period of silence, when they had visited Division A and examined its defense plans, and inspected Division D in its entirety and had returned to the jeep, Rafi said:

"I had only one encounter with Reuveni. One Saturday afternoon I was sitting reading in my room when I heard a knock on the door. Facing me, dressed in a formal suit and grey hat, stood Reuveni. I was perplexed because I knew immediately that he had not come to sing me a love song. For a year I had been Yigal's friend and guide and during that time had not once been in their house or spoken with his father. In the headquarters they had told me that his father opposed Yigal's participation in the youth movement. It did not seem to me at all likely that he would visit the kibbutz—my kibbutz was then in the village—and certainly not on Saturday. I pretended not to know who he was and asked him what he wanted. 'Are you Rafi?' he spat out, 'I am Yigal's father.' I tried to look pleased and asked him to come in. He refused and remained standing in the doorway, full of hostility.

"Many of the people in the village hated and condemned us; and Yigal—whose idol I was in those days—had doubtless told his father about me and tried to convince him of our doctrines, and that of course was the reason for his visit. Since he had made the effort to come, I said to myself, I will try and get some benefit out of the situation and avoid a quarrel. Again, I urged him to come in, I understood that he was tired and wanted to rest for a while.

"I watched his eyes examining the hut, there were two beds, a small wooden table and a bookcase made out of boxes. For a moment it seemed as if the blinkers had been removed from his eyes and that he saw us as ordinary human beings. But suddenly his eyes rested on a nude which was hanging on the wall—in those days we had all discovered Gauguin—now he had found the root of the sinfulness.

" 'Mr.———!' he turned to me drily.

" 'My name is Rafi.' I smiled, but he was not to be caught. 'I wanted to say a few words to you in connection with my son,' he said, going straight to the heart of the matter. 'I hereby inform you that I violently disapprove of any friendship or connection whatsoever between you and Yigal.' "

" 'Why?" I asked quietly. 'Because I am his father!' he retorted, emphasizing his paternity by raising his voice, in which there was a nervous tremor. 'And I oppose this kind of—friendship!' "

"And what if Yigal will want my friendship nevertheless? 'Yigal is a child and does not understand what he is doing.' "

"What is he doing? 'I did not come here to argue with you. I came to warn you that I will not tolerate this, that you are poisoning his mind.' "

"That made me boil. That boy had worked and kept quiet, bearing the upkeep of his family on his own shoulders; and that miserable proletarian, whose God spat in his face, played at being master of the house. That boy was mature enough to understand what his obligations were. 'If he has reached working age then he should also be allowed to think,' I said. It seemed that my words had wounded his most sensitive spot, his tired eyes grew moist and he said: 'God knows, I wanted him to study so that he would be somebody. But even though he supports me I am still his father, and as long as I live I will not allow him to associate with hooligans.' "

" 'How do you know that I am a hooligan? Do you know me? Maybe I can help Yigal.' I was younger then and did not like to keep silent when I was sure that I had something to say and that my intelligence was superior to that of my opponent. 'I am not interested in any benefit which Yigal would derive from friendship with you. I do not want my son's head to be stuffed with Bolshevik lies. I do not want my son to profane the Sabbath nor to be taught to deride my faith. Even though I do not profane the Sabbath in public I can still teach my son something—things which are more beautiful and more important than communist doctrines. I want my son to remain a Jew; that is why I came to Israel.' "

The commander laughed, Rafi had imitated Reuveni's excited tones with considerable talent. "Exactly, when we reached that point— God, Bolsheviks and Judaism—I knew that the discussion was at an end, we would not get any further than that. I declared that I did not force my friendship on Yigal but that as long as he wanted it I would not deprive him of it. At that moment I did not know that the rift between the father and son had already been opened. That same evening Yigal came and asked me to help him to get accepted by a kibbutz because he had left home."

"That boy has character," the commander said, "but only now do several interesting facets of his personality become clear to me."

"From the story?"

"Yes. He was in a unit in my division. As a private he was one of the most outstanding individuals in the unit, as regards social relations, leadership and endurance. But when he came back from an officer's training course and received a command he failed."

"It's understandable. He simply could not delegate duties to others when he could do them himself."

"He's not a leader."

"He's too polite."

"Are you saying that against yourself or against me?" Rafi did not grasp the commander's sarcasm and was silent. An hour later the commander added: "And what is he like on the kibbutz?"

"I don't know. From the time his group went to Tsurim I haven't heard about him. But what do you think about his father, shall we keep him with us?"

"O.K., let's keep him."

IV

Reuveni became a military man. The years melted away amid "the boys," and there was joy in his actions. Most of his work was with the arms stores; he would sit on a box of ammunition, spread a sack on the floor and clean arms, carefully carrying out all the armorer's instructions. On his second day he had put aside the formal suit in which he had set out on his journey. In the stores he had been issued khaki clothes, an army hat, high boots and mess tins—and he had become a soldier in all respects. Because he was working on cleaning arms his trousers quickly became marked with large oil stains which absorbed dust and became black. This merely increased Reuveni's enjoyment. Although he could not see his reflection in a mirror he knew that he had undergone a radical change; in his heart, anyway, there was a great change. Before three days had passed he already knew how to dismantle and reassemble a Sten gun without the armorer standing by him. "Just don't touch the trigger mechanism!" the armorer had warned him, and Reuveni obeyed. He cleaned the barrel and the breech-block and learned the difference between cleaning for storage and cleaning before and after firing. He learned how to load the ammunition belts of the "Beza"; he knew that the thick pipes rearing upward were cannon and that hand grenades required particular attention. He would do all his work with a kind of sacred anxiety, for he had heard stories of a gun into which sand had penetrated and paralyzed its moving parts, and of a "Beza" with whose ammunition American ammunition had been mixed, and when these important instruments had been needed to "support," to "double" or to "block," they had not been able to and had constituted a great advantage for the enemy and had cost many lives.

In the brigade arms store there was enough work for the whole day and the armorer, who had discovered Reuveni's dedication, enslaved him mercilessly. But Reuveni was not satisfied merely with oiling metal parts. The boys of the brigade, all of whom were the same age as his son, liked him and called him "father." This encouraged him so that unimagined resources of energy rose up and spilled over within him. He was always ready to lend a hand and to give others the benefit of his experience. Across the road from the police station they were digging anti-aircraft positions. He stood watching the diggers, the superior smile of a good foreman on his face.

"No, boys," he said, "that is not how one works, you have to know how to hold a spade. Give it here a minute."

He spread his legs, spat into each of his palms, rubbed them together and only then, with a craftsman's grip, grasped the spade. "One must use it as a lever," he explained, "and economize on movements." He brought it up and thrust down, driving it into the ground and loosening a lump of reddish soil. "This is easy ground," he said, perhaps to let them know that he had not completely forgotten how to work on the land; after all, had he not once been an agricultural laborer? In recent years he had become enslaved to a grocery store but that was not the real him, that was because of something else. And as for the operations, he felt no pain now. The sweat collected beneath his hat and his breath grew short, but it was good to stand like this and show his strength to the youngsters. He would be able to do this on the kibbutz too, to stand among Yigal's friends and work, and his son would smile with pleasure.

He straightened up and said, laughing, "Never mind, boys, you'll learn, when you get to be an old worker like me."

Ten days after his arrival a state of readiness was declared, although rumors had been spreading for some time beforehand. The whole brigade was saying that the road would soon be cleared, it was long overdue, it was clear that they would have to begin here, with our brigade. When he heard this in the evening Reuveni ran to the room which he shared with his young friends, those who had met him at the gate of the police station.

"They're beginning!" he cried joyfully.

They were lying on the floor, rolled up in grey woollen blankets, they did not move. Only Chaimke raised his head and, leaning on his elbow, asked: "How do you know?"

"A state of readiness has been announced just now."

"We'll get them this time," Chaimke waxed enthusiastic.

"You be quiet, kid," Shimeleh growled without moving from his place, "war hero!"

"Look at him. What a hero!"

"Do you know what war is, eh?"

Reuveni remained silent. Before the official announcement it had been the focal point of all conversation. And now Shimeleh was talking like this, and he was a veteran and experienced soldier with a good reputation.

"Uzi," Reuveni said, "did you hear?"

"I heard," he said to the wall by his face, in the gathering dusk.

Shimeleh sat up in his bed. The blanket had slipped, revealing his body. Like everyone else he slept in his vest and pants so that they were almost black. He was short with narrow shoulders but his muscles were developed and his skin was dark. The eyebrows shading his narrow eyes and his flat nose frightened Reuveni. All the room frightened him now—the bodies lying next to one another on the floor, the lumpy blanketed forms, the empty shoes, the rifles leaning against the bare walls, the dank smell.

"Why are you looking at me like that, father! Chaimke is only a baby—he left high school a month ago, accompanied two convoys from the sea to the village square and now he's dying to fight. But we who are used to it get pretty sick of it in the end. 'Tomorrow we're going on a little patrol, boys,' 'Tomorrow we're going to explode something, boys'; we go from one action to another, from one hole to another, and it's always the same people. They mobilized me on the first of December because I had been in the Defense Force and the Brigade and I was a veteran soldier. I was mobilized in 'forty-two, when I was sixteen years old and I was frightened that I wouldn't make it. It's been like this for six years—always Shimeleh. Today our brigade consists of less than two companies. I asked them why they don't bring in new people, to give us a bit of a break, so that for three days at least we wouldn't have to be at the front and after that they could bring us back and we would be raring to go. 'There aren't enough people' they say. If there aren't enough people then there can't be a war."

"But we didn't want—" said Reuveni, hesitating and astonished.

"I know it's not us, I know. But how does that help me if it's always me, me, me at the front? When will I be able to live like a human being? When will I have a profession, when will I get married?"

"I don't understand you, how can you talk like that?" said Chaimke.

"Quiet there, kid," growled Uzi.

"You are the commanding officer here, how can we go into action under you if you are afraid? Just because you are scared yourself you shouldn't make others scared."

"Yes. I'm scared. I'm scared before every battle. Each time I'm more scared. So what?"

"Be scared quietly. Don't talk about it."

"But I want to talk about it at the top of my voice, I'm not responsible for the morale of this country."

"You're responsible for your unit."

"You can transfer to another unit, little shitter. I don't sit in Tel Aviv and write stupid articles about the heroism of our soldiers, I'm just scared."

He lay down on his back, pulled the blanket up to his chin and turned on his side. Chaimke followed suit and Reuveni, depressed and ashamed, went to his corner and arranged himself a place on the floor. Shimeleh's words had lowered his spirits and destroyed the image he had created in his mind during the days he had spent with them. But worse than that—he had actually rejoiced in the fact that there would be more battles and that each of these boys would go out to face death. He wanted Yigal, he wanted the road cleared, that was all. But here reality was different, blacker. Shimeleh was his superior in wisdom, war was not a thing which one announced with a joyful voice. And what guarantee did he have that Yigal was exempt from the war? How could he be sure that he was secure in his kibbutz and all his father had to do was to reach him?

He trembled: who had said that Yigal was at the kibbutz? Perhaps he was in one of the brigades, in one of the units. What had become of him after these seven bloodthirsty months? How is it possible, Reuveni said to himself, that this thought had not occurred to him till now, till today? Suddenly he saw his son in all the boys in the room and for a moment terror overcame him. Cruel and terrible pictures, which he had tried to ignore, appeared all around him; Yigal was dead, he had already lost his chance of seeing Yigal.

"We'll go," Shimeleh said suddenly, when it seemed that everyone was asleep and Reuveni had already put out the light. "We'll always go. But there is a moment when I want to run around shouting: I don't want to! I don't want to!" And afterwards he added quietly: "The first action in which I participated was on the Semo in Italy. It was in daytime. The action was an easy one but a few people were wounded and we had to retreat quickly. I was carrying one of the wounded with a friend of mine, together with both his and our equipment, across the rampart. The orderlies were busy and it took some time till they reached us. I stayed with the wounded man in order to rest. I looked at him, his face was shaved for he was a very clean and tidy fellow and had shaved that same morning, half an hour before we left; his eyes were half-closed and there were pieces of earth on his eyelids. His forehead and nose were also covered with earth. I could not understand how anyone could bear to have his eyes full of earth. I started to feel his pulse, I wanted to see where the bullet had entered but couldn't see any blood stains. He looked as if he had just gone to sleep. I unfastened the buttons of his battle jacket, raised his sweater and suddenly my hand sank into something like hot starch. He was dead. My division had already retreated; the tanks which had supported us stood in the field and men were throwing out the empty knapsacks in preparation for returning. Only I remained, so I thought that I would leave him and afterwards the orderlies or someone would come. But what happened? Listen, Chaimke, it's worth your while. I didn't mind leaving him alone in the field because he was already dead. But I saw that there was a watch on his wrist and it seemed a shame to leave it, whatever happened, someone would be sure to steal it. And I had no watch, nor had I ever had one—they had promised me one for my Bar Mitzvah but never got around to buying it. You understand, until an hour beforehand he had been a friend, and suddenly only his watch was left. I took it—but only for a moment. After that moment I became a human being once more. When I reached the rest I went straight to our officer and gave him the watch, I was tired and confused and told him that I had taken the watch to send to his wife. But that moment, till I returned the watch . . ."

"You never told us that story before," said Uzi.

Chaimke was silent and so was Reuveni.

V

A few hours before sunrise the divisions were ready. One by one the boys, somehow different from yesterday, gathered together from the brigade encampments and went out of the gate of the police station. Here a helmet hid unruly hair, there a face had hardened, hand grenades hung at their belts. The boxes containing the machine guns and shells for the action were arranged on the road. The officers inspected the rows; sections, units and divisions had already formed into orderly groups; cannon and medium-range gun crews stood and waited in the heavy and suddenly silent atmosphere.

Reuveni stood to the side, by the edge of the road; he would be staying here with the reserve units. He wished he could go with them and cross quickly to the other side, as if each moment he stayed here brought his son's death nearer. He had hardly dared to express this request when Shimeleh said to him heatedly: "Don't push, father. In the British Army we used to say: 'Never volunteer, never refuse'; soldiers don't challenge their fate."

At twilight they got into the transports. The evening was already misty on the plains; the scene was warm and scented. One by one the transports slipped out of view on the man-made road which stretched out shining and straight. Then it was dark; somewhere a white light shone and went out—a car in the distance. A phosphorescent bullet bloomed like a meteor at the heart of the heavens and vanished. There was a short burst of machine-gun fire. They sat by the gate of the police station and looked eastward as if they could join in the battle and weight the scales with their will power. Someone said: "It's a lovely night." Someone else: "It's starting to get cool." They stood up and went into the building, laid out blankets and dozed, fully dressed.

At dawn the first of the wounded were brought in. From the moment that the sound of the cannon had reached them Reuveni had stood on the roof of the police station looking into the distance, listening to the thundering. He was waiting for a sign, for news, and somehow each time he said "Yigal" he also said "Shimeleh."

They brought the wounded in ambulances, in jeeps, in trucks. Every few minutes a transport would stop at the gate and someone would shout: "Hey, you there by the wall, give us a hand. And you too, your rifle won't run away."

The whole building became a hospital. A wing had been specially prepared beforehand for the purpose, but the other wings were also soon filled, as well as the courtyard. A red-eyed orderly received and classified them according to their wounds. "Tell me," said the driver, "how is the doctor?" "After this slaughter nothing will be able to make him lose his reason."

Reuveni filled every need and complied with every request. But he did not know what had happened that night or what would happen now; no one knew. Wild, contradictory rumors chased one another. He saw only greyish faces and hands on which dried blood had stuck. He threw his jacket into a corner, his shirt had stuck to him with his sweat. In his head one sentence repeated itself incessantly: "Yigal, I must see Yigal, where is Yigal?" And all the time there were the shouts: "Hey, you there—"

Yes, he is going. He will bring water and collect blankets. Tea? Yes. Something to eat too, for you also. Right, of course.

By the end of the morning everything had subsided, no more wounded were brought in. Some of them were moved further on to the hospital, others were bandaged and left to sit in the courtyard. The fighters did not return. A jacket had been left on the road as well as the magazine of a machine gun and an odd shoe. In the courtyard the drivers drank hot tea and told what they knew, and what they did not know.

They got to Vickers. It was sheer slaughter.

A unit reached Bet Tor. The road is ours.

There was no way of knowing anything.

Suddenly Rafi appeared alone, in a jeep. He was completely covered in white dust, even his big mustache was white; his eyes were red and burning.

"Well, Rafi—" Rafi gave him a long look, as if he didn't know him or could by no means understand the question and find an answer. He looked very tired.

"Open," he said, "the road is open."

"Open?" Reuveni was no longer able to master his excitement. He stroked Rafi's hand and his eyes filled with tears. "Open to Yigal?"

Rafi nodded his head, then Reuveni noticed how bloodshot his eyes were. Ashamed, he asked about the others.

"Shimeleh is all right, he always is. Uzi too. Chaimke? That new one? The tall one? Lost a leg, or something like that, I'm not sure. That's all."

VI

The jeep went at less than walking pace. Clinging to the steep road, pulling itself up, stubbornly, hotly straining at its last resources of power, it crawled slowly onwards and upwards. On the slopes of the hill pine trees stopped themselves from falling onto the road. Nearby rose a headless hill; fragments of shattered houses grasped its rocks, like a forest that had been chopped down. A wall supported two storeys of windows on the skyline, like forgotten scenery, the echo of a distant sound. Rafi turned his head: "We'll soon be there," he said.

"What?" During the long journey he had been lost within himself and Rafi, his hands clasped to the wheel, his face turned to the road, had not once bestowed any word on Reuveni. If Rafi had only begun to speak Reuveni would have unloaded part of the burden of his emotions. He wanted to talk to him and ask him: Rafi, what is it that draws me to Yigal? Why are you so quiet? Surely not because you still bear me a grudge? Is it because I have no significance for you? But he is my son. Didn't I have a right to try and guide my son, even if my way of life is not the right one? And maybe it is, for there is one thing that neither you nor Yigal understand—I did not assert that right simply because he is my son but because I had wanted something from my life, something that he and you both want. I find myself strangely drawn to you, but do you feel the same, and will Yigal also sit angrily and silent like that?

"We'll soon be there," Rafi repeated.

A few moments later they turned the last bend in the road. Pictures from another time and place passed before Reuveni's eyes. He was sitting on the narrow porch, it was evening; the smell of dry plaster rose from his white builder's clothes. He was bent over a plate of steaming soup. A little, fat individual was pulling at his trousers. "Daddy, up! Daddy, up!" Dvorka got angry and said: "Let Daddy eat, he is tired." And he smiled, put the spoon down, stood up, picked the child up and sat him on his shoulders. He picked him up. There was a second picture: open-mouthed Yigal was lying in his bed listening to a long story; he did not take his eyes off his father's face. A third picture appeared before him: "What do you want," a tall boy was saying to him, with hatred in his eyes, "I'm not a child."

"Reuveni, we're almost there. You get off here. The settlement is at the end of the fruit garden. I have to go on, I'll be back."

He was left standing alone at the end of the conquered road which had led to this point. He could see three houses and a tin hut, while on all sides mountains of white stone shimmered in the summer heat. Here, on the ridge, there were derelict terraces whose neglect seemed somehow fitting. There were no people. Each mountain angrily kept its secret solitariness as if saying—go and hide yourself, everything else is empty and vain.

Alone, that was how one should live. On a mountain or in an orchard outside the village. That was what mad Shraga had always said. Perhaps he had really been the only wise one. "Leave Dvorka," he had said, "she is beautiful but selfish. Listen to my advice, Reuveni, let her marry Shlomke's son. He will take her to Paris, an Arab woman will wash her floors—that is her dream. And you, escape while you can. Stay in the settlement or chose yourself an orchard like I have done." Where was Shraga now? He had not seen him for years. He was most probably still living in a hut in Shlomke's orchard, guarding, watering and pruning.

What are you talking about, Reuveni? You have a son just two hundred paces from here.

The houses came nearer. People were standing on the roof of a concrete structure, watching him. They watched him walking, sweating under the burning sun, and waited for him. Someone else appeared on the roof, now the courtyard was very clear. Two people were approaching the fence, they also stood and waited.

In the end one of them could not wait until he got there and shouted to him: "Hey, where do you come from?"

"From there," Reuveni pointed to the blue plains which stretched westwards to the sea.

"From the other side?" the man shouted.

Reuveni nodded his head. He was already standing at the gate. The two by the fence came nearer. Those on the roof hurried to descend. Why had everyone congregated together?

"Do you come from the plain?"

"Was there something on last night?"

"Is the road open?"

"What convoy passed here last night?"

Immediately the news spread from one to another and from the small, fenced-in courtyard it echoed to the crest of the hill: "The road is open. They broke through last night."

They did not leave Reuveni alone. They did not let him say who he was and why he had come. First of all he had to tell them what it was like down there—was it true that arms shipments were arriving? And cigarettes? Have you got a cigarette? We haven't seen one for three weeks. You haven't—pity.

"Am I the first person to come here?" Reuveni asked.

"No," they laughed. "People came from all over—from the Palmach and the Field Army; but not from the other side. We would sit here and gaze at the distant plains. Sometimes we could see a car window flashing in the sunlight, in Lod. We heard the sound of cannons from Negba and saw planes going down over Hulda. But everything was from afar, from afar."

Reuveni stood and looked at them, they were children, children like Yigal. What had they done here all the time? He wanted to ask where Yigal was but fear again descended upon him. Why didn't they ask him who he was and why he had come?

"What was it like here?" he stammered a question.

"Boring; we sat and waited. It was lonely—there was no fuel and our pigeon was killed in the shelling. Only our little donkey is left."

"They shelled you?"

"Once, we were lucky. They bombarded us for a whole day. They destroyed the cattle barn and killed the pigeon. But only one of the members was hit. It was an awful bombardment."

"What about Yigal?" Reuveni's voice trembled. "Yigal Reuveni?"

No one answered. Suddenly they all understood who it was who had hurried to reach them from the plain.

VII

Voices came from the courtyard. Hammers beat at the roof of the cattle barn which had been smashed by a shell. On the path a wheelbarrow of stones rumbled to a position not yet completed. In the adjoining room a sewing machine whirred. Reuveni sat on Yigal's bed. The hammers were playing again on the thin metal roof. Yigal was riding a donkey, his feet trailing on the ground, he was laughing. He was a man and here life was still moving. Yigal, what did I want to say to you? Here he stood, his arms around the waists of two smiling girls with white scarves tied to their heads. He had been a man among men. He was a young man and you stayed at the side of the road—that's what the Eskimos do to their old people—to live until the fire goes out.

It was only a photograph album, the smiles were frozen on the shiny papers. Black notebooks lay on the table, smiles and notebooks. Was this Yigal? What had he written in the notebooks? What was within them which you did not know about your only son? Whom would you find in the closely written, crossed-out lines? How many faces did your son have?

Reuveni sat in the room for many hours, and no one came near him. They left him alone with his grief and he sat, afraid to reach out for what his son had left behind. During those two weeks he had known great happiness. Was it because he had found within himself the strength to go to his son? Why? Why had he sought his son? Say, Reuveni, what ate at your heart? Say everything. You loved your son, yet you hated him deeply, a vast envy devoured your life. You will be somebody, you said to him. I will get you work in a bank, you will learn and be an important person. What did you want him to be, Reuveni? Like you . . . ? So that he would not break away? So that he would not be independent of you?

Suddenly he imagined that Yigal had died in order to escape him and avoid a reconciliation. Only one member had been killed here, by chance, he had left the shelter and had been killed. What had Yigal thought of you? How would he have behaved if he had been alone with you in this room, stormily and sensitively alive, not just notebooks which will never change. "Go home now," Shimeleh had said to him at the gate of the police station, "you will cry later." He was not crying but there was an emptiness within him which could not be filled, and he could not breathe. It was a room much like any other, quiet and quite silent. And when they had taken him to a mound of earth it had seemed less real than the reality of his son, who had grown for twenty years in his heart and had put down deep roots there. You climbed the hill and found moments which were like a whole lifetime. You envied and even hated your son, he had hit out at you and at your existence and had stolen your dream. And now he has run away so that he would not have to say that you and he were really the same, that he only continued from the place where you had stood. You are different, the lowest of the low, the weakest of the weak. You are old and have nothing. You are Berkovitz. You are Gold. But nevertheless, Yigal, I am also you, or rather, you are me. That is why I left my home and pursued you; I had a moment of lucidity and I let it flower. I pursued you and that moment which will never return to comfort your old age. Here hammers beat and wheelbarrows roll and Yigal has left you alone. Go and test your strength against that, he has left you. . . . Is that why you mourn, merciful father, or is it for yourself and your own existence? It is not true, Yigal, I am mourning for you. If only we had met just once more. If you had only happened to meet me in the courtyard of the police station with your young friends and seen how I was one of them. Couldn't I have been like that with you, my son? Here young people overflow with youth but who did you join? Only obscene gestures are made at you, pig, old fool. The last notebook is half empty, each night, by the lamplight, he would survey his day. Was it all really worthwhile?

Blood flowed in your son's veins; what was in it that was yours? I say that my son followed in my footsteps, but how? The steps all sink into the tortuous ways of the road, backwards and forwards, to the right and to the left. It is not as simple as all that. Yigal, today you are twenty-one years old. What was I at twenty-one? I was a laborer examining my muscles by the light of the oil lamp in Birza, the labor exchange of the village. The fruit of the lemon has developed a moldering disease. I have failed. I have forgotten what brought me here. That was how things were. When I was twenty years old I was good —and when I was forty? If I had finished when I was twenty I would have been Yigal. If you had finished when you were forty? It is good to end like that, it is easy—

And suddenly everything became quite clear and simple. Yigal was dead, he was no more. All the things in the room were not Yigal. He spoke and the shadows did not answer; he was bereaved and childless, a solitary tree in the desert. It was already evening and he was here alone, no one would come to the door. He had come to Yigal and Yigal was not here, he had left the shelter for a moment, by chance, our only casualty.

Reuveni grasped his shirt beneath the collar and tore at it, rending it. He stopped and carefully, quietly unfastened his shoe laces and pulled them out.

Late in the evening Rafi came to Tsurim. He had known about Yigal's death; on the day the road had been broken through he had reached Tsurim and had heard about it. But when he had returned and had seen Reuveni's joy he could not muster the courage to tell him and had let him go the kibbutz and to exile, for his son was dead. This sensitivity which had not allowed him to tell Reuveni the truth and prevent him from coming was a cruel thing. For he had really come to like this aging man who attached himself to brigades. He had been filled with respect for him, as if he were a saint who suffered and absolved sins which he had not committed.

He knocked gently on the door but received no answer. The lower half of the door was made of wood, the upper of wire mesh; an oil lamp lit up the bare brown wood walls. Reuveni was sitting on a chair which had been placed on its side, he was looking through a thick notebook. He sat between Rafi and the light so that the lines of his face were blurred and only his profile was clear in its dull lifelessness. With the utmost care Rafi opened the door, and suppressing his greeting and anything else he might have said, came to the bed and sat down in silence.

Reuveni raised his eyes a little, they were now very dark and beautiful, like Rafi's, then he buried them in some hidden point. His body swayed to and fro in short, rhythmic movements, like someone praying or mourning. He lowered his eyes once more to the book without speaking.

Yigal's diary, Rafi said to himself; of course, Yigal would keep a diary. He wouldn't be surprised if he had also secretly written poetry. The previous generation had been amazed at every muscle which had developed normally, at a straight backbone or rough speech. Yigal was like that too; he ate plenty of vegetables, walked a great deal, swam in the village swimming pool, played soccer and worked. But was that really Yigal? When he had come to Rafi and said that he had decided to go to a kibbutz they had attached him to a group, and at the earliest opportunity Rafi had gone to see how well he had fitted in. He was not a sociable boy, not what they called a "youth movement type." It was not simply a question of *Weltanschauung*—that's what those who had to say something about everything used to say —with him a more basic emotional force was at work. Yigal had torn the umbilical cord and had severed himself from his home; he had to prove to others, and to himself, that his way was the right one. He would do any work, was a good friend but was often silent. No wonder he had kept a diary. Perhaps a diary was not the best means of self-expression but at least in this way it was possible to write the things one wanted to say out loud when there was no one to tell them to or the right moment never occurred or people were always putting you off. Altogether Yigal had been a very special phenomenon. For him the road to the youth movement had been the road to himself. It had served to unite opposing trends within him—stubbornness, working power and perseverence of the one hand, and an almost sickly sensitivity and moodiness on the other; the unending search had not been for someone else but for himself. Had Yigal been typical of pioneering youth or had he been a unique case?

Reuveni raised his head once more. It seemed as if he had suffered a disappointment and was now complaining about something.

"He had a girl friend." Of course he had. Rafi said to himself. So what? "Why did he leave her? Why didn't he follow her? She begged him to go."

Rafi smiled to himself, it was so typical of Yigal. His success in the group, although he had been an outsider, had been due to the affection he had aroused among the girls, all of whom had fallen in love with him. "And he feels nothing, he's like ice!" one of them had complained to him.

"Why didn't he follow her? Why did he stay here?" Reuveni repeated.

Bereaved fathers were mocked by every detail, if only he had gone there he would not have been killed. As if boys from Tel Aviv were not killed, even in our brigade.

"He was attached to the kibbutz," Rafi ventured a sentence.

"More than he loved any woman," Reuveni said. "I told him: Yigal, you have not been with a woman yet and that is why the way seems so straightforward to you . . . no woman has stood in your way, wanting you with all her might and sweeping you with her. That is what I told him and I was glad . . . because, you don't know, Rafi, but I was jealous of my son. Today I can see the truth and I will speak the truth. Why could he do what I was unable to do? You most probably think—Reuveni is only a shopkeeper, but I did not come to this country as a shopkeeper, no, not as a shopkeeper. I have lived a hard life. I sank and I forgot. And then I remembered and wanted to return to my son, to explain to him." He smiled a strange smile, full of the soul-bitterness of a man who knows that nothing he can do will change his fate. "To explain to him that he is no better than I am. That I am as good as he is. But my son did not forgive me. I wanted to come and say; you have not been tested with all the trials with which I have been tested, and because of that I am entitled to continue now. But my son hears and laughs: no, father, that way is blocked. I did not run away, I never ran away in my life and certainly not because of any woman. Go back to the village, to the generation of the wilderness. You came this far but can go no further, you will not die. Return to the village and live there, day and night; and let this be a reminder of the road on which you went half-way. Father, there is only one moment of mercy, woe to him that misses it."

Rafi listened to the father's wild, strange words spilling out one after another. He is exaggerating, he said to himself, he is on the point of hysteria. But he kept quiet and let him speak, break down and cry for his son. What would such a man do once he no longer had Yigal! What could he do?

Rafi listened quietly and his eyes followed Reuveni's fingers as they played with the thick notebook, measuring it and opening it, pressing and separating it. From there his eyes wandered to the window, the wooden shutter was closed; there were large holes in the rusting wire window netting.

Translated by Dorothea Shefer

Avraham B. Yehoshua

A Long Hot Day

Another hot day, he thinks in his sleep and is suddenly filled with anguish. He turns over, burrows his face in the pillow, flings his arms wide and becomes a limp lifeless cross. And without waking he thinks a wordless curse on the sun plowing the back of his neck with a broad furrow of light.

It is eleven o'clock in the morning.

His wife is long gone. Left the house at six to catch the first bus to Jerusalem for a full day at the university. Like a light bird she has flitted without leaving a trace. Her bed is made, nightdress folded, even the sound of her steps is gone from his mind.

His daughter had blustered about the house at half-past seven, the sweetest time, hour of his true sleep. She had wakened with the ring of an alarm clock, had turned on endless taps, dropped a frying pan in the kitchen, opened and shut the refrigerator again and again. At last, when he had imagined her gone for good, the door of the room had opened softly and she had entered on tiptoe in her school uniform —blue blouse and too-short skirt—to pick up the schoolbooks that he takes from her room to while away his insomnia. Silently she had collected the books and crammed them into her schoolbag. He had lain watching her noiseless movements out of the corner of his eye, impatient to be asleep. Except that suddenly, with that absentmindedness that comes over her so often, she had begun to hum a tune. Furiously he had stirred between his sheets and she had fled the room at once, shut the door carelessly and vanished.

Their street, a blind alley, is very quiet. He had managed to curl back into sleep again but presently, with the light gaining strength, he had begun to swelter in his bed. A man like him—forty-two years old, robust, hairy, an engineer with the Water Company.

Convalescing and hence idle, sleeping badly at night; by his bed— glasses of water, medicine phials, a few scattered pills.

A sweating man who, slowly and with eyes shut, divests himself of the last of his covering. Jacket, trousers and sheet spill about him; naked and bare he wakes.

A few weeks ago his mission to Africa had been cut short due to a false alarm. For nine months he had been employed as a foreign engineer on the construction of a dam some hundred miles south of Nairobi, in a mountain region of mists and forests, strewn with green huts. An Israeli and a Dutch company had jointly obtained the technical supervision of the project. The dam, going up at the junction of two river beds, was designed to hold back the flood waters and create a reservoir. The Israel Water Company, with which he had been connected for many years, had offered him the job, and he had responded at once, enthusiastically. Besides the prestige that went with supervision over such a large project and the release from a round of futile drills in the Negev, he would come in for a considerable raise in salary, enough to trade in his old car by the end of a two-year contract. Naturally he had not been allowed to take his family along, but what would he have done with Tamara anyway in that bleak mountain region? He had therefore hesitated awhile whether to accept, but Ruth had dismissed all his doubts. His trip would lend new life to old plans; she would take another year at the Jerusalem University in her endless rounds of studies. He and the Dutch engineer, a fat and rather lazy bachelor of about thirty-five, had been the only white men in the working village erected on the site. All the rest had been Africans, two or three thousand of them (their number would keep changing). There had been a great deal of work and it had had to be done in somewhat of a hurry. Several stages would have to be completed before the wet season set in.

He had found his niche at once.

His store of broken English had been enough to keep up a limited contact with the native foremen and engineers. The rest of his work had been a matter of maps, blueprints and calculations. Because he had been excited about his job, and had lived in fear of disasters like the sudden collapse of a structure, he had never allowed a nail to be driven in without preparing a sketch first. The Dutchman used to scoff at such formality; but he had been insistent. In addition, he had always tried to stay within reach of the site, and whenever he had been forced to go to Nairobi to order tools or a spare part he had risen at dawn in order to get through his errands in time to be back the same night. He would leave Nairobi at dark, speed along a highway that would presently turn into a wide and empty dirt track, tear past sleepy villages, scare unidentified wild animals with the headlights of his jeep, and when reaching the camp late at night he would not go to bed before he had slipped down to the dam and there, among silent scaffolding and concrete mixers, by the light of a torch and the stars of a tropical sky, inspect the work done that day.

For the rest, he lived in solitude, which to him was freedom. His wages were sent direct to Ruth, and he would reserve only a small amount of pocket money for himself, since his needs were all supplied on the spot. From time to time the Embassy would send him a batch of Israeli newspapers, but their clever-clever articles somehow sounded insipid on the fringe of the great jungle. And, of course, a short letter from Ruth now and then and half a page from Tamara. He, too, wrote seldom. What was there to tell? Each time he would apologize, though no apology was asked for. Sometimes, instead of a letter, he would send a blurred snapshot of himself, down at the dam, on top of the scaffolds, or bent over his plate. One old native laborer used to bring a heavy square English camera to work with him and would photograph everybody, whether they wanted to or not, then sell them the pictures.

Everything would have gone well, except that one night, back in camp from a little native celebration at one of the villages in the area, he had wakened up with a feeling of being strangled. It was as if someone were wedged on top of him and squeezing his throat. It was the same on following nights. Sometimes, without any warning, he would wake in pain, lose consciousness for a few seconds and come to again exhausted, as though rising from the dead.

He, who had never been ill.

He had thought the weather was to blame; the winds at night had suddenly grown cold, heavy with fog. As his temperature stayed normal, and in daytime he only felt slight bouts of dizziness, he had waited for it all to blow over. A few days later he had nevertheless gone to the African medic and told him. The man had listened full of interest, attentive, had seemed embarrassed and had at once spread the news of his illness abroad throughout the camp. The natives had been puzzled, a little worried, had seemed to take an oddly grave view of the matter. They began to inquire about his welfare, dozens of laborers crowded around him to shake his hand and, with queer grins on their faces, to wish him health. They had liked him, apparently. The Dutchman had suggested that he see a doctor, and at last he had indeed gone to Nairobi and seen one, an English doctor. He had been baffled by the English words needed to define the subtlety of his sensations. The Englishman made light of the whole thing, had prescribed a series of sedatives, which had had a drowsy effect. The pains had eased somewhat, but his work suffered. He began to rise late, and was forced go back to his hut for a rest after the noon meal. The native medic began to dog his steps, visit him daily, bring him his meals, crouch on the floor by his bed, his first-aid kit at hand, watching him for hours on end. Laborers would stand and peek at him through the windows. One evening the medic had brought along the old man with the camera, dressed in gay working clothes, jeans and a faded red shirt. After lengthy explanations it appeared that the old laborer was none but a former village witch doctor. He had refused to be examined, of course, had laughed. But the old man had not come to examine him at all. He had stood hesitating on the doorstep, looking at him from afar as though afraid of contagion, then had taken a scrap of dried leather from the pocket of his shirt, placed it on the table among the blueprints, and slipped out. That same night, after midnight, he had detected dark spots in his groin. He had been alarmed, had gone to wake the Dutchman, had lost his head. Next morning, wrapped in an army blanket, placed in the back of a van, his suitcases by his side, he had been borne away to a hospital in Nairobi. The hospital, however, proved to be a small old-fashioned outfit, its equipment dating back to the Second World War and suited mainly for the treatment of injuries. They failed to diagnose his case, and the Embassy people had advised transferring him south by plane to Dar-es-Salaam, to a new hospital built under the supervision of Chinese experts and inaugurated—a blend of barracks and pagoda—but a few months back.

After several hours of meticulous registration at the reception office, an African doctor had come and taken him under his wing. He was a young man, bespectacled, calm, serious-looking. Though the hospital was only half occupied, the doctor had allocated him a bed next to an old dying native.

For three whole days that doctor had not let go of him, had kept at him even at night. He had him undergo dozens of examinations and tests, probed at him with all possible instruments, as though to run in the new equipment. For hours on end the patient had lain naked on the stretcher, had been tossed about, strong lights directed at him, his wrists tied with electrodes. In the course of lengthy examinations the doctor would subject him to political arguments. He had shown himself to hold extremist views, to hate anything Western, to hate particularly anything to do with Whites. Actually he had not argued about his views but had preached them, and in fluent English; detached, unsmiling, as though all this contact with the white body under his hands was a kind of compulsion to him. He considered all white experts dangerous parasites, grieved for Africa. Of Israel he had never heard, nor wanted to. The Israeli had wished to avoid a dispute. Now and then he tried, with his awkward English, with a puckered smile, to come to the defense of the Western world. Never had loneliness been so hard to bear. Without a newspaper, a letter, another human being; in a half-empty hospital smelling of new paint, by the bed of a dying African, wheeled across long dim corridors, between landings; the dumb contact with native nurses who spoke no English. The spots, by the way, had vanished, his pains abated; only a dull fleeting echo at night. Then the examinations were over. At dusk the doctor entered his room, dressed in a gray jacket, without his white coat and with a somewhat formal air about him, to say that he had been found to suffer from cancer and that the disease was in an advanced stage. Tomorrow at dawn he would operate upon him. He even showed him a small colored sketch to explain the nature of the operation. There was no trace of sympathy in his voice, it was just information, flatly delivered. Rain was falling outside, an unexpected tropical rain. Near them, a soft rattle came from the old man's throat. He heard the doctor out calmly, taking deep breaths. The doctor drew nearer his bed, very dark, very quiet, agile. Outside the darkness began to move in on the windows.

The Israeli replied, feverishly, that he refused absolutely to accept the diagnosis. They had made a muddle somewhere. He didn't have cancer, he was convinced of that, and he certainly didn't intend to get up on any operating table here. If die he must, he would die at home. The doctor was stunned, deeply offended. Uncertainly he removed his glasses and began to wipe them, the whites of his eyes showing large. Then he collected himself, spat out a venomous rebuttal, jeered at his patient's conviction, turned and left the room.

The engineer got up at once, dressed, packed his suitcases and placed them on the bed, went down the staircase and after a little wandering found a way out through the garage, escaped into the street. That same evening he sent two long telegrams to Israel—one to the Water Company to ask for a replacement, the other to Ruth to announce his return. To Ruth he wired a whole letter, as she did not even know of his transfer to Dar-es-Salaam to begin with. He gave an account of the findings, asked that a bed be made ready for him in hospital, added a long involved love message, and all of it in Hebrew spelled out in Latin script. It cost him eighty dollars, but he did not care. The astonished clerk at the post office, a half-breed, awed by such a large sum, had risen to accompany him to the door, shaken his hand, thanked him warmly, as though the post office were a private business concern. He drifted through the town, found a hotel and took a room. In his clothes, his shoes, without taking off the bedspread, he lay doubled up all night, not moving, not sleeping, freezing with cold. In the morning he returned to the hospital, slipped in with the first shift of Black nurses. He had thought they wouldn't notice him, but he was stopped at the information desk. It turned out that his refusal to get up on the operating table and his subsequent escape at night, which had been discovered when his old African neighbor had died, had raised a scandal. He turned a deaf ear to what they said, to the lecture they wanted to read him. He settled his account, picked up his suitcases. There was nothing now but this longing to go home.

Soon after midday he already had his flight ticket to Israel via Addis Ababa in his wallet. He wired the flight number to Ruth and returned to the Embassy to wait around in one of the corridors, by a table overflowing with old Israeli magazines. He began digging among the pile and presently it began to slide and totter toward him, as if trying to snow him under. Suddenly he remembered that he had seen nothing of the town, actually, that soon he would be leaving Africa for good. He got up, went to deposit his suitcases at the airport and began exploring the town as though in search of something. As it was he took in nothing. When his eye caught a glimmer of the sea, the Indian Ocean beyond the houses, he began walking toward it in a dream, attracted to the beach, dragging his legs among native huts, a mixture of housing-estate boxes, Arabic arches, minarets of new mosques. Here and there he entered a courtyard, absently winding past doors, wrapped in thought, meaning to see "how the other half lives," and leaving again. After a while he gained a following of children, a flock of starlings trailing in his wake. Adults, too, came out to watch him. Someone even approached to ask what he wanted. He did not answer, pushed the man away. The alarm was up. The children were warned away from him and a little gang of young men, a flock of crows, began to follow him. He drew away from the houses, began walking along the shore, near the water line. A dun sea, glazed over with yellow toward nightfall. A light drizzle came down for a few minutes, and then he had also cried a little, an eerie wail forced out of him. The young men closed in on him, peered into his face, made some obscure threat, then left him. He realized at last that he had long left the town behind. Fields stretched around him, and a desert far ahead. He stopped an old lorry driven by a native who for a fee agreed to take him back to civilization, to the airport.

At Addis Ababa there had been a telegram from Ruth: "Expecting you. Hospital bed ready. Chin up." For about half an hour he wandered round the lounge, past booths selling cigarettes and drinks. Suddenly it occurred to him that he hadn't bought any presents to bring back from Africa. He crossed over to one of the counters and bought ten identical statuettes: little figurines of a grave African warrior bearing red-painted shield and sword. Its face looked familiar. Before boarding the plane he still managed to send a postcard to the Dutchman, in English: "Unbelievable, but it seems that I have cancer. I return therefore to my land. Regards to our dam. Yours . . . "

His plane touched down at Lydda Airport at half-past three in the morning. He had not slept a moment during the long flight, had sat with his face pressed to the window among shreds of cloud and summer stars. And at Lydda, dry grass rustling alongside the tarmac. He had been away for nine months.

The airport was completely deserted, only a weary figure moving here and there, a policeman. Ruth and Tamara waved at him from afar. He was surprised to see how Tamara had grown, a whole head. She had grown thinner too, and prettier, and though only fifteen she was as tall as Ruth. Ruth was in slacks, her hair cut short, her eyes behind new glasses. Yes, they were frightened, and unable to hide it. He approached. The customs official did not even turn to him, let him by without a word. They embraced. Actually he did not embrace either of them but pressed them both together against him. And suddenly Tamara burst into tears, a wild ominous wailing that echoed around the empty lounge. A sleepy policeman rose from his seat and ran toward them. It took them a long time to calm Tamara. At last, abruptly, she was quiet, began even to smile through her tears. Meanwhile a porter had picked up his suitcases. He thought there had been some muddle, but it appeared that Ruth had hired him.

An Israeli night, a summer night flooded with moon. The smell of earth which for months had tasted no rain. They walked to the old car and he insisted on driving, even though utterly exhausted after almost forty-eight hours without sleep. Ruth gave in. He drove slowly, more slowly than he ever had. A faint smell of gasoline was seeping through the car, poisonous, intoxicating. Through the windshield the

moon seemed about to drop to the horizon, huge and oppressive, as
on long nights of guard duty, strained to the edge of wakefulness. He
thought of words, prepared himself to come to the point at once. But
Ruth was trying to divert his attention, prevailing upon Tamara to
talk, and the child, sunk into the back seat, at peace now, began a
laborious tale of a play at school in which she had acted an important
part. He did not hear, was intent upon unfamiliar, ill-boding noises
in the engine.

Home. Everything was as he had left it. Though it was after four
now, they did not go to bed, sat around the table to drink tea. Tamara's chatter lapsed into an obscure mumble. Her head drooped. They
sent her to bed, only a child after all. He went into her room to switch
off the light and found her curled up in her blankets, her room as
always in wild disorder, books and papers littering the desk. He bent
to kiss her. She said: "It'll turn out to be nothing, you'll see." But
there was fear in her eyes, and she drew back from him as though
afraid of contagion. Her eyes closed. His heart contracted. His glance
flitted over the books. Her *Young People's Encyclopaedia* lay open at
the entry "Cancer." In the center of the page—enlargements of cell
tissue. He shut the book, extinguished the light.

A quiet Ruth was waiting for him beside a fresh cup of tea. A deep
silence all over. Now he wanted to start and tell her about the hospital,
but she checked him at once. Not now. Tomorrow. If he must talk,
let him talk about something else, about the dam, say. It's nearly five
in the morning. He was quite ready to talk about the dam, was
wonderfully, burningly awake.

At last they went to their room, prepared for bed. A light morning
breeze blew outside. The orange tree stirred beyond the familiar rec-
tangle of the window, laden with shriveled fruit left unpicked during
the winter of his absence. He said: "Tamara has grown tall, pretty."
She said: "She's got suitors already. Once she made me read a note
she got from some Danny or Gaddy. We had such a laugh."

"And you with glasses," he whispered suddenly and collapsed on
the bed.

Mechanically her hand went up to the frame of her spectacles.

"But you love me like this, too?"

He put his arms about her. In spite of his abysmal tiredness he intended to be with her, to make love to her if only to prove himself still alive. But she pushed him away lightly, kissed the top of his head, slipped out of her clothes, put on a nightdress, got into her bed. He tried to insist. Perhaps it was the so-familiar room that had kindled his desire, perhaps her bare feet. At last he let go. Anyway, there had been trouble even before his African journey. And now, after two days without sleep, at five in the morning, before entering hospital? He gave in. She fell asleep at once. He could not sleep. At six he saw the morning at the window. With staring eyes, desperate, he touched his wife: "I'm not sleeping." She woke at once, talking to him with closed eyes: "What's wrong? Pains?"

"Not pains. I can't sleep."

"Your illness?"

"Not just that."

She was silent. Suddenly she sat up, eyes closed, felt for her slippers, went like a sleepwalker to the bathroom, returned with a glass of water and sleeping pills, put them down beside him, fell into bed, curled up and went to sleep. He sipped at the water, left the pills untouched and did not sleep. Light came bursting through the windows, a hot summer day.

Tamara woke at ten. Ruth gave her a note for the teacher: "Dear Sir . . . Tamara's father . . . etc." He was still writhing between the sheets. Only by eleven did the sounds die down, and he fell asleep. He slept like dead for twenty hours. They had to postpone his admission into hospital by a full day.

Again he underwent the same examinations, though this time the pace was a little hurried. Gangs of doctors and nurses kept coming in and out of his room. An Israeli kind of bustle mingled with the hard light. One of the doctors turned out to be an old acquaintance from his war days who kept scoffing at him and his mysterious aches. "What's all this nonsense?" he would grumble and would handle him with pointed irony, as though this whole illness wasn't worth notice. Nevertheless it proved a long affair. They had him in the X-ray room for hours on end, anaesthetized him, put him under radiation, were even obliged to perform a "teeny little" operation. To everyone on the staff, to the doctors and nurses, he would say again and again: "Look, I'm not afraid of the truth. . . ." But they all made light of his illness. Some queer kind of blood poisoning. One doctor spoke of an ancient African disease mentioned in the travel books. Gradually his mind was set at ease. His friends from the Water Company began to come in droves, ply him with flowers. He would recount the whole story, at length, over and over, would curse the African doctor. Cancer, of all things. Why had the fellow taken it into his head that I have cancer? When they gave him permission to smoke he was convinced.

"Of course, no cancer," he wrote from his bed, on a postcard, in simple English, dripping with sweat, one hot afternoon, to the Dutch-man who had stayed by the dam. He left the hospital after a fortnight. Ruth arrived in the afternoon, shuttled back and forth between office rooms for hours, collected a huge parcel of documents, test results, himself and his suitcase.

She was in a great hurry.

Tamara was at her music lesson.

The sudden encounter with the street tumult made him feel weak. He let her drive, sank into the seat beside her, picked up the parcel of documents and began searching through them, silently, feverishly, ripping envelope after envelope, rifling pages and trying to decipher the doctors' wild handwriting; examining X-rays, urine tests, blood tests. At last he gave up, swore loudly that Tamara would have to go and study medicine whether she'd want to or not. From now on he would need an attendant physician. Then he began listening to the engine, fixing his eyes on the world streaming toward them, which Ruth was pushing through with arrogant maneuvers.

"How the hell are you driving?" he fumed. "They ought to've put you behind bars long ago."

But she smiled, and absently rushed through a red light. Pedestrians swore at her.

Not far from home, near a barbershop where he used to go for his haircut, she stopped the car suddenly and bundled him off.

"Get yourself a haircut, my lad. You look like an animal. And with Africa we're finished and done with."

He glanced into the little mirror floating above the wheel. It was true. A huge wild head, hair like a tangle of forest framing a dusky, deep-colored face. Long manes at the back, adding a softness to his eyes. As though he were an artist. All at once he was sorry to part with his hair. Ruth herself continued toward the center of town, hurrying to buy something for supper before the shops closed. At the barbershop he was given a great reception. He told about Nairobi, about the Indian Ocean, about the dam, the Negroes. He had begun to hatch a pattern by now, stock tales, leitmotifs. Meanwhile they cut off his locks. Twice they had to sweep around his chair. They cut his hair short, a crew cut "American fashion," as the proprietor himself assured him. Then, a slight unpleasantness when he wanted to pay and found himself without Israeli currency, not even small change, nothing but a few Kenyan shillings. They all laughed. No problem at all. He could pay next time. He was here for good now, wasn't he?

By the time he left it was already dark outside. Winds blew round his cropped head. He approached and found the house in darkness. Ruth hadn't arrived yet, nor Tamara. He did not yet have a key. He tried breaking in through the back door, but everything was locked. He squatted on the porch step. A smell of new-mown grass came from the neighbor's flower garden. In the street, close by the fence of their own yard, a figure was outlined, a young man, waiting, waiting for Tamara perhaps, moving about nervously. Perhaps belonging to the house across the road, dark as his own.

At last the car appeared, with Ruth. And he, concealed by darkness, immobile, watched the woman laboring under two heavy shopping bags. She gave a start of fright when she came up against him in the dark, on the step. For a moment she failed to recognize him. Then she laughed, dropped the bags at her feet, stroked the stubble on his skull.

"They've mown off your last touch of exoticism." And suddenly she was angry. How can a man let them do such a thing to his head.

The bags yielded an abundance of delicacies. Exquisite cheeses, expensive salami, the best she could lay her extravagant hands on. Except that she had forgotten to buy bread. He helped lay the table, very hungry. They waited a long time for Tamara. At last, tired of waiting, he was going to start by himself when suddenly they heard Tamara's voice floating outside. He went out and saw her sitting on the curb, against a tree, her bicycle sprawled on the road, a guitar beside it, and standing over her the same young male he had seen loitering about before, his arm around the tree now and swaying it gently. From the doorway he whispered: "Tamara?" The boy, startled, said a hasty goodbye. Tamara jumped up, grabbed the guitar, propped her bicycle against the fence and came in. She looked flushed, glowing with excitement.

Before he could reproach her she had burst into loud laughter at the sight of his cropped head. She sat down at the table and began to eat. Ruth made both him and her get up and sent them to wash their hands. In the narrow bathroom, crowded together over the washbasin, he noticed the thin straps of a brassiere outlined through the taut material of her shirt.

"Who's that kid?"

"Kid?"

"I mean, that young fellow."

"Oh, just someone from the play."

"What's his name?"

"What's it matter?"

"Come on . . ."

"Gaddy."

"Gaddy who?"

"You don't know him. He's from the top grade. He's going into the army tomorrow."

The guitar became the topic over supper. He plied her with questions: Why had she switched to guitar all of a sudden, it had been the piano before his trip to Africa, hadn't it? Since when does one learn to play the guitar? What's there to *learn* about it anyway?

What does he mean! Half the class is taking guitar lessons.

Following which, Tamara gave him a lecture, all about the guitar, and toward the end of the meal she even jumped up from her chair to strum out a little tune, which went nowhere near proving any of her profound theories. For all that, he was pleased to sit and sip coffee while his daughter, in her school uniform, eyes sparkling, sat playing for him. They exchanged some banter. Ruth was quiet, withdrawn, a little sad. The unfamiliar glint of her glasses. She was fetching plates, clearing them away. At last, since she planned to go to Jerusalem the following morning for a long day at the university, she shut herself up in the kitchen to cook a chicken for them both. Tamara suddenly remembered her homework and made a dash for her room. He sank into an armchair for another go at the documents, this time with the help of a foreign dictionary. He came up with a blank, or with plain absurdities.

At half-past eleven they went to bed. He took off his clothes, and a sharp hospital smell rose from his bare body, fumes of ether or iodine or something. He lay down naked on the bed, waiting to show Ruth his new scar, relic of the "teeny" operation. When she still did not come he picked up a newspaper, skimmed its pages, grew tired, sleepy. At last Ruth came, saw the scar, undressed, put on a night-dress, glanced through the paper trailing over the bed. He put on pajamas, Ruth extinguished the light. Everything was so much as usual, it never occurred to him that once again he would be unable to fall asleep, till half-past two, desperate in the dark house, wandering about softly, watching Tamara and Ruth who were sleeping like dead, very much alike in their sleep. He heard crickets, babies crying, the sound of distant cars. In the sky before his eyes a giant moon was born, faint with its own radiance. He did not dare wake Ruth again. This is ridiculous, I'm going to fall asleep any moment now, he said aloud and turned over and over in bed.

When he woke up it was past ten, and he had wakened into a house filled with midmorning silence, into a hot day. Naked he paces through the house, enters each room and closes shutters and windows against the heat. By every mirror he lingers to examine himself, and where there is no mirror he searches for his image in windowpanes. His hair has grown, little by little he is returning to his self of three weeks ago. He brushes his teeth lazily, enters a sun-drenched kitchen and tumbles straight into the chaos left by his daughter. The butter is melting on the table, the milk going sour in the heat, the door of the refrigerator isn't shut properly, jam is dripping over a dry slice of bread, a piece of nibbled cheese on top of a load of dirty dishes—it's as though a band of hoodlums had had their breakfast here instead of one thin, straggly child. The dishes include a whole series of plates, sieves and spoons with which she has tried to get rid of the skin on her milk—in vain. Squeezed between the dishes there is a page covered with figures and formulas, a last-minute attempt at cramming for a test in mathematics set for today. He puts the kettle to boil, moves the entire pile of dirty dishes to the sink and starts chewing at the slice of bread left by her. He eats slowly, without relish, slumped in his chair, sighing once, suddenly. Bread crumbs collect in the tangle of hair on his chest.

Silence. He telephones, in the shuttered half-dark, naked, to the Water Company offices. Once every three or four days he gives them a call. He is passed on from one secretary to another. He is looking for a certain department head who has promised him an answer concerning a new assignment. The fellow isn't there. He talks, therefore, to the secretary, who inquires first of all after his health. He informs her that everything is fine, asks what has been concluded. She goes in search of the file. A long time. The receiver, meanwhile, spills voices, giggles, telephones ringing. Back comes the secretary armed with the file, and she announces that he has been granted additional sick leave. Another two months.

He does not understand, is smitten. Additional sick leave? What for?

She doesn't know, of course. She will ask her boss. There's a shortage of work, maybe it's that. Anyway, the boss'll be back, as she said, in a week.

They chat. She is full of patience (if she knew that he is in the dark, completely naked). He questions her about his replacement in Africa, a young engineer whom he doesn't know. Has he written them yet?

"Sure. He's been sending picture postcards to everyone in the office."

"What does he say?"

"He's having a high time."

"A high time," His heart contracts. "Meaning what?"

"He likes it awfully there. Raves about the scenery. He's been driving around a lot, writes about interesting little villages, about folklore. The other day someone at the office even said: 'What the hell? Did we send them an engineer or did we send them a poet?' "

He laughs, bubbles over with laughter: a poet . . . great . . . "And the dam?"

"The dam . . . " She considers. "The dam's all right, I guess. But it's not going to be finished in a hurry. They've already written to us from the Kenyan Labor Department, asking to renew the contract. They've plans to extend the dam to another river."

He is aroused.

"Another river? Which one?"

"Don't know . . . I know nothing about this kind of thing."

"The one south?"

"Dunno."

Suddenly his voice breaks.

"Sorry to be such a nuisance. But you know, don't you? About this muddle. Such a horribly stupid thing. I was supposed to stay on there."

Yes, she has heard all about it. Those doctors. And what a way to tell a man just like that, right in his face: You got cancer.

"Especially when one hasn't," he cuts in with a hoarse laugh.

"Sure. Specially when one hasn't," she seizes at his words, agitated, her voice shrill. A dowdy little secretary. He remembers her.

And suddenly she has lost her patience. Someone has burst into the room over there, a door is slammed, A concrete mixer trembles, a shout comes.

"Excuse me, I've somebody here now."

"Just, please, don't forget about this job . . . this leave . . ."

"Sure, I won't forget. Just let my boss come back . . . first thing. . . ."

"Me too, I'll look in at the office again one of these days."

"Why bother in this heat."

"I don't mind."

Then again he is pacing softly, barefoot, like a giant cat. Goes to Tamara's room, takes the guitar out of a corner, strips it of its sheath, sinks down on the bed and starts plucking single notes.

A guitar—a folly, a dull affair. What, after all, can he play, slowly, haltingly, groping for every note: a children's song, the national anthem, an old dirge? After five or ten minutes he would grow bored, abandon the guitar and go in pursuit of fresh occupations. During the first days after his return from hospital he would rummage through drawers, spy into everything. He reread all the letters he had sent from Africa, inspected the blurred snapshots. After that he started to ransack bundles of old letters: his own letters from the war, before their marriage, his queer confessions of love, his passionate, clamorous wooing of a hesitant Ruth. Letters written her by others in the same period. Numerous letters from girl friends; involved, facetious styles and tiny script. Among them, a whole collection of poems composed by a girl who had obviously been in love with Ruth.

Apart from all these—documents. Ruth's school reports by the dozen, her military insignia (she had been an officer), their marriage contract, her birth certificate, Tamara's (where's his?), the title deed to their house. Every scrap of paper connected with her past was deposited here. He meant to tidy up, wondered what he could destroy.

After long deliberations he threw away the envelopes. Strange, these mornings suffused with drowsiness and heat. He would wake between ten and eleven in a house invaded by a hard sun, the windows wide open. At once he would stuff up every crack, attack each ray of light. Then he would wander naked through the illusory darkness, lone among beds, chairs, illustrated magazines. Odd, this silence, new to him. The house without Ruth. It's as though they weren't living together anyway. Four days a week she will make the trip to Jerusalem, spend the day at the university from morning till night, between lectures and reading rooms. A not-so-young woman moving among the young. In the two days left she goes looking for work, solicits from office to office. Apart from that—her shopping. In the evenings—in the kitchen or studying for her exams. And on the Sabbath, after washing her underwear, she suddenly discovers the abysmal depths of her fatigue, collects newspapers into a pile, sinks into them, drowses on the couch, or in the sun, prostrate on the little square of lawn left in their yard. Her body exposed, naked almost, greased with lotion, not wearing her glasses and hence dizzied, squinting, a small transistor radio playing between her legs. For hours and hours. There is no knowing whether she is conscious or not. Once in a while she exchanges a few words with her old, silent parents who come to see them regularly every Saturday, sitting very still on the balcony and awaiting the favors of Tamara, who would on Saturdays run to particularly giddy moods, tearing like a whirlwind through the house, making endless telephone calls, seeming to rally whole crowds to meetings.

And just on these Saturdays, amid this unaccustomed stir, he would find himself full of animation. He would come up with schemes, would suggest going to the beach, to the woods, to Eilat, Jerusalem, to the Syrian border. In vain would he appeal to the glistening limbs, the slim, somewhat boyish but already deeply furrowed body. His wife swooning fervently under a heavy sun.

After her parents have left he flings himself down by her, silences the radio, tries to sleep by her side. But he ends up studying her at length, he passes his hand over her hair, tries to rouse her with new ideas that he whispers at her: for instance, that they have another child together.

Then she murmurs:

She knows. It's Saturday. But he can see for himself, she is dead tired. And a merciless week is ahead. Yes, a crazy spell. Just let her get through with her studies and the exams, and then they will go not just to the Syrian border but beyond it. For the time being, why doesn't he go to see friends? Where are all his friends? Pity that he's neglected friendship . . .

They have not made love, not since his return.

Then she apologizes:

True, he is right, impossible to go on like this. But he hasn't quite recovered yet, has he? And she, oh well, he can see, ready to drop. He's right. It's wrong. There's no excuse. It's all evasions. What's to be done? And if he were to pretend he isn't back yet? He came back by mistake, didn't he? What would he have done if he'd stayed on in Africa?

And at night, she gropes for his head, she kisses his eyes, tries to take him in her arms and gradually falls asleep, and he still responding.

Those mornings of drowsiness and heat. His new solitude, his superfluous thoughts. The feverish hunt for spots on his skin. Above all, the deep hush reigning in their street. It is a marvel to him. No children's voices, not a human being. Now and then the sound of a car caught up in a traffic jam. Such mornings he seems to be the only one left. In sudden agony he slips on some light clothes and goes out to wander among the small semi-detached houses, along hedges, avoiding the battering sun as much as possible. Cats peer at him out of bushes, follow his movements anxiously as though he were an actor tramping a bare stage, against a backdrop painted for sky.

He escapes to the small orange grove that seals the street; it is all that is left of the vast plantation that used to cover this whole area. And there, between rows of trees choking off light, he drifts through a warm green haze, from shadow to shadow. At last he seats himself on an upturned crate, near a puddle fed from a dripping tap. With a dry twig he starts scratching at the loose soil, carves a little ditch, diverts the water to a slope, directs it to a basin, casts in pebbles and builds a dam. Then he rigs up a bridge of leaves. He rises, wipes it all out with his shoe and clears off through an old gap in the fence.

By the letter box in front of his house he lingers, looks at his watch, opens the box, closes it. Since his return from hospital he has begun loitering by the letterbox. Here, every day toward noon, he intercepts letters addressed to Tamara. That kid, youngster, soldier, that Gaddy, is apparently falling in love with the child. And in his torment, his longing, his hope, he sends her a letter a day.

The child: yes. Grown slimmer, taller, prettier, learned to play the guitar: but she has also become independent, breaking loose, slipping his authority.

She would return from school at irregular hours. Sometimes he would wait till four in the afternoon. When she appears she is always "dead beat," flushed and excited for obscure reasons. She drops her schoolbag at the door as though it were beyond her strength to carry it another yard, slips out of her sandals and leaves them beside it, and barefoot, blindly, she makes her way to the refrigerator, clasps the cold-drink bottles. Then she attacks the morning paper. Meanwhile he warms up dinner, which as a rule will not be to her liking. She picks a bit here and there, chews listlessly, leaves the main dish untouched, pronounces herself not hungry, and makes a dash for the telephone to talk to girl friends she has just now parted from. Breathless whispers, giggles, veiled confessions, inanities.

If she happens to have a guitar lesson she shuts herself up in her room, practices for about half an hour, then vanishes with her bicycle.

If she doesn't have a lesson she takes off her school uniform, puts on a light blouse and briefest of shorts, spreads herself on the couch and plunges into illustrated magazines or a love story. When he talks to her she replies in grunts.

Only when the sky begins to fade a little does she betake herself to find out what homework there is to be done. She drags the schoolbag to her room as though it were a heavy cross, heaps a plate with grapes or cherries, spreads all her books and copybooks across the eternal confusion of her desk, starts losing things, despairs.

She calms down for a while, till all of a sudden she discovers that actually she doesn't know what the teachers want of her. Back to the telephone, long discussions, clarifications.

She comes back, sits still awhile, and now she gets up to buy a new exercise book. Not a day has passed since his return from hospital that she did not need a new exercise book. She takes some change from the pile on the cupboard (the last of his African salary) and returns after a long absence, laden with good things: bars of chocolate, sweets, two dripping ice-cream cones, an evening paper. Sometimes the one thing she would forget to buy would be the exercise book.

She would make him join her "party," eat the ice cream, share the chocolate with her, nibble the sweets. Afterward they would both get absorbed in the evening paper, wordlessly swapping pages.

The hard light would break.

The sky would lose its color.

Suddenly, without reason, she would be gripped with anxiety, would fling down the paper, fly to her room.

She would always embark on her English lessons first; one hand plucking grapes, and in shouts across the whole house she would dump obscure words in his lap, demanding explanations. Words from poems by Byron, Wordsworth, Shelley, words from tragedies by Shakespeare: names of plants, clouds, subtleties of light, distant scenery, castles and English lords.

Words of whose meaning he had no idea.

He would try evasion, would ask to hear the full sentence, then the word spelled out, and all of it in loud cries, shouts trumpeted across the rooms. At last he would jump up, go to her room, bend over the open book, glance at the difficult word, read whole verses of the poem, consult the poet's biography, study his portrait, scratch his head and offer assumptions that would at once be proved wrong. Extremely annoyed at being shown up in his weakness, he would counter-attack.

Well, what the hell are dictionaries for?

But the dictionary reduces Tamara to gloom.

In the end she hangs her arms around his neck, implores him, pleads for her life, cajoles, heaps words on him, sits him on her bed, brings him a newspaper, settles a pillow behind his head, presses grapes on him, invites him to take more chocolate. Finally she lays the dictionary on his chest.

He shall do the looking up for her.

Well, has he anything better to do?

Idler that he is.

Outside the sun is beginning to set.

The poems one and all seem to be nothing but a string of hard words. He curses the poets. At slack intervals he will delve into other textbooks, read a bit about Africa in her geography (what do they know about Kenya?), leaf through biology books, study the human body.

Sometimes the telephone rings and Tamara leaves him for a long time, and only his threat that he will abandon the dictionary there and then will bring her back. Occasionally, girl friends come to see her. Two fat girls materializing suddenly on the threshold of the room, having crept in softly, without ringing, through the open doors. They would find him sprawling on the bed, the dictionary lowered on his belly, books scattered about him, the evening paper fluttering around his head. The pair of them, acutely embarrassed, would greet him, inquire nervously after his health. He knew already that on the day his African wire had arrived Tamara had wept in school, had moreover informed the teacher and the entire class of the exact diagnosis. This had brought on a storm of emotion. Everyone had wished to share her grief. During recess, in a corner of the playground, bosom friends had huddled around to weep with her.

Perhaps these very girls had wept for him, and he watches motionless how the two gather the hems of their skirts, sit down nearby, fix their eyes on the floor in a silent, polite stare.

He, his chest naked, bare feet stuck out in front of him and planted on the window ledge, smiles at them.

He would wonder if Tamara had taken the trouble to say that the whole thing had been a mistake.

Through the open window, leaves are trembling in the warm twilight breeze. The edges of the curtain glow a soft pink. He remembers the dam near Nairobi, chokes with the misery, the longing. He thinks of the Africans, smiles secretly to himself. Hadn't thousands swarmed around him there, foremen followed him about?

Tamara does not mind his staying among them, listening from her bed to their conversation. The two girls, though, are ill at ease, but eventually they recover, forget his existence and open out, telling stories, cursing the teachers, gossiping about the boys: first about the boys in their class, then about strange boys, young men from the upper grades, from other schools. He listens with half an ear, grows bored. His eyes close, he nods a little, emits a light snore. Out of the corner of his eye he discovers his feet wandering away from him, sticking high into the heart of the darkening sky.

Occasionally he ventures to join in the conversation. Feebly he defends the teachers.

Tamara shakes with laughter, while the girls turn to him and, very politely, backing up one another, prove to him how wrong he is. It's a fact: all teachers are bastards.

At last he gets up and goes to the balcony to wait for Ruth. The English gets done somehow, followed by the rest of the homework. Afterward—supper, chitchat, idling around. He would be waiting for his hour to strike, the hour of maths—Tamara's weakest subject. Such blatant ignorance! Apparently the many rehearsals for the famous school play had regularly been held during the mathematics hour, and Ruth, ever absent, had let matters slide. Tamara hadn't a notion. She was already called upon to solve equations of three unknown factors, but wasn't even able to divide fractions. It had therefore been decided, without the least spark of zeal on Tamara's part, that each night before going to bed they would sit down together to work out problems.

She would try to wriggle out of it in a hundred ways, put off this hour until far into the evening. When at last he would be called to her room, after all the other homework had been done, at the close of a hot day, he would find her dull, listless, unable to concentrate, her head nodding. Her room would be a shambles, her desk littered with books and exercise books, crumpled pages, chocolate wrappers, the skeleton of a bunch of grapes; the statuette of the brave African warrior toppled from its base. Through the open window the blind stirrings of night, pierced by hot stars.

He would fetch a second lamp from the living room, place another chair by hers, attach the wires, cast a strong light, pull out white pages, ruler and compasses, and be set for battle. And she, barefoot, light, brittle, huddling between her frail shoulders, nervously biting her pen and already in despair, shrouding herself in a fog of stupidity.

Those hours would become an endless source of wrangles between them. In no time he will have lost his temper, started scoffing, despising her; and she, put in the wrong, defiant, catty, beginning to argue about every figure. Presently they will have worked up a bitter hostility between them.

It sometimes happens that the lesson ends with Tamara in a fit of sobbing; and Ruth, exhausted after a hard day, rushes to part them.

She's just a baby, he would think, pacing in the garden on hot nights, round and round between trees, car, hedge and strip of lawn; watching the lights go out one by one in the little houses, in his own house. And as though the telephone calls, the girl friends, the chocolate and the newspapers weren't enough, there still would be clamoring for her, here in the letter box, day after day, love letters. If he did not dam their tide, they would flood her altogether.

And, anyway, she would never have been able to decipher Gaddy's handwriting, the words, the dreams, the lovesick harangues. Yes, and she would have gone and bothered Ruth with the letters yet, asked for advice. And at night she would have sat and composed replies, prepared envelopes, licked stamps; and perhaps fallen in love herself, in a fit of absent-mindedness. . . .

And he, here alone, racked, drifting under a sultry fan. He would run his eyes over Gaddy's letters cursorily, standing there, right by the letter box, exposed to the sun. Then he would fold them and stow them away in the car's toolbox. Never did the letters cross the doorstep. Nights when he could not sleep he would sometimes go out to the car, and there, by the light of a small electric torch, would leaf through the letters again. The pages were getting shuffled, the days confused. For the youngster, in love as he obviously was, would write to Tamara every single day.

He had opened the first letter by mistake. Home a few days from hospital, still new to the morning hush, wrung by the dry desert heat. Between a telephone bill and a municipal bulletin there had been an envelope with a military postmark. He had torn open the envelope, slid out the pages, run his eyes over the writing, unable to make anything of it, and then he had discovered that the letter was addressed to Tamara and had wished to return it to its envelope at once. But upset about the torn envelope, he had folded up the lot and thrust it into his pocket. He had meant to hand the whole thing over to Ruth, except that she had returned near midnight, and by then he had forgotten all about it. At night, when he remembered, she had been asleep. He had got up, read the letter and wanted to destroy it at once, then decided to stow it in the car. And what if the letter had got lost? Such a letter would only have made Tamara laugh anyway.

Gaddy himself had written:

You may be surprised getting a letter from me. It'll probably make you laugh.

That talk by the fence that your father interrupted.

Of course, you may not answer.

Me, I shall go on writing.

Actually your silence makes it easier for me.

And so, day after day, he would be sending letters and the father would entrap them all, towards noon of each hushed morning.

At first he had found it difficult to decipher the handwriting, since Gaddy wrote mostly in the field, in the short breaks between drill periods, on his pack or his helmet, by the light of sunsets, moonshine or perhaps by the stars alone. Soon he grew accustomed to the cramped, crooked writing, read it with a practiced eye and even picked out a few spelling mistakes here and there, when the training got tough.

The pretext for the letters—that play in which they both had appeared and whose rehearsals, coinciding with the mathematics hour, had drawn them so close. What play had they put on, anyway? Tamara had mumbled something on his first night back, on the ride from the airport. He had not caught the name of the show. He must ask her again.

Apparently she had been the true love of a brave underground hero who throws himself under the wheels of a train he has dynamited. Quite a daft story no doubt, seeing that Tamara could not even recall the author's name.

But Gaddy would sing paeans to the play:

Little is left of our play; nevertheless at night, in my tent, I repeat parts to myself; mine, yours, others. Something has caught in me and will not be resolved.

At times he would even sit down and quote whole passages, in order to arouse her memories.

"Run to the river and wait for me there, by the big dam. Don't open fire any of you. . . . Be very still. . . . Hold back . . . I alone shall wait here for the train. You too, my beloved. Go with them. Do you hear me? That's an order! Leave me by myself."

He asked Tamara to let him see the full text. It turned out that, careless child, she had thrown it away after having learned her own lines by heart.

Apart from that, Gaddy would write at length about camp, tedious accounts of his tentmates, conjectures to the ounce about the weight of the equipment laden on his back, complaints about his shoulder bruised by the recoil of the rifle butt. The smell of brushwood. His denunciations of the platoon commander, stray reflections, words.

As though he were writing himself a diary.

Just out of high school and still reluctant to part with his pen, Gaddy.

From time to time he will hint at her silence, but forebearingly, without taking offense. Figuring that the little girl needs time to digest his ideas. Sometimes he would be blaming himself, in his despair. "I am boring you," he would write again and again on the small military pages smelling of rifle oil. For all that he would not stem the flow of his words, would still add his reflections about death, as though he were wandering behind enemy lines and not in a rifle range set among orange-grove country. "What, after all, is so fearful about death?" he would write with the matter-of-fact simplicity of the soldier-savant, wishing at any price to soften the heart of a girl who has never even received his letters.

In one of the letters he suddenly remembered to inquire after her father, ask about his illness. Hoping, he wrote, that he had not been made to enter hospital again.

That same evening, at supper, he put her through a cross-examination. Ruth followed it with amazement.

What had gone on at the play? What had her part been exactly? How much had she been onstage? Just in what way had she been involved?

It turned out that in one scene she had been embraced, had even had to be kissed.

He was stunned.

How had it gone?

Ruth intervened, said that, as far as she was concerned, the scene had been perfectly natural, a mark of the director's talent. Tamara on her part blushed a deep red; her pupils dilated, she told with an uncertain smile about a big ado at rehearsals, about the others' glee. She herself hadn't been able to control herself either, would burst into laughter right in his face.

"And how did Gaddy manage?"

A hush followed this outright mention of the name. Even Ruth was taken aback. Does he know him, demanded Tamara tensely, very flustered.

He is surprised: She's talking about him all the time, isn't she?

"Me? . . ." Tamara wonders at herself, and gradually she calms down.

And after a brief silence:

"Oh, he was quite all right. So serious always."

Just so, his seriousness, that's what's frightening. Each day at noon he resolves to destroy the passionate letters, but by evening he has changed his mind again. In another few years Tamara will be older, he'll let her read them. To make her laugh.

Sheer nonsense, the whole affair. He is wandering around, at a loose end all day, else would it ever have occurred to him to waste time over it? And so he spends his white nights huddled in his car, huddled over the letters. There is quite a pile of them by now.

The boy is in love, after all, lonely. All these words of his are a kind of fraud, though not a big one. If Gaddy knew that only I read his letters, he thinks, and he is sick at heart.

With the temperature soaring, the sky swept bare of clouds, the air solid with the intensity of the light, the impact of the letters grew worse. And the letters themselves, filled with despair, sadness, grew shorter and shorter.

"Nothing is left of our play," he would write, a soldier baking on a hill in the Negev sands.

And suddenly the letters stopped.

Though he felt certain that the kid hadn't got himself shot on maneuvers, he grew restless. Besieging the letter box, pursuing the postman.

A number of days now.

His much-blighted car, his crippled steed, overheating, gasping uphill, drowsing in the morning. Even on that first drive home from the airport, in the stillness of the night, by Ruth's side, he had realized that the car was on its last legs. Ominous throbs in the gearbox, creaks in the clutch, rattles in the engine.

Ruth's verdict: sell it, get rid of it fast.

He said: fix it. There's still hope. Why be left without a car? Look, he'd fix it himself.

After his return from hospital he had appropriated the car from Ruth. And each blue sun-charged morning he puts on some old rags, approaches the silent car, throws open door and bonnet and worms his way in between the wheels. However he lacks the tools.

Every few days, therefore, he descends on the garage to look for what he needs. The people there put up with him patiently. Hadn't he bought the car at this very garage?

And though many years have passed since, he still repeats to them with half a smile: It's you who are responsible.

He appears just before the noon break, when all eyes are down, faces averted from the harsh sun. Softly he edges the car in, parks it in the yard, out of the way; walks leisurely into the dim garage like a man with all the time in the world. He saunters among the mechanics, from pit to pit, watches the work in progress, bends over a stripped engine here and there, collecting gear as he goes. Back to the car in a wide arc, and with harsh jerks he disconnects, say, the whole electric system, hauls it over to a dark corner and takes it apart.

Moving among them, he is quite at home. The workers are tolerant with him. The boss himself, a veteran mechanic always under pressure of distant business and rarely to be found on the premises, had come over to him on one of the first days for a cordial handshake, had even received a little story from East Africa. Since then he has given him the run of the garage.

From time to time, reaching a dead end, he will talk one of the mechanics into coming to listen to the engine, step on the pedals, turn switches. They will say whatever they say, invariably adding that the car is going to pieces anyway, better get rid of it.

And he, stung, will retort that indeed, that much he knows himself. How much would he get for her, by the way? He is taken aback by the low figure.

For the time being he isn't losing money, inasmuch as these wanderings through the garage don't cost him anything. Only rarely does he pay a few pennies for a screw or a little tube. Sometimes, in the noon break, when the garage is empty, he may coax one of the apprentices to stay behind, and together, in the still garage, they hoist the car up on a winch and investigate its underside.

The boy will always be eager to give his opinion, trying to figure as an expert. And he listens without a word. In these peaceful hours he would sometimes contrive to get to the heart of the engine, to the cold twisted steel. Finally he began to renounce even the boy's services. He would arrive exactly at breaktime, tie a gray apron around his middle and fall to work. A great plan was taking shape in his mind: to take the whole car apart and put it together again.

But today, in the silent garage, with him crouching greasily in a corner, fussing over a tiny screw, a heavy hand suddenly grips him and there is the boss in person, quiet, easy, at leisure, giving his shoulder a fatherly squeeze, asking gently:

"Trouble?"

And the engineer gives a sad nod, lets go of the tools in his hand. To his great surprise the boss offers to take him out for a run in the car so that he can sound her out himself.

The boss at the wheel, he by his side, they set out at snail's pace, the mechanic steering with one hand, with the greatest of ease, as though he were driving a toy. He had expected them to take a turn around the block and back, but apparently the boss has a longer drive in mind, makes for the highway, lunges through the burning noon hour, in the very face of the sun, aiming for the sea. At first they both keep silent, intent on the engine. Then the boss begins to talk. He is speaking of Ruth:

"She's basically sound. After all, I've seen older cars than this one keep going. But when a car gets to be this age she takes on a personality of her own. She gets capricious, has whims. Say, one of the gears will get obstinate, will have to be shifted just so, with a certain twist, say. Well, that's not so terrible, the driver must just be a bit gentler, a bit more patient. Being an engineer, you know what I mean. But your wife, let me tell you, she took this car while you were away and drove it like it was, oh, the latest model Jag or something. Hell for leather she rode it. Look, I'm sorry, I'm not talking of the pedestrians, that's not my affair. But the car suffers. She would slam her foot down on the accelerator in one go, and so hard as to bust the whole car up. About once a fortnight we'd have to clean the carburetor for her, and then she'd still put the blame on my lads. I myself, with my own hands, took hold of her foot and laid it down the way it should be. I even took her shoe off and joined her bare foot to the pedal so she'd feel the proper motion. Nothing doing. A question of reflexes, that's what it is. And me, I have no patience with women. The more so as she didn't seem to get my intention. She would keep arguing with me, like all of them. Hasn't the faintest grasp of machinery. Doesn't even know how to change a wheel, your wife doesn't. Sorry, I don't want to speak ill. . . ."

"No, that's all right, go on."

"You see, every fortnight or so she'd bring the car in for repairs. I'm not thinking of the expense, that's your affair. But the nuisance, the phone calls, the times she got stuck. And it wasn't always the car's fault either. The craziest things would happen to her. The clutch'd get jammed, wouldn't disengage, particularly in winter, on cold days. Time and again I'd have to send someone after her to get her out. At nights I'd go myself and tow her. Look we even scratched my private phone number here on the wheel . . . so she'd remember."

He looks, and there it is. Tiny figures scored into the steering wheel. All at once his heart swells with pain.

"Didn't she tell you? Must have been ashamed. Yes, some nights, right in the middle of the night she'd call for me."

"In the middle of the night?" he whispers, stunned, his eyes on the sea that has suddenly appeared in front of them.

"One time she called me to fetch her at two in the morning, on the Jerusalem highway. I found her by the roadside, shivering in the car. Wouldn't turn to anyone else at such an hour. I trust no one but you, she said. Thank you very much, I said, and towed her to the garage, and then I had to take her home still. Those weeks I never went to bed without checking the fuel in my tank. In a state of alert, I used to be . . . ha-ha, up in arms. All it lacked was for me to sleep in my clothes . . . ha-ha, in my shoes . . . ha-ha-ha. I said to my wife: Right here's the reason I'll never let you drive. So you won't get like her.''

His heart beating hard. Drops of sweat blinding his eyes. His head swimming. Suddenly his old pains seem to well up in him.

The sight of the calm sea, blue and pretty, drives him mad, makes him sick.

He smiles.

The boss, utterly serene, cruises down a deserted side road alongside the beach, like a youngster delighting in his first turn behind the wheel. All of a sudden he swerves the car and takes a steep dive, down a slope and straight on to the sea, drives along the beach, very close to the water line. He is driving in zigzags, pulling the wheel from side to side in a slow dizzying roll. Meanwhile he chatters on, drivel about other women, other cars giving him trouble. At last, by way of finale, he points the car with its nose to the sea, makes headlong for the waves, stops, makes a wide U turn. Back up the steep slope and the car is screaming with the strain, strange high wails, and nevertheless she obeys the quiet unperturbed mechanic, makes the climb in a single rush. Then they are on the road once more. The way back seems short, suddenly.

The mechanic falls silent, thoughtful, increases speed a little to cut the time short.

The engineer sits and stares into the sweltering air that is making the road wave and contort.

He has calmed down already.

He even considers speaking about Africa.

Furtively he draws a few sheets of Gaddy's letters from the toolbox under his seat, glancing over familiar lines. By the time they arrive at the garage the work there is in full swing, workers and clients milling through the yard. The boss parks the car at the entrance, goes out without a word and beckons to one of the apprentices. He orders him to tighten one nut in the engine, turns to the engineer, gives him a little absent smile.

"Well, you've seen for yourself. Nothing wrong with the car, is there? That's what I always say: it depends who's driving her. . . . Leave her alone. Better not take her apart every day. She'll do fine. Just keep your wife away from her."

And suddenly he extends a hand, shakes his to indicate a final goodbye, disappears into the garage. And left there, stunned, the engineer hasn't even managed to thank him.

Translated by Miriam Arad

Natan Shacham

Coming Home

I must have been sunk in dreams. Dazedly, I felt my neighbor tap me on the shoulder.

"He means you," he said, pointing behind him with his thumb.

I looked at him. My glance must have been vague and uncertain for he smiled at me mildly and explained:

"He, the driver."

At that moment everything became clear to me. The bus had stopped, the driver was waving to me and all the passengers were looking back at me with impatience, while I was sunk in dreams.

"You get off here," the driver called to me with annoyance.

It was true. I was surprised at myself. We were standing on the road to Valley Gate and I had not realized it. I hastened to get out, dividing up the extent of my confusion into the detailed attentions which I devoted to my belongings.

"Go straight ahead on the road in front of you. From the hill in front of you, you will see Valley Gate. Better hurry before it gets dark. Otherwise you're apt to get lost on the way," the driver called after me politely.

Even though I am extremely fond of polite ways and you can always win me with politeness I felt angry at him. Who was he to come and teach *me* how to reach Valley Gate? Did I seem as foreign to this landscape as all that? Could the few years which I spent in Europe have blurred the characteristic marks of a product of Valley Gate? And I had been thinking that the clothes I was wearing, so distinctly European, made me look like "a cat in a turban." In general, I had always thought that my face revealed whatever there was about me that I failed to proclaim for fear of being thought arrogant. And I had always thought that my face and my way of speaking enabled me, from the beginning, to behave with people as I do, for they always compliment me, from the beginning, for whatever a person of my kind might have said or thought in the past. And whenever someone comes along and makes some mistake concerning my background or age, I realize my mistake and the fact that, at first, in any case, I have no choice but to behave with people as they expect me to, and to avoid all those manners which well-behaved young girls call "unsuited to you." This is the only way in which I can explain the inexplicable gloom that descended on me when the driver gave me instructions, as if for a child, on how to get to Valley Gate. This gloom, having planted itself in a damp and suitable place, began striking roots. I flung a part of it to the evening wind and broke the other part up into memories.

Every square foot here was as laden with memories as two grandmothers. And I was a very young man, in the bloom of youth, straight-backed and somewhat amazed at myself. I had, it was true, lived in Europe for some years, had treated myself with some respect, acquired the marks of sobriety and pride; I had managed to learn the art of scorning anything beyond my immediate reach; I had acquired the faculty of being pleased with what is useful; but whenever I returned to this landscape I felt as though I was still the helpless boy whose work-tools seemed to laugh at him, abusing his untoughened hands. But this kindness of youth which I felt for the landscape seemed to be one-sided. It had not kept faith with me. It had made several changes in its appearance, having crowned itself with orchards and lawns, multicolored with various sorts of green, and having grown a small forest on its crown, with roads cut into its tangled heart and a new settlement on one shoulder, with well-spring eyes in its forehead, so that it could contemplate all the fair doings around it with joy.

Nevertheless, the patient, compassionate countenance which it showed in the evening, the tender coolness which used to have such an effect on the complicated mechanism in my chest, the serenely tired

redness of the color spread over its hills, and the luminous and lovely
confidence which rose out of the east even before the west had sunk
its head, all this still remained and dwelt here. Remained and dwelt
here so much that I felt as nothing before them. I ceased to be that
same complete and finished, self-loving thing; instead, I seemed to be
a confused bundle of memories and place-marks seeking to find a
motto for itself before it is bound away in leather stamped with gold.
I felt that I had to arrange this confusion in my soul according to an
order which I could call beautiful. But this uncorruptible landscape
which revealed to me both those stretches of land which spoke in
praise of me and those which shamed me did not let me have my way.
This stretch of land did not allow me to build myself an imaginary
world out my own self-indulgent vanity. It insisted on revealing things
as they were. Before me were the eye-witnesses and the ear-witnesses
and the whole *corpus delicti* of my follies. The hedge which I had
destroyed by driving into it five years ago was still shorn and forsaken,
demanding satisfaction, and everyone who passed, coming or going,
cursed my recklessness. I have mentioned the hedge in order not to
mention worse things.

As I remembered my follies I fell into an unreasoning confusion
again and felt as though the ground were slipping from under my feet.
I wondered how old I would have to be in order to rid myself of this
confusion which knifed me in the back whenever my mind was unoc-
cupied. I felt as though it had mounted on my back and weighed on
my shoulders like a heavy load. I slowed up my pace.

How would the friends whom I had left years ago receive me? What
would I say to them and what would they say to me? Doubtless
something of the same kind had grown up inside them. What I saw
in myself I called development, but what I saw in them, dropping
upon them suddenly in this way, I called change. Where once the flap
of a tent waved in the wind, revealing secrets, a cement wall, no doubt,
would stand today; and where once there was a window, there was
probably a thicket; and where once a field full of ears of corn stood,
as if at prayer, today the fat and well-fed minnows were swimming;

and if they did build a fast cement road, it meant that the friendly walks of old, under a pensive moon were over.

I remembered a letter which I had written to my comrades. This was my last letter. I saw the letter standing before me and each word in it passed in front of me to my great dismay, for I feared that it was too full of friendliness in a way that was not suited to my comrades and, hence, not suited to me. I am fond of friendly talk. But if one says too much, one is a babbler. I respect the gift of speech too much to allow myself any babbling. This is my way of thinking; those who think otherwise are from the beginning doomed not to be my friends. And if they don't care, I certainly don't.

I had written:

Dear comrades,

(Who the devil led me into using that accursed word? So I thought at the beginning, but then I remembered that silent, cold, foreign night and the snow that fell and pressed directly onto my heart beneath three suits of clothes and two coats despite the miserable fire I had burning in a stove, and the tremendous loneliness that overcame me suddenly as I parted from the wonderful woman who had helped me in my work. That whole dim frozen experience itself demanded precisely that word, that word and no other. "Dear" I wrote, and my hand did not mock my thought, and no wretched little devil sat in my brain to remind me of so-and-so's stupidity or so-and-so's coarseness and the other things that can embarrass the heart's language and make you hate everyone and yourself.)

"Here, in this valley of fir-trees, with its snow-clad mountains and the strong fortress standing above it like the prince of its dreams, and the pure lake in its heart, and the wonderful trees out of fairy-tales, and the black skies, like the villain of the story, which swallow up the fortress and darken the lake in the valley and strike at it with black swords, so you can only see the point of the fortress' sword, stuck in the heart of the ravaged fog, like a threat and a promise; and after that they become reconciled and the skies turn a shining face again and become the grooms of the valley and the fortress, and seem to carelessly throw white bridal ribbons at them and the lake grows still and children skate upon it, and the gay chime of bells is carried through the air—here in the valley of fir-trees you can forget everything. Everything! Everything pleasant and everything unpleasant, whence you came and whither you are going and what you expect of the morrow. You are as free as a bird here, alien to your brother and alien to everything. Only the world of false gods welcomes you. It is strange to what extent a landscape can affect me; I had thought that I was made of harder metal. It may be that I have neglected my duties. It is my belief that I could not have done otherwise than I did. There is such a disharmony between the life here and the earth which supports it. Beauty against ugliness; the most lofty and the most degraded. And I, of course, am drawn to beauty by my nature—but enough, why should I multiply words? It is true, nevertheless, that here, in the valley of fir-trees, into which all the splendor the mind can imagine has entered, *here* you can forget everything. Yes, *here,* but all the while the heart, the heart, if you will forgive the expression, is not *here* at all but in Valley Gate, at home, and you can forget nothing. . . ."

This is what I had written. And now the letter, word by word, rose before me. Some of the words blushed.

I knew that I had had a perfect right to write a letter "like that." Not everyone had the right, but I had. I tried to imagine how everyone would have laughed, how I should have laughed, if someone else had written the letter, exactly the same (that is to say, of course, it would not be possible, but the same tone, the tone . . .) if, for example, Berke had written it, he whose heart is bound up in his machine and his soul —a motor with four pulses; suction, compression, action, release. Or, for example, Zimmerman, that slow-witted creature, or Shmuel, or Zimbeleh, or many others. . . .

I knew that the community was ready to forgive me all sorts of mistakes. I even had the right to enter into a general discussion and to say things that depended on feelings and they would make sense. I didn't know in what way I had come to this; I didn't remember that I had intended it but, in any case, I did have that position. In exactly the same way no one would pay any attention to me if I should raise some point about buying and selling. I was sorry about this. But it was a fact. You cannot break out of your "position" unless you have made some serious changes in yourself.

But now, as I returned after a long separation, would they still allow me to be myself, did I have the right to be that sum of errors and charms and something more that is hidden from the eyes of some and not hidden from the eyes of others that one calls roughly, character, or nature, or temperament—all those things which enabled me to behave as I behaved and to talk as I talked and to carry the burden of life as lightly as I used to in those days.

I thought of Zimmerman and I remembered that I did not like him. I remembered him and I remembered his wife who was ugly and nasty and disgusting to me, so that whenever I saw her coming near me I disappeared. I remembered other people of whom I was not fond and I was ashamed to have revealed something of my soul to them. Had I "revealed something of my soul?" And what had I said? Actually I had said nothing. Nevertheless, Masha had written me afterwards: "Ah, how well I know you, how well I know you. This letter is so much you. Ah, Menachem, the heart, if you will excuse the expression —you have not changed at all. . . ." I felt uncomfortable. What does that mean? What gives her the right to say that? (Except, perhaps, her own desire . . . .) Nonsense, as if this letter were enough to give me away. Ah well . . . as if anyone really could know me, as I really was, or better, as I can be if you are able to make me speak. . . .

I went on until I came to the fields of the farm. Out of the gateway a horse came clattering with a small child astride its back. I did not recognize either the child or the horse. At the time when I left they were probably taking their first steps on the quaking ground. I gazed out at the fields and noticed how many things which I had made were there still. I had fixed that pipeline. A great deal of water had flowed through it in the meantime, but it still bore me friendship. I saw fenugreek and clover and vegetables in the garden. If someone had been walking beside me I should certainly have advanced my opinion about a furrow that was not as straight as it should be and crops that were not coming up well for one reason or another, and irrigation that was best before the sowing or after the sowing, and other such-like things about which I knew very little in general, except that they served to refresh my feeling of not being entirely cut off from the soil. And more than any intention to voice an opinion or to argue with my companion would have been my effort to show that I had not forgotten my training and that my mind was still given to farming matters as had been the case a long time ago. Now that I was walking by myself what was left to me?—nothing except to breathe deeply of the pure air which, on its way from my nostrils to my lungs filtered fresh scents and quiet smells into my heart. . . .

I had entered the gate leading into the courtyard. A group of youngsters stood there and barred the way in front of me. I tricked them and tried to get away. They stood before me like a wall and played a game in front of me. This amused them greatly, but did not amuse me. I was tired and too old to devote myself to a game for long. Finally they allowed me to pass. But in payment for this they demanded satisfaction for their curiosity.

"Comrade, whom are you coming to?" cried one of them and leapt back in front of me.

I thought to myself: To whom do I come?

"To everybody," I replied.

I thought then that they would let me alone. I took one child on to my shoulders, like the spoils of battle, and started to go on. But he began to hit my chest in such a way that I was forced to give in quickly. I let him go. My answer, however, did not appear to satisfy them.

"Where will you sleep?" they asked me.

The youngsters felt that "everybody" was a very vague address.

"In the straw-barn," I replied. I smiled to myself and went on.

"Comrade, comrade!" they shouted after me. I considered carefully. Should I turn around or not? I weighed educational reasons against reasons of prestige and realized that it was important for me to have their friendship. I turned around.

"Don't smoke cigarettes in the straw-barn!"

Just when you are in the throes of an unreasoning fit of sadness, you find that everyone seems to greet you with precisely those words which tend to make you feel melancholy. Why had I said "a straw-barn?"

I walked through the yard and saw that there was a new barn and new granaries and a storehouse for grain (finally) and two trucks and some very modern agricultural machines. I stood there and counted everything that was strange to me. I noticed with affection some scraps of iron that had belonged to the old tractor. To what a state had I come! These were my possessions, but I had not struggled to build or buy them and hence they were not to be considered as my *creations.* While all my comrades preferred the newer things, my eyes gazed fondly at the old things which were nearer to me. An enormous tractor stood in the covered stand and stared at me like a bulldog squatting in a doorway, eyeing strangers wth hostility. While I was examining its insides a real dog barked at me from behind. Although it barked like an ordinary dog it seemed to me that its barking was infused with a special kind of anger. As if to say: let him be killed before he goes by. I lifted a stone. A young girl came running, seized the dog and embraced it: "Zeri, Zeri, be quiet now, stupid, it's nothing."

She meant me. She was a pretty girl and I wondered who she was. I stared at the wealth of curls falling over her bent head; I saw whatever else there was to see and congratulated myself on the fact that this young palm-tree had grown up in our neighborhood. After she had calmed the dog, she raised her head to look at me as well. She had very bright eyes with a very direct glance and a dancing light of understanding in them. Suddenly she leaped up, shouting "Mendel!" She jumped up at me, and began embracing me as though I were her nearest relative. She squeezed my hands violently and my eyes grew wet as a result (or so I said to myself). No one ever called me Mendel except with great affection. I am generally too much Mendel, or Naksho, or simply Scander (so I was called at times) to be Mendel consistently. Only when my behavior was funny to the point of absurdity did I become Mendel for a moment. Only my closest friends used to call me Mendel. The name rang in my ears as if all the bells of Valley Gate were ringing to announce my return. So this was Ronit. She had been a little girl and was now a full-grown woman whose affectionate ways spoke straight to my heart. She walked alongside me, amusing herself with youthful mischief. And all the while I felt her pure and spring-like body so desirable that it hurt me. You fool, I said to myself, what are you warming your heart for, over nothing? After you have spent two days here she will cease thinking about you. This is simply the result of the unexpected meeting, no more than that. Go and cool your heart off with things that make sense. I took her arm in mine and went up the slope of the sidewalk. We met some young lads who gazed after me in anger. We reached a place where some people were standing and she said: "I brought him over," as though she were proclaiming her right over me. And then she disappeared.

My old friends were standing there as well as some people whom I did not know. Out of politeness I shook everyone's hand. Thus my friends were not able to distinguish the degree of warmth that entered into each hand-clasp.

"Yes, I have returned," I replied.

I did not intend to annoy anyone, but I was still in a state of confusion and did not know what to say. I was afraid that they might try to twist the meaning of my words. There was an instant of strange silence. I realized that they were occupied with something and, smiling foolishly, (or so it seemed to me) I said:

"I'll go and settle down."

And I went on. Actually I did not know where to go. But after I had said that I would go, I had to go. Hayim Ahronson ran after me and said: "I'll go with you." I am not sure if I had always preferred Hayim Ahronson to the others, but at that moment I was certain that I had always felt a special affection for him. He took over and led me to an empty room and helped me to unpack my belongings. He noticed what I needed and went off to get it. I sat in the room and took off my shoes. Someone I was not acquainted with entered the room, carrying a bundle of sheets under his arm; he stood there a moment, stared at me and asked:

"Do you live here?"

"I think so," said I.

"That's too bad," said he with touching candor, "I had intended to make use of the room myself."

He stood there a little while, staring at me with undisguised regret, as though waiting for me to leave. I hardened my heart. Suddenly he turned quite red, stammered a few words, among them a request to be excused, and went off.

Soon my friends began to appear. I got tired of shaking hands. But I was fond of all of them. I told them everything I could and their silence flattered me to the point where it drew out everything that had grown up inside me. Those whose habit it was to do so asked questions that did not require an answer, but were intended to attest to the perceptive powers of the questioner, and those whose habit was otherwise asked questions and received answers. Then I held my tongue. If I tell you everything at once, now, I will be emptied out from now on and you will no longer be interested in me tomorrow, so I said to myself, and then regretted it. I was already about to overdo it.

"We can hear it over again, too," said Chana to me. Her eyes were very kind. This comely and vital young woman, eager for young men, had reached a certain lovely and finished maturity together with a kind of composure. Her limbs had grown rounder and softer and the mischief in her eyes had changed to generosity. After having seen many beautiful and insolent women, the sight of her tranquil grace moved my heart.

"No!" said I, "you talk first. Where is Hayimke, by the way? Why isn't Hayimke here?"

"He left," they told me.

Many of them said, *He left*. Some of them in anger, some with a sigh, as though they were mourning someone dead. My sympathy was with those who sighed. Hayimke was one of the best of the boys. If he had left, there must have been something wrong. "And Berkovich?" I asked.

"He's working." They said.

I was insulted. I had just arrived and Berkovich was at work. What kind of work could he be doing that he couldn't drop?

"In Bir Keziv," someone remarked, as though reading my thoughts. The lands of Bir Keziv were the most remote we owned. The whole of Valley Gate could be wiped off the face of the earth, and towards evening a field laborer would return from there quietly without knowing anything about it.

"And Rachel?" I asked.

At that moment I saw her standing in the door.

"You can congratulate her," someone told me, "she got married a little while ago."

A boy standing next to her smiled like a victor. (He had the right to be proud.) She looked at me with a heavy and almost frozen glance, which I could not explain except as the result of confusion. For surely she could have no quarrel with me for having gotten married. I realized that everyone was expecting me to blush; I hastened to do so. Actually I felt no need for it. If I had been apt to blush I would not have asked a question that would have put me in such a ridiculous position. After I had blushed—I felt embarrassed. She looked at me with a kind of melancholy that I should like to explain like this: if I had known that you were capable of falling into confusion because of me, I should not have done what I did. I realized that I was the target of excited curiosity. I got up from my place, walked up to her, pressed her hand in an exaggerated way and said:

"I have not congratulated you yet. Good luck."

My voice almost gave me away. But it did not. Her hand melted in mine, soft, helpless, friendly. The blush left my face; I obscured it with my hands as I held them to my face, lit a cigarette and continued to press my comrades to tell me what had happened in my absence.

In the evening they prepared a "spontaneous" party for me. The most endearing thing about it was the bad organization. What I said there and what they said to me I shall not record, for reasons of modesty. It was a full evening. After the party my friends sat and sang and I sat to one side. I did not sit this way intentionally, but having

done so, my friends decided that I wanted a little privacy in their
midst and with extraordinary delicacy they refrained from approaching me. As a matter of fact I wanted to talk and chatter about one
thing or another, and not to be alone and brood, but as my comrades
did not approach me I sat to one side. They sang new and old songs.
Songs which I knew and songs which I did not know. I like new songs
which come as a surprise. I also prefer to hear others' singing to
singing myself. (My voice is not suited to it.) But this time, whenever
they sang new songs which I did not know and could not sing, it
seemed to me that they were using these songs to annoy me. After that
they sang one very sad song which spoke straight to my dejected soul.
Some young people got up and danced dances which I did not know
and which did not suit my mood. I felt as though everyone were
conspiring to say: You are a stranger. I felt as though I were standing
to one side and life were rushing forward without me. For although
I had travelled and had seen a great deal, life here had surged on
differently and now I was "the fly of yesteryear." When I got to the
point of remembering the stories of my childhood I was past all
remedy.

I slipped outside. My mood had become rotten for no adequate
reason. It was a black night. Silhouettes of trees, black on black, rose
up before me out of the darkness. I walked a few steps and ran into
a barbed-wire fence. What was a barbed-wire fence doing here? There
had never been a barbed-wire fence there before. I was nearly ready
to believe that they had only put a barbed-wire fence there in order
to exasperate me. I felt that part of my clothes which had come in
contact with the fence and found that my trousers were torn. Even
if I had intended, secretly, to return to the party, I had no other choice
now but to go and hide in my room.

I went on, the torn trousers on my mind. I saw a field which had
run wild and I said to myself, look, you, too, are like a field run wild.
You cannot simply let it alone and hope that it will yield produce. You
must clear the stones away, pound at the hard places, break the
ground, plough and sow; you must work at it. You cannot come into
contact with people and make friendship grow immediately. If you

break off the continuity of work, you will lie waste even if you are choice soil and there is plenty of moisture in you and you are fertilized by an abundance of memories.

I saw a room with light in it and entered. The *sadran* (the member of the kibbutz responsible for work assignments) and the heads of the different branches of work sat there and argued. Even though they were involved in a dispute they received me warmly. I felt that if I were to be idle the next day I would destroy myself with excessive brooding. I realized suddenly that I must get up early next morning and go to work without any delay, to make the waste field in my heart bloom very soon.

"Arrange work for me tomorrow," I said to the *sadran.* Everyone looked at me in amazement.

"On the first day? Already? Not by any means. You must rest," he told me generously.

"I request it; I must work tomorrow" I pleaded with him.

"Well, all right," he said and wrote my name down before him.

I went out feeling that I had done a great thing. I knew that my comrades would attribute this demand of mine to my exhibitionist tendencies, to my peculiar liking, well-known as of old, for strange and surprising actions, and would count it among my follies. But, one way or another, they would forgive me as time went on.

Translated by Hilda Auerbach

The Third Hill

When we were small we used to play in the road that climbed up and up past the synagogue. The Arabs sold vegetables and eggs, and their donkeys raised the brown grey dust as they passed.

It was never winter. The sun shone all the time, and reduced the range of vision. Rifra, the fat Arab woman who worked in the house, sprayed the courtyard and the cracked steps to lay the dust, and thin streams of water trickled out into the road. Grandmother spoke to her in an Arabic mixed with Russian words that sounded like Yiddish, and my aunt taught her geography and told her of distant lands, more distant even than Mecca.

She smiled with her one blurred, watery eye, its fine colours flowing into each other, and I hummed to myself "tender the eyes of Leah."

We talked Hebrew, and she called us *m'tumtamim*—daft. We played in the long road, running and shouting, and bruising our knees.

There were days when I just lay about in the courtyard—washing days—and then Ralia and Khadra would join us. When she wasn't occupied with the washing, Khadra used carefully to gather together the sparkling medals my father had brought back from the last war. She had the face of a nun, and her eyes smiled sideways. Ralia was a sturdy, merry girl, full of vitality, and moved with a glowing abundance. They busied themselves with adult matters, but translated everything into Hebrew; they talked of wedding-nights in the village, and—in a whisper—of Ahmed, who was childless, and of many varieties of potions.

Ahmed would pass by, muttering "Women, women," in a cracked voice, and I knew this voice was cracked because of the potion he had drunk at a gulp, though intended for his wife.

Tall and bony, he came past the yellow wall where I was sitting, looked at me for a moment with flushed eyes, and said something in Arabic aimed not at me at all but towards the cowshed, into an expanse of white light. He had never had any children. The laughter of the women in the courtyard rang out, rose and fell, and my aunt, who was hanging up the washing, turned her head and I could not see her face. The courtyard was full of the smell of washing drying in the sun, and soap, and the water pouring out of the copper bowls whispered like snakes on the dry ground.

Abd frequently came into the courtyard to talk to his mother. He was the younger son, and several years older than me. He had one leg that was dead straight and thinner than the other, and he limped. He had a narrow, brownish face; they said his leg was tubercular, and that he had water on the knee. Once I saw the sac of water, bright and transparent gathered in his bare knee, like a crystal ball. He was talking Hebrew and smiled towards me, and I got up in haste from the rough stone wall. Rifra was standing by him, looking at me with her one eye, and I threw the ball that was lying by the steps towards the children. Abd looked at us, but didn't kick the ball.

Abd has a wife now, and children to support, but his leg is still straight and thin, and his body leans heavily on it.

It was hot and we played games. We mimicked the Arab who sold eggs, we scared the donkeys and we threw stones into the courtyard of the settlement slaughterer. He came out of the house and called us by name in a funny sing-song, but we were already hidden behind the eucalyptus trees. I pictured to myself his long sharp fingernail piercing and cutting the necks of the chickens and the pigeons that were then thrown twitching into the middle of the blood-stained courtyard, and I picked sharp, hard stones to throw at him the moment he turned away.

Abd came along the street and looked at me again, but I lowered my eyes and busied myself collecting stones, and he limped off towards the Arab village.

We had been invited to a wedding-feast in the village. The large copper bowls which served for the washing in the courtyard were full of food. The hide of the horses glistened with sweat, and their hooves pounded the ground. My father was talking Arabic to everybody in a pronounced Russian accent. My mother acknowledged the food, stood to one side and didn't touch a thing. She said the food was filthy. The children laughed and shouted. I stood alone, pulling at my new blue skirt which didn't cover my knees, and gazing from the horses' hooves towards the entrance to the house. Rifra came out in a blue embroidered dress and kissed me. My mother took out a handkerchief and wiped my face. When we arrived home, she washed my face and rubbed it with alcohol.

On the border of the colony, on the Third Hill (to this day I don't know why it was so called or where the first and second hills are) lived a tribe of watchmen. One Shabbat we went to visit them. The yellow dogs barked and prowled angrily around us, and Amer came down the hill to greet us, tall and slender, his black moustache gleaming. He was said to be the most handsome of the watchmen. I looked at him and saw him galloping up one day on horseback to offer my father the bride-price. The dogs had calmed down, but still looked at us suspiciously from time to time. By the tents a fire was blazing and on it stood a steaming black cooking-pot. A similar cooking-pot stands today in my home beside the thin legs of cold polished furniture.

My father talked with them and they laughed. The children gathered round the tent and looked at us with large, curious eyes. I didn't go out to play with them. The air was full of a blend of smells, food and spices and ovens. To this day it remains among the new white houses that have been built on the Third Hill, and though the thistles have been cleaned and weeded, they still persist in growing. Only the dogs apparently have died with the passing of the years.

Our kitchen was full of pots and pans. I used to sit beside the wide wooden table, stuck to the oil-cloth, and look at the engraved silver sugar bowl which my grandmother had brought with her from Russia. Rifra was washing the dishes. Her back was turned towards me. My aunt opened the window and said I should be playing outside with the children. I remained seated and listened to the conversation between her and Rifra.

They were talking of Mecca, and how Rifra could get there. Rifra asked the same questions over and over again. My aunt brought a map, showed her the way through the different colours, and began to mark it with a thick pencil line. Rifra smiled to herself, still not really convinced; I saw her walking along with the rest of the faithful, wrapped entirely in white, across the sandy tracks of the great desert, towards the black rock shining in the sun, and we both looked from the map towards the window and the dazzling light of day.

Outside too it was hot. I sat on the cracked steps, drawing in the sand with a eucalyptus branch. Amer galloped by without looking at me. Ahmed was leaning on the creaking wooden gate, his lashless eyes gazing towards the village, dreaming of his unborn children. Rifra pushed back the gate, gathered up her dress and ran towards the clinic where Abd was waiting for her. The outlines of the drawing were lost in the sand. I struck the steps with the eucalyptus branch, but no one heard. Ahmed was absorbed in his own strange thoughts and the noonday sun enwrapped us all. Rifra knelt on the cold floor and spoke with God. Ahmed spread something red in the courtyard and also knelt in prayer. Rifra spoke with God in a whisper, but could tell me nothing of what she said. In her Hebrew such matters could never find expression. I leaned heavily against the white-washed wall, waiting for her to rise and shake down the embroidered dress she had lifted and tucked carelessly under her wide belt. The porch was full of the presence of God, and the pigeons flew in the courtyard. The door opened and the local slaughterer came in, his white beard reaching almost to his waist. He looked for a moment at Rifra kneeling and muttering on the floor, and then passed into the kitchen to talk with my aunt and look occasionally at her legs and breasts. When he saw me, he suddenly wagged his finger at me reprovingly, the nail gleaming and flashing in the sun. I screwed up my eyes and, when I reopened them, God had vanished. The chickens lay twitching in the courtyard, fluttering from place to place, their cut throats dripping with blood.

Yussuf came to see my father; they sat on the wooden bench outside the house and talked and talked. Yussuf was already an old man, and ruled over the watchmen of the Third Hill. Not all his children, so they said, were known by him. Now he sat and whispered with my father, and his white horse tied to the eucalyptus tree drummed its feet and whinnied. In the colony they said there was trouble coming, and Yussuf had no love for the Arab villagers.

My father came into the house and said they would be loyal. When I asked him to whom, he made no answer.

In the kitchen Rifra was sitting by the table drinking a glass of tea, her hair tied up in a fine, bluish head-scarf. I wanted to tell her what my father had said, to ask her why Yussuf didn't like them, and whether they knew about the trouble in the village too, but she sat there in silence, holding her glass in both hands and noisily sipping the sweet tea—I sat down opposite her without a word.

The scars on my knees had almost vanished. In the settlement they had begun paving roads and the newspapers appeared with black borders. At night men went on guard, many orchards had been partly cut down and the roads strewn with nails. In the streets of the colony there was no sound but that of bulldozers, and there was a depressing silence. The sellers of vegetables and eggs had disappeared, the balls we used to play with lay rent apart in corners. The Arab village was remote as some inaccessible enchanted castle where all lay in prison. Amer and Yussuf galloped through the streets of the settlement without a sideways glance. Only the dogs barked at night and the sound came through to us, prolonged and mysterious. I wrote a long letter to Rifra and Abd, but hid it in the yellow stone wall; then we left the colony.

I came back during the holidays. Rifra hugged me, was amazed how I had grown, and went on washing the many dishes piled up in the sink. I wanted to tell her everything, about the new school, and the white house we lived in, but I couldn't speak Arabic. Abd was already married; he lowered his eyes and gave me a hasty greeting whenever he appeared in the courtyard. Ahmed had gone, and his place in the courtyard was taken by Fawzi. He spoke a fluent Hebrew, twisted his moustache, and didn't like us. Rifra had come back, and perhaps wanted to forget, but between Abd and Fawzi and myself lay long, summer days, dazzling and cruel. I found the letter I had written in the stone wall, and tore it into tiny pieces.

The last time I saw them, there were children playing ball in the narrow street that climbs up and up past the synagogue, and raising the dust as they ran. The local slaughterer dragged his feet along the road, his shoes creaking strangely. He didn't call me by name in a sing-song voice; he didn't even recognize me.

The squeaky wooden gate at the entrance had been taken down, the grey steps were without cracks and the yellow stone wall had been repaired and was now completely smooth, with no irregularities. In the yard, by the cowshed, Fawzi was unloading clover from the wagon with quick sharp strokes of his pitchfork, but without looking towards the house.

Rifra, in a new embroidered dress, her greying hair dyed with henna, was sitting in the kitchen drinking tea from a blue enamel cup. She asked me why I wasn't married, and shook her head sadly. Abd already had five children. This time she didn't kiss me, merely shook her head from side to side and went back to sipping her sweet tea.

I went into the settlement to visit the cemetery. All those who had known how to speak Arabic were long buried there.

It was hot, and the dazzling white light reduced the range of vision. The village houses had become part of the hill-side. Cactus bushes were growing wild and tall thistles turned yellow in the sun. Stones had crumbled from the houses and lay along the side of the road. In the silence the enchanted castle vanished like a childhood tale.

Long lines of new white houses stood in neat rows on the Third Hill and the air was clear, and bright and free from smoke.

Translated by A. Levenston

Yitzhak Orpaz

The Wild Plant

He knocked on the door. Silence. He entered the house, and his footsteps re-echoed from the bare walls; there was no one at home and his step was hard and even; the large rooms of the house surrounded him, staring at him curiously, so that he stopped short, embarrassed, in the middle of the big room. Muddy boots, red clay footsteps, egg-crates, milk pitchers, empty sacks: a friendly simplicity in the air of the house which somehow was not quite in place there.

In the middle of the large empty wooden table, a glass vase with great protruding handles flashed the newcomer a fetching white smile: "Mumu," it called the newcomer by name, "look at me."

Mumu glanced at it briefly; he was disillusioned with white smiles. Leaving the big room, he passed through the kitchen and out into the farmyard. Looking cold and reserved, he ignored the antics of the puppy, the protests of the horse and the cackling of the hens; then he sank into the suffocating smell of potash fertilizer, until it was diluted with the scent of new mown hay, cut that very morning perhaps. At the entrance to the building which served both as barn and stable, a small man and a big horse were so preoccupied with one another that they did not see him coming, even though it seemed to him that the sound of his footsteps filled the whole farmyard. The short thin man was bent over the wounded front leg of the horse, which was emitting snorts of bitterness which shook him from his trembling nostrils to the tip of his smartly clipped tail.

"Whoa, you old beast," shouted the short thin man, his hands and eyes darting about with diabolical nimbleness. His simple, easygoing face was as tough as the leather of his shoes; and he obviously belonged to the house—his self-assurance was like that of his toothless upper jaw out of which his cries of "whoa!" kept wheezing out like an oboe. Later Mumu was to hear how the man had lost his teeth years ago as the result of a punch in the jaw from a friendly Australian soldier. This was back in the days when the tavern he ran for war-weary soldiers had been a better paying proposition than anything else on his farm. The experience had left him with the wide brimmed Australian hat he was now wearing, the shoes on his feet, his wheezy cry of "whoa" and his childlike bare-gummed smile.

Without further ado, the man said, "Grab his head, my boy. Whoa! Grab his head, if you know what a horse is!"

They hadn't looked at each other but Mumu was in no doubt about who had spoken and to whom. The horse's big head threshed about in pain and from time to time beat out its protests on the short man's shoulder, interrupting his work.

Mumu passed his sure hand over the proud neck of the horse and fondled it; after that he looked into the big horsey eye and, in a whisper, promised him the same fate as Stashek. Stashek, he whispered to him, had been a donkey in the institution. One day he had halted in the shade of a carob tree and refused to budge; he had tried hitting him with a stick, then prodding him with spurs, and finally he had scratched his back with dry branches until he bled—Stashek hadn't protested; he had just lain down on the ground very humbly and never got up again; but Mumu remembered him kindly; he remembered his last look—a look of patience and surrender. He was prepared to remember the horse just as kindly. Now the horse's head was quiet in Mumu's hands, and his eyes rolled in surrender.

"You have a sure hand," said the short man, leading the horse to the trough. "A horse can always tell. What's your name?"

"They call me Mumu." From the other side of the wall came a long drawn out "moo," as heavy and listless as a yawn. Mumu too drew out his words in a heavy, listless drawl. "You're a relative of mine—that is, if your name is Shmuel Korn."

"Sure we're relatives." He shook cordially. "But who are you, I mean, what's your last name?"

Mumu was silent. It seemed to him that he had never had a last name. "Mumu the knife-grinder?" Maybe that was it, Mumu the knife-grinder. No one knew the color of his eyes because he never looked anyone straight in the eye. Knives, scissors, the flash of blades, the volley of sparks and the eye of the revolving grindstone—the eye of oblivion.

A red orange hung from one of the trees in the nearby grove, glowing like a small sun. A dry, rotten sun. He felt for his knapsack and thought of going away. But Shmulik spoke first; from a pile of green and fragrant fodder which he had just set down in the troughs, he wheezed, "Look at me standing here and asking you questions. It's a sure thing that you're a Korn—one of the Korns, just like me. Bruriah, we have a visitor."

"Coming right away," came the voice of a woman from the hatchery.

Not taking his eyes off the red orange, Mumu said: "I've come to work for you—I mean if you have anything for me to do."

"Good for you. The Korns are working people. Are you a farmer?"

"Yes."

"I don't do much farming here—just what you see, and a fodder patch for the animals, and that citrus grove over there."

"I can do any kind of outdoor work."

"I'm sure you can. The trouble is that we usually manage to get along by ourselves, especially now that we have Shaul with us. You'll meet him. A lad with a head on his shoulders. He's in charge of the grove. Bruriah!" he called out, "this is a relative of mine, Mumu Korn. You see, a Korn can be tall, too."

Bruriah had burning eyes and a huge bosom. You could not be near her without feeling the impact of her breasts. He felt her breasts on his face and he felt her blood pulsing in her palm. She said something friendly and her hand quivered in his—as if she were afraid of him. He stared at the red orange, his whole body paralyzed. The slightest move and he'd run plump into that enormous bosom. The glowing orange shifted into the shade, and was extinguished. An excited whispered conference was taking place, to the accompaniment of stamping hooves, snorts and sneezes. "We'll find something for him to do . . . are you sure that . . . nobody ever gets lost here . . . that's nothing."

They invited him to lunch, "and then we'll see."

"Micha'le, Micha'le," called Bruriah. And Micha'le, a boy of about seven, appeared from the orange-grove, dancing around a stone like a small flame. "Micha'le, lunch is ready, come quickly," called Bruriah. Mumu realized that he had never had a little brother like Micha'le and felt that he was hungering desperately for something— something more than his lunch.

Frisking and capering around the stone, Micha'le yelled: "Come on out, snake, come on out!" and his raven hair flew about his head like black doves.

"Leave the snakes alone, Micha'le," Bruriah's voice struggled through the air as if the space surrounding them was saturated with the venom of asps. Shmulik made a dash for the stone with Mumu close behind him.

"But daddy, it's only a little adder," said Micha'le, still capering.

"Get out of the way!" Shmulik yelled. He moved the stone, caught the snake skilfully by the tail, and, first making an arc with it in the air, brought its head down on the stone. But the snake slipped away from him and coiling itself, began darting its triangular head back and forth in perplexity. Mumu held up a small stick in front of the snake's eyes and gave it a cold stare. For just the fraction of a second the snake was frozen to the spot, but it was long enough for Mumu to grab its head between his figures and separate a downward wave of frenzied wriggling from the quivering fangs above.

Squealing with joy, Micha'le looked admiringly at the big, handy fellow, but he wanted to stick up for his father too: "Daddy's killed loads of snakes, maybe a thousand, do you believe me?"

"Yes," agreed Mumu.

"You'll give me the snake to put in a bottle, won't you?"

"All right."

"You're going to stay here with us, aren't you?" asked the boy.

"Shaul, come and eat," called Bruriah, her voice muffled and warm, like a cow mooing over a full trough. The puppy whiffed the smell of the voice, a smell of bones and scraps of meat, and whined hopefully.

A voice called from the grove, clean and shiny as a razor blade: "Who's going to finish this row if I come and eat? Work is work." It was a well-groomed, affected voice, like an ornamental glass-flower. A tremor of his jaw told Mumu: you hate Shaul; he is your enemy. And little Micha'le, his hair a crown of flying doves, said: "Shaul is a coward, he runs away from snakes. I've seen him myself."

Mumu was silent. He walked evenly and confidently.

"You're staying here, aren't you?" the boy persisted.

Shmulik, who, in the meantime, had had time to feed the calf, gave her a kick in the rump and shut the wooden wicket.

"Daddy, he is going to stay with us, isn't he?"

A slight hesitation hung in the air, elastic like a drop of water about to fall from a leaking faucet. "Of course," answered Shmulik, "he's staying with us. Of course. He belongs to the family." The drop fell, tinkling like the clapper of a silver bell.

Mumu wanted to lay his hand on the boy's head, but for some reason he could not. Then he finished killing the snake on the doorstep, and the house lay open to him.

He spent the rest of the day exploring the neighborhood. He made the acquaintance of Nati, the elder son; he listened a lot and spoke little. He daydreamed under a fig tree and tried to believe that the past was forgotten and perhaps, perhaps, his life was about to take a new turn; but all the while a yellow parrot was screeching in his ear: "Don't you trust them, don't you trust them."

When he got into his soft bed that night he heard the puppy scratching at the door, begging to be let in. He remembered a boy who had knocked at a strange door and asked to come in; when they asked him why, he replied: "I'm not comfortable sleeping out in the street, that's all." At that time the boy had been Micha'le's age—could it have been himself?

He fell asleep and dreamed that he met the small eyes of the puppy, and they were wide and excited like the bellies of frolicking rabbits; immediately he recognized Micha'le's eyes; he wanted to caress his bunched up hair. . . . He woke up, intending to open the kitchen door for the puppy, but for some reason he could not.

II

The days were thick and scorching, like Bruriah's vegetable soup; and her soup was good—it burned Mumu's tongue and palate and gave him an excuse not to speak without his silence falling like an angry stone amid the constant chatter at the Korns' table. Bruriah laughed a great deal, her laughter bursting straight out of her huge bosom, thick, warm, provocative and disquieting. Shaul would pinch her, laughing and teasing, and his quick, subtle tongue would fill the house with its noise, irritating Mumu and making him more taciturn than ever. Then Mumu would mutter through compressed lips, "Going to sleep . . . got to get up early tomorrow," and escape to his bed and the thriller that was always under his pillow. The next day, up early it would be, along with the morning mists; and then you could pick up the long hours, salty with sweat and heavy with heat, and carve a world of dull forgetfulness out of them. And sometimes there were salty hours when the sky grew gentle, and the head of Stashek the donkey gazed down at him from above, patient, submissive, appeased.

Now the hours of appeasement became more and more frequent at the Korns; something was changing; he still had not caressed Micha'le's shock of hair, but he knew that he wanted to; once, he even caught himself staring at one of Shmulik's smiles and admiring his heartwarming, tooth-denuded childishness, but he immediately refocussed, sliding his gaze into space along a line of vision which evaded and avoided all human beings.

It was not surprising therefore, that while he hated Shaul, he did not know the color of his eyes or which hand he used to hold his spoon while eating Bruriah's soup, and, although he knew exactly how many trees there were in the third row in the grove and how many sacks of fertilizer there were in the storehouse, he had no idea of the color of Shmulik's hair or whereabouts exactly on Bruriah's body those splendid, massive breasts were suspended. But he heard Bruriah's laughter echoing richly throughout the house and yard, as if calling to him: I am here, I am there, where are you—but some-

one seemed to be treading down upon the nipples of her laughter
. . . someone . . .

As we have said, the days were thick and scorching in the grove.
His hand pruned and hoed and fertilized and irrigated and hated
Shaul who was always working nearby, just a few rows away from
him.

One morning Shmulik was in the clover patch, Bruriah in the
chicken coop, Nati on the river sailing boats, Shaul and Mumu in the
grove, and little Micha'le, who had become Mumu's inseparable companion, was running around close by. Micha'le would open or shut
the slide-valve at Mumu's bidding and between times dig worms out
of the damp earth, watch a procession of ants, or worry Ludar with
a great shepherd's staff. Ludar was a tremendous, mean-natured dog,
a sort of cross between wolf and fox; like the coward he was, he was
capable of attacking another dog from behind and finishing him. After
a pedigree dog had been done to death in this way, Ludar's master
was forced to chain him up. His master, too, was no ordinary character; he raised strawberries and gladiolas exclusively and his livestock
consisted of Ludar and a few cats—no cows and no chickens. Naturally, the neighbors' children delighted in annoying the pair of them
—Ludar and his master as well. The most active in this sport was little
Micha'le, who wielded his staff so sprily and so dexterously that
Ludar usually ended up with his voice gone, his hair bristling, and his
face twisted into a crazy grimace.

Mumu was resting on his back at the far end of the grove, relaxed
and cool as a trickle of water in the irrigation ditch, when a blast of
cries and growls broke about his ears and awoke him. There was
Micha'le before him clutching the big shepherd's staff, his breath
surging in his throat.

"The old man got awfully angry and said he'd let Ludar loose.
D'you believe he'll do it?" His panting was as gentle as the chirping
of birds, and a fragrant citrus blossom fell on his face.

"Maybe," he answered.

"But Ludar is awfully big and he's probably as strong as the wolf
that got into Shifra's chicken coop."

"Ludar barks all day and barking dogs don't bite." The thought passed through his mind—maybe Shaul is like that too.

"But Ludar hates me and he's surely as strong as the wolf that got into Shifra's chicken coop."

O God of Stashek, how was it possible for man or beast to hate this boy? If he put his head a bit closer at this moment he would caress him. Or would he? What a pity that his hand wasn't used to it.

"Micha'le, tell the story about the wolf and Shifra."

"But I've already told you."

"Never mind, tell it again."

So Micha'le told him the story that was famous throughout the valley of how Shifra from Kibbutz M. had come into the yard of the chicken coop and found a big angry dog there. She asked him to get out; he wouldn't; she told him to get out; he wouldn't. She threw a stone at him. Then the big dog got angry, went over to her, threw her on her stomach and started eating her behind. Shifra yelled and fainted. Some people from the farm came and killed the wolf—for in the meantime it had turned out that the big dog was really a wolf. It happened that her husband's name was also Wolf. From then on all the children in the neighborhood used to sing in unison: "What made Wolf get mad at Shifra and eat up her behind?"

"Wolf get mad at Shifra and eat up her behind," repeated Mumu and giggled. When he was with Micha'le he sometimes giggled. And Micha'le loved to see Mumu giggle, like the sun coming out from behind a cloud.

"You know," said Micha'le suddenly, "I hate Ludar and Ludar hates me. And when he's not chained he doesn't bark either."

Micha'le was afraid.

Mumu listened, cocking his head at a point below the surface of the ground. He heard something besides the sounds of the water flowing along, of the soil absorbing it, of the loam crumbling and of the worms rustling underneath. He heard something else and lifted his head: a few steps behind Micha'le stood Ludar, all his muscles taut, tail between his legs, muzzle on the ground, his eyes two bloodshot slits —a tense bundle of hatred. Mumu grabbed the roughly knobbed shepherd's staff and leapt at the dog. Ludar crouched low, contorted his face, bared his teeth and growled. Mumu stuck the knobbed end of the staff between his teeth, Ludar bit into it. There was a crunch and a yelp, but the stick held firm and the knob twisted into a dough of flesh and saliva. The dog opened his eyes slowly and met Mumu's gray-green stare; the dog shuddered, a wave of trembling shook him from head to tail; he lowered his muzzle, opened his eyes wide in terror, and started submissively wagging his tail.

But Mumu didn't trust Ludar. The dogs legs were fixed to the ground, his whole body tense. Mumu couldn't remember Shaul's face; he had never looked at him directly, but at that moment he was certain that this was Shaul's face. Don't trust him, the wheel of the grindstone shrieked in his ear, he's going to spring at you! He raised the staff and with a powerful swing brought the knob down on Ludar's head. There was a noise of smashing bones like a rumble of thunder, and then everyone seemed to come running. Mumu put down the staff and with a cold expression on his face went back to his nook at the far end of the grove. His eyes sought the boy but he was already gone. He lay on his back and wrapped himself in a heavy cloak of indifference. All around him he heard the stamping of feet and cries of "what a hoodlum!" and noisy arguments and wrangling and then questions as soft and sticky as tar: "Why did you do it, why did you do it, why did you kill Ludar?"

Afterwards came the coaxing and cajoling, going to his head like a drag: "Why don't you apologize. Why don't you say you're sorry, or something?" And to add to it all, Shaul's honeyed entreaties and Bruriah's long drawn out uddery mooing. He himself remained a lump of silence amidst all the confusion. Micha'le was now there, not far from him, looking at him sorrowfully and trying to explain to the grownups that Ludar had been going to attack him; but the grownups were as deaf as the wall. So he sat not far from Mumu, looking at him sorrowfully and not saying anything.

Afterwards he heard the carcass being dragged along nearby, and a roar of fury: "That's a murderer you have in the house, not a human being!" and again the frightened whisper of Nurit, his little sweetheart, hummed in his ears: "I'm afraid of the way you look at me," and then afterwards: "Let me go, you're worse than an Arab."

The grindstone sharpened his temples until they ached. He jumped to his feet and his blood shrieked: "What do you want from me. Leave me alone!" But no sound broke from his sealed lips, and his features remained apathetic from force of habit. It was just as well, because at that moment Shmulik approached him, and little Micha'le who was trailing behind skipped forward, calling to him on the run: "Daddy made up with the old man. He promised him a pedigree boxer."

Shmulik approached with quick even steps, his huge Australian hat moving before him like a sanctuary of shaded repose and sympathy.

"Are you finished with the watering, Mumu?"

"No."

"Why waste time. Get on with the watering, Mumu."

"O.K."

Shmulik continued on his way as if nothing had happened, and Micha'le sang gleefully: "What made Wolf get mad at Shifra and eat up her behind? Isn't that great, Mumu?"

Something inside him rasped and was released, like a rusty shutter creaking open into the air outside. And someone giggled at the joke as if nothing had happened.

To hell with it! Something had happened, and to hell with the secrecy and the fear and the shame and the secrecy and the fear. To hell with it all!

He would tell Shmulik everything, everything he had wanted to conceal and to forget. He would tell him tomorrow, maybe even tonight—after the porcupine hunt.

III

Evening descended on the Korn house, cool and fragrant. Mumu and Nati returned from the hunt bearing a huge porcupine. The air was clear, one could see for miles around; only Mumu's hands were thick with the blood of the porcupine. Never mind, he would wash them and then go and talk to Shmulik. They trussed up the porcupine on to a tree and proceeded to skin it and remove the outer layer of fat.

"Give me your knife, Mumu," said Nati. "I want to do it alone; just watch, I won't leave a scrap of fat on it."

"Here, take it."

It was easier than usual to hand over his only possession—the knife with the silver handle; and as he looked at the silver moon he felt wealthier than ever before. The moon laughed at him toothlessly, like Shmulik's laugh. The twinkling lights of the far off city blinked at him with hope, hope that was as gentle and submissive as the head of Stashek the donkey lying at the threshold of the house. But a repressed thought, cruel and reptilian, kept licking at the soles of his feet, like the smooth heads of asps whose fangs have been drawn; something was happening to him, something deep down inside. Quickly, Mumu withdrew his feet from the strange, inimical thought and went into the house. "Home," he whispered, "home."

He turned on the light in the kitchen and hurried to the faucet to wash the blood off his hands; but before he could turn it on, there was a burst of laughter from the next room which froze his hands in mid-air. Shaul and Bruriah and Shmulik were laughing, and the walls and the tea in the cups all joined in: "Mumu," they said, "Mumu-Mumu-Mumu"—and they laughed. And when the laughter died down Bruriah said: "Go on, Shaul, finish the story. I was always a little afraid of that boy. . . ." The porcupine had also been afraid of him—it had lifted its tail and spread it out like a fan, but that only served to bare its rear end and provide a perfect target for the bullet. But that was a porcupine, Bruriah.

"I want to hear the rest of it, Shaul!"

"I've been hesitating whether to tell you or not. After all, he's a relative of yours. But today, after what happened with the dog, I thought to myself, today it's a dog, tomorrow it will be—well, who knows?" Well, everyone knows, everyone sees what he's driving at. What happened with the horse was just typical. "Imagine, he grabbed a broken harness and hit the horse until it bled. And why? Because the horse kicked him. He was thirteen at the time, and the counsellor explained things patiently the way they always do at a children's institution. He said to him: 'A horse isn't a human being; sometimes he kicks.' Do you know what he answered him? He said that he didn't like the way the horse looked at him!"

He didn't like the way the horse looked at him. Quite true. That's what he had said. And they had expelled him from the institution. That's right. And they waited for him to apologize and say he was sorry, but he hadn't said a word—he didn't like to be looked at, not even by horses.

They were all laughing, even Shmulik was laughing, though Shaul wasn't even talking to him. He was telling the story to Bruriah and plucking at her breasts and she was roaring with laughter, ha-ha-ha, ha-ha-ha! Whoever else she was afraid of, she wasn't afraid of Shaul, that was clear.

"Go on, Shaul, tell us the rest."

"Tell us the rest, Shaul," echoed Shmulik. And Shaul continued: "At the agricultural school they called him 'silent Mumu,' until one day he showed his teeth. He was sixteen at the time, and they expelled him for rape."

"Rape?" they chorused excitedly.

"Rape, beatings, scandals and tears."

And tears and flight in the thick darkness from the shed to the fields. She and he, she and he after her.

"Nurit, wait for me, wait for me, I won't hurt you."

"Leave me alone!"

"Nurit, wait for me. I didn't mean to—"

"I'm afraid of the way you look at me—"

"Nurit, wait for me—" She stopped. And the night got down on its knees. "I didn't mean it. You asked me to come to the shed—and I love you."

She chirped: "You behave like a hoodlum. You're even worse . . . you're worse than an Arab—"

He hit her in the face and she fell to the ground and began to wail. He didn't say anything, but the red night raged all around him: revenge, revenge. He was silent afterwards too, when he rose from her side, left her and went back to the dormitory to take his knapsack. He left the school at dawn.

"Poor girl," said Bruriah. "He's a wild beast. Shmulik, you never told me that there are fellows like that in your family." And they all sipped their tea, with a heavy and terrible feeling, perfectly dreadful for them, and then they sipped their tea again, and Shmulik opened his mouth, bare-gummed like a black moon, and—and he had nothing to say. He looked around, and then he looked at the glass vase, and there was Stashek the donkey peeping out of it, but Shmulik didn't know Stashek the donkey, so there really was nothing to say. The black sheep, the black sheep.

Bruriah sighed: "It's a shame about the children. They listen to him. Just a shame. Well, after what you told us about his mother, it's not surprising!"

The green mother burst forth out of oblivion like a huge toad, and her love descended on him like a thousand tons of yellow sky; the burden weighed on him, pulling him down. He looked at his hands thick with blood; his legs buckled and his head was drawn irresistibly to the floor. The yellowness was crushing and the stare of the toad burned the back of his neck like the lash of a whip. He was too tired to flee—he had fled to suburbs and to petty thievery, to the houses of strangers and to prison, to the field and to exhaustion and the silence of the lonely; but she always found him in the end and brought him back to the inferno of her love. But one day she had departed from the world, and then they all stood beside him, the stepfather and the others and the grindstone, wringing their hands and grimacing righteously. "It's not our fault, actually we're not involved, so how are we to blame?" And the green mother said, "I shall return to you, dear, I shall return," and left the toad's skin on his back as a remembrance. Then they all filed by him, righteously wringing their hands, and so out into the night.

And he after them . . .

But on the threshold he collided with Nati, who rushed into the house at a gallop, and immediately all the doors flew open. The light of the big room fell on Mumu like the sun on a glass roof; there was nothing in him that was not illuminated.

Nati called excitedly: "A great hunt, we caught an enormous porcupine." But his words were drowned in a strange silence, a silence which gazed blindly into the shining vase on the wooden table.

Mumu quickly withdrew into himself, looking at the spots of clotted blood on his hands; then said: "You didn't tell them everything, Shaul. You didn't tell them that when I was eight years old I gave myself up to the police for stealing apples. The policemen ate the apples, and they put me in jail for the night; so all of us were satisfied —they had the apples, and I had a roof over my head for the night."

The room froze in the silence. Mumu broke loose from the room and threw himself on his bed, shivering and feverish.

When he awoke he heard the puppy scratching on the door.

IV

Mumu was an old hand at leaving without saying goodbye.

When the night of hallucination and nightmares lifted, and he arose into the dawn, silence hung over the Korn house. He removed his shoes and walked on tiptoe. In the big room he encountered the breathing of Nati and Micha'le and found his knife with the silver handle. The glass vase was also there and looked at him with an azure, yearning eye; it was waiting for him. So Mumu took the knife with the silver handle and put it near Nati's bed. Then he stayed for a moment to caress Micha'le's light breathing as it floated off in the air. Returning to the room he picked up the vase by its ears, the great ears of Stashek the donkey. Patient and submissive, the vase slipped into his knapsack, and together they escaped from the Korn house into the dawn. Mumu was used to going away without saying goodbye. In fact, he could hardly remember ever saying goodbye before leaving. And it was always at this hour between night and day: only at this hour between night and day, the time when hope blossomed, was he capable of leaving.

Sometimes he left when the air was like intoxicating wine; sometimes he left, crawling on his belly into a white frost, when the eye of dawn was crimson with shame; and sometimes he left on a bridge of crutches when the horizon was aglow with hope. This time he simply went out into a void—a void that was empty and pallid and hollow like the thin blast of a ram's horn. What lay beyond? Emptiness. And beyond that? Still emptiness, always emptiness.

Mumu tried to run, but it was hard to run in emptiness, constantly pulling at his skin which was caught, damn it all, on some thorn back there in the house from which he was fleeing.

He left the plain of white sand and went into the fields, and from there he got onto a black road over which the night threw a faint sheen; he came upon a large truck which was out collecting empty milk cans, and the moving shadow of houses on the road, and a small cloud that had put up for the night on one of the trees in the road and having awakened was now fleeing to the sea, pursued by a light breeze, as light as Micha'le's breathing. . . .

But it was only when he came to the main road, and the sea swelled before him, deep and promising as a black womb, that the poisoned arrow whined in the void: Never again, never again the not caring, the not expecting anything from anyone, and the closing of memory's eyes to everyone and everything. Never again, because the Korn house was inscribed in clear letters on the black womb and there was no escape. Micha'le—Nati—Shaul—Ludar—Shmulik—Bruriah—and all the rest, and the smells and the sights and the awakenings—oh, how he hated them, hated them! But for all his hatred, there would never be any escaping them. Never again.

The winds blew wildly in the empty space, and when they calmed down a little, the black road was lighter. He wanted to flee to the dark warm womb of the sea, but that too had become lighter in the meantime. He looked around him and saw how the void had turned into a glass roof and the new day was looking into him and seeing everything.

Mumu remembered the glass vase and looked behind hem. Maybe they were chasing him. Yes, they were certainly chasing him—they probably thought he had stolen the glass vase. But the vase had been waiting for him; it was his. It was good that the crossroad was just ahead—from there he could get to any part of the country. But where? What did it matter. Anywhere, anywhere. Just to get away, that was all.

"Where's the money for the ticket?"

The ticket office looked at him with a glassy stare, and a kiosk opened with maddeningly hot rolls on display, and a gabbling, milling crowd collected, and the roof of the station was tired and bepissed with the dew of the sky, and the sky was dizzily high, and everything beneath it was an utter blank.

He sat apathetically, his feet in a ditch, and let the images come. And come they did, some astride laughing goats and some on the backs of light clouds, and Shaul came by riding Ludar, and after him Bruriah, floating on her breasts, proud and overflowing and mooing like a cow. "How do you come by a man like that, Shmulik —it's a pity for the children—the children." And Shaul was laughing in his face: "You don't even have the money for a ticket, you pauper, you!"

"Leave me alone," said Mumu. He got up and turned to go. But just at that moment, Shmulik's jeep pulled up next to him and the Australian hat over the bare-gummed smiling mouth emerged from it.

Mumu drew back a step and his face was impassive as always; then he took the glass vase out of his knapsack with a slow dull movement. The vase writhed in his hand: no—it was Stashek rolling his eyes.

"To hell with it," exclaimed Mumu, lifting the vase and throwing it at Shmulik's feet. "To hell with all of you! What are you all running after me for?"

The vase shattered into tiny fragments that sprayed through the air, white as dead doves:

"Now you know who I am."

People began to gather and an agile policeman pounced on Mumu. Shmulik stopped him: "Just a moment, officer, this is a family matter. If he hadn't smashed the thing, I would have. He's my son."

"His son, his son," a murmur went through the crowd and the policeman asked them all to disperse. Shmulik and Mumu were left alone, face to face.

"What are you waiting for, Mumu. Come on, hop into the jeep— or we'll never get that grove watered today." Mumu stood riveted to the spot and the emptiness of the world stretched taut as a drum. If he spoke, every word would resound inside him with a blare; but not a word could he utter.

"Come on, will you. Shaul is leaving today. He's going to his own place and there'll be no one but you in the grove. Besides, Micha'le is sitting at the table and says he won't touch his breakfast until you're back with him. So hop in, let's go home."

Home . . .

His hand trembled with a yearning to squeeze Shmulik's hand, but since he didn't know how to go about it, he just climbed into the jeep and kept silent.

Translated by T. Zandbank

Nomad and Viper

The famine brought them.

They fled north from the horrors of famine, together with their dusty flocks. From September to April the desert had not known a moment's relief from drought. The loess was pounded to dust. Famine had spread through the nomads' encampments, and wrought havoc on their flocks.

The military authorities gave the situation their urgent attention. Despite understandable hesitations, they decided to open the roads leading north to the Bedouins. A whole population, men, women and children, could not simply be abandoned to the horrors of starvation.

Dark, sinuous and wiry, the desert tribesmen trickled along the dirt tracks, and with them came their emaciated flocks. For most of their way they meandered along gulleys hidden from town-dwellers' eyes. An intermittent, persistent stream twisted northwards, circling scattered settlements, staring wide-eyed at the astounding sights. The dark flocks spread into the fields of golden stubble, tearing and chewing with strong, vengeful teeth. Their masters' bearing was stealthy and subdued; they shrank from watchful eyes. They took pains to avoid your encounter. Tried to conceal their presence.

If you passed them on a noisy tractor and set billows of dust loose on them, they would courteously collect their scattered flocks and make you a wide passage, wider by far than was necessary. They stared at you from a distance, frozen like statues. The scorching atmosphere blurred their appearance and gave a uniform look to their features: a man with his staff, a woman with her babes, an old man with his eyes sunk deep in their sockets. Some were half-blind, or perhaps feigned half-blindness from some vague alms-gathering motive. Inscrutable to the likes of you. How unlike our well-tended sheep were their miserable specimens: knots of small, skinny beasts huddling into a dark, seething mass, silent and subdued, humble as their dumb keepers.

Only the camels, the camels alone spurn meekness. From atop tall necks they fix you with tired eyes brimming with scornful sorrow. The wisdom of ages seems to lurk in their eyes, and a nameless tremor runs often through their skin.

Sometimes you manage to come up on them unawares. Crossing a field on foot you may suddenly happen on an indolent flock standing motionless, noon-struck, their feet apparently rooted in the parched soil. Among them lies the shepherd fast asleep, dark as a block of basalt. You approach and cover him with your strident shadow. You are startled to encounter his eyes wide open. He bares most of his teeth in an appeasing smile. Some of them are gleaming, others decayed. His smell hits you and you grimace. Your grimace hits him like a punch in the face. Daintily he picks himself up, trunk erect, shoulders hunched. You fix him with a cold blue eye. He broadens his smile and utters a guttural syllable. His garb is a compromise: a coarse, patched European jacket over a flowing desert robe. He cocks his head on one side and an appeased gleam crosses his face. If you do not upbraid him he holds out his left hand and asks for a cigarette in rapid Hebrew. His voice has a silken quality, like a woman's. If your mood is generous you put a cigarette to your lips and toss another into his wrinkled palm. To your surprise, he snatches a gilt lighter from the recesses of his robe and offers a furtive flame. The smile never leaves his lips. His smile lasts too long, is unconvincing. A flash of sunlight darts off the thick gold ring adorning his finger, and pierces your squinting eyes.

Eventually you turn your back on the nomad and continue on your way. After a hundred, two hundred paces, you may turn your head and see him standing just as he was, his gaze kneading your back. You could swear that he is still smiling, that he will go on smiling for a long while to come.

Do not forget their singing in the night. A long-drawn-out, dolorous wail drifts on the night air from sunset till just before dawn.

The voices penetrate the confines of the kibbutz, and charge our nights with an uneasy heaviness. No sooner have you settled down to sleep than a distant drumbeat sets the rhythm of your sleep like the pounding of an obdurate heart. Hot are the nights, and vapour-ridden. Stray clouds caress the moon like a train of gentle camels, camels without any bells.

The nomads' tents are made up of dark drapes. Stray women drift around at night, barefoot and noiseless. Lean, vicious nomad hounds dart out of the camp to challenge the moon. Their mongrel howls drive our kibbutz dogs insane. Our finest dog went mad one night, broke into the henhouse and massacred the young chicks. It was not out of savagery that the watchmen shot him. There was no alternative.

II

You might imagine that the nomad incursion enriched our heat-prostrated nights with a dimension of poetry. This may have been the case for some of our unattached girls. But one should not overlook a whole string of rather prosaic disturbances, such as foot-and-mouth disease, damage to crops, and an epidemic of petty thefts.

The foot-and-mouth disease came out of the desert, carried by their livestock which had never undergone medical inspection. Although we took early precautions, the virus infected our sheep and cattle, reducing the milk-yield and killing off a number of animals.

As for the damage to the crops, we had to admit that we had never managed to catch one of the nomads in the act. All we ever found were tracks of men and animals among the rows of vegetables, in the hayfields and deep inside the fenced orchards. What was the point of wrecking irrigation pipes, plot-markers, farming implements left out in the fields and other such innocent objects?

We are not the kind to take such things lying down. This holds especially true of our younger men. Decency constrains me not to dwell in detail on incidents of cattle-rustling, on the stoning of a nomad boy, or on the beating senseless of one of the shepherds. In defence of the perpetrators of the last-mentioned act of reprisal, be it said that the shepherd in question had an infuriatingly sly face. He was blind in one eye, broken-nosed, drooling, and his mouth—on this the men responsible were unanimous—was set with long, curved fangs like a fox's. Such a man was capable of anything.

The pilfering was the most worrying aspect of all. They laid their hands on the unripe fruit in our orchards, pocketed the taps, whittled away piles of sacks, stole into the henhouses and picked off the poultry, and even made away with the valuables from our little houses.

The very darkness was their accomplice. Elusive as the wind they passed through the settlement, evading both the guards we had posted and the extra guards we had added. Sometimes you would set out on a tractor towards midnight to turn off the irrigation-taps in an outlying field and your headlights would trap fleeting shadows, a man or a beast. A hot-headed guard was prompted one night to open fire—and merely killed a stray jackal.

Needless to say, the kibbutz secretariat repeatedly called in the police, but their tracking-dogs betrayed their masters and showed open sympathy for the enemy. Having led the policemen a few paces outside the kibbutz fence, they raised their noses from the ground and simply stared foolishly into space.

Spot raids on the tattered tents revealed nothing. It was as if the very earth had decided to cover up the plunder and brazenly outstare the victims. Eventually the elder of the tribe was brought to the kibbutz secretariat, flanked by a pair of inscrutable nomads and spurred on by short-tempered policemen.

We received the elder and his men respectfully, welcoming them with sympathetic expressions and with a pot of steaming coffee, brewed by Geula with her own skilled hands. The old man responded with elaborate courtesies, favouring us with a smile which he kept up from the beginning of the interview till its conclusion, and answered us in mild and ceremonious Hebrew.

It was true that one or two of his young men had laid their hands on our property. Boys will be boys. He had the honour of begging our pardon and restoring the property. That was the way of it. What could one do about the hot-headedness of youth? He deeply regretted the trouble to which we had been put. He put his hand into the folds of his robe and drew out a few screws, some gleaming, some rusty, a pair of pruning-hooks, a stray knife-blade, a broken hammer, and three grubby banknotes, as a suitable recompense for our loss and worry.

Etkin spread his hands out in embarrassment. For reasons best known to himself he chose to ignore our guest's Hebrew and to reply in halting Arabic, the residue of his studies during the time of the riots and the siege. He opened his remarks with a frank and outspoken statement about the brotherhood of nations—the cornerstone of our ideology—and about the quality of neighbourliness of which the peoples of the East had long been justly proud, and never more so than in these days of bloodshed and groundless hatred.

To Etkin's credit let it be said that he did not shrink in the slightest from reciting a full and detailed list of acts of theft and sabotage which our guest—as the result of oversight, no doubt—had refrained from mentioning in his apology. If the plunder were returned and the vandalism stopped, we would be wholeheartedly willing to open a new page in the relations of our two neighbouring communities. Our children would doubtless enjoy and profit from an educational courtesy-visit to the Bedouin encampment, the kind of visit which broadens horizons. And it went without saying that the tribe's children would pay a return visit to our kibbutz home.

The old man neither relaxed nor broadened his smile, but kept it sternly at its former level as he remarked with an abundance of polite phrases that the gentlemen of the kibbutz would be able to prove no further thefts beyond those which he had already admitted and for which he had sought our forgiveness.

He concluded with elaborate benedictions, took his leave and departed, accompanied by his two barefooted companions wrapped in their dark robes.

Since the police had proved ineffectual, and had washed their hands of the affair, some of our young men suggested making an excursion one night to teach the savages a lesson in a language they would really understand.

Etkin rejected their suggestion with disgust and in no uncertain terms. The young men, in turn, applied to Etkin a number of coarse epithets which decency constrains me to pass over in silence. Why then did Etkin reluctantly agree to put their suggestion before the kibbutz secretariat? Perhaps he was afraid that they might take matters into their own hands.

Towards evening Etkin went round from room to room and invited the committee to an urgent meeting at eight-thirty. When he came to Geula, he asked her to bring along a pot of black coffee and a lot of goodwill. Geula replied with an acid smile and eyes bleary from ravaged sleep. While she changed her clothes the night fell, damp and hot and close.

'II

Damp and hot and close the night fell, and tangled in the dust-laden cypresses. Frantic sprinklers scattered water onto the thirsty lawn, and the parched grass swallowed it till it left no trace. A busy phone rang vainly in the locked office. The walls of the houses gave out a damp vapour. A stiff column of smoke rose from the kitchen chimney and gently headed southwards. From the greasy sinks came the sound of a shattered dish, followed by a shout of reproof and an angry snort. A fat house-cat killed a small snake and dragged the corpse onto the baking concrete path to toy with it lazily. An ancient tractor rumbled and belched a stench of oil, then moved off in a hurry to deliver an evening meal to the second shift, toiling in the outlying fields. Geula prodded a discarded bottle, shiny with the remains of a slimy liquid. What made her kick it? She kicked at it furiously, but instead of shattering the bottle rolled heavily into the middle of the flower-bed till it came to rest, its belly hidden among the shrubs. Geula picked up a stone to throw at the bottle. She missed, of course.

Geula was a short, frail girl of twenty-nine. Although she had not yet found a husband, one could not deny her positive qualities, such as the energetic dedication which she lavished on local social and cultural activities. Her face was thin and pale. None of our other girls could rival her in brewing strong coffee, the real thing. A pair of bitter lines were etched at the corners of her mouth.

On summer evenings, when the rest of us would stretch out casually on one of the damp lawns and launch bursts of cheerful song heavenwards, Geula would shut herself up in her room and not join us until she had prepared the pot of scalding coffee, which she served with a dish of cakes.

What had passed between Geula and me is another story and need not be gone into here. Long ago we used to stroll together to the orchards at evening time, tossing not entirely outworn political ideas to one another and exchanging views on the latest literature. Geula's literary taste was sensitive but firm, and I would find myself agreeing in confusion with her sharp judgments. She did not like my stories, because of the extreme polarity of situations and characters. Sometimes I would lay a conciliatory hand on her neck, till she relented and gently leaned against me. Sometimes I would take her hand and count her fingers, making absurd mistakes. Naturally our affair was destined to come to nothing. She religiously cut my stories from the periodicals and arranged them in a locked drawer which she devoted to them. I continued to buy her a book of poems for her birthday. I crept into her room when she was out and left the book on her table, without any inscription or dedication.

Sometimes we would happen to sit together in the dining hall at supper-time. I avoided her glance, so as not to have to face that quiet, mocking sadness. On hot, damp summer days sweat disfigured her face and brought out her reddish spots. Some days she would go out at sunset to wander in the orchards. She went out alone, and alone she returned. In fairness it must be said that she did not stay there long.

IV

Viciously Geula picked up another stone to hurl at the slimy bottle. This time she did not miss, but she failed to hear the shattering-sound she craved. The stone grazed the bottle, tinkled faintly and disappeared deep in the bushes. A third stone, heavier than the other two, was launched from much closer, so close that it was nothing to boast of. The bottle naturally shattered this time with a harsh, dry rattle, and the explosion brought no relief.

Damp and close the night fell, its heat pricking the skin like broken glass. Must get out.

Geula retraced her steps, passed the balcony of her room and tossed her sandals inside. Barefoot she passed the older members' houses and barefoot she went out onto the dust track.

The clods of earth tickled the soles of her feet, and the soft breeze soothed her sweaty skin. Her rancour lent urgency to her pace. Beyond the rocky hill the shadows of the orchard were waiting for her. With determined hands she widened the gap in the fence and slipped her short, wiry body through. Must get out.

A gentle breeze was roaming aimlessly in the fields. An old sun rolled westwards, trying to be sucked up by the dusty horizon. A last tractor chugged its way home to the depot along the dirt road from the outlying plots. It was hard to make it out clearly because of the dust, but it stood to reason that this was the same tractor which had taken the second-shift workers their supper.

Geula bent down and picked some pebbles out of the dust. Absently she swung her arm and threw them back again one by one. Her lips soundlessly whispered snatches of poetry, some by the young poets, others her own. At one of the irrigation-pipes she paused to press her lips to the tap. The pipe was hot, the tap rusty, the water tepid and foul. Nevertheless she bent her head and let the water pour over her face. A sharp rust flavour filled her throat. For a few moments she kept her eyes closed. Neither cooled nor refreshed. Must hurry to the orchard. A cup of hot coffee might just bring relief.

V

The orchards were heavily laden and fragrant. The heavy branches converged to form a shadowy dome. The large clods of earth retained a measure of moisture. Geula picked a plum and crushed its pulp. Dark juice dripped onto the clods. With an air of decision she dropped to her knees and sketched twisted shapes in the soil. She clasped a dry twig in her hand and drew lines on the surface of the earth. Straight lines shooting off at an angle or zigzagging aimlessly. A distant bleating invaded the orchard. Dimly she became aware of a sound of bells. The nomad stopped behind Geula's back, as silent as a phantom. He dug at the dust with his big toe, and his shadow fell in front of him.

The girl was blinded by a flood of poetry. For a long time she continued to kneel on the ground and draw winding lines in the dust with her twig. The nomad waited patiently. From time to time he closed his good eye and stared in front of him with the other, the blind one. Finally he reached out and bestowed a long caress on the air. His answering shadow moved in the dust. Geula started at the shadow and leapt to the nearest tree, letting out a low sound. The nomad let his shoulders drop and put on a faint smile. Geula raised her arm and stabbed the air with her twig. The nomad continued to smile. His gaze dropped to her feet. His voice was hushed, and the Hebrew he spoke exuded a rare gentleness:

'What time is it?'

Geula inhaled to her lungs' full capacity. Her features grew sharp, her glance cold. Clearly and drily she replied:

'Half past six.'

The Arab broadened his smile and inclined his body as if to acknowledge a great kindness:

'Thank you very much, Miss.'

His bare toe had dug deep into the damp soil, and the clods of earth crawled at his feet as if they concealed a nervous reptile.

Geula did up the top button of her blouse. There were large perspiration stains on her shirt, drawing attention to her armpits. The nomad closed his blind eye and looked up. His good eye blinked. His face was swarthy. Creases were etched in his cheeks. His nose was long and narrow and a faint moustache showed beneath it. His cheeks were sunken, and a firm chin jutted out below. His lips were thin and fine. The man was repulsively handsome, Geula decided to herself.

Unconsciously the girl responded with a mocking half-smile to the nomad's persistent grin. The Bedouin drew two crumpled cigarettes from his belt, laid them on his outstretched palm and held them out to her. Geula dropped her smile and accepted one. For a moment she ran the cigarette through her fingers, ironing out the creases. Then she inserted it in the corner of her mouth. Before she had noticed the man's sudden movement a tiny flame danced in front of her. Geula drew a light, then another, from the lighter, and the nomad lit his own and bowed politely.

'Thank you very much.' He threw the words out quickly.

'Thanks,' Geula replied. 'Thank you.'

'You from the kibbutz?'

Geula nodded.

'Very nice.' A sound slipped out between his gleaming teeth. 'Really nice.'

The girl eyed his heavy, dark robe.

'Aren't you hot in that?'

The man gave an embarrassed smile, as if caught red-handed, and took a light step backwards.

'Not hot. Really not.'

The treetops grew darker. A first jackal sniffed the oncoming night and let out a tired howl. The orchard filled with a scurry of small feet. All of a sudden Geula became aware of the throngs of small black goats bursting in in search of their master. They swirled silently in and out of the trees. Geula pursed her lips and let out a short, surprised whistle.

'What are you doing here? Stealing?'

The nomad cowered as though a stone had been thrown at him, and glanced behind him. His hand beat a hollow tattoo on his chest.

'No, really not,' he swore anxiously, and smiled once more. His blind eye winked nervously.

An emaciated goat darted forward and rubbed against his leg. He kicked it away and swore again with exaggerated fervour.

'Not steal, truly, by God not steal. Forbidden to steal.'

'Forbidden in the Bible,' Geula replied with a smile. 'Forbidden to steal, forbidden to kill, forbidden to covet. The righteous are above suspicion.'

The Arab cowered before the onslaught of words and looked down at the ground. He kicked at the clods of earth with renewed energy. He was trying to ingratiate himself. His blind eye narrowed. Surely an undisguised wink. The smile left his lips. He spoke in a soft, drawn-out whisper.

'Beautiful girl, truly very beautiful girl. Me, I got no girl yet. Me still young. No girl yet. Yaaa,' he concluded with a guttural yell directed at a goat that had rested its forelegs against a tree-trunk and was munching at the foliage. The animal cast a pensive eye at its master, shook its beard and solemnly resumed its munching.

Without warning, and with amazing agility, the Arab sprang forward and seized the beast by the hindquarters, lifted it in the air, let out a guttural screech and flung it away with a wild heave. Then he spat and turned to the girl.

'Beast,' he muttered. 'No brains. No manners.'

The girl let go of the tree-trunk against which she had been resting and leant towards the nomad. A slight shudder ran down her back.

'Another cigarette?' she asked. 'Have you got another cigarette?'

The Bedouin replied with a look of deep anguish. He apologised in broken tones and explained that he had none left. All gone. What a pity. He would gladly, very gladly, have given her one. None left. All gone.

The beaten goat was getting shakily to its feet. Treading circumspectly it returned to the tree-trunk, keeping a disingenuous eye on its master. The shepherd watched it without moving. The goat accordingly reached up and once more began munching indifferently. The Arab picked up a heavy stone and swung his arm wildly. Geula seized his arm and restrained him.

'Leave it. Let it be. It doesn't understand. It's only a beast. No brains, no manners.'

The nomad obeyed in total submission and let the stone drop. In his surprise he uttered a rapid phrase in his own language. Geula let go of his arm. Once again the man drew the lighter out of his belt. With thin, pensive fingers he toyed with the gilt object. He accidentally lit a small flame. Geula blew hard, and the flame widened slightly, slanted and died. Nearby a jackal broke into a loud, piercing wail. The rest of the goats had followed the example of the first and were absorbed in their rapid, silent munching.

A vague wail came from the nomad encampment away to the south, the dim drum beating time to its languorous call. The dusky men sent skywards their single-noted song. The night took up the strain and answered with dismal cricket-chirp. Last glimmers of light were dying away in the far west. The orchard stood in its darkness. Strange noises sounded all around, the wind's whispering, the goats' sniffing, the rustle of ravished leaves. Geula pursed her lips and whistled a soft tune. The nomad listened, surprised, his head on one side. The girl glanced at her watch. The hands responded with a phosphorescent glint. The Arab turned his back on Geula, dropped to his knees, touched his forehead on the ground and began mumbling fervently.

'You've got no girl yet.' Geula broke into his prayer. 'You're still young.' Her voice was loud and strange. Her hands were on her hips, her breathing still rhythmical. The man stopped praying, turned his head and muttered a grumbling phrase in Arabic. He was still crouched on all fours, but his pose suggested a certain suppressed joy.

'You're still young,' the girl repeated happily. 'Very young. Perhaps twenty, perhaps thirty. Young. No girl for you. Very young.'

The man replied with a very long and solemn remark in his own language. The girl let out a nervous laugh.

'What's the matter with you?' she enquired, laughing still. 'What do you want, anyway?'

Yet again the nomad's reply was in Arabic. A note of terror suddenly filled his voice. With soft, silent steps he edged further and further away from her. His one eye glowed like a firefly. Geula sensed the nervous tension within him was freezing his muscles. In an instant he would run for his life.

A single wild syllable escaped from the shepherd's mouth, apparently aimed at the goats. The goats responded and thronged round him. Their nimble patter filled the orchard. The crickets fell silent as at a secret sign. The goats huddled into a dark, quivering body. Slowly they withdrew into the depths of the orchard, with their routed master in their midst.

In the clear sky above the treetops passed an airplane, rumbling dully. Its lights blinked alternately with a rhythm as precise as that of the drums: red, green, red, green, red. Involuntarily the girl looked up, and stared curiously at the plane. When she eventually looked down again, the goats were swallowed up in the night, and the night had covered their tracks. A quiet breeze was wandering alone in the tangled orchard. The girl's body filled with revulsion, even though the nomad had not laid a finger on her.

Fear hit her like a sudden blow. She fled at a run, pursued by the sawing of the crickets.

VI

Got to have a shower and go to the committee meeting.

Geula was not one to be late. Punctuality was in her blood. Since she had been asked to take a pot of coffee with her to the meeting, she put business before pleasure and put the kettle on to boil before she went out to the showers. Outside the cool of evening had set in, but indoors it was still close and muggy. Geula's body was sticky from her frantic running; her armpits exuded a strong odour, and the spots on her face were glowing from the sweat. Her movements were angry and abrupt. Hurriedly she put the coffee on, and counted the number of times it boiled. Coffee which has not boiled seven times is not coffee. With pursed lips Geula counted as the black liquid rose and subsided, rose and subsided, bubbling fiercely as it reached its climax. Finally she let the crust floating on the brew overflow the edge of the pot, letting off a glowing aroma. Just as the coffee was on the point of erupting and boiling over she removed the pot and hastily covered it. From now on it would start getting cold. It didn't choose to boil and it didn't choose to get cold. Time to pick up my evening clothes and hurry along to the showers. Must get out.

What has Etkin called this meeting for? The boys want to tackle the Bedouins and beat them up once and for all. So what? I'm not keen on violence and I'm not in favour of terrorist tactics, but this time things have gone too far. What does Etkin think, that they can rob and rape and destroy and make an unholy mess of our fields, and we'll dress up in our Sabbath best, go out and admire their exotic camps and preach the brotherhood of nations? Etkin is an intelligent man, and I don't doubt the purity of his motives. If it weren't for the frightful thing that's just happened to me, I'd probably toe his line. But he hasn't got so much as the foggiest glimmering of an idea about primitive psychology. The nomad sniffs out weakness from a distance. Weakness simply makes them even more brazen, till they end up committing actual crimes. It'll be very interesting to see what Etkin has to say when I tell him how a shepherd tried to rape me in the orchard.

How foul these showers are! The drain's clogged up, and the bench is greasy and filthy. Where can I put my clean clothes down? Imagine, Etkin, a girl goes out, all innocent, for a walk in the orchard, and suddenly she's pounced on by a savage. I'm shaking all over. Not from the cold water, from disgust. Just like an animal, the way he carried out his filthy scheme. Dragging me down onto the ground, grabbing me by the throat, forcing his way onto my stomach. Horrible. He was so skinny, and small as a boy—but so strong. A savage.

No, I won't tell them. I haven't got the strength to face their inquisitive stares. It's enough that I've told you, Etkin. You can tell them yourself. Tell the boys to go out to the camp tonight and break every bone in their bodies. I've been scraping my stomach, but I still can't get rid of the feel of that loathsome touch. How slimy these showers are. Must get out.

VII

Geula left the shower, and nausea took hold of her. She tried to overcome it or ignore it, and quickened her pace. The man's face appeared before her and made her weak at the knees. She leant against a tree, bent over and retched.

First of all came a long, loud groan, followed by a violent spasm. Then a series of acrid vomit-blasts, rising in her throat and bursting out, until her tears got the better of her, and overflowed her eyes, pouring down her cheeks and rushing along the bitter furrows embedded at the corners of her mouth. She dragged herself in among the trees and sat down in the shadows. A cup of strong coffee would have put her right, but she did not have the strength to reach her room. She stretched herself out in the depth of the thicket, and rubbed against the bushes till her skin was covered with red scratches. Her tears had run dry, but her teeth still continued to grind. A great feeling of pity welled up inside the girl and washed over her; her hand went up to her face and began stroking it gently.

It was possible that all those planes had been sent here on a night-bombing exercise. Every now and again they flew among the stars, keeping up a constant flashing, red, green, red, green, red.

Out of the pitch-dark night came the persistent sounds of the nomads' song. Their drum-beat set time to the urgent inner throbbing. One, one, two. One, one, two.

VIII

From eight-thirty until nearly nine o'clock we waited for Geula. It was not like her, not to turn up to a meeting. Since she did not appear, Etkin embarked on a brief résumé of the damage caused by the Bedouin tribesmen, concluding with his objections to the improper course of action to which the younger men wanted to resort. Etkin's intention was to deter them from violence not by outvoting them but by dissuading them. He rightly reminded us that the conflict between herdsmen and tillers of the soil was as old as human history, citing in evidence the story of Cain, who rose up against Abel his brother. It was fitting, in view of the social gospel we had adopted, that we should put an end to this ancient feud, too.

An air of tension pervaded the overheated room thanks to the aggressiveness of Rami, who heckled Etkin continuously and even went so far as to call his statements hypocrisy and cant. Etkin in turn raised his voice and pounded the tattered table-top with a furious fist. He refused to stand there and face a battery of insults. The young men's attitude was hooliganistic; he was not afraid of calling a spade a spade.

If you take into account, besides the violent exchanges of words, the rivers of sweat streaming from the participants and the absence of Geula, which deprived us of our customary coffee, you will not be surprised at the bad feeling which pervaded the room. The exchange of words which ensued between Rami and me demolished the last barriers of decency.

Although in age I belonged with the younger men, I did not agree with their proposals. Like Etkin, I was absolutely opposed to answering the nomads with violence, for two reasons. When I was given an opportunity to speak I set forth both my arguments without hesitation, and that was what set loose the furore. In the first place, I urged, the use of violence was beneath the dignity of the kibbutz, and, secondly, nothing really serious had happened so far. A bit of stealing did not add up to rape, pillage and murder.

Hereupon Rami broke in excitedly and asked what I was waiting for: for the police, who had failed and abandoned the case? For the insolence to get worse? For something terrible to happen? Wasn't it bad enough that our lands had been taken over and that no one could go out into the fields alone? It was high time to put a stop to things once and for all.

I replied by protesting against Rami's exaggerations. It was not true that our land had been taken over. It was wrong for us to work ourselves into a frenzy by exaggerating. It was still possible for a girl like Geula to go for romantic walks through the orchards every evening and come back safe and sound. Not a hair of her head had been touched. Everybody knew that.

Rami in turn shot me a furious glare and demanded with a sneer whether Geula, and I too for that matter, were sitting back waiting for a rape actually to happen so that we could brood on it, I in my stories and Geula in her poems.

Etkin responded to this outspokenness by silencing Rami and me and attempting to restate his position. Rami and the other young men exchanged glances. In the middle of Etkin's speech they stood up and stalked out of the room with a contemptuous look, leaving Etkin to direct his harangue to four elderly veterans.

After a moment of indecision I too rose and followed them. True, I did not share their views, but I too had been unfairly deprived of the right to speak.

If only Geula had been present at the meeting, she might have managed, in her usual way, to restore calm and good order. The coffee, too, would have helped to soothe our tempers. Pity.

IX

The highly prized coffee did not help to soothe tempers, for the simple reason that it was still standing in Geula's room. And, naturally, it was getting colder and colder.

Geula herself was lying all alone among the bushes watching the flashing lights of the planes in the night. She was filled with a silent emptiness. Repose had not yet engendered a state of liberation, but it was somewhat soothing. Soothingly she stroked her own cheeks and comforted herself with snatches of poetry soundlessly caressed on her lips. The savage who had overpowered her and ravaged her body would not leave her alone. In his ears she whispered her poems. Now and again she closed her eyes and rebuked him sadly. The cold was already stealing among the bushes, bringing relief to the girl and to the broken glass, the remains of the slimy bottle Geula had shattered with a stone a few hours before.

The earth had not succumbed to the cold, but continued to exude a subdued warmth. Red, green, red, green, red winked the planes in the sky. The flashing lights did not distract the viper crawling alongside the girl's body. Rage swept over the serpent, who raised his head and shot out a forked tongue. The viper's anger was not capricious.

The girl had chosen to stretch out in the thick of the bushes, and in doing so had blocked the entrance to his hole with her body. He wanted to return home, but he could not. His eyes bulged with a dull glassiness. He could never close his eyes, for the simple reason that he was not endowed with eyelids. His body was grey-green and out-stretched. The zigzag line stressed his outstretched pose and exaggerated it by contrast. Lost in her poetic reverie, the girl was unlikely to notice the snake. Her eyes were shut, and they did not open when the viper thrust a pair of sharp, venomous upper fangs into her ankle, the lower ones lending stiff support. Geula lifted her foot at the sudden pain and rubbed it with a warm hand. She tried to pull out the thorn which had been thrust into her flesh.

Freed of his venom, the serpent experienced release. In lazy loops he made off from the scene. Exhaustion prevented him from going far. Near the broken glass of the bottle he curled up and buried his head in his trunk. Satiety cast a deep slumber on him. How can we know at which precise moment the slumber overcame him. His eyes were ever-open. Geula's eyes, too, were open. A heaviness pressed against her ankle. A dull pain, a tender pain penetrated her bloodstream and soothed her whole body, while a sound as of distant bells warned her to get up and look for people. The heaviness overpowered her, and her eyes closed once more. Her knees betrayed her and refused to bend. Weakly she rolled over on her side, curled up and rested her weary head on her arms. A shudder of pleasure rippled over her skin. Now she could listen to the sweet wave sweeping through her body and intoxicating her bloodstream. To this sweet wave Geula responded with complete surrender.

Geula still retained a vestige of lucidity, by means of which she could perceive a group of young men passing close by with excited voices and great commotion. The young men were crossing the flower-beds on their way to the fields, to punish the nomads. We had short, stout sticks in our hands. The mounting excitement made our chests swell and the pupils of our eyes dilate.

Far off in the dusky orchards dark, dust-laden cypresses stood, waving to and fro in calm devotion.

Because of the searing pleasure Geula did not come out to send us on our way and wish us good luck. The pleasure flooded the girl and sent a soothing coolness coursing through her. She was still clutching a dry twig in her hand.

Her hand felt very soft, soft and full of pleasure.

Translated by Nicholas de Lange

Yoram Kaniuk

The Parched Earth

I sat on the parched earth. All about me burned the evening's dark autumn, my vast evening, belonging to me alone. I seized it with both my small hands, not letting it escape. I loved it.

The short street ended in a small square in which a tree stood, a black sky hanging in its crown; in the middle of the sky there was a yellow hole. The moon had no face, no eyes, no teeth, no mouth; two clouds tickled it. "It will rain tonight," I said. In the square stood the twins, peeing their names in the sand: Meshulam, Yeruham.

Aunt Shlomit stood at the window. Without knowing it, she looked pretty in the light of the lamp that shone behind her. Her head celebrated itself, casting its own halo, singing itself songs. I longed madly to pull her hair with tenderness, but I was on the parched earth and saw an insect walking between its cracks. The house behind me did not stir. Only Aunt Shlomit stirred and ended the light.

"Why aren't you 'making' homework, Yosef?" she said suddenly.

"Don't want to," I replied. I would have preferred to hold back the answer, but my tongue would not obey; it leaped up and ruined my plan. Someone like me on the parched earth has nothing but plans anyway, plans that are never realized and remain clouds melting in the wind. Then why try? Don't ask.

I was a good child, obedient and quiet. Sometimes I was stubborn, like my father to whom everything was a challenge. If someone said to him, "Alex, you can't jump off the roof," he would instantly jump to show he could. Once, after the Arab riots in '36 he went to Café Pilz, picked up a glass from the bar and asked, "How much?" The barman said, "Two *grush*." He gave the man the money, then hurled the glass at the wall, shattering it to bits, just like that, because someone told him he wouldn't dare. At night, my father draws. No one knows. No one, that is except anyone between here and Rehovot. He knows that they know and they know that he knows that they know, but he doesn't mind.

"Don't want to *do* my homework," I shouted to Aunt Shlomit. I was teasing her. I said *do* and she had said *make*. Her Hebrew is translated from Russian: "Yosef, open the light!" I taught Aunt Shlomit to say "hole in the sky" rather than "moon." I have scores of names for the moon and more names for other things. On our street they call her Mrs. Hole-in-the-Moon; they are so poetic. At least ten poets should come out of this neighborhood. But in the meantime, they cackle and buy and sell. Mr. Abramowitz is already looking for a match for his daughter who is in my class. She invited me to go to the woods with her. I said no, I don't go to the woods with girls. On our street they used to sing a song about Aunt Shlomit, especially in the summer when the iceman came and everyone would stand in line. At night we all die, Aunt Shlomit once said. They used to sing to her. Especially the "pariah" . . . he was the first to sing to her:

> "Hole in the moon-oo-on, he—oo-le in the m-oon,
> hole-in-the-moon/ hole in the—moon/ hole in . . ."

"When your father comes home, I'll tell him," Aunt Shlomit said angrily. "I'm scared to death," I answered in my indifferent voice, feeling very manly and grown up. I was thirteen and would have no Bar Mitzvah. I didn't want a Bar Mitzvah. I had this "bug" in my mind, a sort of madness that gnawed at me in the night like a swarm of ants on the parched earth. My mother wept. It was Father who consoled her. "Don't want to . . . don't have to!" my father had told me. I couldn't explain that I wished they would insist. I saw I had lost and didn't say a word. So that was that.

"Why won't you do it?" Aunt Shlomit asked.

"Do what?"

"Your homework. I suppose you're dreaming, for a change? I talk to you about homework and you start to 'what' me. Such a brat . . ."

"Because it's all silly," I said. "What do I care about one-point-four divided by zero-point-three? We won't get rid of the British through the square root of three."

"When you grow up, you'll see it's important. Look at your father. . . ."

"I drink cod liver oil because it makes me grow, but what does this have to do with my father? He makes picture frames and he doesn't care at all about how much is six squared multiplied by zero point hole-in-the-moon." I swallowed the last words so I wouldn't offend her and so I could really laugh; I laughed so much I almost burst. But the twins were gone. I thought of their names peed in the sand. The thought flashed through my mind: God has dealt the same with me because of the Bar Mitzvah I will not have.

"Look at your father! What intelligence. You can see it on his face: such intelligence . . . You're no Jew . . . I'm bringing up a regular *shegetz.* "

"I'm glad," I told her. "Want to sing with me? I want to be an electric pole, a thorn, a grey bush in the Moslem cemetery. All right?"

Then I ran out of the yard. The ground was cracked all the way to the street, where the unfinished road begins. Everyone is building. Not a single empty lot is left. All around me stands Tel Aviv, the city that my grandfather and old Izmuzik built so they wouldn't have to live in filthy Jaffa. They stood on the hills, were photographed, drove stakes, and behold, a city, the city of Jews. Let the gentiles deal in finance. The Jews will sit singing songs, making bonfires, roasting gentiles. In the meanwhile, we need a gentile to do the work forbidden to Jews on the Sabbath. What do we do? Form a City Council which makes an agreement with the Holy-One-blessed-be-He. For the sake of the city, light must be installed. That's why I don't want a Bar Mitzvah. They say, "Emergencies defer the Sabbath," because they made this agreement with God. If you can make agreements with Him I don't want to give Him my chastity and promise to grow up for His sake. . . .

Oh, Tel Aviv, Tel Aviv, Mound of Spring, your hot winds are not spring, your spring is short and fleeting. Two jasmine can make a man crazy, so says Aunt Shlomit, stacking plates one on the other as she does with the days, years, moments of her life.

"What a spoiled child," she said. "If I were your mother, I would teach you respect."

"Auntie dear," I said, "did you see what the twins did?" She fled to her room, and her window shut. But the cracked earth continued to the edge of the city. Tel Aviv began at the point where the unfinished road was washed out by the great flood, when we rowed down Bugrashov Street in boats not knowing if the end of the world was upon us. Tel Aviv, your winters drip and it is c-c-cold. The houses are unheated, for this is the East and in the East it is warm: it says so in books. What the books forget is that once all these hills were covered with forests that blocked the wind. Now there are no forests and the wind is an ignorant wild devil. Not without cause do they call you the Mound of Spring. Sad loveliness of mine, they build you so fast that the last new house considers the next-to-last a mound to be searched for antiquities.

Our house used to be far north of the city. Walking from the house to the city was an adventure—lonely vineyards with dusty broken branches surrounded by graves. Then the boundaries were set. One section was to be called city, the other graveyard. Now the city races after us, the wasteland retreats and I shout "Ayyy," because I was born here. If I had been born in Germany, I would say "aow," in America, "ouch." Here dreams are buried—so my father, who made frames, used to tell the Germans who wanted to hang drawings on the walls of their homes. This house, beside the parched earth, beside the ants, beside the yard with the twins' tree, beside Aunt Shlomit, between a street that is no street and another street which is a boulevard without a street—what boy is growing here? I am growing and I will have a Bar Mitzvah without a Bar Mitzvah. When Dumbo reads his Portion, which could have been mine, I'll go to the Arab village of Samuil and eat sesame seeds. They won't give me presents; fine, so they won't. They won't give me the *Complete Writings of Ber Borohov* and three fountain pens. What can one write with them anyway?

The Bible is all written, so are the poems of Bialik, even Shlonsky's. What is there left to write? Letters? Where am I going? Running away? All the ways are closed: mountains are in Beirut, and in the south the Egyptian river. Where to? The North Pole? I don't know the way. At best I go to Samuil or to Jasmine Street, or to Treetop Street, or to Raven Street. Before they gave the place a name, ravens used to cackle from the top of a sycamore tree. Once the sun died on the treetop, the ravens cried and flew away.

Where else does one go? School? There, too, I have nothing to write. If I write, I remember; then it is harder to forget.

Put me in the black-sooted kerosene stove. Burn my limp body with last year's papers, burned-up news that took its own life because it couldn't run as fast as time. Once newspapers discovered time; now they can't compete with it. I wish I were no longer here, on the parched earth. For Aunt Shlomit, it is better not being than being.

My marvelous city, my wonderful city, my city of empty lots. They are filling your emptiness. Rabinowitz, the pariah's father, Rabinowitz's brothers, all come and build houses. One house, then another. They bring death to the lots. The wild visions of pioneers roasting potatoes in the wilderness, and a people becoming its own Messiah, turn into the reality of balconies. Old Rabinowitz, along with young Rabinowitz, paints his balcony the color of the murder of beautiful wastelands. The wasteland cries. How sad the cry of this wasteland in the mouths of jackals at night: yuhuuuuuuu.

"Go get some bagels," Aunt Shlomit called to me. I ran to bring her bagels. Had they not taught me what "bagels" are I would place a wreath at the wasteland's grave. But I was taught language precision. "Take the bagels," I say, "it's a tradition, my friend!" In Jaffa there are markets where a great secret lies, containing itself with caution and patience, ready to erupt like the shriek of a citrus grove's well at night. From the murky depths the edge of our dreams peers up. And Aunt Shlomit wants *bagels*.

On every second lot they build a house; on every other a billboard is erected: one side is used to post notices, the other to do what the twins did near the tree. Sometimes the sides are reversed. The houses are white, glistening shrill-white, not the whiteness of the dainty moon, but more like the brazen sun. Houses shriek of whiteness like the jackals. Every apartment has its balcony, each balcony a table. I sit on the parched earth, talk to the ants and drink the yellow hole with my eyes, debating whether to kill Aunt Shlomit or simply beat her or strangle her. Nonsense, I can't even raise my hand against a fly. Except for the pariah. I could castrate him. He told the class I masturbate at night. I don't mind *what* others think of me; I mind that they do at all. There are things which are all mine, absolutely private. In the bathroom I am king.

All around are balconies, on every balcony a table, at each table sit our people in a cloud of night butterflies, eating finely chopped vegetables with yogurt. The roofs are covered with white laundry. Old Yemenite women, their faces drawn, cheeks ridged, do the wash in giant gray basins; from time to time they pour some bluing into the suds. The blue turns white. Soon roofs will be swept into flight by the multitude of sheets that hang flickering in the sun by day and the moon by night. Everything here resembles itself, imitates itself, looks in a mirror. Winter and summer, night and day; only night is somewhat darker. Day is night minus darkness. Daytime: father goes to his work, mother to hers and Aunt Shlomit gets on my nerves. "What are you digging for in your nose? Gold?"

Night gathered unto itself and away from evening, and said to me: "Yosef, there is a bed upstairs. To sleep!" I went up. My mother sighed. "How is it in the yard?" she said, "did you see Aunt Shlomit?" "Go to the window and call her," I answered, "she's sitting in the dark, insulted, thinking about things." Then I prepared my body for the altar of night. I moved with mincing steps, touching, yet not touching, doe-like, and said, "Goodnight, Mommy, goodnight, Daddy." They said, "Goodnight, my child, pleasant dreams."

I always dream pleasant dreams. I fly wherever I want to, as if I were an ant with wings. I hover above and go mad in the sky, pluck stars, do multiplication without numbers, silently steal close to Saul, King of Israel, who lost his world because he spared the king of Amalek out of pity. We are a pitying people! Mommy and Daddy have other dreams. They sleep in separate rooms and all night they sigh and groan in their sleep. Sleeping with a door between them, two parted worlds and their dream is one. What a strange lot fathers and mothers are. Dumbo has silkworms that dream themselves into cocoons and return to the world of butterflies. Tiny eggs emerge from them. A million, maybe more.

If only tomorrow were Saturday. But tomorrow is not Saturday, nor is it Rosh Hashanah or even Arbor Day, or Remembrance Day. If it were I would go to Abu-Shaluf Sumale, shoot pumpkin seeds dizzily into my mouth, drink Turkish coffee, belch out groans straight from the belly where all the years I have yet to live are sleeping. Days arranged like sliced bread, for meat, for cucumbers, for apples. And old Abu-Shaluf would tell me about Juha, the Arab Charlie Chaplin. What did Juha do? He went to the *muhata*—station in Arabic. Why? Because the wife he was buying was coming from Beirut on the train. What a vision did he, Mr. Juha, see in his mind (which was as open as the mouth of a woman) of this wife and how she would look inside his bed! What did this Juha do? He tied his donkey to a stake and waited with vee-rry great patience, *il-has-la*. Suddenly, the train was coming, the one that was bringing him the woman he had bought in Beirut, and sounding its whistle: tooo! tooo! The donkey, that old donkey, what does it do? Aaay, aayaaay, its whole jaw quivers like a whore's behind. Juha is angry at him and says, "Ya-donkey, who is this woman for . . . you or me?"

Indeed, the day waxed weary with age. That is fine speech. Mother uses fine speech. She doesn't say, "in mine bed." Father uses fine speech. My speech is wild. It comes with the hot winds, the raindrops, the sun that dries everything, manes of cypress that ask the sky questions, pointing upward as if they were fingers of schoolkids playing dumb, jasmine that inhales its own perfume, carobs that smell like a dirty joke, cactus thorns with which our dainty bodies were decorated. Mother says our land is the land of milk and honey. But what do we say? Land of donkeys and asses. She speaks from her heart, we from our eyes. We were born here, without ideals; she came here on the wings of ideals. The question is, which is greater: the thing that is, or the thing that can become? They came because they had to, therefore they could. We, however, can, because we have to. Mother has a world of her own. My world is the world of the parched earth to which I am tied with an umbilical cord. But the earth is not my teacher, and does not come home in the afternoon to ask me, "Haven't you prepared your lessons?" And of course Mother can't be fooled. Dumbo can tell his mother anything, but I can talk only to the parched earth. For Mother, I am a pedagogical laboratory. And why does she hang around during recess with Mr. Broshi, the teacher? The wildness of our speech is an outrage, Mother says. Aunt Shlomit agrees in simpleminded Hebrew. Outrage! An exquisite word. Such words, along with names like Rio de Janeiro, can redden a long winter night under the feather quilt Aunt Shlomit gave my mother, this feather quilt being the pearl of Broshi's Hebrew. My teacher, Mr. Broshi, will say: Flowers appear on the earth, buds are in bloom . . . the feather quilt having settled in his eyes like a color film. My name is Yosef. I am the pearl of the outraged language, the outrage of the pearl of language, or . . . But today's not Saturday, and I must get up.

I crept from beneath the covers, bare, into the chill of the room. Outside, the parched earth and the one-sided street, the tree—the twins must be getting up too. If only I had a twin brother. We would divide the world in two and drink it up, each one a half. Together. You have to brave the chill of the room. Like a refrigerator. Dress fast, swallow the cold that sits in your eyes like a bird singing songs. Gideon's brother can imitate a bird's songs. The pariah can't do anything. If it was Lag b'Omer I would hang him in a bonfire and run around it, me and all my twins. It is he who sings 'hole-in-the-moon' to Aunt Shlomit. Suddenly Aunt Shlomit matters to me. Anyone who is being mocked is my pal.

I sat down and swallowed my breakfast. Cereal, pale coffee, a warm roll. I kissed Mother and Father good-bye, and slammed the door. That life was left behind, a faint wail. God had spread Himself before me. I could have ridden on His back to the end of the world. This is the spot where I pick berry leaves to feed the silkworms. In a moment,

I was at the seashore. One step more and I could swim to America and kill Indians. Two waves laughed at me. They were white and full of roaring foam. They crashed against the sand and released a handful of seashells. It was autumn and the land, which yesterday was cracked, now spewed moist greenery in which the clearness of water was fixed. When I stand and look at it, what do I see? A picture of myself, one more precise than what the mirror yields. Mother says, look at the photograph of Uncle Yasha on the horse. It is as if he were looking at a mirror. The mirror is crooked and the clock does not tell time. Everything depends on something else. The image in a mirror is untrue, it is reversed. How much better to be on the parched earth. One day I will go there. To rest.

Autumn, enchanted, marvellous, is spread upon the seashore. Two sparrows cried the birth of autumn from the Book of Legends. The water is cool. Wind blows sand. I might find something left by last summer's bathers. All the children dash to the beach as soon as the autumn winds begin to blow. Hundreds of children from all over. What a sight—a battlefield. They scurry across the sand searching for dreams; the dreams sit laughing in the holes of the ring-shaped money, the *grush.* Arab women hang *grushim* in their nose, we hang our dreams in the hole of the *grush;* Mother, in the hole of the bagel. Father says, how do they make bagels? They take holes and set them in dough. That's Father, a framemaker. That is why he says these things. Think it over; they take some plain canvas with a nothing-like picture of a chicken, one that is worthless, that can't even cackle, let alone be eaten. Around this a frame of gold is constructed. Then what does one say? Look at the picture! But where is the frame?

One child found a *grush.* Someone else found a bracelet, or maybe a wind, and flew off with it. They all find or say they find. I go to the beach every morning, betraying my sweetheart, the parched earth in the yard, giving up my place in the world to come, failing to sing my Portion of the Torah, renouncing my chance to become Bar Mitzvah. What do I find? I find someone who had found something and has run off leaving his secret behind. When I was born, my godfather said, "Today is the sixth of Nissan, a marvellous month, one with the fragrance of citrus flowers and many scented bloomings; a sun bathed in the flighty beauty of silver color mixed with lemon, delicate as my mother's face when she is asleep and not dreaming . . ." I was born under the sign of spring. They call me Yosi. "When he grows up," my godfather said, "call him Yosef and when he grows wise—make it Yehosef."

Yehosef-ele Gretz-ele the children called me with malice in their eyes. If their eyes were daggers, I would have died long ago. Therefore, my only love is the parched earth and my life's dream is to be an ant—whose lot is better, having no truck with children who go to school by way of the beach to search for a *grush* and to laugh at Yehosef-ele Gretz-ele. "Just because his mother is the teacher . . . Just because . . . Just . . . ." Just because I go to school and know that something horrible will happen, every day something horrible happens at Mother's school.

On the way to the beach, Mrs. Birnbaum emerged from the bushes that enclose her home like an envelope and swooped down on me, clinging to me as the sun clings to some poor creature on the street. "What happened, Mrs. Birnbaum?" I said hurriedly, rushing my words. "They were here again. The lions," she said.

She began to weep her special gems, the ones the husband she doesn't have any more kisses away—salted tears, Birnbaum tears. She wiped her face with a faded apron. A car passed. She started in terror.

"Nerves," she apologized. "Nerves . . ."

"They're frayed," I said.

"Frayed, shattered. Someone opened the sky and rained troubles on my head. There were lions here tonight."

"Lions again," I said. I was the adult here. Everyone has his moment. The shoemaker, Yehoshua, when his moment comes, sews a song. The sister of Nehama Meyerowitz refuses to give her body to British soldiers on the hill in the Muslim cemetery, at the foot of a stone engraved with scythes and swords and pictures of wild horses frolicking.

"There are no lions in this country," I consoled her. "Maybe Giladi's rabbits were scratching at the wall of the rabbit house. Maybe a jackal lost his way. What time is it?"

"High time," she said and cried a mound of stone tears.

A landslide, I thought, and was reminded of the pariah, wishing he were caught in such an accident.

"No, no," Mrs. Birnbaum implored. "I'm alone, all alone. There is nothing. Only lions come at night and roar into the darkness."

"It's the parched earth," I said, "crying for rain."

"What a country," said the old woman, Mrs. Birnbaum, whose husband did not come with her, but stayed in some faraway place. "What a country. Every year drought."

"An awesome word," I told her, "and full of glory."

"I like furniture," she said, "because of its quiet."

"And beauty." I smiled my cute smile, the one I leave outside so Aunt Shlomit won't fall on her knees in thanks to God that I-can-be-so-cute-when-I-want-to-be. But the drought is as full of glory as an eagle.

"Eagle," mumbled Mrs. Birnbaum.

"There is 'eagle' and there is yogurt. Two sides of the same coin. Beauty has but one opposite: splendor. In the middle, hope is pressed."

"Which?" she asked.

"Of a land in the midst of the East."

"This is our land," she said and repeated, "our land, the land of Israel . . ."

"Many thanks," I said. "Mine too. I was here before, because I didn't know where to go. Suddenly, the stork came and told me: come out. I came out. Know what I did then?"

"No," she said.

"I let out an awful scream, from my stomach. Father fainted, almost."

"A good memory," she said.

"Yes, but there are no lions here."

"No, no. Yes, Yes . . . that is, my father was a hunter. He hunted them in the jungles of Africa and sold them to zoos. They will come to find me, to revenge . . ."

I began to run for my life. "There are no lions here," I repeated, shouting back to her.

Nor are there bears or Red Riding Hoods. There are no jungles. Only a couple of small groves that we, the children, plant. I have planted at least four of these with my own hands. Every month, besides, I collect my money and give it to the fund that plants a tree in my name on Arbor Day, the 15th of Shvat. Holiday of Trees, New Year for Foliage and Yom Kippur of the Earth. They are slaughtering the great earth with these trees. The groves are all planted. A week later goats come and eat the seedlings. Again we plant.

Mrs. Birnbaum settled into her sooty house and I whistled myself back to the beach to look for those who find things there. I place my book on my head as the Arab women do with their water pitchers, took off my shoes and hung them on my Scout belt, and walked splashing through the chill water, my feet pricked by broken shells. It felt good. I began to sing aloud, trying to outdo the noise of the sea, to subject it to my own voice. But my voice was hushed, like the breath of a swallow, by the wondrous murmur of the seaside morning, the shore, Jaffa with its towers behind, the world before; Tel Aviv, sprawled to my right; to my left, waves; fish cried, cranes cray-crayed, seashells shelled themselves; I sang:

"Tel Aviv, city of endless sky,
White roofs and the shoe-shine boys' cry . . ."

"Oh, Yehosef-ele Gretz-ele . . ." I heard the call, not knowing whence it came. Maybe God was talking with me as with Moses. With Samuel. But, He didn't actually speak with Samuel, for Samuel thought he heard the voice of his master. Of all the people in the world, only with Moses did He speak directly, and with me. But no. It was not He. Two inverted bodies came up from behind, legs up, hands leading. The twins: Meshulam and Yeruham, walking on their hands.

"What's up down there?" I asked.

"Funny. Oh, how funny is this Yehosef-ele Gretz-ele," Meshulam said from the depths.

"What if, one day, you would start to walk like the rest of us, on your feet?"

"It would be the same, but you would never know. What's new, Yehosef-ele? Look there, in the harbor. See a boat?" Yeruham pointed with his foot toward the dock.

"I see."

"It's bringing holes. A boatload of holes."

"Good it didn't sink," I said. I was clever. I knew something they didn't know I knew.

"It's no joke, Yehosef-ele Gretz-ele."

"Was I laughing?"

"No," they gestured, both of them. Their mouths were full of sand.

"Speak up," I said.

"See the second boat?" I looked. "It's full of needles. The government ordered a boatload of needles. It came and the inspectors went to work. What did they find? Needles without eyes. Beautiful needles, sharp, gleaming, perfect—but no holes. What did they do? Ordered a boatload of holes."

"Have a good walk," I said, waving good-bye to them.

I continued on my way, sang again, inventing a tune. By the time I found words to fit I was at the fishing boats. Some workmen were repairing a large vessel. They said to me, "Hey kid . . . hey kid . . ."

"What?" I said.

"Study hard. If you're late, you'll end up fixing fishing boats." For some reason this sentence made them laugh. If I hadn't passed them on the run, my book already in my hand, my shoes rocking back and forth on my Scout belt—though I wasn't ever in the Scouts—I would, probably, hear them laughing to this very day. It's lucky that I ran from there.

I passed two British policemen at the entrance to the harbor, climbed up the hill and whistled to Dumbo. He came laughing. He probably heard the joke, I thought. "What are you laughing at?" I asked and didn't wait for an answer. "We'll be late for school," I said.

"It will wait," said Dumbo, who was a giant. His stomach was large, his nose a marvellous hump, like a ram's horn held backward.

"My mother had a dream," he said.

"I suppose she heard lions in the yard," I said.

"No, if she saw a lion she would think it was a big dog. That's why she didn't see a lion. If she saw a big dog, she would die of fright. No, she dreamed that the English left the country, that only Jews were left. She cried in her sleep. 'Who will there be left to curse,' she shouted. 'Who? Weizmann? Shertok? Ben-Gurion?' "

"She really dreamed lions," I told him. "It's frightening."

"Why are you so strange?" Dumbo suddenly said and stopped running.

"It bores me not to be," I said.

"Oh, that's another matter." We began to run again.

We were almost late when we got to school. Dumbo wanted to wrestle with me on the grass. Everyone wants to wrestle on the grass. The grass, apparently, likes people to wrestle on it. But we were in a hurry. So we didn't wrestle on the grass. Not in the hallway either. We barely managed to break a coat hanger or two and, at top speed, we flew into class. The bell sounded for the last time and thrust us into the room. In class I was transformed. I assumed another expression, went quietly to my place and sat down. Ninety eyes were fixed on me. I paid no attention. I took a book from my briefcase, sharpened a pencil.

"How is your mother today?" Hedva asked.

"She's not my mother. She's the teacher," I said brusquely.

"Yes. But she's your mother."

"Hedva, by the laws of *your* logic, she's my mother because she gave birth to me, because at home she feeds me, because last night I heard her groaning in her sleep. But, by other laws of logic, those that *you* are incapable of grasping, here she is the teacher, Miss Mira. The people who bring us into the world do not always remain mother and father. Sometimes something happens. The frames change. For example, in dreams I have a different mother."

"You told me you don't dream."

"I said I don't have nightmares."

"Oh."

The teacher entered. "Good morning, children," she chimed, scanning everyone with all-seeing eyes. She sat down in her place, the blackboard drawing her in clear and solid lines. Brightness on a ground of black, just like in dreams.

To me she said, "Gretz!" her voice tarrying a second though she did not look up. I answered, "Present." She noted this and continued, "Herma, Lubianiker. . . ."

We sang a song:

> "The wheels of the world (since the world
> is round it has square wheels, maybe)
>
> Grind with force as they work (stick a tack
> in that seat and you'll force the works—)
>
> In song every muscle shall sway (muscles
> that sway in song need medical attention)"

We were excited. We built with all our dreams and hopes; Tel Aviv harbor—we hewed large rocks, our arms struggled with their heavy weight. It was wonderful to be such heroes. The voices soared, passed out of the classroom, flitted over the bare hills to the left, congregated at sea, raced toward distant lands, circled in the skies of reverie, played football on the sandy lot where later the army camp was built.

"Mr. Broshi taught her the song," Ehud said. "Mr. Broshi must have taught it to her."

"Stop it. Can't you see Yehosef-ele Gretz-ele is blushing," Ahuva said.

"So what if he's blushing."

"Yes, but . . . Maybe Mr. Broshi is really his father."

"He has two fathers. Mr. Broshi and his other father at home."

"Who's talking?" the teacher asked.

"Teacher, I have a question," said Hedva.

"Ask it."

"Why do Arab women veil their faces?"

One day I was walking on Herzl Street with my mother. We went into a store to buy material. My mother was bargaining with the storekeeper. I was ashamed. Buy it already, buy it already, I said to myself. Then I went out. An Arab woman passed; her eyes, above the veil, were blue, her skin was brown, her hair was like the board behind the teacher—the color of slate. She raised a hand and motioned me to follow her. We disappeared into the secret alleys of Jaffa. Meat was sold in the streets there. In the spice market I was drunk with the smell. I hung onto her dress. She smiled at me and then she ran away laughing. I cried. Not to my mother, not to my father, not to Aunt Shlomit . . . just to her, whose beautiful face I never even saw. She was gone like the wind, false as a dream. This is my first memory of childhood. Before that everything is dark and unknown.

"Now children," the teacher said, not answering Hedva's question and raising her face from the desk and shifting it from one to another of us until she settled in a smile which grew, balanced itself on the tip of her nose and slowly covered her entire face, expanding it into one beaming melon field, every fiber smiling. "Now, I would like to have a talk with you. Close your books and anyone who has written answers to arithmetic problems on his fingernails may erase them." We closed our books and gave her our attention. A gentle gladness passed through the class, made our eyes tremble. We were pigeons circling over a crumb of bread. Outside, the sky seemed bluer.

"Every boy and girl," said the teacher, "each one of you sits here seven hours a day. In the afternoon you gather in playgrounds, on the streets, go to the swamps in the north to collect tadpoles. Each of you is born of a moment of mute loneliness." There was silence in the room. It was possible to hear the parched earth singing its lone song.

"You came into the world alone. Only your mothers and fathers were there to welcome you. Every mother and every father," the teacher continued as we listened intently, "has his personality, his scent, his culture. Here, in school, seven hours a day, we live in another world, a world of togetherhood, forgetting where we have come from and where we are going, speaking 'as if' and thinking with intimacy. Our senses are not individual, but belong to the collective 'us,' the group, the National Council, the general committee. Education is not contact with the individual. For the individual, every single one of you, is swallowed in one lake. And now (she stole a glance at me; I looked down and broke the point of the pencil), I would like some of the children to get up and tell about their homes, their parents, the furnishing in their houses, a private clock that gives the room an earnest mien, a grandfather face, the deep secret of slow budding which is one human truth, so precious . . ."

She smiled suddenly, then laughed. Her laugh glided through the room like the delicate north winds of a summer night. "I am using dreadful words," she laughed. "Even the teacher has moments when she reaches into the store of aphorisms. Please get up and speak. In this way, we will know one another with greater breadth, understand more, live a few of our separate moments together."

The children were inspired. They were swept by the stream, resounded in the wind, their hair grew furrows leading inward. Dumbo got up, sharpened his nose, polished his hunched form and said,

"My father . . . my father does something as a worker in the port. I have a brother too, Nehemiah. You all know him. He is the fastest bicycle rider. Once we rode to Herzliah, the two of us went together. We hiked all around. We slipped and fell. Together. Really the main thing is—my father, on Purim, you should see the funny mask he has . . ."

He went on and on. The more boring it was, the closer we felt to him. Suddenly, we were together with his father . . . and if we were his mother, we would have given birth to him, Dumbo, right on the table. The class was open to every wind. And every wind brought a fine smell, the scent of home, delight of a tune far beyond all the seas, the murmur of the heart on a moonlit night.

Dumbo took his seat. Nehama got up, lanky as a tree. Her hair was always falling over her eyes so that she would say "oof" and brush it behind her ears, only for it to fall back again. She told about her mustached uncle, Amiel, a watchman in the Galilee; how he took her to the Galilee where Arabs stopped to greet him, raised their hands to their foreheads, said *ahlan we sahlan hawaja Amiel* with great respect. He took her on his horse to the waterfall called "the stove" and showed her what a waterfall is. "In the stove the water burns with cold," she said.

One by one, the children rose and offered the breath of their homes to the class. It was as if the room melted with Tel Aviv, as if Tel Aviv broke into the class and snapped all the coat hooks so that the coats flew back home. Where to? Russia, Poland, Tunis, to the orphanage, to find a source of the wounds, the roots. Everyone has a root, a place he comes from. Why? Because! The wind howls upon walls which fall under the weight of hanging blueprints. We build the land with diagrams, loop the ridges of wadis with dreams and build houses to cover them up. So they will not be.

I didn't know what was happening to me. At the beginning, I raised my hand. Many others raised their hands and were called before me. When it was my turn, at first no one paid any attention. Not I, not the teacher, not Amihud, nor Dumbo nor Hedva. I rose to my feet, I was trembling, wind swept me. I saw my body stretched out on the parched earth, the twins writing their names in sand, the treetop praying to clouds, to wind, to God knows what. Among the hills I was lone as a tree. Alone, like a lone undertaker, like my own undertaker. Anyone in his own mother's class, the ants said, can have no friends, can have nothing but the earth all about. Here I was, standing before the teacher, surrounded by forty-five idiots. I began to speak.

"Father makes picture frames. At night, secretly, he draws. We have a large green bookcase and lovely, lovely books. I have a phonograph at home. On Friday night, Father arranges a concert. Afterward, we sit on the balcony and drink the sea, the thundering sea. The sea is the music, the music of the balcony. The Rothschilds play cards on the balcony across from ours, surrounded by a cloud of butterflies. Night butterflies have private stars. They fly into light and die. How they love to be burned and die! Father plays the guitar and sings in a low voice."

"Stop it, Yosef," the teacher whispered as if trying to tell me a secret. But she was too late. The children began to smile. The magic fainted and broke. A thin rustle rose from the benches. I was silent; I felt nothing. I saw a flame; in it an Arab woman, her face veiled. In my ears, guitars played the love songs of Mozart. It was so right to drink the perfume of summer evenings from the yellow fire which played across from me. Below, under our balcony, the pariah is doing exercise like an idiot: hohp-hohp-hohp, a future champion. To the left is Gilboa's house, firmly planted. Gilboa has an awful voice. Every evening he sings furiously.

"Stop," his wife shouts. "Stop it already."

"Stop," the neighbors yell.

"Go to Hell," says Gilboa.

In Gideon's house, pigeons are roasted in the yard. Next to them lives Mrs. Birnbaum, whose husband didn't come to this country with her. Every night she hears lions coming.

"Yosef, that will do," the teacher said. Her face was pale. By now the children were laughing out loud. Outside, the sky was red, the windows drew a crooked frame for the red sky. Dumbo tapped me lightly.

"And Father . . . Oh Father draws at night," I said. "In green. He's mad about green . . . and Mother laughs. He draws with green, paints green the color of Satan's eye. And she laughs."

"Yosef!! Yosef!!"

"But, Teacher, every child told his story and you didn't interrupt."

"That's right, Yosef, but you must understand . . ."

"Understand what?" I shouted. "Understand, understand . . . it's not . . ."

"Father gets up early in the morning," I continued, "earlier than the sun, the morning, the birds, Gilboa's rooster, before Gilboa's cricket, before Mrs. Birnbaum's lions, before the pariah, and goes to the sea. Every morning, he goes there, alone, only he and the water. He says he loves the sea in its nakedness. That's what he says. People come to the sea and make a bath house of it. The sea is beautiful because it is solitary, alone, vast, embraces the sky, jumps white, jumps blue, drowns the kisses of the stars. It is beautiful because it is cold as the winter sun and loves to be alone. When Father goes for a dip in the sea, he asks its permission to honor his own aloneness. And Mother . . . Mother lights candles on Friday night. We sit at the table. The candles flicker. Two trees shouting their treetops; two candles rending the darkness. Is it true that darkness puts out candles on winter nights? Just as the parched earth drinks the rain, just as the ants build and never sing 'Wheels of the World'? We sit around the table, Father, Mother, Aunt Shlomit, Uncle Bomak, singing. If I had a brother, we would sing in six voices. If I had a brother my age, I would be in another class."

"If Grandma had wheels she would be a car," said Amihud.

"Genius," I said. "What a genius."

"Yosef, stop it. I warn you . . ." My mother's face was red.

"You have no right to warn me," I said.

"She's got no right," Rina teased.

"No right," the twins said. They weren't there. They went, on their hands, to another school where the very same things are said. In Tel Aviv everyone says the same thing in different words. That's why there is so much politics but only one idea.

"On Saturday we sing: '*Uvyom uvyooom uuuvyom uvyommm ha-Shabbat . . .*' "

"Leave the room!" the teacher cried. "Out! Out!"

Her voice trembled. Her eyes, the pupils, the brows, quaked like the crown of the tree on the one-sided street. She stood up. The class stopped laughing, stared at me. A tremor passed through me. All at once, I became conscious of the moment. I leaped from my place, my eyes filled with tears. I went up to the teacher's desk, clenched my fist and pounded with all my might. Everything jumped: dust, books, calendar. The sparks in the teacher's eyes. The stupefaction of ninety other eyes. The hills framed by the crooked windows. The grass. Everything.

"Why did you let me make a fool of myself, Mother? Why? Why?"

I ran out, tearing the door from its place. Outside stood the row of hangers. I broke three or four of them and ran back and forth: from the classroom door to the principal's room, from the principal's room to the door of the class. If only I was the lion cub Mrs. Birnbaum dreamed . . . Now I was the pariah. I hated myself. My mother came out, deep in thought, her face white as the reverse of the blackboard. She ran after me, seized my arm and began to fuss with my hand which was bleeding from the force with which I had pounded the desk.

"What did you do to your hand, child?"

"I killed it," I said.

"What did you do?" In her face there was terror. Her voice implored, broke into a thousand fragments.

I stared at her. There was a dull ache in my chest. I stopped crying. Even the blood stopped its flow. I stared at her and, suddenly, a smile streamed across my face. "Go back, fast, Mommy dear. Go back in. Otherwise, they'll run wild in there. The children will make you miserable, and they'll go at me again with their nasty tongues. Go back. Go back fast. And at recess—stay away from Mr. Broshi!" I swallowed the end of the sentence and smiled.

She looked at me, her face recovering its color, her eyes soft, two tears fixed in them like marvellous jewels. She wiped blood from her lip and returned to the class. Saying "Thank you, Yosef," she went back. As soon as the door swung behind her, I burst into tears.

I stood outside. The parched earth died in my dimmed eyes.

The stubborn "I" was thinking, son of my father, the picture-frame maker. I have a special sort of father. Even though my mother won't let me tell of him. In this framework she is my teacher, most accursed teacher. Still, I *am* allowed to tell, to drink his spirit, to mumble hello to him. For, if Mother really did become my teacher, then it would all be possible. If it is impossible, then everything is impossible. Apart from what I will find on my own road, the handful scooped out of loneliness, mine on my cracked earth, in the secrets of my precious heart. I must know that it is precious, accursed teacher.

During the main recess, when the children joked about Miss Mira and Mr. Broshi, I no longer felt hurt. I smiled a forced smile and forgave them. When school was over, I went home, hoping Aunt Shlomit would be there.

School was over, the morning was over. The sun hung in the sky without knowing why it had destroyed the dainty autumn. It was sad. I wanted to search for autumn, for the days preceding morning. I could not find them. I stood there in the center of the sad world and knew that they had gone with what the twins did near the tree, with the dead ant in the cracks dried by sunlight.

I did not go home by way of the beach. Let the beach go to Hell!

Soon the waters will dry out and then everything will be salty. If I were a bird, I would drink the sand and sing an ode to the life of the days that did not return. The sun laughed at me. Aunt Shlomit put me in the pantry and turned off the light. In my eyes, all that was left cried for its mother never to come again.

Translated by Zeva Shapiro

Next of Kin

The rain reached Beersheba six hours after we did. I watched the first drops splatter on the sidewalk and reflect the light from the lamppost outside. Soon the water lay glistening in large puddles. I sat by myself in the officers' cafeteria at five in the morning, drinking a cup of black tea which was too strong and too sweet. The cafeteria had stayed open for the members of the staff, who worked through the night. They were all anxious to close the case, and agreed that preparations should be made for both funerals to be held sometime during the day.

There was a continual bustle of activity throughout the brightly lit building. My own presence was unnecessary, so much so, in fact, that I was the only one to notice it. I bothered no one. Three or four times I declined the offer of a bed, though it was made by one of the friendliest sergeants I had ever met, and apparently came on orders from above. Someone had remembered to look after the guest. By five o'clock streaks of rain were visible beyond the perimeter of the street lamp, silently etched against the soft, gray morning. I made up my mind to go home. Half-an-hour later there were signs of life in the parking lot. A car drove up, men left the building. I went to the door. Joe sprang toward me through the puddles. "Come on," he said. An army poncho was slung across his shoulders to keep off the rain, and rolled up under his arm was another for me.

We set out in a convoy on the Hebron road, Joe, a reporter and myself in the first car. At kilometer 48, on the border, we were to pick up two bodies, a boy and a girl, in exchange for a live Arab infiltrator, who was somewhere in the back of the convoy. Officially, the bodies were also listed as infiltrators. The long wait had, after all, not been in vain and I began to feel better.

The windshield wipers fought the rain with a steady, patient squeak. When the motor was cut they screeched even louder. "Here we are," said Joe, and everything came to a halt but the rain. We were on a deserted stretch of road. Joe's marker had been a signpost, planted off to the right of the highway some twenty feet from where we were parked. It was most probably the border warning. While Joe lit a cigarette, I wiped the fog from the rear window. The van behind us was a small new carry-all with a sturdy canvas roof. In the cabin I could make out the driver, chubby and fuzzy-cheeked like a boy, and beside him, an open morning paper, spread across the face of whoever was reading it.

Through the glass pane I saw the stocky figure of a girl in khaki slacks and a khaki sweater emerge from the back of the van. The first to venture into the rain, she looked down the road and began walking forward to get a better view. Passing alongside us—wet hair stretched shapelessly downward, mouth on the small side, chest too hefty—the girl strode on toward the pockmarked sign. She stopped to read it. The years had blurred its letters, bullets and stones had chipped away at them, but one could still make out: "Halt. Border Ahead."

"That's the sister," Joe said, as the girl crossed in front of him, "Tamar."

I watched her walk across the road, hands in her pockets, shoulders bunched, oblivious to everything. Around her neck she had knotted the sleeves of a blue cardigan which barely covered her shoulders. "His sister or hers?" asked the reporter.

"Hers," answered Joe. "Tshernobilsky from Migdal. His name was Chafetz. When it comes to identifying bodies," he continued, turning to me because he disliked journalists, "we prefer to bring the younger relatives. Brothers and sisters are best. Parents get so flustered you can't get a word out of them."

The reporter persisted: "Who's coming to identify the boy?"

"He was an only son," said Joe, still talking to me. "We've brought along his father, old Chafetz. If you're interested in queer characters . . ."

"The point is," said the reporter, leaning forward toward Joe, "if you have no idea who the bodies are, why did you insist on these people coming to identify them?"

"Five days ago," answered Joe reluctantly, speaking with exaggerated patience, "a family from Migdal came to the police in Tiberias and reported a daughter of theirs missing in the company of a boy from Jerusalem. The names and information were checked and forwarded. Actually, it didn't cause much of a stir at the time. The affair was considered to have—how do you fellows say it?—a 'romantic' background. The day before yesterday the U.N. contacted us. An Israeli boy and girl were found murdered on the road to Hebron, robbed, practically stripped of their clothing, without identification. We put two and two together. As far as I can see, ninety-nine chances out of hundred it's a sure thing."

"What do you think happened to them?" the reporter insisted.

"I have to get in touch with Jerusalem," Joe snapped, and left. I opened my door and stepped out after him.

The four cars stood in a row. Behind us was the army van, and behind the van, a police wagon which had a wireless connection with Beersheba. Behind that came a staff command car. I crossed the road as far as the ditch and looked back at the cars huddled together in the rain, at the dead shrubs from the season before strewn by the roadside, and at the girl's heavy even footprints. Her name was Tamar, Tamar Tshernobitz, or something longer. Had a giant door been blocking her way, it might have explained her nervous pacing back and forth. But there was only the road, running on monotonously past the sign, then dipping suddenly out of sight and reappearing on the crest of a ridge, one of the foothills in the steady ascent of the Hebron range. The wet earth cast a yellow sheen back at the sky, streaking the countryside. Further off, the land grew gray and indistinct, retaining its pleasant softness beneath the falling rain. The girl had finally stopped with her back to us, and stood gazing at the distant hills, rising dreamlike from the mist on the horizon.

Joe returned from the radio car. "The U.N. just notified us that they won't be here before eight," he said. The girl turned about wearily and came toward us. "They won't be here before eight," he called to her.

She shrugged her shoulders and kept on walking, passing us by and going on down the line.

Joe did not bother to follow her movements. "You're fond of queer characters," he repeated. "Here's a real strange one for you. A school-teacher, would you believe it? Teaches nature and geography and what-not. I couldn't get much more than that out of her. We really didn't talk as much as we should have. The old man, as I told you, is all confused. Look, let's go to Beersheba. There's no sense in wasting a whole hour here."

He didn't seem to care when I turned down the offer and said I would remain. "I'll send along some food and something to drink," he said, shutting the door behind him. His car spun around; as it picked up speed he disposed of me with a careless wave of his hand. Wheels showering the roadside with mud, the command car pivoted and followed. The police wagon maneuvered strenuously until it, too, headed the other way. Now I caught my first view of the Arab prisoner. Tired and haggard-looking, he stared out at the receding landscape. I noticed Tamar; her eyes were fixed on the same stark shape, growing distant inside the green car. Absent-mindedly, she came and stood beside me. "It must be the infiltrator," I said. My uncertainty won her confidence. It proved that I, too, was an outsider. "What can he be thinking?" she asked, averting her glance from me. "That they're taking him back to jail . . . ?"

We were still talking when the police wagon stopped short with an unnerving suddenness that was almost comic. At first nothing happened. Then a door slammed, tires squealed and the car sped off again, leaving an old man behind on the road. He came toward us, hunched beneath a dark raincoat and crumpled hat. I knew at once who he was and I pictured to myself the scene which must have taken place in the front seat when the old man, realizing belatedly that they were leaving, that they might be gone for an hour, had demanded that they stop and let him off. He headed straight for the van, which was now the only shelter against the wind and rain. I lost sight of him and noticed that Tamar had again gone off toward the border. They should both be put in the driver's cabin, I thought, but one look in that direction

was enough to change my mind. The morning paper had disappeared;
in its place, sporting a handsome beard, sat a pale-faced young rabbi
who had been assigned to accompany the corpses.

Gusts of wind drove thick sheets of rain across the road. I motioned
the girl to climb into the van. If her duty was to wait for her sister,
mine was to see that she as least acted sensibly. But she gave no
indication of having understood. She seemed lost in herself as I approached, yet was not startled when I brushed her wet sleeve.

"Get inside! Hurry up!"

"Thanks. I'd rather not."

"Save your thanks. You have to. Hurry up!"

"I don't want to." It went on stupidly for a few minutes. Finally,
I threatened her: "I'll call the officer and we'll make you get inside."

"Do you know who I am?" she asked suddenly, returning the
threat.

"Certainly I know. But that has nothing to do with standing in the
rain." I grabbed her by the arm and pulled. Her obstinacy had led me
to expect more of a fight, but she let herself be dragged along easily,
submissively. When we got to the truck, however, she stiffened and
balked.

"What's the matter?"

"You mustn't tell him who I am."

"Tell who?"

"The old man. Doctor Chafetz."

I hadn't realized that he was a doctor or that he didn't know who
she was. The question troubled me: Why didn't he know? Why
mustn't he be told? But, since to wait for an answer meant standing
with her in the rain, I nodded my silent consent. She didn't need any
help, but I boosted her onto the platform of the truck, jumped in after
her, and slid the wooden bench around from its place by the wall. She
chose to sit at the back of the truck next to the tarpaulin, where she
was hidden from the old man's sight.

The old man's broad-brimmed, shapeless gray fedora lay on his
matted hair as if it had been dropped from above and was too small
for such a head: unruly white shocks protruded from beneath it in all

directions. The bench rattled under us as we sat. His quiet, blue stare came to rest on me, the eyes marked by deep wrinkles. He was ill at ease. Removing his glasses, he shut his eyes and polished the lenses slowly and carefully. When they were bright and shiny he replaced them deliberately, and asked, so abruptly that I was taken aback, "May I presume you, then, to be the relations?"

He was alluding to us both, and I more than kept my word to Tamar by answering, "No." "My son," he said, gesturing vaguely toward the Hebron hills, "Yehoyariv. Yehoyariv Chafetz. I am among the relations requested to appear for the identification. If you will pardon a trite phrase, there yet remains a shadow of doubt and, truthfully, I ask myself whether his name has not been mistaken for someone else's. The fact of the matter is, he went to the Galilee. The girl's relations . . ." he broke off uncertainly ". . . not one of them has come?" He looked at me, then stared at the girl, studying her hair and shoulders. Like most old teachers who have lectured a great deal, he made little distinction between a question and a statement of fact, talking as if to himself, sometimes pausing to reflect, sometimes challenging his own assertions. His voice was quite pleasant, unhurried and inoffensive. But behind that exterior, it seemed to me, a mind schooled in abstractions was racing madly to protect itself against naked reality. Beyond the façade of hair and shoulders to my right, I could sense the fear-glazed eyes of the girl staring into the rain, all too aware of the truth.

"And you, sir, if I may be permitted to ask, who are you?" The question gave me a start, though the style of delivery was by now familiar; clearly, this was how he addressed his students. "I'm from the government," I said, suddenly content with the small, honest affirmation.

"The government." He broke the word into syllables, as if demonstrating its pronunciation. "In that case, perhaps you know for what purpose we are being kept waiting?"

"I don't suppose it depends on us," I said.

"But on some other government," said the old man, filling out the sentence to suit himself. "The Lord be praised, every people has its government. Or on the rain." He talked into the gloomy shelter, which grew murkier as the sky outside darkened and the front windshield fogged over. "The night rains," he continued, "can wash out all the roads below Hebron. The Hebron-Beersheba road runs, does it not, through the center of the southernmost portion of the Hebron basin, in distinction to its northern counterparts, which all face in a westerly direction. On its way to the Basor this basin amasses huge quantities of run-off, coming from two divides, the Artzit, and the one between the Shikma and the Basor. We should not forget that near Hebron are two isohyetic areas of eight hundred millimeters each. One night of solid rain isolates the villagers on Mount Hebron, and delays all traffic to Beersheba by half a day at the very least. Flash floods . . ."

The old man had a tendency to ramble on. Piqued by the girl's presence, he sought to gain her attention, in such a way that her stubborn silence, too, became part of the conversation. A professional vice, I thought to myself, at the same time trying to read something of her mind. "When will he shut up," she seemed to be thinking. "Who can listen to all these lectures?"

"Since you seem unable to enlighten me in regard to the present and why we are waiting here, certainly you will be equally at a loss in regard to the future and how long we shall have to wait. Perhaps, however, you are in a position to shed some light on the past. Quite frankly, I know less than nothing." Without waiting for an answer, he continued. "Yesterday evening there was a knock on the door. 'Does Yehuda Chafetz live here?' The policeman confused the name. 'Yehoyariv Chafetz,' I said. 'What is the matter?' The policeman didn't know, he was only sent to inquire whether Yehoyariv was at home, and if not, where was he. Shortly after he left, someone more important came, an officer. He went over each question again, as if nobody had been there before him. Since then I have repeated my story countless times, but like water poured upon sand it falls on deaf ears. To be sure, my son Yehoyariv left a week ago, but his travels led him northward, to the Galilee. To the best of my knowledge, in his own words—which were always precisely chosen—his plan was to tour the Galilee, starting from the Valley of Genosar and working northward through Migdal to Nahal Amud, in order to make a survey of the plant life there. We have a journal called *Land and Nature* and our correspondent in the Galilee was to go with him, our correspondent on weather, nature, geographical data of all sorts . . ."

The girl's shoes scraped against the metal bumper at the rear. She barely raised herself from her sitting position, and slid outside, feet first. The old man was upset. "Has anything happened?" A car was approaching from the direction of Beersheba. "Perhaps the relations have arrived," he said, glancing first outside and then back at me, as if to appeal to my better judgment. As before, he did not wait for an answer. "We didn't know her. Not even by name. We only knew her address at the district school and her initials, M.G.D., short for Migdalit, which is how she signed those articles of hers, so terse and lucid. We knew she was a schoolteacher, we thought she must be shy. Even if I could be led to believe that my son might have reversed his direction and gone south to the Judean hills, crossing through Jordan from Hartuv to Ein Gedi, still it violates all logic to suppose that she . . . that it's possible . . ."

His hands, which had been clasped between his knees, spread apart tremulously, palms upward, to express his bewilderment. "I don't understand, it makes no sense, I simply refuse to believe . . ."

Two sisters, I thought. Both schoolteachers. One is successful, talented, writes articles. The boy from the capital asks her to come camping and exploring. The other is jealous, she tries to tag along. They give her the slip. Instead of going north, they head south. It's obvious, I thought. She must feel guilt-stricken.

The army rabbi approached from behind, surveyed us both, and addressed himself to me. "Bread and tea have arrived, if you want any." I brought the old man some tea in a flat military bowl, and thick slices of bread and sardines. He placed the bread beside him on the bench and buried his face in the tea, tilting his head slowly backward until he had gulped it all down. He laid the bowl down by the bread and stared outside. The storm had lifted and the sky was clearing. "The relations, then, have not arrived?" He had found his tongue again. "We didn't know if she had any relations, and if she did, whether they were parents, sisters, brothers . . . We never knew. We only corresponded, and of late it was Yehoyariv who undertook this. In his last letter he wrote: 'I should like to catalogue the flowers and plants of the Galilee.' As usual, she answered punctually, 'Let's go together.' And they went . . ."

When I returned the empty bowl I inquired whether the girl had drunk anything. "What girl?" I was asked. She was standing by the border sign again. They filled a bowl of tea for her, and after thinking it over, I made do with that. If she wants to eat she can come over here. I brought her the bowl without spilling a drop; the air was still damp, but the thick liquid surface of the tea was unruffled. She accepted it silently and took two careful sips.

"What are you staring at?"

"You can have something to eat if you want," I said.

"Who asked you to look after me?"

I reached for a cigarette, my first since leaving Joe's car. "Smoke?"

"No," she said; all her feelings toward me were bound up in that one word. I smoked in silence, making it clear that I was only waiting to return the empty bowl. "Go to the old man. You'd better look after him."

"He asked about you again," I replied gingerly, "about the relations. He talked a lot about your sister. With great respect."

"He's never even seen her, how can he talk about her?" She had been gazing down at the road, at the wet, cracked asphalt and the muddied patterns. Now she shot me a wild, quick glance. "Take your tea. Get out of here!" She flung the bowl onto the pavement and it rolled about clattering on the ground. She ran after it immediately, bent over, picked it up, and handed it back to me. "What do you want? What business is it of yours? Who asked you to get mixed up in this?"

I crushed the cigarette under my heel and turned to go, gripping the bowl in my hand. It's all right, I thought, it's understandable.

I returned the bowl to one of the soldiers, who tossed it over his shoulder into the open compartment. The old man sat in the van chewing on a piece of bread, the bearded rabbi beside him. He stopped when he saw me and motioned with his hand, searching for an opening word. "I beg of you," he said, gesturing with his bread toward the rabbi. "Observe what these gentlemen have been saying. The dead girl was apparently a soldier. From the army. So you see, it can't be our couple after all . . ."

"Can't you leave him alone for a while?" I asked the rabbi angrily. I didn't like him, and now that I felt responsible for the two of them, I couldn't stand the way he picked at their wounds, first feeding the old man all sorts of stories, then scolding him for being confused.

"He thought I was one of the relatives," the rabbi said, jumping to the ground. My manner had convinced him that I was important, and he followed me obsequiously across the road, tendering apologies. "He asked me, am I related, so I said I'm a chaplain and he asked what's a chaplain. I explained to him . . . the burial unit . . . when a soldier gets killed. He said my son isn't a soldier. So I told him it's a girl, that's all I know, and he kept asking me questions . . ."

It was nearly eight o'clock. Slowly, the sky began to brighten. The convoy returned: first police wagon, then Joe's sedan and the staff car filled with soldiers.

"They're coming!" someone yelled, pointing up the road toward Hebron.

In the distance we made out the white cars of the U.N., and Arab Legion jeeps escorting a truck. "Well," said Joe, "this is it. Who's coming with me?"

Accompanied by a staff Major we advanced past the sign. Where the road dipped lay the border, sealed by steel spikes heavily laced with barbed wire. Fifty meters further off was a second roadblock, theirs, where men were working to clear a path. Halfway between the two barriers, beside an open car, U.N. officials and Legion officers waited with their credentials. An amiable French Colonel presided correctly over handshakes and salutes, and apologized for the delay.

"Of course," I said. "The rain. Flash floods . . ."

"But yes," he said, pleasantly surprised. "How did monsieur know?"

He spoke to his chauffeur, who reached into a hand-tooled liquor cabinet and brought out several glasses. The Colonel filled them himself, telling us about the floods, which were so bad that they had to wait for the water to drain off the roads and bridges. "But not a drop got into the brandy," Joe quipped, and the Colonel laughed heartily. I gladly accepted a second glass.

"Would you like to see them?" the Colonel asked.

"No," said Joe, "the next of kin have been waiting for hours."

The Legionnaires expressed their sympathy. The Colonel corked the bottle and handed it back. The chauffeur collected the empty glasses. The Legion officers saluted and left. We remained behind by the car. "Send blankets with the stretchers," the Colonel advised, ignoring our parting handshakes and walking alongside us. The glasses tinkled as they went back into the cabinet. "The black devils wouldn't even let us have a closed truck," he confided. "I argued with them for an hour. They said that on rainy days only open trucks were available. I wanted you to see them before the next of kin . . . very well, send dry blankets . . . the blankets on them now are soaked through."

The Major volunteered to see to it. He saluted and strode quickly back towards our lines. We followed behind.

At the border the Colonel took Joe's hand in his own detaining him for a brief moment. "She was one of the loveliest girls I have ever seen in this land, and I am not one to go about with my eyes shut. She could not have been more than eighteen." He spoke gently, with compassion.

"Nineteen," Joe said.

"A fine fellow," he said to me, once we had recrossed the barrier and slowly climbed the hill. "A good friend and a good drinking companion—and once even a good soldier."

"According to the old man," I replied, groping for what was baffling me, "I had the impression that she was at least twenty-five."

"What does he know about it, the old man? He doesn't even know her name . . ."

I flushed with surprise, as if the two glasses of brandy had gone to my head.

"But he knew that she taught school, she wrote nature columns for his journal. It's not in character for a nineteen-year-old girl . . ."

"So he confused you too? The poor fellow. It's Tamar here who's the teacher, the sister . . ."

"But . . ." I didn't finish, perhaps because there was something I wanted to know which even Joe didn't know.

"But what?" he asked, half indifferently. I didn't answer. Still I needed to be sure. "Perhaps they were both teachers?"

"Ziva Tshernobilsky was in a Nahal Brigade," said Joe, closing the argument. "She belonged to a unit at Ein Gedi. A short furlough home—then she decided to hike back, by the direct route across Jordan. She took her boyfriend along . . ."

Hers or her sister's? I nodded automatically, but I no longer heard what Joe was saying. God forgive me, I felt happy inside. Something was approaching fulfillment. With a cool, imperturbable desire, I wanted Tamar to know that I, and only I, shared her secret.

I bided my time. At the top of the hill Joe grew philosophical. "There's really nothing left for me to do here. Two long funerals now, and then it's over."

At the signpost we came across the old man. Craning his neck, he licked his dry lips without daring to speak. But he couldn't restrain himself entirely. "What," he asked, "what? Are we going for them? Not yet?" We stopped beside him.

"Soon," Joe said, and added encouragingly, "but we needn't go ourselves. The police will bring them." His words were inadequate, but he was afraid to say more; anything else would have been just as bad.

A column swung by, four soldiers led by an officer, with two policemen carrying folded stretchers and blankets over their shoulders. They marched forward, then halted at an outcry from below in English and Arabic. "Only the police!" yelled Joe, running after them. "Only the police with the stretchers. The army isn't allowed here. A demilitarized zone . . ." I had to strain to catch his last words. The soldiers returned; the police hesitated, then started out again. The old man fidgeted. He wouldn't let them out of his sight. Each time I tried to restrain him he squirmed loose and trotted after them. The stretchers spoke a language which he finally understood. At a vantage point overlooking the scene below, we caught up with Joe.

Two U.N. officials, their dress uniforms gleaming in a sudden burst of sunlight, stepped forward to help the stretcher-bearers. The stretchers were extended full-length now, although still empty. They advanced toward the Jordanian ranks, and the old man trembled as they disappeared among them. Joe tried to calm him. "They'll be back in a jiffy. Soon they'll bring them." He stared back uncomprehendingly, unable to decide which of us had spoken. "It makes no sense," he mumbled, "none, none at all. At this very moment they are somewhere in the Galilee. It is inconceivable that they should have forgotten the December issue. It was to be specially devoted to our Galilean flora. And she said they would go together, she wrote him, 'I'll take three days off from my teaching' . . ."

The truth was right under Joe's nose, and I stole a glance at him, suspecting that now he would grasp it. He raised his eyebrows at me over the old man's shoulders. "Didn't I tell you—he's out of his mind." I nearly laughed out loud.

"Here they come!" I cried exultantly, and was immediately ashamed of myself. They came in twos, walking slowly and with difficulty, carrying one stretcher after another. The rabbi appeared at our side, his face sweet and composed, fingering the book which he held in his hands. He opened it to the correct place, smoothed out the page, and then closed it, using his finger as a placemark. Obviously, he was a man of some experience. When the stretchers passed the second roadblock he opened the book again and began reading silently to himself.

"Are you a relation?" the old man asked him, his eyes on the book.

"I've already told you, from the army," whispered the rabbi, "on a military assignment, the Lord is my Rock and my Fortress." He stood chanting at the approaching stretchers.

"You, sir, are a relation!" The old man held on to me in a daze, tremors passing from his body into mine. "You have no right to conceal the facts from me any longer. How could it be, it's not possible, through what error could they have come here, my son and your good daughter . . ." He may have been angry or simply bewildered. Torn between pity and apprehension myself, I pulled him closer, keeping my footing and managing to support him at the same time. Joe must have thought I was squeamish; this time I was sure he would suspect something, but he was too busy with the stretchers to notice either of us. The old man, too, loosened his grip and watched with rapt attention. The stretchers sagged heavily beneath the weight of the bodies, swaying perceptibly despite the bearers' efforts to keep them straight. On the steep grade the bodies jiggled and slid back. The corner of a blanket hung down from the second stretcher and a naked foot flashed whitely. They passed before us in a miniature procession. The rabbi, the old man and I joined at the rear.

Following Joe's directions, the driver skillfully maneuvered the van until its back faced us. Joe and his crew stepped aside, the rear flap was opened noisily, and the stretchers were brought into position. The end of the first stretcher was heaved onto the truck; one of the bearers jumped onto the platform and pulled at it from inside, while another continued to push. Then, the second stretcher. The old man came forward, stopped, rested his elbows on the floor, and buried his head in his hands. Beneath the blanket, the two bodies were indistinguishably alike: a head, knees, hands and feet. "It's impossible," he said, and nobody heard him. "I can't, I can't . . ."

The U.N. officials smoothed the creases out of their jackets and surreptitiously rubbed their hands, which were numb from exertion. There was an awkward moment of indecision, of covert glances. By the time Joe realized that the old man would not be able to go through with it, it was too late to have the stretchers lowered again. "Where's the girl?" he asked. "Here!" She was right behind us. "Put him in the cabin." The driver and the rabbi led the old man away. He was weeping uncontrollably.

"I can manage by myself," Tamar said, when Joe and I tried to help her up. She moved forward two steps, knelt on one knee by the corpse on the left raised the corner of the blanket ever so slightly, then immediately laid it back in place. Motionless, she choked back a cry. Her other knee sank to the floor.

"I was absolutely certain," whispered Joe.

She straightened up slightly and turned to the stretcher on the right. This time she raised the corner of the blanket and held it a long while, straining to absorb all she could in the dim light. "What's going on there?" Joe whispered. "Have you any doubts?" he demanded of her. Frightened, she dropped the blanket and lifted her face towards us, her eyes shut against the sunlight. She half rose and moved heavily toward the back of the van, avoiding us with her eyes. "What doubts? I never even saw him."

"Good enough," said Joe, "We'll finish up in Beersheba. Close the door. Let's get going." Silently, Tamar let me help her down. We heard the door slam shut. Joe was already somewhere else, but she continued to answer his question anyway. "They arrived in our village together, by accident, on the ten o'clock bus. She was on leave from the army, he had come from Jerusalem . . ."

From beyond the van a detachment of police brought forward the infiltrator; afraid to outdistance his escort, he waited after every order to make sure it was all right to go on. Joe directed the operation from behind. "Let him go," he said in Hebrew and then, to the two U.N. officials in French, "Everything is in order. You may take him."

"I had made all the necessary preparations for the three days I would be away. At eleven I left the school. Mother and Father were out in the orchard."

The Arab walked north between them like a sentenced man, hugging his arms close to his body as if they were still in chains. His fear had yet to wear off.

"She left a note, and her uniform, and they were gone before any of us came back. They went straight down the road, to the south . . ."

Translated by Hillel Halkin

About the Writers

CHAIM POTOK, who offers the foreword for *Firstfruits*, is a distinguished novelist whose widely acclaimed works include *The Chosen, The Promise,* and *My Name Is Asher Lev.* Dr. Potok serves as editor of The Jewish Publication Society of America.

JAMES A. MICHENER, noted Pulitzer Prize author, has edited *Firstfruits* and has contributed a moving introduction to its contents. Michener, who first won worldwide notice with his *Tales of the South Pacific*, is the author of many books, including *The Source*, a novel that spans the history of the Holy Land.

BENJAMIN TAMMUZ ("An Enigma") is a well-known Israeli sculptor, novelist, and literary critic. He has written several novels, including *The Life of Elyakum* and *Castle in Spain.*

ASHER BARASH ("Hai's Well") was a poet and novelist who died in 1952. Barash wrote with great feeling about the Jewish pioneers in Palestine. He also translated *Uncle Tom's Cabin* and *Robinson Crusoe* into Hebrew.

SAMUEL YOSEPH AGNON ("Tehilah"), who died in 1970 at the age of 82, was a giant of contemporary Hebrew letters. In 1966 he was awarded the Nobel Prize for literature. His works include *The Bridal Canopy* and *A Guest for the Night.*

YITZHAK SHENHAR ("On Galilean Shores") settled in 1924 in Israel, where he worked on farms and in the government. Later he became an editor for a major publishing company. His novels include *Basar Vadam, Me-Eretz Le-Eretz,* and *Ehad Me-Elef.* Shenhar translated stories by Gogol, Kafka, and Balzac into Hebrew. He died in 1957.

AHARON MEGGED ("The White City") is an author, editor, and playwright. His books include *The Spirit of the Sea, Hevda and I,* and *Fortunes of a Fool.*

HAIM HAZAZ ("The Sermon"), until his recent death, was one of the leading figures in Israeli letters. He won the prestigious Bialik Prize, the Israel Prize, and the Ussishkin Prize. He was a member of the Hebrew Language Academy and the author of such classics as *Ya'ish, Daltot Nehoshet,* and *Beketz Hayamim.*

YEHUDA YAARI ("The Wanderer and the Blind Man") is a diplomat and writer whose works include *Bein Ashmorot, Be-Ohalim,* and *Darkei Ish.* He lives in Jerusalem.

HANOCH BARTOV ("In a Son's Footsteps") is a journalist and author. He was born in Petah Tikva and educated at Hebrew University. His books include *Hacheshbon Ve-Hanefesh, Shesh Knafaim La-Echad,* and *The Brigade.*

AVRAHAM B. YEHOSHUA ("A Long Hot Day") is one of Israel's younger writers. He is a graduate of Hebrew University and teaches world literature at the University of Haifa. "A Long Hot Day" is included in his book *Three Days and a Child.*

NATAN SHACHAM ("Coming Home") is a playwright and novelist whose writing is largely focused on the problems of Israel's young people. He has published twenty-four books, and his story collections include *Dagan ve-Oferet* and *Ha-Elim Atselim.*

HEDDA BOSEM ("The Third Hill") is a native Israeli born in Tel Aviv and a noted member of a small group of Israeli women who follow the writing profession. She has written for newspapers, where she has served as literary critic.

YITZHAK ORPAZ ("The Wild Plant") came to Israel from Russia in 1938. He studied at Tel Aviv University and started his writing career in the literary supplements of the newspapers. His short story collections include *The Death of Lysanda, Skin for Skin,* and *Wild Grass.*

AMOS OZ ("Nomad and Viper") has been widely acclaimed as one of the foremost Israeli writers of our time. His novels, including the well-received *My Michael,* his novellas, notably *Crusade,* and his social and literary essays in leading Israeli publications have brought him worldwide attention.

YORAM KANIUK ("The Parched Earth") was born in the Tel Aviv of which he writes in "The Parched Earth." *The Acrophile* was his first novel to be published in English.

MOSHE SHAMIR ("Next of Kin") is an editor, author, and playwright. He won the Bialik, Brenner, and Ussishkin literary prizes and his books include *Hu Halakh Ba-Sadot, Bemo Yadav,* and *Milhemet Bnei-Or.*

Acknowledgments

Many hands have helped in fashioning this book. The Jewish Publication Society of America expresses its special thanks to Acum, Ltd., of Tel Aviv, and to its director general, Menachem Avidom, for permission to include in this collection the following stories: "An Enigma," by Benjamin Tammuz; "Hai's Well," by Asher Barash; "On Galilean Shores," by Yitzhak Shenhar; "The White City," by Aharon Megged; "The Sermon," by Haim Hazaz; "The Wanderer and the Blind Man," by Yehuda Yaari; "In a Son's Footsteps," by Hanoch Bartov; "Coming Home," by Natan Shacham; "The Third Hill," by Hedda Bosem; "The Wild Plant," by Yitzhak Orpaz; "Next of Kin," by Moshe Shamir; and "The Parched Earth," by Yoram Kaniuk. "Tehilah," by S. Y. Agnon, is reprinted by permission of Schocken Books, Inc., from *Israeli Stories,* edited by Joel Blocker, copyright © 1962 by Schocken Books, Inc. "A Long Hot Day," by Avraham B. Yehoshua, is reprinted by permission of Doubleday & Co. from the book *Three Days and a Child,* copyright © 1970 by Institute for the Translation of Hebrew Literature, Ltd., published by Doubleday & Company, Inc. "The Nomad and the Viper," by Amos Oz, is included by permission from Deborah Owen, Ltd., of London. The English translation by Ouzi Nistar first appeared in *Israel Magazine.* It has been revised by Nicholas de Lange with the permission of *Israel Magazine.* A word of thanks, too, to the helpful staff of the Zionist Library and Archives in New York and to Mr. Zvi Gabay, consul of Israel in Philadelphia.

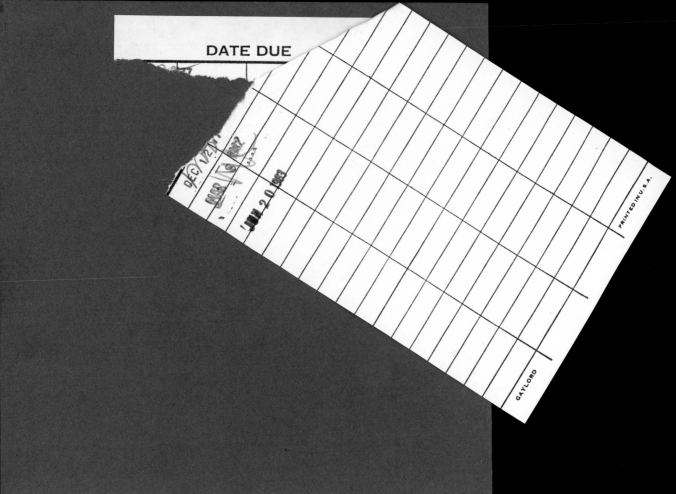